Building a Christian World View

Volume 2
The Universe, Society, and Ethics

W. Andrew Hoffecker
Editor
Gary Scott Smith
Associate Editor

Presbyterian and Reformed Publishing Company
Phillipsburg, New Jersey

Copyright © 1988
Presbyterian and Reformed Publishing Company

Unless otherwise indicated, Scripture quotations in this volume are from the New American Standard Bible.

Manufactured in the United States of America.

Library of Congress Cataloging-in-Publication Data
(Revised for vol. 2)

Building a Christian world view.

Includes bibliographies and indexes.
Contents: v. 1. God, man, and knowledge — v. 2. The universe, society, and ethics.
1. Theology—History. 2. Knowledge, Theory of—History. 3. Bible—Criticism, interpretation, etc.—History. 4. Cosmology. 5. Ethics. I. Hoffecker, W. Andrew, 1941–   II. Smith, Gary Scott, 1950–
BR123.B77   1986   230'.044   86-91437
ISBN 0-87552-281-5 (v. 1)
ISBN 0-87552-282-3 (v. 2)

Contents

Acknowledgments

Completing this second volume of *Building a Christian World View* has been possible because of the continued cooperation and good spirits of my colleagues at Grove City College. Teaching and working together with them for more than a decade has made my task as editor easier. Familiarity, it is alleged, breeds contempt. Not so when a genuine spirit of congeniality and Christian fellowship characterizes relationships—even academic ones! I thank the contributors for stimulating my own thinking and working diligently to make this volume available for a larger public. Our staff meetings, phone calls, and impromptu discussions in front of the faculty mailboxes have always been characterized by a desire to reach a common understanding that would improve our work. While the volume is made up of many parts, we have attempted a coherent expression of the Christian world view that will help others who struggle with similar concerns.

I express heartfelt thanks to Gary Smith, who has been unflagging in his editorial suggestions to make our chapters clear and unified. His willingness to help me research and add minor points during the final stages of preparation is especially appreciated. I also thank Carrie Barr, Stephanie Dittrich, and Heather Ketler, who have typed the manuscript and endured the agony of deciphering unreadable mazes of arrows and changed wording.

Finally, I thank my family, who have suffered patiently the foibles and idiosyncracies of a husband and father who has to "work on the book again tonight" (or tomorrow or next week or . . .). May you receive the reward due to your understanding.

W. Andrew Hoffecker
Grove City, Pennsylvania
July 4, 1987

Contributors

James Bibza, Ph.D., Assistant Professor of Religion, Grove City College, Grove City, Pennsylvania.

Dale R. Bowne, Ph.D., Chairman, Department of Philosophy and Religion, Professor of Religion, Grove City College, Grove City, Pennsylvania.

John D. Currid, Ph.D., Assistant Professor of Religion, Grove City College, Grove City, Pennsylvania.

Ross A. Foster, Ph.D., Vice President for Student Affairs, Associate Professor of Religion, Grove City College, Grove City, Pennsylvania.

W. Andrew Hoffecker, Ph.D., Professor of Religion, Grove City College, Grove City, Pennsylvania.

Charles S. MacKenzie, Ph.D., President, Grove City College, Grove City, Pennsylvania.

Alan W. Rice, Ph.D., Professor of Chemical Engineering, Grove City College, Grove City, Pennsylvania.

Gary Scott Smith, Ph.D., Associate Professor of Sociology, Grove City College, Grove City, Pennsylvania.

Preface

W. Andrew Hoffecker

In the preface of *Building a Christian World View: Volume 1, God, Man, and Knowledge* we defined what a world view is and how important understanding world view issues is for contemporary Christians. A world view consists of ideas (presuppositions), convictions, and commitments that shape our outlook on life. Although it might seem that only professional scholars—those who make their living as researchers, teachers, and writers—think about things such as basic assumptions and presuppositions, everyone has a world view. Even though they rarely reflect self-consciously on their basic convictions, all people hold fundamental beliefs that contour every aspect of their lives—their thoughts, work, leisure activities, feelings, values, and attitudes.

World views are pretheoretical—they are so fundamental to what we believe and know that they actually precede our conscious acts of thinking. Our world view determines which ideas we consider to be most important. These fundamental assumptions are more than abstract, inert ideas. Like sunglasses, they "color" how we perceive the rest of the world. But unlike sunglasses, which we consciously put on or take off as we choose, our world view is such a part of us that we rarely reflect on how it shades our perception of all things. Only with conscious effort can we isolate, identify, and then evaluate the fundamental ideas, convictions, commitments, and feelings that constitute our world view. Only our unique human capacity of self-transcendence enables us even to think *about* the ideas *with which* we think.

Because a person's world view is all-encompassing, affecting every aspect of life, it is fundamentally religious in nature. The term "religious" is often thought to describe only those who believe in God, belong to an institutional church or sect, and exercise an identifiable piety or form of worship. Though popular, such an understanding of "religious" is very misleading. It implies that people who do not believe in God or belong to a church or practice a certain piety are not religious. And yet such people may religiously pursue wealth, prestige, and material well-being or fervently commit themselves to secular values that direct every phase of their lives.

The term "religion" is derived from *religare*, which means "to bind or to commit oneself." Although supposedly "unreligious" people recognize no transcendent values and may appear to be antireligious, in reality they are simply devoted to a different kind of religion. All people are religious because they hold a world view that by its very nature commits them to certain beliefs, presuppositions, or basic convictions. Regardless of their vocations or avocations in life, people religiously embrace an interpretive framework that directs how they reflect on reality and their experiences within it. In this sense, a world view is indispensable to life.

The questions raised in these two volumes force readers to recognize that they hold world views. Only after understanding their fundamental commitments can individuals self-consciously affirm, deny, or alter them. The process of Christian maturation demands that we become aware of our basic ideas (cf. I Cor. 2:1-6; 14:20; Eph. 4:13, 14). As followers of Jesus Christ, we are to surpass our secular counterparts in understanding and analyzing worldview issues.

In this volume we attempt to complete the building of a Christian world view, which we began in volume 1. While self-consciously affirming our commitment to the biblical perspective, we surveyed in that first volume the world views of prominent thinkers whose theological, anthropological, and epistemological presuppositions have shaped Western culture. In each section we noted that a person's views of God, man, and knowledge are correlative. What we believe about God (Is there a God or not, and if so what is God like —impersonal, abstract, and aloof from mankind or personal and capable of revealing Himself? Is God more like a watchmaker, an all-encompassing absolute, or a sovereign but gracious Lord?) has direct implications for our view of human nature and human capabilities (Do humans share a common human nature? Is man more like a beast, and therefore untamable, or like a god, and therefore destined for greatness? Or is man neither a beast nor a god but a unique creature who is self-conscious, can reason, and can reflect God's image? Has human nature remained the same over time? Does the human condition in all its diversity represent the "normal"? Can human nature be changed or altered? If so, how and by whom?).

Our views of God and man have implications for knowledge and vice versa (What is knowledge and what are its sources? How can we verify what we know? Is there certainty? What part does God play in these endeavors? How can man know and communicate with God?). We concluded that our understanding of God, humanity, and knowledge are inseparable. It is impossible to isolate any one element from the other two. Even the suggestion that we do so reveals something fundamental about one's world view—that one's ideas are merely interchangeable integers and that elements of a world view need not be integrated with each other. Presuppositions, however, are not bits of intellectual data separated from one another in airtight compartments; they mutually support each other. Isolating one from the other is like disconnecting a speaker in a stereo system and still expecting to hear stereophonic sound or taking one of the three primary colors out of a photograph and still expecting to view all hues of the color spectrum. As in each instance sound or color loses an indispensable quality or characteristic, so our perspective is severely distorted if one or more areas of thought are missing.

The two basic alternatives we summarized at the conclusion of volume 1 are (1) a view of ultimacy or transcendence as limited or nonexistent, combined with a belief in unlimited human autonomy and knowledge or (2) a view of ultimacy as unlimited and sovereign, held in conjunction with belief in human dependence and limited human knowledge. Between these two extremes are numerous mediating views, which involve compromising the unlimited nature of transcendence or human autonomy. We also noted that cultural development is often a barometer of the health of society. When people share a common world view, their culture is unified, coherent, and meaningful. When sharp divisions erupt over world-view issues, society is frequently fragmented and declines culturally and morally.

In the three units composing this volume—the universe or cosmos, society, and ethics—we build on the foundation laid in volume 1—theology, anthropology, and epistemology. Cosmology (the study of the world or cosmos—its character, origin, etc.), society (the study of the basic structures or institutions of the public order), and ethics (the study of right and wrong moral behavior) are interwoven with each other and with our previous discussions of God, man, and knowledge. In the past many scholars have failed to see the necessity and value of this integrated approach. They have assumed that the various disciplines in education can be neatly compartmentalized. They have, for example, accepted Immanuel Kant's argument that science and religion should be totally isolated from one another. If scientists and theologians would simply stick to their own areas of study and not make pronouncements in the other's domain, all controversy between these two fields would gradually cease. Scientists would be free to expand our knowledge in the empirical sciences and create technology to make life better, and theologians would be free to further our understanding of morality, theology, and spiritual needs. Kant's approach, however, produced the modern dualism of the phenomenal (material) and noumenal (mental) worlds, and the contemporary belief that we must always isolate science from religion for the good of both. Present-day controversies in bio-medical, business, judicial, and technological ethics result largely from modern thinkers' acceptance of the Kantian dichotomy between the empirical sciences and other disciplines. While the compartmentalization of disciplines has made academics neat and tidy, it has dangerously fragmented thinking. In virtually every area of public life—education, politics, business, medicine, research, and technology—people note the paucity of moral teaching because the Kantian separation of the two realms has made scientific studies dominant in our cultural activity. Moral and theological commitments are viewed as hopelessly mired in subjectivism and relativism.

But many scholars, especially Christian thinkers, correctly challenge such a separation of ideas and thus of academic life into distinct compartments. This fragmentation of knowledge brought about by specialization prevents efforts to develop meaningfully coherent philosophies capable of spanning disciplines. Specialization is the process resulting from the exponential growth of our knowledge in the past century. Academic study has proliferated at such a rate that intellectuals have increasingly narrowed their study in the general disciplines such as biology, political science, and mathematics by creating separate subfields with the result that scholars are almost totally ignorant of research done by colleagues unless they are in the exact same specialized field. Trivialization of knowledge—the pursuit of a discipline for its own sake and not for any transcendent end such as the glory of God—has been a direct result of specialization. Knowledge has become a mere accumulation of facts or trivia, rather than a unified and meaningful perspective reflecting the nature of reality as created by God. Current trends in specialization and trivialization of knowledge further imply that what we think does not necessarily influence how we live. But our study of biblical epistemology in volume 1 demonstrated exactly the opposite. What we think affects our lives directly. What we believe in our hearts, our ultimate commitments, guides our actions. Moreover God holds us accountable for the ethical implications of all that we know. Inasmuch as part two of this volume essentially examines social ethics and part three covers individual ethics, this volume emphasizes how our ideas affect ethical behavior.

While all six of the subjects we have mentioned mutually influence each other, for purposes of simplicity we suggest the following scheme as a means of relating the elements of a biblical world view:

THE PRESUPPOSITIONS OF	INFLUENCE THE STUDY OF
THEOLOGY	COSMOLOGY
ANTHROPOLOGY	SOCIETY
EPISTEMOLOGY	ETHICS

This chart shows how theological presuppositions are particularly relevant to the study of cosmology. Such a correlation does not mean that anthropology and epistemology are divorced from our study of the world. But the existence or nonexistence of God and the nature of God's character if He does exist are very pertinent to our understanding of the world we live in—its origin, nature, significance, and purpose. Similarly, anthropological presuppositions are decisive for any view of society. Our beliefs as to what society is, its aims, basic institutions, and controlling ideas such as justice, peace, and order are directly related to our view of human nature, whether man is free or determined, and whether he is fundamentally good, evil, or amoral. Finally, any examination of ethics, while related to our views of man and God, is most intimately related to epistemology, for the most crucial and troubling questions in ethics are about the basis and nature of authority on which ethical decisions are made.

We will continue the historical approach adopted in the first volume and survey various perspectives that have dominated Western thinking.[1] Our study compares and contrasts various world views and evaluates them on the basis of the biblical perspective. Our primary purpose is fourfold: (1) to help readers understand the leading thinkers and philosophers that have formed Western thought; (2) to enable readers to comprehend major issues and questions involved in cosmology, society, and ethics; (3) to present readers with a biblical analysis of these areas; and (4) to challenge readers to clarify their own perspectives in each of the areas of study.

We stress in each unit how one theme dominates the Western mind since the Enlightenment—autonomy. Autonomy has replaced the Judeo-Christian God as the single most important world-view issue. As the interpretive principle in every field of thought—cosmology, society, or ethics—autonomy has been the framework by which people have understood modern life. Through the medieval and Reformation periods, biblical themes frequently checked rising pressures from a minority of philosophers who

---

1. See the introduction to vol. 1, pp. 3-8 for chronology charts that identify the major time periods we study and thinkers whose ideas best illustrate dominant world views characteristic of each era.

advocated independence of the cosmos, human institutions, and morality. But more recently secularists have pushed aside traditional categories. The physical and biological sciences now probe the origin, nature, and operation of the universe as if it were totally self-contained and self-determined. Political theorists, economists, and other social scientists discuss social institutions without any reference to transcendence. Their ruling assumption is man's independence—his capacity to understand and transform institutions as if human beings were free of inherent evil and could build a just society without divine assistance. Ethicists consider human beings to be morally autonomous. In both individual and public life moral thinkers reject transcendent norms out of deference to immanent ethical principles. In summary, autonomous man lives within an autonomous universe under his autonomous moral authority.

As we begin this second volume, we remind readers that Christians will be most effective when they understand not only their own world view but also other views competing for the contemporary mind. We therefore urge our readers to be alert to autonomous claims wherever and whenever they appear and to be ready to respond with a defense of biblical truth.

PART ONE:
THE UNIVERSE

Introduction

W. Andrew Hoffecker

Cosmology is a branch of metaphysics—the field of philosophy in which scholars reflect on the meaning, structure, and principles governing whatever exists. Cosmology (from the Greek *kosmos*, "universe," and *logos*, "study of") deals with the world or universe, particularly questions of origins and ultimate principles governing objects and events within the universe. Because the Greek *kosmos* is all-inclusive, cosmology encompasses the totality of our experience. Cosmologists attempt to construct a conceptual framework that explains everything from the vast galaxies in space to the smallest subatomic particle. Cosmologies include such subjects as the origin, size, and nature of the universe; the nature and type(s) of being(s) in it; its governing principles; and its ultimate meaning. Underlying cosmologial inquiry are logically prior questions about God. Is there a God? Did God create the universe, or is God coexistent with the world? If God created or crafted the world (two significantly different positions, as we will see), what is the relationship between God and the world? Is the world orderly or chaotic? If it is orderly, does it govern itself or does God continue to control or guide the cosmos? What are the properties of physical reality, and are physical beings and material things the only reality? If other beings exist, what is their nature and what is their relationship to the operation of the cosmos? What about causality? Do laws govern the existence and behavior of objects and people? If so, are laws merely descriptive (explaining why certain events happen) or are they causative (actually causing events or behavior)? Does the universe have an overarching purpose so that events within the universe are meaningful, or is the cosmos as a whole, as well as individual things within it, merely the result of random chance?

Although "cosmology" may be a familiar term, "cosmogony" (from the Greek *kosmos*, and *gonos*, "origin" or "birth") is less so. A cosmogony is an account of the origin of the universe and thus is a part of a larger cosmological framework. Ancient peoples created imaginative stories describing how gods made the world out of carcasses slain in heavenly battles. Modern scientists construct models of origins based on their knowledge of elements presently existing in the universe. Cosmologies have always included accounts of how the cosmos began—except those devised by people who thought the universe had no beginning. But even philosophers who have regarded the world as eternal (for example the ancient Greeks), have usually argued that it now differs from its original form.

Cosmogony and cosmology, therefore, cannot be separated. A cosmogony is meaningful only within a larger context provided by a cosmology which, in turn, is dependent upon a theology. Contemporary debates over the teaching of evolution and creation in the public schools are often superficial because people fail to acknowledge that a proper understanding of origins is related to issues that teachers never openly discuss. For example, our nation's schools presently teach the Big Bang theory as the most probable account of the beginning of the universe. By deliberately focusing only on cosmogony or origins (because to go deeper would raise cosmological world-view or religious issues), contemporary educators prevent students from learning about larger frameworks that could be used to evaluate the Big Bang theory. By omitting cosmological questions, teachers imply that we can understand how our universe began merely by learning what contemporary scientists and philosophers now believe is the most acceptable theory, without knowing the cosmology and theology underlying that theory. Only by directly confronting the questions raised above can a person pass judgment on accounts of how the universe came into being.

Our study of cosmology and cosmogony is designed to highlight differences between naturalistic and supernaturalistic perspectives, whether ancient or contemporary. Chapter 1 deals with mythical cosmologies of the ancient Near East. Ancient cosmologies from

Egypt, Mesopotamia, and Canaan are among the oldest written documents in the world. Their cosmologies are mythical accounts of a polytheistic universe. Each myth ties the origin and meaning of the cosmos to forces of nature that personify the gods. By understanding the origin of the gods and the forces that govern the gods (magic), people could understand the origin and operation of everything within the cosmos itself. All aspects of human existence in polytheistic societies—political, familial, and agricultural activity—relate directly to observable powers in the cycle of nature, which, in turn, reflect the life of the gods. Only magic, an impersonal, abstract, and amoral force or power, is greater than the gods. In polytheistic cosmologies human existence consists largely of man's attempts to order his world by placating or manipulating gods through religious rituals.

In contrast to these mythical cosmologies, which base the cosmos on magic and the life of the gods, classical Greek philosophers founded their cosmologies on philosophical speculation (chapter 2). Pre-Socratic thinkers were philosopher-scientists who sought to explain the universe by identifying the ultimate stuff or essence out of which everything in the cosmos was made. Monists proposed one element (earth, air, fire, or water), and pluralists claimed that several or more essences were ultimate. Ancient Greek cosmologists were totally unconcerned about origins. They thought the cosmos was itself in a sense divine, not because a god or gods created it but because some element within it was ultimate. Even Plato and Aristotle accepted the explanation that the world was eternal. Plato proposed a Demiurge, who crafted the world out of preexistent materials, and Aristotle devised a philosophy of causation in which a final cause, an unmoved mover, drew everything to its final end or purpose. But neither Plato nor Aristotle believed his deity to be a transcendent creator who brought the world into existence out of nothing. Nor were their deities providential governors of the universe. As with other aspects of their world views, Plato and especially Aristotle established cosmological principles that dominated philosophy well into the Middle Ages.

Chapter 3 presents a sharp contrast to ancient mythological and philosophically speculative cosmologies. The Bible describes a cosmos that sprang not from a battle among many gods or from abstract rational principles but from creation out of nothing by an absolutely sovereign God. Biblical cosmology is historical, moral, and revelational. The cosmos had a distinct beginning; it provides the time and space framework in which God's sovereign plan is worked out (the fall and redemption); and it is moving toward a glorious consummation. Moreover, the universe does not operate under the influence of competing nature deities or magical forces. Nor is it subject to an abstract rational ideal. Rather the cosmos is the setting wherein God works out His personal moral purposes. Goodness and righteousness (the kingdom of God) will prevail over the forces of evil. Biblical cosmology reveals the nature and attributes of God who created it. The chapter analyzes current debate over different ways of understanding the creation account in Genesis 1, architectural imagery the Bible uses to describe the cosmos, and various Christian interpretations of the consummation of the universe.

Our final chapter on cosmology (chap. 4) begins with a summary of medieval cosmology and moves forward to cosmologies of the twentieth century. With the rise of modern science cosmological speculation assumed less from traditional world views (such as Aristotle's final cause or biblical creation out of nothing) and presupposed instead that empirical observation combined with human speculation could discover the origin, nature, and operation of the universe and objects within it. We examine in passing discoveries in the eighteenth and nineteenth centuries that led scientists to assume an orderly cosmos determined by natural law. In greater detail we probe the Darwinian theory of natural selection and macroevolution and the Big Bang cosmogony. Of special interest are the unquestioned and often unmentioned assumptions underlying both cosmologies, which presume the autonomous nature of the cosmos. How, for example, do both Christians and non-Christians account for chance or random events in the universe? We conclude with an evaluation of various options available to Christians on the origin of the universe.

I.
ANCIENT NEAR EASTERN
AND GREEK WORLD VIEWS

1
Cosmologies of Myth

John D. Currid

Introduction

Since his creation, man has pondered the origin, operation, and meaning of the universe, and his particular place within it. So, for example, the Mesopotamian *Epic of Gilgamesh*, one of man's first written stories, dating from about 2000 B.C., describes the quest of a man named Gilgamesh to understand the cosmos. Gilgamesh travelled across the earth seeking to discover the significance of the universe, life, death, and immortality. From ancient times until today people individually and collectively have sought to understand these same issues.

This chapter will examine and explain how ancient man understood the origin and workings of the universe. It focuses upon three of the most important and influential societies of antiquity: Egypt, Mesopotamia, and Canaan. A secondary purpose of this study is to provide a historical and cultural context that will enable readers to understand the Hebrew view of cosmology, which will be discussed in chapter 3. Only by grasping the major features of the thought and culture of the surrounding nations can we fully apprehend Israel's cosmological perspective. Egypt, Mesopotamia, and Canaan had the greatest contact with and impact upon the Hebrews.

Egyptian Cosmology

Ancient Egyptians believed that the universe consisted of four principal elements. The first element was the earth, which was thought to be shaped like a dish with raised or corrugated rims. The central, flat part of the dish represented the Nile Valley (Egypt), and its raised rim symbolized the mountains of countries bordering Egypt. Below the earth lay primeval waters, the second main element of the universe, from which life first sprang and upon which the earth floated. Above the earth was the sky, the third element of the universe. The universe's outer limits were bounded by inverted plates, which established the size of the cosmos (both above and below). The diagram below portrays the ancient Egyptian view of the cosmos.

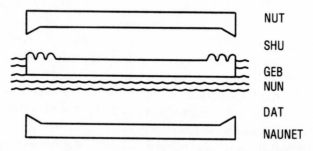

Each element represents a different god; their names are listed on the right. Between the uppermost plate of the universe and the earth was the air-god Shu, who upheld the suspended plate so that it did not come crashing down upon earth. The deity Nut, the sky-goddess, personified the upper plate. Remaining elements of the universe also correspond to Egyptian gods as depicted above.

Although not included in the illustration, the sun (represented by the god Re) was the most important object in the ancient Egyptian cosmological scheme. Egyptians believed that the sun journeyed nightly into the underworld signifying its death, and then was reborn each day out of the waters of Nun, the source of life. This emphasis upon daily rebirth of the sun exhibits ancient Egyptian belief in a cyclical view of time and history. In other words, they perceived reality to be a repetitive cycle of birth, life, and death.

Moreover, the whole natural order reflected an unending cycle. For example, the seasons continually moved from spring (denoting birth) to summer and fall (symbolizing life) to winter (depicting death). Furthermore, objects within nature such as flora followed a similar pattern. Even man himself lived according to a recurring cycle: he was born, lived, and died, but while living he gave birth to offspring, which in turn continued the pattern.

Egyptian cosmology, therefore, did more than describe the universe's structure. It also explained how Egyptian life—its religious, economic, and social relationships—was directly tied to nature.

Given the Egyptian view of the cosmos, it is not surprising that this nation's life, including religious, economic, and social relationships, directly related to principal changes in nature. By arranging their lives so as to be in harmony with the cycles of nature, the Egyptians believed that their chances of success in any undertaking would be greatly improved. For example, when a new Pharaoh was to be coronated, the ceremony was usually scheduled for the beginning of the natural cycle (which signified birth) in order to provide the new reign with a favorable starting-point. Likewise, New Year's Day, because it marked the beginning of the natural cycle, was regarded as the most important celebration in Egypt. Elaborate festivities took place, many of them based upon the theme of battles between good gods (such as Re), who desired rebirth, and bad gods (such as Dat), who did not.

Egyptian Cosmogony

The ancient Egyptians believed that life originated from pre-existent primordial waters (Nun). Out of these waters first appeared the "primeval hillocks," or islands shaped like mounds or hills. According to Egyptian myth, the creator-god Re came into existence upon these "primeval-hillocks." The sun-god Re entered into the universe through self-creation; as an Egyptian text stated, he "became, by himself." The creator-god's principal functions were twofold. First, Re brought order out of chaos by seizing control over the eight preexistent gods (such as Kuk, who represented darkness, and Amon, who symbolized chaos). Second, the sun-god called into being other gods who, like him, each personified a different element of nature.

Three basic accounts describe how Re created these other gods. One of them pictures Re squatting on the primeval hillock, pondering and inventing names for the different parts of his own body. As he verbally identified each physical part of his body, a new god sprang into existence. Another legend portrays Re as violently expelling gods from his own body, possibly by sneezing or spitting. A third myth describes Re creating the gods Shu and Tefnut by an act of masturbation. These gods in turn gave birth to the other gods.

The Egyptians had no separate or specific account of the creation of mankind. To the ancient Egyptians such a creation story had no real purpose since man could not be entirely distinguished from the gods. That is to say, because creation started with the gods, it was thought to continue directly to man.

Mesopotamian Cosmology

The vast majority of cosmological systems throughout history have divided the universe into the animate and the inanimate, the living and the nonliving. The ancient Mesopotamian view can be easily distinguished from the mainstream, however, because Mesopotamians believed that each thing in the universe—human beings, animals, plants, ideas, concepts (such as goodness and justice)— had a will and character all its own. In other words, Mesopotamians regarded each object and idea in their experience as being alive, as having its own will and personality.

Mesopotamians thought that all these individual wills and personalities were "living" together in the community of the universe, in the same manner that a human state or society exists. This cosmic state was, according to one expert, set up as a Primitive Democracy, in which those with the greatest power ran the universe. Thus, such natural, powerful elements as water, the sky, or the earth were understood to be political leaders, which wielded the most power in the cosmic society. Other components of the universal state, which had less natural power, such as rocks and trees, had no political influence at all. Man belonged to this latter group; he was considered a slave in the cosmic society.

Mesopotamians regarded and revered the most powerful natural forces that directed the Primitive Democracy as gods. Hence, the highest and most authoritative of the gods was *Anu*, god of the sky. His duty was to maintain order in the universe and to establish the laws of the cosmic society. *Enlil*, the second most powerful god, was personified by the storm; he enforced the decrees of Anu and the assembly of the gods. Considered almost as powerful as Enlil, *Ninhursaga* was Mother Earth who gave birth to all that had the breath of life. Because water was so essential to sustaining life, the water-god, *Ea,* was as mighty as Mother Earth. Clearly, then, ancient Mesopotamians believed that the gods were totally immanent in nature.

These four gods, along with three others, made up the divine assembly of the Primitive Democracy. This assembly had power to decide destiny, determining both great and small events of the future.

Mesopotamian Cosmogony

According to Mesopotamian belief, this Primitive Democracy, which controlled the universe, was established as a result of a cosmic struggle between order and chaos at the dawn of creation. Order's conquest over chaos produced a cosmic hierarchy, which assigned each facet of the universe a proper place.

The *Enuma Elish* describes the ancient Mesopotamian account of creation. The epic begins as follows:

> When a sky above had not [yet even] been mentioned
> (And) the name of firm ground below had not [yet even] been
>   thought of;
> (When) only primeval Apsu, their begetter,
> And Mummu and Tiamat—she who gave birth to them all
> Were mingling their waters in one;
> When no bog had formed (and) no island could be found;
> When no god whosoever had appeared,
> Had been named by name, had been determined as to (his) lot,
> Then were gods formed within them.[1]

These opening lines picture the universe as being originally chaotic (before the appearance of order), a place where only primeval waters existed (cf. Egypt above). The watery chaos consisted of three gods: Apsu, a male deity representing the sweet waters; Tiamat, the goddess of the sea; and Mummu, who probably was the god of mist.

According to the myth, Apsu and Tiamat created other gods

1. Henri Frankfort et al., *Before Philosophy* (Baltimore: Penguin, 1951), p. 184.

through sexual procreation. The series of gods they generated each symbolized one important element of nature (e.g., sky, water, and earth). These created gods came into immediate conflict, however, with Apsu and Tiamat. The former wanted to work actively to preserve order, while Apsu and Tiamat preferred an inactive role, which produced chaos. Note Apsu's complaint to Tiamat in this regard:

> Abhorrent have become their [the created gods] ways to me,
> I am allowed no rest by day, by night no sleep.
> I will abolish, yea, I will destroy their ways, that peace may reign (again) and we may sleep.

Their different goals produced a cosmic battle between the gods of chaos and the gods of order. Ea, god of water, killed Apsu and locked up Mummu by securing a rope through his nose as a leash. Marduk, king of the gods of order, then slew Tiamat, last of the gods of chaos, in a fierce battle:

> They [Marduk and Tiamat] strove in single combat, locked in battle.
> The lord (Marduk) spread out his net to enfold her,
> The Evil Wind, which followed behind, he let loose in her face.
> When Tiamat opened her mouth to consume him,
> He drove in the Evil Wind [so] that she [could] close not her lips.
> As the fierce winds charged her belly,
> Her body was distended and her mouth was wide open.
> He released the arrow, it tore her belly,
> It cut through her insides, splitting the heart.
> Having thus subdued her, he extinguished her life.

After obtaining victory, Marduk used Tiamat's remains to create the cosmos. Ironically, Marduk established the Primitive Democracy (order) by using the body of Tiamat who personified chaos. Among the many things Marduk created and placed in their proper position in the cosmic state was man. His life was to be uncertain, dependent only upon the whims and fancies of the higher gods:

> [Marduk says:] Blood I will mass and cause bones to be,
> I will establish a savage, "man" shall be his name.
> Verily, savage-man I will create.

He shall be charged with the service of the gods,
That they might be at ease!

Significantly, Ea and Marduk were victorious not only because they were inherently more powerful than the gods of chaos but also because they were better magicians. Ea slew Apsu, for instance, after reciting a magical spell that rendered the god unconscious:

He [Ea] of supreme intelligence, skillful, ingenious,
Ea, who knows all things, saw through their scheme,
He formed, yea, he set up against it the configuration of the
    universe,
And skillfully made his overpowering sacred spell.
Reciting it he cast it on Apsu,
Poured slumber over him, so that he soundly slept.

Marduk, furthermore, fought and killed Tiamat while holding a red paste between his lips. The color red in ancient Mesopotamia symbolized the art of magic. Thus, Marduk conquered because of his superior magical skills. Marduk also used magic to pass a test devised by the gods of order to see if he should be their king. They took a piece of cloth, laid it in front of Marduk, and said to him:

Lord, truly thy decree is first among gods
Say but to wreck or create; it shall be
Open thy mouth: the cloth shall be whole!
At the word of his mouth the cloth vanished.
He spoke again, and the cloth was restored.
When the gods, his fathers, saw the fruit of his word,
Joyfully they did homage: "Marduk is king."

Marduk attained the highest station in the Primitive Democracy primarily because of his innate power over nature as the storm-god and his ability as a magician.

In reality, magic was the ultimate power in the universe, even above that of the gods themselves. All other things in the cosmos— people, animals, plants, rocks—were dependent upon magic to secure their proper place in the Primitive Democracy. The more magical ability each had, the greater was its position in the hierarchy of the cosmic state. Ultimately, therefore, the key element in Mesopotamian cosmology was a force external to the universe: *magic*.

Cannanite Cosmology

The Canaanites' view of cosmology is expressed principally in a group of texts called the Ugaritic Myths, which explain how the universe operates. Like Egyptian and Mesopotamian cosmological stories, the Ugaritic Myths focus upon the life of the gods (as personified by the forces of nature), who ran the universe.

One particular text, entitled the Myth of Baal, provides a striking picture of the Canaanite world-and-life view. This story describes Baal (the god of rain, vegetation, and fertility) and his consort Anath (the goddess of love, fertility, and war) building a palace. As they do so, Mot (god of summer drought) slays Baal and takes him to the underworld. Anath retaliates killing Mot, and Baal is resurrected and reclaims his palace. The Myth of Baal explained why nature moved through a cycle of seasons. Drought blighted crops in Canaan each summer because the drought-god Mot conquered the fertility god Baal. But the rainy season appeared each fall because Anath slew Mot, and Baal, the god of rain, was restored to power.

Canaanites believed that this cycle occurred each year (though at times variations occurred as when, for example, there was extended drought; such a deviation was explained by Mot's holding Baal captive for a longer period of time). This all-pervading cyclical view of life was also reflected in Canaanite religious practice and ritual. Through their religion Canaanites sought to help the yearly cycle continue and attempted to control this cycle, thereby making the gods more favorable towards them. The discussion below explains the relationship of Canaanite worship to this unending cycle.

Canaanite Worship

The religion of Canaan revolved around an elaborate system of ritual. Primarily, the Canaanite cultus centered upon forms of worship that promoted sex and fertility. Such an emphasis sprang logically from their belief that sustaining the cycle of life and death was absolutely necessary for the fertility of their flocks, fields, and wives. These rituals aimed chiefly to invoke the gods' favor upon worshippers. By manipulating the divine (also known as *magic*), productivity was assured.

The Canaanites practiced child sacrifice, especially the offering of firstborn sons to the gods. Members of this ancient society believed that if people gave the first of their produce to the gods, then the gods would continue to grant fertility to Canaanite women. By sacrificing children, the Canaanites also hoped to compel gods to intervene into life-threatening situations (see II Kings 3:27). Archaeological discoveries at Carthage reveal hundreds of charred remains of child sacrifices. Historical records and stone monuments from this children's cemetery indicate that these victims were sacrificed in order to gain certain gods' favors and intervention.

Temple prostitution was another common practice the Canaanites used to gain the gods' good will. According to this custom, male and female harlots were attached to central religious sanctuaries and shrines. Members of this ritual order were known in the Old Testament and Canaanite literature as the *qadeshim*, quite literally the "set apart ones." They were individuals "set apart" for the special function of ritual prostitution. The Canaanites thought that committing acts of whoredom at these sacred precincts would guarantee the fertility of all their people, land, and animals.

It was likely that temple prostitution in Canaan centered on the worship of the divinity Baal Peor, a name literally meaning "Lord of the Opening" (a reference to the female vagina). Numbers 25:1-3 reports that by fornicating with the followers of Baal Peor, the Israelites were seduced into worshiping this god. In other words, this illicit sexual act symbolized Israel's unfaithfulness to her God *Yahweh*. The passage strikingly relates this infidelity and perversion by using the sexual language "coupled or joined together" to indicate Israel's union with Baal Peor. As verse 1 relates, Israel "began to play the harlot with the daughters of Moab," even though God had strictly forbidden the Jews to do so. (For other instances of such unfaithfulness by Israel, see Deut. 4:3; Ps. 106:28; Hos. 9:10.)

Canaanite religion was also idolatrous. Its various gods were depicted in human form, fashioned out of wood or stone. The goddesses of Canaan were generally represented in iconography as naked females with exaggerated, distorted sexual parts. Also, cult objects such as lilies (representing sex appeal) and serpents (symbolizing fertility and fecundity) were often associated with the worship of Canaanite goddesses. Hence, the Canaanites' almost singular obsession with sex and fertility was further demonstrated in their idols.

Most Canaanite worship occurred at "high places," sacred areas where they placed altars for sacrifice, ritual pillars, and idols (see I Kings 14:23). One of the more important objects at the "high place" was the sacred tree or grove, a physical representation of the goddess Asherah. This female deity functioned mainly as the goddess of fertility. Thus, when Canaanites went to the "high place" to worship Asherah, they approached the deity to persuade her to make their families, land, and animals and themselves fertile and productive.

In addition, numerous biblical references indicate that the Canaanites engaged in soothsaying, divination, sorcery, witchcraft, and necromancy (communication with the dead) (Deut. 18:9-11). Moreover, they ritually beat and cut themselves during worship (see I Kings 18:28; cf. Lev. 19:28). All of these were magical acts intended to discover what decisions the divinities might have made concerning particular situations in life.

Conclusion

In this chapter we have discussed cosmological views of the ancient Egyptians, Mesopotamians, and Canaanites. Although the three systems have obvious differences, they rest upon the same basic principles:

1. All three believed in *polytheism*, the worship of many gods. These polytheist religions identified the gods with powers and elements of the universe. In other words, they gave names to natural phenomena and endowed them with personalities. Polytheists regarded the gods, therefore, as totally *immanent*—merely part of the universe. The life or cycle of nature was the life of the gods.

Each god was restricted to the capacity of the natural element he personified, so that a god's power never exceeded the power associated with the natural phenomena (except by magic as we have seen). Thus, the gods were not all-powerful. Rather, nature deities were severely limited in what they could do. In addition, their characters were generally depraved and perverted, often reflecting the debased lifestyles of mankind.

2. The *continual movement of nature through the seasonal cycle* was extremely important to polytheists. Since nature's cyclical progression was synonymous with the life of the gods, ancient polytheists attempted to understand and explain life by influencing and manipulating the powers of nature following their never ending cycle. The personification of gods as forces of nature was reflected in the literature of Egypt, Mesopotamia, and Canaan, which described the operation of the universe in mythical fashion. Life and history were cyclical, dependent entirely upon nature's rhythm.

3. According to ancient polytheism, *the true power of the universe was magic*. Thus, the god who was able to perform the greatest magical feats was considered most powerful. Ancient peoples also relied on magic (i.e., omens, sorcery, divinations, and necromancy) to manipulate nature for their own benefit. Consequently, the ultimate power over the cosmos—magic—was an element external to the cosmos.

4. In ancient Near Eastern societies *man was basically viewed as insignificant* in the overall scheme of things. He possessed little dignity and worth and was thought to be merely a slave to the gods. Man had no freedom either, since the whim and fancy of the gods decided the direction and outcome of his life.

These four points produced a distorted and perverted world-and-life view. Particular emphases upon sex, fertility, and magic can appeal only to the baser side of man. Moreover, ancient beliefs reflected a mythological understanding of the operation and origin of the universe. Mythological world views eventually gave way to philosophically speculative cosmologies. In the next chapter we examine how ancient Greek thinkers approached cosmological questions from a totally different perspective.

For Further Reading

Frankfort, Henri. *Kingship and the Gods.* Chicago: University of Chicago Press, 1948.

Frankfort, Henri and H. A., J. A. Wilson, Th. Jacobsen, and W. A. Irwin. *Before Philosophy.* Baltimore: Penguin, 1951.

Heidel, Alexander. *The Gilgamesh Epic and Old Testament Parallels.* Chicago: University of Chicago Press, 1942.

Pritchard, J. B., ed. *The Ancient Near East: An Anthology of Texts and Pictures.* Princeton: Princeton University Press, 1959.

Thomas, D. Winton, ed. *Documents From Old Testament Times.* New York: Harper and Row, 1958.

Wright, G. E. *Biblical Archaeology.* Philadelphia: Westminster Press, 1960.

2
Cosmologies of Philosophical Speculation

Ross A. Foster

Introduction

The term "cosmology" means the study of the world. As an academic discipline, cosmology is a branch of metaphysics, distinguished from ontology, theology, and psychology. Cosmology is also a science in which astronomers and physicists attempt to explain the cosmos as a whole. Scientists and philosophers who study cosmology continually discuss whether its results are philosophical speculation or a scientific description of this universe. Is cosmology an explanation, or a theory, or a law?[1]

For centuries men have sought to discover the nature of reality and its ultimate source. As will be discussed in more detail in chapter 3, the Bible presents an approach to cosmology completely different from the ancient mythological cosmologies of Mesopotamia, Egypt, and Canaan and the philosophical speculations of the Greeks. Whereas the latter systems arise from man's search to understand reality, the biblical cosmology is based upon God, the Creator, revealing to man, the creature, the nature of truth and the universe. Although human beings are made in the image of God and intuitively know Him, they reject His revelation. Romans 1:19-32 declares that God has revealed Himself through His creation, the cosmos. From the biblical perspective, God's revelation, not human speculation, explains the origin and nature of the universe. Wanting to be independent of their Creator, however, people have continually ignored the qualitative distinction between God

1. Students interested in the problem of method and investigation of the cosmos should read "Cosmology" in *The Encyclopedia of Philosophy*, vol. 1 (New York: Macmillan, 1966), pp. 237-43.

and themselves and have reflected, analyzed, and probed the nature of reality apart from God's truth and grace. The Bible asserts that the universe displays God's character and power. "For since the creation of the world God's invisible qualities—his eternal power and divine nature—have been clearly seen, being understood from what has been made, so that men are without excuse" (Rom. 1:20, NIV). Denying God's involvement in the world, man examines the universe as brute facts, not as God's creation. Rejecting God's revelation in history people draw conclusions about the world based solely on their own speculations.

This chapter examines the Greek understanding of cosmology, which established the method and foundation of more sophisticated cosmologies that follow. It also critiques Greek cosmology from a biblical perspective.

Unlike ancient Egyptians, Mesopotamians, and Canaanites discussed in the previous chapter, Greeks were naturally curious and inquisitive about the nature of life and the structure of the universe. How they understood the gods was strikingly different from other ancient peoples. Greeks advocated no particular view of the origin of the world. They believed Greek gods were limited in power and therefore did not create the universe out of nothing; the cosmos had always existed.

The Greek deities were also delightfully immoral. Among their normal activities were perjury, war, and adultery. To the average Greek, the gods appeared as magnified human beings, not spiritual beings. But the religion of the average person was quite different from that of the educated thinker, the philosopher. Because belief in gods was so widespread, philosophers were generally reluctant to attack them. Thus they frequently used allegories to explain their existence and actions. Other philosophers became skeptics, convinced that human beings could know nothing for certain. Skepticism was especially dominant in the fifth century B.C. during the height of Athenian civilization.

Monist Cosmologists

The Greeks developed, among other things, what we today call science and philosophy. Science began with the Greek investigation of the world in the sixth century B.C. Many of these early scientists lived on the Greek coast of Asia Minor and in the Greek cities of Southern Italy. By the fourth century B.C., however, Athens had become the center of Greek philosophical thought.

Thales of Miletus introduced a new way of thinking about cosmology. Before Thales, cosmological questions were addressed primarily through myths such as those we discussed in chapter 1. The earliest Greek cosmology was polytheistic and tied to the cycle of nature. With Thales, however, an emphasis on rational order emerged. He assumed that he was investigating an orderly universe, a system governed by laws that could be discovered by observation and logical thought. Greeks such as Thales built upon the remarkable discoveries that Egyptians and Mesopotamians had made by observing the regular, systematic movement of nature. But Greek thought differed from polytheistic nature religions by emphasizing not imaginative mythical accounts of the gods but rational speculation of the human mind.

Early Greek cosmologists did not think of themselves as philosophers and initially they did not use philosophical terms to explain such concepts as "substance," "matter," "mind," "element," "atom," "force," "thing," or "event." But as Greeks gradually developed a speculative world view, they invented such terms to express their ideas. What they sought in their speculation was the *arche*, the first (not in time, but in importance) or basic principle of the cosmos, which could explain not only the universe as a whole but also every object within it—what it is, why it functions as it does and so on. Greek philosophers also built on the ideas of those who preceded them. As we will see, Plato and Aristotle attempted to resolve problems raised by their predecessors centuries before them.

In the first half of this chapter we will briefly examine the teachings of major Greek thinkers who sought to find the underlying nature of reality, the "*phusis*," the "essence of things."

Milesian Cosmologists

Thales of Miletus (c. 610-545 B.C.) thought that water was the fundamental basis or substance from which all things proceeded, a conclusion he reached by speculation. He believed water to be a single, living substance. Although the world appears to consist of a vast variety of objects, in reality water is the *arche*, the fundamental element that explains all others. It explains motion (he observed the tides and flowing rivers); it is essential to life (all animals need it); and since it exists in solid, liquid, and gaseous states, it may well be the basic element in all other things.

His good friend, Anaximander (c. 610-c. 546 B.C.), who also lived in Miletus, taught that the material cause and the element underlying all things was the "indeterminate boundless." This "boundless," or, as we would say today, the "infinite," was not an element, like water. It differed from all substance and gave rise to the heavens and the worlds within them. Eternal and ageless, the infinite moved eternally to spin off the earth, which was suspended in space and shaped like a cylinder. Anaximander did not consider any one determinate element such as water to be primary. His conception that all things come from the indeterminate infinite was an early attempt to explain how the cosmos developed (cosmogony). Besides his speculative contributions to cosmology, Anaximander made maps of the Greek world and a spherical model of the heavens to illustrate his cosmology.

Anaximenes (died c. 528 B.C.), also from Miletus, agreed with Anaximander that the underlying source of all things was one and infinite, but he argued that this source was a determinate substance, air. The process of condensation and rarefaction explains how air was and is the source of all things. When air is condensed, it grows colder and thickens. Condensed air forms clouds, clouds become water, and water, further condensed, turns to earth. When air becomes dilated so as to be rarer, it becomes fire. Thus Anaximenes explained what became known as the four elements: earth, air, fire, and water. But for him the *arche* was air.

With the fall of Miletus in 494 B.C., the "school of Miletus" evidently came to an end. Its proponents' explanation of the underlying nature of all things provided an excellent foundation for more sophisticated cosmologies that followed. Unlike Near Eastern cosmologists the Milesians seemed little influenced by the popular mythology of their day. Most significantly, Thales and Anaximenes reduced the vast multiplicity of everyday experience to one material substance and source. Thales' claim that "all is water" and Anaximenes' contention that "all is air" contradict the biblical distinction between the Creator and His creation. Because Milesian philosophers made God, man, and all reality, one, they were corporeal monists—they reduced the vast diversity of reality to a single physical essence or stuff. Though they debated what element is ultimate, they agreed that everything is reducible to a single essence.

Anaximander, however, denied that everything could be reduced to water or to air and went beyond the world of sensation, beyond what is observable, to the infinite. Nevertheless, like other Greek cosmologists, his approach rested upon pure speculation. While the Greek cosmologists were obviously working with what we have called general revelation (God's revelation in nature, history, and the human mind), they did not base their views on special revelation. Their search for an ultimate essence actually functioned as a form of idolatry because in seeking to identify the *arche*, they ascribed ultimacy to what was created rather than to the Creator. All of them rejected the biblical teaching that man can only know the infinite God through revelation.

Ionian Cosmologists

The next important "school" of philosophy was the "Ionians," a group of thinkers who lived in Greek cities in Southern Italy. With the Ionians, philosophy for the first time became a religion or a way of life. Milesian philosophers were not interested in being "saved" from anything. They spoke about gods, but not in a mystical or reverent way. In Greek mythology the Greek word *theos*, "god," generally means either a force of nature or the personification of some force, such as Zeus, Hera, or Aphrodite. During the seventh and sixth centuries B.C. Greek cities of Italy and Sicily experienced a religious revival, producing much more devout worship of gods such as Apollo and Dionysius. During this period the philosopher Pythagoras (born c. 570 B.C.) supposedly established a brotherhood with secret initiation ceremonies and strict vows. Similar to medieval monastic orders, it stressed rigorous self-examination.

The cosmology Pythagoreans developed reflected their religious ideals. As in ancient Persian religion, their view of reality was dualistic, although the Pythagoreans expressed this dualism in mathematical terms. Their dualism involved a conflict between two forces: "the unlimited" and "the limited." The unlimited represented the principle of chaos and aggression, and the limited stood for order. Before the cosmos came into existence, the unlimited ruled in complete darkness and disorder. The limited arose with fire and light in opposition to the unlimited, and the cosmos was born. Metaphysical dualism created moral opposition in the universe. The unlimited stood for evil and wickedness and was symbolized by feminine qualities. The limited represented goodness and was symbolized by masculine imagery. This view is quite similar to the great ultimate of ancient China with its concept of yin and yang. Their strong emphasis on mathematics led the Pythagoreans to teach that all things can be expressed by numerical relationships. From the fact that number accounts for harmony in music (for example in octaves, fifths, and fourths) Pythagoreans believed that number was the key to order or harmony in the entire cosmos. To them, number was the source of all reality, including good and evil as discussed above. Thus they showed that philosophical speculation can be an end in itself.

Heraclitus (c. 504 B.C.) of Ephesus[2] argued that behind change lay unity. What is fundamental to all being is not a "stuff" or essence, but a process. According to Heraclitus, the universe is constantly changing. He used the images of a river and of fire to explain his view. One cannot step into the same river twice because the river is constantly changing as water flows through its bed. In other words, the source of all reality is dynamic, never in a state of rest, never inert. Fire is the source of all, but behind fire is process. The cosmos is characterized by constant flux, a state of "becoming" — not "being," which is unchanging.

Opposed to Heraclitus was the cosmology of Parmenides (born c. 515 B.C.), the first logician, who denied the existence of change. His system of thought depended entirely on logical deduction. Parmenides thought it impossible to conceive of "nothing" as

2. Although Ephesus is in Asia Minor, not southern Italy, Heraclitus's thought most resembles Ionian cosmology, and we therefore discuss him in this section.

"something" that exists. Being, the source of reality, is the *one*. Anything that comes to be arises from either being or nonbeing. If it comes from being, then it already is. If it comes from nonbeing, it is nothing, because from nothing comes nothing. Parmenides affirmed being as the only reality. Whereas Heraclitus said that everything changes, Parmenides claimed, "Whatever is, is." Becoming is, then, illusory, as is all change. Motion and change are inconceivable to Parmenides, and if sense perception suggests to us that things change, then our senses are deceiving us. Reason shows that there is not, nor will there ever be, anything apart from being. Parmenides' view of reality challenged the concept of Heraclitus's changing cosmos. Parmenides rejected the evidence of the senses and relied on his abstract premises and reason, which show us there is no change, no motion, and no creation.

From the biblical perspective, Heraclitus's and Parmenides' disagreement over being and becoming as fundamental to the cosmos is not as important as the ideas they share in common. Both taught that there is no "creation out of nothing" (*ex nihilo*), a fundamental premise of biblical cosmology. God is the source of all reality. According to the doctrine of creation, God is not what He created, and what He created is not God. That doctrine affirms the Creator-creature distinction, which is basic not only to a biblical cosmology, but also to a biblical understanding of knowledge and ethics.

Pluralist Cosmologists

In the fifth century B.C. a new group of cosmologists arose, the pluralists, who argued that the universe has more than one underlying substance. Empedocles of Akragas, Sicily, was deeply religious (influenced by the Mystery Religions) and believed himself to have been reincarnated several times. As opposed to the one substance theory (monism) of Thales and the Milesians, Empedocles taught that all reality sprang from four "roots"—earth, air, fire, and water. These eternal and unchanging principles neither came into existence nor pass away. Two forces in the cosmos account for change and motion—"love" and "strife." Love, representing the power of unity and cohesiveness, attracts particles of earth, air, fire, and water, allowing them to combine. Strife, or hate, representing diversity and separation, divides particles, thus causing the destruction of objects. Empedocles appealed to the mythological forces of love and hate to explain natural change in the universe, but he failed to explain how the cyclical processes of nature take place.

Another pluralist, Anaxagoras (born c. 500 B.C.), influenced many Greek philosophers to consider the concept of *mind* the original cause of the cosmic process. Arriving in Athens in 480 B.C., Anaxagoras made it the principal center of philosophical speculation. He agreed with Parmenides that being is and that nothing can be added or subtracted from what is. Disagreeing with Empedocles' four "roots" theory, he argued that matter is a continuum, infinitely divisible so that each part of matter contains elements of every other part. Thus, by "mingling" and "separating," elements move and change. Anaxagoras also rejected Empedocles' argument that the forces of love and hate formed things out of the first shapeless mass. Instead, he contended that the principle of *nous* or "mind" has power over all things. *Nous* is present in all living things, according to Anaxagoras, and is the same in all. It, however, does not create matter. Matter is eternal; the function of *nous* is simply to stimulate motion. Later Greek thinkers criticized Anaxagoras for failing to develop a philosophy based on *nous* as the organizing principle of the cosmos.

A third pluralist, the leading advocate of atomic theory and the most consistently naturalistic of the pre-Socratics, was Democritus (born c. 460 B.C.). Democritus asserted that atoms are the source of all reality. For Democritus, atoms are invisible and have magnitude, yet cannot be divided. They are solid entities, unlike our conception of atoms today. Motion is inherent in the atom and is eternal. Democritus considered the universe a giant mechanism, which by necessity produces motion. His mechanistic view of the cosmos reduced all qualitative features to merely quantitative arrangements of atoms and spaces. All differentiations in our experience— everything from seeing the color of a sunset and tasting a cool, refreshing drink to loving a child or anguishing over a tragedy—are simply mechanical modifications of atoms. His atomic theory was reductionistic and naturalistic.

The monistic Milesians and Ionians and the pluralists helped to advance the development of Greek philosophy. While not providing fully satisfying answers to cosmological questions, they built a foundation for future Greek speculation. By raising questions about the relationship between being and becoming, they moved Greek thought beyond the early religious mythology. Their work contributed to subsequent epistemological theories, the formation of logic, and the progress of the natural and physical sciences.

In the fourth century B.C., philosophers with very different assumptions and concerns came on the scene. Holding a much higher view of man than the earlier cosmologists, they directed attention away from the universe to man's needs and desires and to the social order. Nevertheless, later Greek thinkers, especially Plato and Aristotle, did develop cosmologies as intricate parts of their systems of philosophy.

Plato and Aristotle

In the fourth century B.C. the Sophists, a group of popular teachers, redirected the emphasis of philosophy from cosmology to the nature and problems of man. They made philosophy more practical and functional by discussing morality, justice, education, war, and other issues not considered by earlier cosmologists. Although they held diverse views, the Sophists concurred that man is the measure of all things. Socrates strongly attacked their relativism and humanism, arguing that man could know absolute truths, especially through self-examination.

Plato

Building on Socrates' critique of the Sophists, Plato (427-347 B.C.) developed a dualism that he believed reconciled the views of Heraclitus and Parmenides and accounted for both permanence and change. He postulated the existence of two different dimensions—the ideal world and the real world. The world of "forms" or "ideas" is changeless, eternal, and perfect. The physical world is a copy of the ideal world. His understanding of the world of forms was derived from his epistemology and from his understanding of the soul. The world of sense experience is a world of change, the phenomenal world, where everything that exists is a copy of the forms in the world of ideas. What man experiences on earth is an imperfect, shadowy, changing copy of reality.

According to Plato, our knowledge about the universe comes not by revelation from a personal Creator, but rather by human reason apprehending impersonal, abstract forms. Plato argued that the Demiurge crafted the world of experience, a copy of the real, from preexistent forms. As an architect or builder, not a creator, the Demiurge fashioned chaotic or unorganized matter to form the world according to preexistent blueprints or forms. Man can know the world of forms because he has previously experienced it through his immortal soul. Prior to entering the body in the world of sense perception (the physical world), the soul passes through the river of forgetfulness (see the "myth of Er" at the conclusion of Plato's *Republic*). All that it has known of the "real" is forgotten. By experiencing copies of the forms in the phenomenal world, however, man remembers the real that he knew before birth (in a previous life). The soul, which the body holds prisoner, has within it certain universal principles not derived from experience, but recalled through experience. Plato wrote:

> The soul then, being immortal, has come to birth many times. It has seen what is here and in the underworld and all things, and there is nothing which it has not learned. . . . For all research is but recollection.[3]

In short, Plato's world of forms depends upon his understanding of knowledge, his theory of recollection, which, in turn, rests upon his understanding of the soul. In fact much of Plato's philosophy is based on his concept of the soul.

Plato believed that his dualism of (1) the perfect realm of eternal, unchanging forms and (2) the realm of matter—the world of sense experience, constant flux, and the source of illusion—actually unified philosophy and reality. He believed that the debate between Parmenides and Heraclitus was resolved by this dualistic conception of the cosmos. The cosmologies of Parmenides and Heraclitus each described only a portion of reality, not the whole. Parmenides' cosmology correctly depicted the world of forms. Heraclitus's views

3. Plato *Meno* 81-c.

accurately pictured our world of sense experience. But neither being nor becoming accounts for both aspects of reality, which Plato believed are totally separate from each other. Although Plato in later life emphasized mathematics as the symbol of the structure of reality, he continued to argue that the phenomenal world of experience contains only shadows and copies of the real.

Aristotle

The most unsatisfying feature of Plato's philosophy in many people's opinion is the separation or sharp discontinuity between being and becoming. As a student of Plato, Aristotle (384-322 B.C.) agreed with Plato that universal essences are the primary objects of knowledge. For Plato, being, universals, and truth, exist only in the world of forms, which are completely transcendent. In his *Metaphysics*, however, Aristotle argues that Plato's forms solve neither the problem of change in the phenomenal world, that is, the problem of coming-to-be, nor the problem of knowledge. Platonic forms do not help us to understand the nature or substance of particulars. Plato merely postulated entities in a transcendent, other-worldly existence equal in number to objects that he explained. Aristotle developed his doctrine of substance in order to retain form within change.

The "really real," (Plato's forms) according to Aristotle, is contained *in* the things of the universe, not in some transcendent realm. He substituted the term "substance" for Plato's "forms" to explain what is most real. The idea of substance also suggests a different form of knowledge. For both Plato and Aristotle, it is the form, the essence of a thing, that is knowable. For Aristotle, being and substance are associated with what is permanent or what persists through change. How then do we know the really real, the substance, the being? For Plato it was by recollection, dialectic or eristic reasoning (see vol. 1, chap. 10). For Aristotle we come to know the form, the essence of a thing, the universal by first studying concrete particulars using sense experience and reason. His basic principle was that the universal (idea, form, essence) exists only in the particular, never apart from it. Ideas, forms, or essences exist within concrete things. In all substances, animate or inanimate, form does not exist without matter, nor matter without form. Knowing an object, therefore, must involve both perception by our senses (which works on matter) and intelligent apprehension by reason (which apprehends internal form.) In the case of living things, in addition to the matter of the organism we can distinguish a soul, an inner form or activity without which it would not be living. The soul is a living being's "entelechy" (literally "having the goal inside of"), which makes actual what is potential in the organism. Assuming various types of soul (for example, vegetative, animal, and rational) as essential to life, Aristotle was thereby a vitalist. For him, organisms have an internal form or entelechy that accounts for their life and cannot be explained in terms of their material properties.[4]

As a metaphysician, Aristotle argued that earlier cosmologists did not distinguish between the various "causes" of what we experience by sense perception. He studied cause and substance in themselves, not as attached to any particular event or object, in order to know and understand being. Aristotle wrote,

> Some things are said to be because they are substances, others because they are the attributes of substances, others again because they are a process toward substance [i.e., a coming to be] or destructions or privations or qualities, or productive or generative of substance or of things related to substance or negations of one of these things or of substance; for we say even of not-being that it is not-being.[5]

Because earlier cosmologists failed to distinguish between causes of things that exist, of things coming-to-be, or of things passing from existence, Aristotle developed his doctrine of four causes. Previous cosmologists discussed change either in relation to opposites or as the result of pairs of opposites. Aristotle did not deny these explanations but added to them. For example, water (matter) is hot or cold as a result of opposites—the result of one being form (hot

4. Vitalists believe that there is something other than matter that governs the movement and development of living organisms. We will note in the next chapter that vitalism is under attack by some modern biologists. Although they are primarily thinking of Christians as supporters of vitalism, others such as Aristotle would oppose the contemporary belief that life can eventually be "explained" in terms of biochemistry alone.

5. Aristotle *Metaphysics* 1003 b6ff.

water), and the other privation (cold water). But he argued for two additional types of cause: the moving or efficient cause and the final cause. Thus he stated his doctrine of four causes: *material cause* (the matter or "potential" from which the object is made), *formal cause* (the shape, pattern, or organizing principle that distinguishes it from other bits of the same matter), *moving or efficient cause* (the agent who brings the object into being or imposes the form on the matter), and *final cause* (the purpose or goal for which the thing is produced). These four causes apply to all that is and all that is coming-to-be, all change experienced in the phenomenal world.

Consider the example of a table. What causes the table to be as it is? The material cause of a table is the wood from which it is produced (oak, maple, or pine); the formal cause is the idea or pattern in the mind of its maker, giving rise to its specific shape; the moving or efficient cause is the carpenter who uses his tools to craft the table; and the final cause is its purpose: utility, decoration, or sale. Or consider a game of tennis. Its material cause is the equipment used to play the game. The formal cause is the rules of tennis. The efficient or moving causes are the players and the referee and linesmen (if any) who interpret the rules. The final cause might differ radically depending on the purpose of the participants—professionals Ivan Lendl and Chris Evert play to make a living; amateurs play to achieve a ranking; and everyday "hackers" to get some exercise, improve their skills, or enjoy competition. To understand change (that is, any event or new circumstance in the universe) properly, people must analyze these four causes. Although the four are logically distinguishable, they are not always distinguishable in fact. Aristotle emphasized final cause because he regarded that goal or purpose to be the deepest explanation of things.

Most important, however, is his belief in the unity of matter and form. Matter and form always co-exist and are never apart from each other. Matter gives the substance to things and represents the potentiality of a thing; form is the outline, pattern, and boundary of things representing its actuality. If something were pure matter, possessing only materiality but no form, it would be indescribable, indistinguishable from anything else. If something were pure form, it would be like a concept of a perfect circle or square. It exists only as an idea in the mind. Only Aristotle's unmoved mover, which he considered beyond the world of material things and, as we shall see, the final cause of all things, is pure thought or conception. But everything in our experience has matter (or potentiality) and form (actuality). Aristotle's unity of matter and form through actuality and potentiality replaced Plato's dualism of the two worlds of being and becoming.

Because he emphasized the final cause or purpose, Aristotle argued that purpose is conceived in the mind, and form always precedes matter—thought precedes deed. The chicken indeed is before the egg! The egg exists only because there is an actual chicken to produce it, and it is produced with the goal (final cause) of becoming another adult chicken. Man is prior to boy; human being is prior to seed. Until the artist has an idea enabling him or her to work with oils on canvas, there is no painting. Everything that exists moves toward its end, its purpose. Man does not see in order to have eyes. He has eyes in order to see. A thief does not become a thief because he steals. A thief steals because he is a thief. A hero does not become a hero by doing heroic acts. He does heroic acts because he is a hero. Actuality always precedes potentiality. Everything moves toward a goal, and that goal, therefore, is logically the cause of all movement. Aristotle used this concept of progress toward a goal to explain all motion in the cosmos.

The cosmos or visible universe seems to be naturally divided into two regions. The terrestrial region, consisting of the earth and its atmosphere, is constantly changing, and the objects in it are impermanent. Yet above the cloud-filled atmosphere is the celestial region, where the sun, stars, and planets move in a stately procession. Aristotle taught that these celestial objects were not subject to change or destruction; hence they were eternal. As the moon shows regularity of motion and changes in phase, the boundary between the two regions was thought to be near the moon's orbit.

Aristotle accepted Empedocles' idea that everything in the terrestrial region is composed of four elements. Observation shows that they tend to arrange themselves naturally according to their density, with earth at the bottom, water above earth, air above water, and fire above air.[6] Aristotle observed that objects in the terrestrial region move toward their proper level in the universe; when they find their proper place, they have no more inclination to move and therefore remain at rest. Rocks will fall through air and water to get where they belong, at the bottom of things. Thus the center of the spherical earth is the very bottom, the lowest point in the spherical universe. From that point there is nowhere to go but up. Furthermore, the earth itself must be stationary because the element of which it is made is in its natural place and has no inclination to move. The Aristotelian doctrine that the earth does not move, based upon such reasoning and later supported by misconstrued biblical texts, persisted into the sixteenth century.

Aristotle observed that within the terrestrial region natural motion eventually ceases. Terrestrial objects slow down and stop if they are left alone. To keep an object moving requires a mover. On land, oxen keep carts going. On the seas, boats are kept going by winds or by rowers. If the mover stops, so (eventually) will the cart or the boat. The bright objects in the celestial region, however, do not slow down. They are so regular in their motion that their location· can be predicted in advance, and therefore there must be a steady mover in the heavens.

Above the earth and past the moon, Aristotle taught, all objects are composed of the noble element ether. In particular, there are nine transparent spheres, concentric with the earth, and nearly weightless. Connected to each of the first seven spheres (perhaps by means of an additional, rotating sphere) is a bright and lightweight object, which appears to be a planet. This bright orb represents an intelligent being (intelligence increasing with distance above the earth). In order, these spheres belong to the moon, to Venus (the goddess of love), to Mercury (the god of speech), to the radiant sun, to warlike Mars, to regal Jupiter, then to wise old Saturn. Beyond Saturn, at an immense distance, is a rotating sphere containing the fixed stars, all of which are lighter than fire. And beyond that is the first moving sphere (with nothing attached), the primum mobile, which is the largest object in the universe. The universe is huge, but

6. Elemental fire is more refined than flames, and though it rises to its place above the air, it cannot be seen to glow in the sky at night.

finite. To be beyond the primum mobile is to be beyond the spatio-temporal creation. There is light there, but it is pure intellectual light, the light of the greatest intelligence, of Aristotle's unmoved mover. The primum mobile's motion is the fastest of all the spheres. Its high speed results from its intelligent love for, and aspiration to be like, the divine intelligence, which is everywhere at once.[7]

The lesser spheres are also moved by a similar intelligent love for, and resulting imitation of, the divine intelligence, but their speed is less because the spheres are smaller and closer to the earth.

The brightness, clarity, and orderly movement of the higher regions of the cosmos reflect the activity of the celestial intelligences. The sphere of each intelligence imparts motion to the sphere below it. By the time of Cicero (50 B.C.) it was believed that subtle influences shone from each planet, affecting human fortunes. The celestial region seemed to be one of unchanging perfection, and the motions of the heavenly objects supposedly manifested that perfection and constancy. Therefore the planetary motions were held to be various combinations of motion in a circle (a perfect shape) at constant speed.

The unmoved mover is not an efficient cause, *pushing* the world of being, but a final cause, *drawing* the cosmos to its state of actuality. It is pure actuality, moving the heavenly bodies as final cause through its attractiveness as a desirable goal.

Is Aristotle's unmoved mover equivalent to the God who has revealed Himself to humanity in history as proclaimed by the prophets of Israel? Not at all. As pure actuality and final cause, the unmoved mover is pure reason and thus thinks without having any knowledge of the world of human experience. The unmoved mover is not the Creator, sustainer or revealer, but merely the highest intelligence of all, which all other intelligences in the universe love, admire, and aspire to imitate as nearly as their natures will permit. The existence and character of the unmoved mover are inferred logically, not known from acts of God in history interpreted by God's

7. High speed over great distances was held to be the way these intelligent beings approximated the ubiquity of the unmoved mover. For a helpful description of this cosmology as seen from the Middle Ages, see C. S. Lewis, *The Discarded Image* (New York: Cambridge University Press, 1967).

appointed prophets. Aristotle's god is a necessary logical consequence of his conception of the cosmos.

Aristotle's cosmology prevailed for almost two thousand years. It
was based on the assumption that autonomous man can know the
real through sense experience and reason. For Aristotle, man could
use reason to examine the particular in order to know the universal.
Because of the nature of what is knowable, the unity of form and
matter, the doctrine of causality, and the nature of substance, man's
reason makes known what is knowable, and makes what is potentially intelligible actually intelligible. For Aristotle, as for other
ancient Greek cosmologists, divine revelation was considered
unnecessary to provide a true understanding of reality, because, as
the Sophist philosopher Protagoras put it, man is the measure of all
things. Purpose or teleology, not necessity, dominates Aristotle's
philosophy—a purpose inherent in the structure of the universe,
not furnished by a transcendent, all-powerful Creator who reveals
His will and love for human beings.

For Further Reading

Burnet, J. *Early Greek Philosophy*. London: A. and C. Black, 1930.

Clark, Gordon H. *Thales to Dewey*. Boston: Houghton Mifflin, 1957. Pp. 30-61.

Copleston, Frederick C. *A History of Philosophy*, vol. 1. Garden City, N.Y.: Doubleday, 1962.

Edwards, Paul, ed. *Encyclopedia of Philosophy*, vol. 1, "Cosmology." New York: Macmillan, 1966. Pp. 237-43.

Guthrie, W. K. C. *A History of Greek Philosophy*. London: Cambridge University Press, 1962.

Lewis, C. S. *The Discarded Image*. New York: Cambridge University Press, 1967.

Lloyd, G. E. R. *Aristotle: The Growth and Structure of His Thought*. New York: Cambridge University Press, 1968.

II.
THE BIBLICAL
WORLD VIEW

3
A Cosmology of History: From Creation to Consummation
James Bibza and John D. Currid

Introduction

The biblical conception of the universe differs radically from the ancient mythological and Greek cosmologies discussed in chapters 1 and 2. Whereas ancient Egyptians and Mesopotamians sought to explain the structure and operation of the universe by the gods who were personified in nature, the Bible speaks of a Creator God who is apart from the universe. While ancient pagans speculatively searched for elements that order the universe internally, the Scriptures present an external force who created and continually sustains the cosmos. Because both testaments of the Bible stress this viewpoint, we will examine each testament's teaching separately and extensively.

Ancient Jewish cosmology rests upon the Hebrews' unique belief in a single God (monotheism) who began the universe and is completely sovereign over its operation. Old Testament writers taught that the unique, singular God called a people (Israel) out of the midst of pagan nations in order to be His peculiar and distinct agent in the world. Leviticus 11:44 reads: "For I am the Lord your God. Consecrate yourselves therefore, and be holy; for I am holy." The word "holy" in Hebrew (*qadash*) literally means "to be set apart, separate, distinct, and unique," indicating God's command that Israel repudiate the ways of pagan nations and follow His statutes only.

All of the thoughts and actions of the Hebrews were to be different from their neighbors, such as the Mesopotamians, the Egyptians, and the Canaanites. Magical acts, which underlay ancient pagan religions, were forbidden in Israel (Deut. 18:10-11). So were pagan rituals such as temple prostitution and child sacrifice (II Kings 23:4-10). The God of Israel is a sovereign deity who cannot be manipulated by such rites (see Exod. 7:8-13, in which God is shown as sovereign even over magical powers of Pharaoh's court magicians).

Furthermore, unlike ancient polytheists who believed that history follows the unending cycles of nature, the Hebrews understood history as linear. Time and history begin at the creation and are continually moving toward consummation. The Hebrews thus assumed history had both a specific beginning and an end.

Although, like ancient mythological cosmologists, the Hebrews emphasized the origin of the universe, their understanding of that beginning differed dramatically from other ancient views.

Hebrew Cosmogony

The name of the first book of the Hebrew Scriptures, Genesis, literally means "origin, beginning." It narrates the Hebrew view of the creation of the universe, as well as the beginning of the human race, the nations of the earth, and God's covenant people, Israel. A careful examination of the first chapter of Genesis reveals the basic features of Hebrew cosmogony.

Genesis begins by introducing us to the power and glory of God: "In the beginning God created . . . " The narrative exalts the great *Elohim*, in His eternal aloneness. Through the divine revelation, we hear and see Him penetrating the universe's silence, shining into the primordial darkness, in order to create a sphere where He might display His sovereignty, incomparability, and power. Through creation God reveals Himself and His glory. "The heavens are telling of the glory of God; And their expanse is declaring the work of His hands" (Ps. 19:1).

Genesis 1 describes God's creation of the "heavens and the earth." Here we have a figure of speech called a merism, a set of opposite terms with an all-inclusive character.[1] The phrase "the heavens and the earth" is used here and throughout the Old Testa-

---

1. Cf. the merism in Ps. 139:8: "If I ascend to heaven, Thou art there! If I make my bed in Sheol, Thou art there!" (RSV). Where then is God? Everywhere.

ment to teach that God created everything that exists, (e.g., Gen. 14:19; Exod. 31:17).[2]

How did God create? The third verse of Genesis 1 indicates that God declared, "'Let there be light'; and there was light." By simply speaking God created the universe and all that is in it. Numerous other biblical passages demonstrate that God's speaking is the method of creation. In Psalm 33:6, the psalmist declares that "by the word of the Lord the heavens were made." And Psalm 148:5 extols God's name, "For He commanded and they were created." Summarizing the New Testament view, Hebrews 11:3 reads, "By faith we understand that the worlds were prepared by the word of God."

Furthermore, God's verbal fiat resulted in the creation of the universe *ex nihilo*, "out of nothing." The Hebrew term *bara* ("create") in Genesis 1:1 supports the idea that all reality (other than God) arose from the nonexistent. A variety of ancient Hebrew words express the idea of forming or making, and they may have either God or a human agent as their subject (see Gen. 3:21; Exod. 38:1-3). But the subject of the word *bara* is always and only God, never man. And the word never refers to creation out of a preexistent material. It is applied only to creation *ex nihilo,* which no one but God can do.

Each act of God's creation *ex nihilo* in Genesis 1 follows the same pattern:

1. Pronouncement: "And God said . . . "
2. Command: "Let there be . . . "
3. Completion: "And it was so."
4. Judgment: "And God saw that it was good."
5. Temporal Framework: "And there was evening and . . . morning, one day" (etc.).

Evangelical Christians today disagree over the precise duration of the creation. The three principal evangelical views depend mainly upon different understandings of the Hebrew word *yom* ("day").

---

2. This proposition directly contradicts the pagan beliefs we surveyed in chapter 1. The pagan cosmogonies emphasized the origin and descent of the gods (theogony), and how the universe was created by means of the gods' quarrels, battles, and affairs.

1. *The Literal View.* This interpretation states that each day mentioned in Genesis 1 is a literal twenty-four-hour period. Moreover, each twenty-four-hour day of creation is reported chronologically, so that during the first twenty-four hours of time God created light, in the second day the firmament, and so forth until the completion of creation after six twenty-four-hour periods. The Genesis 1 narrative, therefore, is quite simply understood as history.

This interpretation has had the greatest support throughout the history of the church. The majority of the Reformers, for example, held this view. John Calvin asserted, "Let us conclude that God himself took the space of six days [for creation], in order to accommodate his works to the capacity of men."[3] Many modern commentators also accept this view.[4]

Critics, however, expose some striking problems with the literal perspective. First, natural laws must be discounted to accept this interpretation. Indeed, according to a chronological understanding of Genesis 1, some things are created prior to other things upon which they are naturally dependent. So, for example, light is created on day one while the sun is not created until day four. Second, critics argue that the accounts of creation reported in Genesis 1 and 2 present different orders (see, for example, 2:19, where the animals are created after mankind). If Genesis 1 is literal history, how is one to interpret the chronology of events in Genesis 2? Third, many suggest that the seventh day is not a literal twenty-four-hour day, but God's eternal Sabbath rest in heaven. If this is true, the other six days may also be figurative as well. Last, some interpreters argue that geological evidence that the earth has existed for about 4.5 billion years and man for approximately 2.5 million years contradicts a literal six-day creation.

Although modern commentators vehemently attack the literal view, the position has some strong supportive data. First, there is no indication of figurative language in Genesis 1. If the narrative is to be considered imagery, one would expect to encounter many of the

3. Calvin's Commentaries on the *First Book of Moses Called Genesis,* vol. 1 (Grand Rapids: Eerdmans, 1948), p. 78.
4. Cf. C. A. Simpson, C. T. Fritsch, Keil and Delitzsch, and most notably E. J. Young. See E. J. Young, *Studies in Genesis One* (Grand Rapids: Baker, 1964).

essentials of figurative language (e.g., schema, metaphor, and other tropes), but there are none.[5] Second, other biblical texts seem to indicate that the first chapter of Genesis should be read literally. Advocates of the position often point to the Sabbath command in Exodus 20:11, which says, "For in six days the Lord made the heavens and the earth, the sea and all that is in them, and rested on the seventh day; therefore the Lord blessed the sabbath day and made it holy." In the context of the Decalogue this command demonstrates that the seven days of creation in Genesis 1 are to be a pattern for each Israelite week (i.e., six days of labor and one day of rest). It is not likely that a nonliteral seven days would serve as a proper or useful paradigm for the Israelite week; thus, the defenders of the literal position argue that Moses understood creation to have occurred in six literal days.

2. *The Day-Age View (Concordist Theory)*. In this interpretation, the Hebrew word *yom* is understood to refer to an indeterminable length of time. Each "day" of creation, therefore, is figurative, indicating a long time rather than a literal twenty-four-hour period. The chronology of the days remains the same, but the days themselves are extended. First proposed in the nineteenth century in response to new scientific discoveries regarding the age of the earth, this position attempts to harmonize geological research and Scripture. Concordists insist that the term *yom* can be used to describe periods of time extending to four billion years.[6]

In the Old Testament the term *yom* is sometimes used to indicate a lengthened period of time (see Prov. 25:13). Psalm 90:4 is a good example: "For a thousand years in your eyes are like a day [*yom*] . . . " (NIV). Henri Blocher also points out, "The text of Genesis provides a very valuable indication that this must be the case with the seven 'days'. Indeed, the seventh day does not conclude with the

5. Although figurative language is not present, opponents of the literal view point out that strophic structure, parallelism, and refrain lines indicate that Gen. 1 contains poetic literary elements and is not simply prose writing.

6. Bernard Ramm, *The Christian View of Science and Scripture* (Exeter: Paternoster, 1955), p. 211. Ramm identifies the first advocates of the concordist view as J. Dana, J. Dawson, and Hugh Miller. See Derek Kidner, *Genesis* (London: InterVarsity, 1967), pp. 55-56.

formula, 'there was evening and there was morning', from which one must with Augustine deduce its permanence. . . . If the seventh day extends across thousands of years of history, the six others can [also] cover the millions of centuries of cosmogony."[7]

Several objections, however, are frequently raised to the day-age view. (1) The use of a number in conjunction with the word *yom* (i.e., first day, second day. . .) occurs over one hundred times throughout the Pentateuch, and in every instance it refers to a twenty-four-hour, solar day. (2) Likewise, whenever the word *yom* appears in the plural in the Old Testament (about seven hundred times) it always refers to literal twenty-four-hour, solar days. Thus, when Moses comments in Exodus 20:11 that "in six days the Lord made the heavens and the earth," he likely understands that creation occurred in six literal days. (3) There are many Hebrew words that the writer could have used other than *yom* to indicate that creation took place over a long period of time, such as *'olam* ("age, forever").

3. *The Framework Hypothesis.* This view asserts that Genesis 1:1-2:3 is a literary work using poetic elements to arrange creation by topic, not by sequence or chronology. Thus, the order of the Genesis 1 account is figurative, as is the use of the term *yom* ("day"). The lack of a complete chronological sequence in no way implies a lack of historicity. The topical structure of the Genesis narrative is as follows:

KINGDOMS RULED BY KINGS

KINGDOMS (DOMAINS)	KINGS (RULERS)
Day 1. Light: Gen. 1:3–5	Day 4. Light Bearers: vv. 14-19
Day 2. Sea, Sky: vv. 6-8	Day 5. Fish, Birds: vv. 20-23
Day 3. Land: vv. 9-13	Day 6. Land Animals: vv. 24–31

Day 7. Sabbath

7. Henri Blocher, *In the Beginning* (Leicester: Inter-Varsity, 1984), p. 44.

In the six days of creation, there are two sets of three: the first triad (days 1, 2, 3) establishes the three kingdoms, and the second triad (days 4, 5, 6) creates the rulers over those kingdoms with a direct correspondence between days 1 and 4, 2 and 5, and 3 and 6. Hence, the author of Genesis (Moses), according to the framework view, explains creation by presenting pictures of what happened in the creation, with the refrain line "And there was evening and there was morning, the first day" (etc.) telling the reader that the first frame is over and the new picture is about to begin.

As Henri Blocher points out, the framework theory is not as recent an interpretation as many have supposed.[8] St. Augustine seems to have held to this view in a very primitive form (see his *De Genesis ad Litteram*), as did Thomas Aquinas. In the modern era, such respected evangelical scholars as H. N. Ridderbos and Meredith G. Kline favor the framework hypothesis.

The literary view allows for a harmonization between the events recorded in Genesis 1 and general revelation. Thus, the framework view alone allows for the possibility that the sun is older than the earth, a position most modern scientists think almost certain. Furthermore, the glaring differences between the Genesis 1 and Genesis 2 accounts of creation no longer cause difficulty, with Genesis 2:5 presupposing that God sustained His creation using ordinary, providential means whereas both the literal and day-age views presuppose extraordinary providential care.[9] Moreover, the fact that some of Scripture is topical and not chronological (material from the Old Testament prophets, for example) seems to support the framework view. Chronology seems to be of little consequence in the artistic arrangement of Genesis 1.

Even though some of the advocates of the framework theory refuse to acknowledge any weaknesses in the position,[10] it does

8. Ibid., pp. 49-50.
9. One of the greatest problems for the literalist and concordist is how to harmonize Genesis 2:5 with a literal week for the creation of the universe. Regarding this issue, see M. G. Kline, "Because It Had Not Rained," *Westminster Theological Journal* 20 (1957-1958): 146-57.
10. See Blocher, *In the Beginning*, pp. 39-59, who vigorously attacks the concordist and literalist views, but does not admit even one failing of the framework hypothesis.

suffer from a few problems. First, the argument that Genesis 1 presents a poetic structure in which the kings of days 4-6 rule over the kingdoms of days 1-3, is a bit strained. In what manner, for example, are the birds and fish (day 5) rulers over the sky and sea (day 2)? Certainly the fish and birds dominate those areas in numbers, but how do they govern them?[11] A second criticism has already been mentioned: the text of Genesis 1 contains no indication of figurative language, such as schema and tropes. Opponents argue that the Bible is emptied of its true meaning and power when it is taken figuratively, because it was never meant to be interpreted so. Finally, a few interpreters argue that if Moses used poetry as a means of describing the creation event, his account cannot be chronological. However, much of the Old Testament that was written in poetic style, such as the book of Job, is also historical and chronological.

Clearly, each of the positions we have considered has advantages and disadvantages. Christians can hold to any of the three and still maintain a high regard for the authority of Scripture. All three positions assert that Genesis 1 teaches that God is the Creator and sustainer of the universe. It is He "who made heaven and earth, the sea and all that is in them!" (Ps. 146:6).

Hebrew Cosmology

Having analyzed the nature of God's creative act, we now consider the Hebrews' understanding of the cosmos He created. Frequently the Old Testament uses a building motif to describe the universe.[12] It repeatedly presents the universe in figurative terms as a three-storied building, composed of the heavens above, the earth beneath, and the subterranean sector below the earth (see Exod. 20:4). The heavens consist of vaults (Job 38:22), in which windows are secured, held up by columns that reach to the earth (Job 26:11). The heavens are compared to a veil or tent, which God has stretched over the earth (Isa. 40:22; Ps. 104:2). The earth itself is

11. It might be better to speak of days 1-3 as *dwellings* and days 4-6 as *dwellers*. In this case, domination and rulership would not be necessary elements of the relationship.

12. For a more developed presentation of this view, see M. G. Kline, *Kingdom Prologue I* (unpublished manuscript, Gordon-Conwell Theological Seminary).

supported by pillars with foundations extending into the subterranean sector (Job 9:6; 38:6; Pss. 18:15; 104:5). The subterranean area, called *sheol* by the Hebrews, is the place where man descends after death (Gen. 37:35; 42:38; 44:29; Num. 16:30-33). Deep beneath the earth where darkness reigns (read Ps. 88), *sheol* is sometimes pictured as a prison with gates and bars (Isa. 38:10; Job 38:17).

Even Genesis 1 contains architectural imagery, demonstrated by its division of the world into compartments or "rooms" for habitation by various creatures. As well, the sky, which stretches over the earth, is a canopy-like covering ("the firmament") serving as a roof for the cosmic structure. Lights are installed in the roof in order to provide light.

The Hebrew conception of the universe as an architectural structure is clearly figurative. Architectural imagery means that the cosmos is designed and constructed with the same care and planning as a building. That the universe was intricately planned and designed emphasizes God's role as designer. The Old Testament repeatedly explains that God is the great architect and builder of the universe. In Job 38:4-10, God questions Job: "Where were you when I laid the foundation of the earth! Tell Me, if you have understanding, Who set its measurements, since you know? Or who stretched the line on it? On what were its bases sunk? Or who laid its cornerstone?" Such rhetorical questions indicate that God Himself, figuratively speaking, laid the earth's foundations and determined its measurements with plumb line in hand. Likewise, Proverbs 8:30 states that God is the master builder who used His wisdom to construct the earth.

The cosmic structure that the Lord created was designed to house more than earth's creatures. It was built as a holy abode for the living God Himself! Psalm 11:4 says, "The Lord is in His holy temple; the Lord's throne is in heaven." Thus, the universe is God's kingly residence where He dwells and His royal court where He presides. Consequently all of creation is to serve Him. "Thus says the Lord, Heaven is My throne, and the earth is My footstool" (Isa. 66:1).

Invisible angelic beings who attend the Lord also reside in the cosmos. Nehemiah 9:6 affirms this point: "Thou alone art the Lord, Thou has made the heavens, The heaven of heavens with all their host." The latter part of this verse suggests that "all their host," which refers in part to the invisible angels, were made by the Lord and dwell in the heaven of heavens (i.e., the cosmos). In addition to the angels who attend the Lord, evil spirits also reside in the cosmos. Satan (a title meaning "adversary") is a rebellious spiritual being who dwells in the cosmic house and roams about the earth seeking to wreak havoc on mankind (Job 1:7).[13] Moreover, he seems to have access to the Lord, sometimes appearing before God's very throne (Job 1:6ff.; 2:1; Zech. 3:1).

Cosmological Implications of the Fall in the Old Testament

When God created the cosmos, He made man ruler over the rest of creation. Genesis 1:28 clearly identifies man's intended position: "And God blessed them; and God said to them, 'Be fruitful and multiply, and fill the earth, and subdue it; and rule over the fish of the sea and over the birds of the sky, and over every living thing that moves on the earth.'" Psalm 8 comments on man's status at creation, explaining that God "hast made him a little lower than God, and dost crown him with glory and majesty!" (v. 5). God appointed man over creation, to be overlord and overseer of the cosmic house, crowning him with glory, and giving him dominion over all creation.

Man, however, failed to exercise dominion over creation and allowed a lower creature to dominate him (i.e., the serpent of Gen. 3).[14] Instead of responsibly governing creation, he yielded to the enticements of the great tempter. The results of man's fall into sin are tremendous.

First, the fall affected *man himself* in many ways: (1) As a result man and woman are *alienated from God*. Genesis 3:7-11 describes this separation, depicting Adam and Eve as hiding from God imme-

13. The view that Satan is an individual being and does not merely represent the concept of evil is supported by the occasional use of the definite article with the term Satan ("the Satan"). See, for example, the references occurring in Job 1-2 and Zech. 3. The New Testament evidence confirms this understanding (cf. Luke 4; also Rev. 12:9, which incidentally connects Satan with the serpent who tempted Eve in the Garden of Eden).

14. The serpent undoubtedly tempted the woman first in order to undermine the original authority structure that God had appointed, in which the man was the highest authority in creation.

diately after their sin. (2) The man and woman are *alienated from each other.* Prior to sinning they were vulnerable, open, and intimate with each other, symbolized by their physical nakedness. After sinning they covered themselves and Adam blamed Eve for his sin. (3) The man and woman were *alienated from eternal life.* Death is a result of sin, as the apostle Paul wrote: "The wages of sin is death" (Rom. 6:23). (4) They were *alienated from the Garden of Eden.* God drove them from the garden and never allowed them to return (Gen. 3:24).[15] (5) Adam and Eve were *alienated from themselves,* evident in their inability to accept responsibility for their action when God confronted them.

Second, not only man but *the entire cosmos* was affected by man's sin. Genesis 3:17-18 discusses how creation is subjected to vanity, futility, and frustration because of man's fall: "Cursed is the ground because of you; in toil you shall eat of it all the days of your life. Both thorns and thistles it shall grow for you" (Gen. 5:29). Commenting on the Genesis 3 event Ecclesiastes declares: "'Vanity of vanities,' says the Preacher, 'Vanity of vanities! All is vanity.'" The universe's continuous cycle of birth, growth, death, and decay demonstrates this vanity, futility, and frustration to which God has subjected nature. The universe is in a process of deterioration (what Paul in Rom. 8. calls "slavery to corruption"), and it appears to be running down. Nature, like man, is in a state of decay, deterioration, pain, and futility.[16]

---

15. Other effects of the fall, such as the imputation of Adam's sin to all of mankind, are very important, but space demands the limitation of our discussion.

16. Some commentators argue that nature was not greatly influenced by man's fall into sin. Arthur H. Lewis, for example, observes, "Nothing in the narrative suggests that the realm of nature has been altered in a fundamental way" ("The Localization of the Garden of Eden," *Bulletin of the Evangelical Theological Society* 11 [1968]:174). Meredith G. Kline, *Kingdom Prologue I,* p. 81 agrees: "The Bible does not require us, therefore, to think of the character and working of man's natural environment before the Fall as radically different from what is presently the case." However, when Paul comments in Rom. 8:20 that the whole created order "was subjected to futility," he is really saying that nature did not remain the same after the fall. There is indeed a change, and it is what Paul calls "slavery to corruption" (Rom. 8:21).

The Cosmological Redemptive Hope in the Old Testament

The Old Testament teaches that the present futility to which the whole cosmos is subjected is merely temporary. A time will come when the universe will be saved from corruption, delivered from decay, and restored to its proper order and structure. That is to say, Old Testament writers prophesy that one day the effects of sin will be removed from the cosmos, and the universe will be regenerated. Isaiah describes a redeemed future condition of the whole creation as follows: "For behold, I [God] create new heavens and a new earth; And the former things shall not be remembered or come to mind. But be glad and rejoice forever in what I create; For behold, I create Jerusalem for rejoicing, And her people for gladness. I will also rejoice in Jerusalem, and be glad in My people; And there will no longer be heard in her the voice of weeping and the sound of crying" (65:17-19).

Two principal elements of the future regenerated cosmos may be identified in the Old Testament. First, God will redeem His chosen people, restoring them to a proper relationship with Himself. Ezekiel speaks of redemption this way: "And I [God] will make a covenant of peace with them; it will be an everlasting covenant with them. And I will place them and multiply them, and will set My sanctuary in their midst forever. My dwelling place also will be with them; and I will be their God, and they will be My people" (37:26-27). The prophet Jeremiah provides another description of mankind's future redemption:

> "Behold, days are coming," declares the Lord, "when I will make a new covenant with the house of Israel and with the house of Judah, not like the covenant which I made with their fathers in the day I took them by the hand to bring them out of the land of Egypt, My covenant which they broke, although I was a husband to them," declares the Lord. "But this is the covenant which I will make with the house of Israel after those days," declares the Lord, "I will put My law within them, and on their heart I will write it; and I will be their God, and they shall be My people. And they shall not teach again, each man his neighbor and each man his brother, saying 'Know the Lord,' for they shall all know Me, from the least of them to the greatest of

them," declares the Lord, "for I will forgive their iniquity, and their sin I will remember no more" (31:31-34).

These are but two of many Old Testament prophecies that describe the future salvation and restoration of God's chosen people (see also, Jer. 24:7; 32:40; 33:14-16).

Second, the Old Testament prophets announce that God's entire creation will share in the redemption of His people. The cosmos, now subjected to futility, will someday be restored to harmony. As D. Martyn Lloyd-Jones explained:

> It is only then that creation will really be free to develop as it was meant to do, as God created it to do. It is only then that it will be entirely delivered from every element of disintegration. We saw that, at the present time, it is "subject to vanity", that there is a kind of futility about it, that there is this element of decay and putrefaction in it. Then, it will be free from everything of that nature. There will be no more strife, no more discord, no more disease.[17]

We read in Isaiah Chapter 11, verses 6-9:

> And the wolf will dwell with the lamb, and the leopard will lie down with the kid, and the calf and the young lion and the fatling together; and a little boy will lead them. Also the cow and the bear will graze; their young will lie down together; and the lion will eat straw like the ox. And the nursing child will play by the hole of the cobra, and the weaned child will put his hand on the viper's den. They will not hurt or destroy in all My holy mountain, for the earth will be full of the knowledge of the Lord as the waters cover the sea.

Isaiah provides a further description of the restored creation in chapter 35:

> The wilderness and the desert will be glad, And the Arabah will rejoice and blossom; Like the crocus It will blossom profusely And rejoice with rejoicing and shout of joy. . . . No lion will be there, Nor will any vicious beast go up on it; These will not be found there. But the redeemed will walk there, And the ransomed of the Lord will return, And come with joyful shouting

---

17. D. Martyn Lloyd-Jones, *Romans: An Exposition of Chapter 8:17-39* (Grand Rapids: Zondervan, 1975), p. 76.

to Zion, With everlasting joy upon their heads. They will find
gladness and joy, And sorrow and sighing will flee away (35:
1-2a, 9-10).

This overview of Old Testament cosmology clearly demonstrates
that the Hebrews maintained a historical conception of the universe: the cosmos was created and is now moving toward a climax.
Such a view strikingly contrasts with views of Israel's contemporaries. Whereas the Eygptians, Mesopotamians, and Canaanites perceived the universe as locked in the unending cycles of nature, never
heading anywhere, the Hebrews saw the universe as moving according to the plan of God, the Lord of history.

The Hebrew conception of reality conflicts with Greek cosmologies, as well. The Greeks were primarily interested in presenting a
rational description for the order they observed in the cosmos. Working only with general revelation, which they naturally suppressed,
they sought to understand the cosmos by speculative reason. Most of
their cosmologies were preoccupied with principles found within the
universe. The Hebrews, however, believing that the universe was created and sustained by God, had little desire to probe the hidden
mechanics of the universe. They were more engaged with understanding God's revealed nature and how He works within His created
order, especially His relationship with man.

New Testament Cosmology

Strong elements of continuity exist between the Old and New
Testaments on such matters as the nature of the use of architectural
imagery for the cosmos, the role of angels, and the consummation
of the cosmos. However, the New Testament further reveals the role
of Jesus Christ both in the creation of the earth and in the consummation of human history. This is exactly what we would expect since
God progressively revealed more and more of His will and His
nature as He guided His people throughout history. What is incomplete and partial and anticipatory in the Old Testament is now
fleshed out or completed in the New Testament. Thus, the promise-
fulfillment motif, already seen in our previous study of theology,
anthropology, and epistemology, is also evident here.

Christ and Creation

Like the Old Testament, New Testament writers clearly teach that God created the universe. The New Testament does not even hint that the creation might be co-eternal with the Creator. Christ explicitly affirms God's separation from His creation in Mark 13:19 ("from the beginning of the creation which God created," RSV). So does Paul, who states that God revealed Himself in creation (Rom. 1:20) and that the root sin of mankind is worshipping created things instead of the Creator (Rom. 1:25).[18] Furthermore, Hebrews 11:1-3 confirms the Old Testament teaching both that God created *ex nihilo* and that "the universe was formed at God's command, so that what is seen was not made out of what was visible."

A new dimension is added to the Old Testament teaching about creation, however, by the New Testament's insistence that Jesus Christ played an active role in creation. Nowhere does this come out more clearly than in John 1:1-3, which asserts that Jesus, "the Word," existed from "the beginning" and "through Him all things were made" (NIV). To underscore this point, John, using synonymous parallelism, continues, ". . . without Him nothing was made that has been made" (NIV). John's phrase "in the beginning" (emphasizing the preexistence of the Word) uses the same formula as Genesis 1:1, thus clearly referring the reader to the precreation state. The contrast between light and darkness, prominent in both Genesis 1:3-5 and John's prologue (1:1-18) shows further a parallelism between the two texts. Moreover, Genesis 1 describes God's speech as the agent of His creative activity, and John 1:3 depicts the *Word* as the agent through whom "all things were made," showing the strong linkage between the two passages. What in Genesis is described only as God's spoken word, in John is explained to be literally the preexistent Word or Son of God. Paul expresses the same point in Colossians 1:16 when he says about Jesus, "For by him all things were created: things in heaven and on earth, visible and invisible . . . all things were created by him and for him" (NIV). The author of Hebrews continues this theme,

18. Other specific passages asserting that all things were made by God include Acts 17:24; Rom. 11:36; I Cor. 8:6; 11:12; Eph. 3:9; Rev. 4:11).

declaring that God, the Father, made the universe through His Son (1:2).

Yet this emphasis upon the creative activity of Christ, the Son, in no way lessens the creative activity of God the Father, since the creative act is seen as a unity, and the Son and the Father are also understood as sharing an essential unity. John 1:1 hints at this by stating that the Word is both God and "with God." John's assertion certainly involves the mystery of the Trinity. While distinctions can be made between the Word and God, in essence they are one, and so there must be unity to their creative acts as well. Hebrews 3:3, 4 makes the same point even more explicitly, stating that Jesus has greater honor than Moses, just as the builder of a house is greater than the house, itself. However, in 3:4 our author says that "God is the builder of everything" (NIV). This interchanging of Jesus and God is common in Hebrews and points to their fundamental unity as architects of this world. In 1 Corinthians 8:6 Paul links the creative and sustaining activity of the Father and the Son.

One additional theme of some significance is that the New Testament not only affirms Jesus' role in creation, but also teaches that the created order exists for the sake of Jesus Christ. As Colossians 1:16 puts it, "All things were created through Him and *for* Him" (RSV). Pauls phrase "all things" includes everything visible and invisible, both in heaven and on earth. In other words, the entire creation is Christocentric (Christ-centered) not anthropocentric (man-centered). All things, including every aspect of our lives, are to center on Jesus Christ. Focusing our attention on Christ in cosmology helps us to see ourselves properly. Although as God's image bearers we are the crown of creation, we and the world as a whole serve a greater purpose: the glory of the risen Christ.

Christ and the Cosmos

As does the Old Testament, the New Testament uses figurative architectural imagery to describe the universe. Thus Paul, in II Corinthians 12:2, while referring to a vision he has had, states that he was "caught up to the third heaven." Jesus, in discussing the events before His return, proclaims: "At that time men will see the Son of Man coming in clouds with great power and glory. And he will send his angels and gather the elect from the four winds, from the ends of the earth to the ends of the heavens." In fact, several of the "building" images used in the New Testament are connected with the end of this present age. Thus, in John 14:1-3, Jesus tells His disciples not to be troubled because He is going to prepare a place for them: "In my Father's house are many rooms; if it were not so, I would have told you" (NIV). In Revelation 21, John describes the New Jerusalem as having twelve gates, one for each of the twelve tribes of Israel, and the walls of the city as having twelve foundations, corresponding to the twelve apostles. He then describes the measurements of the city and the various materials used in its construction. John depicts the eternal house of God in Revelation 21 and 22 as a restored and consummated paradise of God. This suggests that the original creation of heaven and earth was also a "process of divine housebuilding—the original construction of a dwelling place for God."[19] Here, again, we find both continuity with and fulfillment of a basic Old Testament motif. This theme thus begins and ends the Scriptures (in Gen. and Rev.).

The New Testament also makes use of architectural imagery in a somewhat different fashion from the Old Testament. This is seen most clearly in Hebrews 3:1-6, where the author speaks of the house of God (again figuratively), but this time as the people of God. The author compares Jesus and Moses, concluding that both were faithful over God's house. However, since the builder of a house receives more honor than the house itself, Jesus is worthy of greater honor than Moses. The author declares, "And we are his house, if we hold on to our courage and the hope of which we boast." This statement corresponds nicely with Paul's proclamation that Christians are members of God's household, "built on the foundation of the apostles and prophets, with Jesus Christ himself as the chief cornerstone" (Eph. 2:19-21, NIV). Changing the metaphor slightly, Paul continues, "In him the whole building is joined together and rises to become a holy temple in the Lord. And in him you too are being built together to become a dwelling in which God lives by his Spirit" (NIV). The Old Testament teaches that God dwelt with His people

19. Meredith G. Kline, *The Structure of Biblical Authority* (Grand Rapids: Eerdmans, 1972), p. 86.

in a special place, the Holy of Holies, a sacred part of a physical temple. Now the New Testament emphasizes that God actually dwells spiritually within His people.

In the twentieth century the Bible's architectural language and teaching of an open cosmos—that God and other spiritual forces may influence events in our space-time history—has been persistently criticized. Critics often allege that New Testament writers present a "primitive" picture of the universe, which their contemporaries accepted literally. The modern scientific explanation of the cosmos as a closed system of natural causes (see our next chapter), critics claim, demonstrates that biblical teaching on cosmology and related matters is simply outmoded, the result of ignorant, superstitious people.[20]

Denunciations of the biblical cosmology as "primitive" and prescientific, however, are open to serious question. First, as C. S. Lewis has pointed out, "If we are going to talk at all about things which are not perceived by the senses, we are forced to use language metaphorically."[21] In order to be understood, the biblical writers could talk about God and supernatural reality only by using words that refer to God's activity as if it were open to our ordinary sense experience. In fact, when people attempt to eliminate either architectural or anthropomorphic language, Lewis notes, they merely substitute other images for the ones discarded.[22] For example, even though we may not believe in a local heaven "up there" or a hell "down there," what will we substitute for the imagery of Christ's incarnation (His "coming down" and taking on human flesh), His death and descent

20. Rudolf Bultmann's classic criticism of New Testament (and Old Testament) cosmology reflects an absolute acceptance of a natural order in which God has no part. Bultmann not only dismissed architectural imagery and the existence of spiritual beings but also denied any possibility of miraculous acts: "Now that the forces and the laws of nature have been discovered, we can no longer believe in spirits, whether good or evil. . . . The miracles of the New Testament have ceased to be miraculous, and to defend their historicity by recourse to nervous disorders or hypnotic effects only serves to underline the fact. . . . It is impossible to use electric light and wireless and to avail ourselves of modern medical and surgical discoveries, and at the same time to believe in the New Testament world of spirits and miracles" ("New Testament and Mythology," in Kerygma and Myth [London: SPCK, 1964], pp. 4, 5).

21. C. S. Lewis, Miracles (New York: Macmillan, 1947), p. 74.

22. Ibid., p. 75.

into hell, and His resurrection and ascension back "into heaven"? We can explain the incarnation and ascension as Christ's "entering and leaving" the cosmos (substituting a sideways motion for descent and reascent). But we are still confronted with the fact that biblical writers affirm miraculous events caused by God in an open universe, events that our normal scientific categories cannot explain. Christ's ascension into heaven was observable and "miraculous" to its original observers and still would be today if it occurred in view of our foremost scientists. Lewis states that we have to "explain" each of these events in ways that are consistent with our present understanding of the cosmos, but we must not "explain them away."

Second, Lewis argues that it is "quite erroneous to think that man started with a 'material' God or 'Heaven' and gradually spiritualized them," as critics frequently assert.[23] Rather, these concepts and other related ones originally had within them the ideas of both the physical and the spiritual. In time people distinguished between the material and spiritual. Lewis puts it well when he concludes that "the material imagery was never taken literally by anyone who had reached the stage [of philosophical thinking] when he could understand what 'taking it literally meant.'"[24] Thus, as our scientific and philosophical knowledge increases, Christians will have to explain their continued use of biblical cosmological language. But they must also continue to insist that the cosmos is open to the activity of God, who maintains it by His providence and does His mighty works for our benefit.

In a manner analogous to the Old Testament, the New Testament teaches that both faithful angels and Satan and his demonic followers inhabit the celestial cosmos. Although angels are mentioned frequently in the New Testament, every reference is incidental to some other topic. In other words, God's revelation never intends, as its primary purpose, to teach about the nature of angels. Therefore, some of our questions about angels must remain unanswered. However, the New Testament states enough for us to piece together some picture of what angels are and what their function is.

23. Ibid., p. 79.
24. Ibid., p. 80.

Angels are created by God (Col. 1:16), and they are clearly spiritual beings (Heb. 1:14). Although in most cases angels are invisible, they have the ability to appear to humans (Mark 16:5; Luke 24:4). Angels are personal beings who have both will and intelligence (Rev. 22:9). While angels have both superhuman knowledge (Matt. 24:36) and superhuman power (II Pet. 2:11), both capacities, unlike God's knowledge and power, are limited. Angels know and do only what the Lord permits.

The function of angels is to praise and glorify God (Rev. 5:11-12; 8:1-4). They also serve as messengers of God and communicate His message to humans (Acts 8:26; 10:3-7). Their ministry to believers includes protecting them from harm (Acts 5:19; 12:6-11) and caring for their spiritual needs (Luke 15:10; Heb. 1:14). Angels also bring judgment against God's enemies (Acts 12:23; Rev. 8:6-9, 21; 16:1-17).

Angels are prominent at several crucial points in the life of Jesus. They deliver the initial birth announcements to both Mary and Joseph (Matt. 1:18-21 and Luke 1:26-38). They instruct the shepherds to go and worship the infant (Luke 2:8-14). And they tell Joseph to flee to Egypt to escape Herod's massacre of babies in Bethlehem (Matt. 2:13-15). At the beginning of Jesus' public ministry, angels are sent to attend Jesus after He successfully conquered Satan's temptations in the wilderness (Mark 4:13). Finally, at the tomb of Jesus an angel declares to the women that Jesus is risen and reminds them of His predictions made in Galilee (Matt. 28:1-8).

However, not all angels are obedient to God; some are fallen angels. Rebellious angels are called demons, and their leader is referred to as the devil, Beelzebub, or Satan. New Testament teaching progresses well beyond that of the Old Testament on this issue. In the Old Testament Satan is mentioned infrequently, and only two cases of demon possession are mentioned in the entire Old Testament.[25] In contrast to this, Jesus states unequivocally that His coming has resulted in a battle between the kingdom of God and the kingdom of Satan (Matt. 12:22-29). The casting out of demons, a prominent part of Jesus' ministry, demonstrates that the kingdom of God is the stronger of the two. Here we see a vivid differ-

25. Those two are Saul in I Sam. 16:14f., and Ahab in I Kings 22:22f.

ence between biblical cosmology and that of other ancient societies. In various pagan cosmologies, the gods are part of the cosmos, not supreme over the cosmos. Jesus, however, is the transcendent one who has become incarnate and who intervenes in the affairs of both men and angels!

II Peter 2:4 and Jude 6 both indicate that demons are angels, created by God, who were originally good but who have sinned and thus become evil. The term, Satan, means an adversary, an opponent, and that is how he is portrayed by the New Testament.[26] Satan and his forces tempt people in many different ways, afflicting them with various physical ailments (Mark 9:17, 25; Matt. 12:22; Acts 8:7). Most of all, they oppose the spiritual progress of God's people (Eph. 6:12). One of the primary means Satan uses to accomplish these purposes is deception. He often appears as an angel of light and his demonic servants disguise themselves as servants of righteousness (II Cor. 11:14-15).[27] The destiny of all demons, including Satan, is certain doom. Both Satan and his demonic angels will be thrown into the lake of fire forever (Rev. 20:10 and Matt. 25:41). The decisive battle between the forces of God and those of Satan was won in the crucifixion and resurrection of Jesus Christ. Though Satan's influence and power are still considerable, his defeat is certain.

Christ and Consummation

Central to New Testament cosmology is the return of Jesus Christ and the consequences this will have for the entire cosmos. Christ's work on the cross was not simply to save sinners. God's redemptive program is cosmic in scope.[28] Genesis 3 teaches that humankind actively rebelled against its Creator and will therefore suffer certain types of punishment. It also explains that the earth, itself, is cursed and needs to be "redeemed." Christ's work will

26. Francis Brown, S. R. Driver, and Charles A. Briggs, *Hebrew and English Lexicon of the Old Testament* (New York: Oxford University, 1955), p. 966.

27. Millard J. Erickson, *Christian Theology*, vol. 1 (Grand Rapids: Baker, 1983), p. 448.

28. For a very helpful discussion of this, see Anthony Hoekema, *The Bible and the Future* (Grand Rapids: Eerdmans, 1979), pp. 274-87.

"redeem this entire creation from the effects of sin."[29] Christ not only ministered to sinners' souls, but also will give believers new resurrection bodies to be used on a new heaven and earth.

The promised return of Jesus Christ has generated much controversy throughout the history of the Christian church. Although there are different variations of these positions, essentially there are three primary views concerning the return of Jesus.[30]

The most popular position today in America is the *premillennial view*. According to this view, God's primary concern is with the nation of Israel. The church is simply a kind of parenthesis in God's plan. While on earth Jesus offered the kingdom of God to the Jews. They rejected His offer, and so He turned to the Gentiles. However, some time after Israel is re-established as a nation (this occurred in 1948), Christians will be removed (raptured) from this earth. Immediately following the rapture, a seven-year tribulation period will begin. During this period many Jews will become Christ's disciples and will suffer intense persecution at the hands of the Antichrist. At the end of this tribulation period, however, Jesus Christ will return to earth, defeat the Antichrist, and establish His kingdom, with Jersualem as His capital. Christ's reign will last one thousand years (the millennium) and will be characterized by relative peace and prosperity. After the millennium will be the final judgment and the establishment of the new heavens and earth.

Opponents of this premillennial position argue that it is based on an overly literal interpretation of passages in Ezekiel, Daniel, and Revelation, which clearly contain figurative (apocalyptic) language. In addition, no biblical evidence indicates that the church is merely a parenthesis in God's redemptive program. Moreover in

29. Ibid., p. 275.
30. See the helpful book edited by Robert Clouse, *The Meaning of the Millennium* (Downers Grove, Ill.: Inter-Varsity, 1977) for a presentation of these major positions by adherents of each school of thought. Actually, as Clouse's book indicates, the premillennial view has two different branches, the dispensational branch and the historic premillennial view. For the purposes of this chapter, we have used the term "premillennial" to describe the predominant premillennial viewpoint, which is dispensationalism.

Romans 2 and 9 Paul identifies the true Israel as those who shared the faith, not the ethnic descent, of Abraham.

These difficulties with the premillennial position and other reasons have led some Christians to adopt *postmillennialism.* Advocates of this position argue that the biblical passages premillennialists use to develop the doctrine of a "tribulation" refer instead either to the war between Rome and Jerusalem in A.D. 66-70 or to a brief period of tribulation that will take place not before but immediately after the millennium. As their name implies, postmillennialists believe that Jesus Christ will return to earth only *after* the millennium. Moreover, they expect increasing medical advances, technical innovations, and evangelistic expansion gradually to usher in the millennium. Material and spiritual conditions will progressively improve until much of the earth is brought under the spiritual rule of Jesus Christ. Although the two world wars dealt a severe blow to this viewpoint, during the past twenty years some who are discouraged by premillennialism's pessimistic assessment of human history have become postmillennialists.

However, postmillennialism suffers from a rather forced interpretation of many of the tribulation passages. Of even greater significance is that postmillennialism appears to destroy the attitude of expectancy that passages such as Matthew 24 and I Thessalonians 5 clearly teach. That is, it makes no sense for Christians eagerly to await the Lord's return if a thousand years of history (the millennium) must first intervene.

These difficulties with both premillennialism and postmillennialism and their understandings of Scripture have led still other Christians to adopt what is called the *amillennial view*. This position simply states that *no literal future* one-thousand-year millennium of relative peace and prosperity will occur. The millennium, which is mentioned only in Revelation 20, refers to the time between the first and second comings of Jesus Christ. According to this view, there will be a time of tribulation (though not a literal seven years), which all people will endure, and then Christians will meet Christ in the air as He returns to earth as the conquering king (I Thess. 4:13-18). After this will come the final judgment, with the separation of believers and unbelievers (Matt. 25:31-46), and the establishment of the new heavens and earth where Jesus Christ and His people will dwell forever.

Many critics of the amillennial view argue that it spiritualizes passages that should be taken literally. However, the amillennial position appears best to take into account the literary genre of Daniel and Revelation. And it seems to be most consistent with the teaching of Jesus and Paul. All three views, however, represent efforts by conservative Christians to interpret the Bible faithfully and accurately, and therefore are worthy of serious consideration.

Despite their differences, all three views teach that Jesus will return to earth and eventually establish a new heavens and earth. What results will Christ's return bring? Romans 8:19-21 and Revelation 21, 22 express the major biblical teaching on this subject, but other texts are also important. In many ways both the Old and New Testaments prophesy the establishment of a new heavens and earth. Genesis 3 describes the fall of humankind and the resultant cursing of the earth. Genesis 3:15 provides the first redemptive promise, as God states that the seed of the woman will crush the head of the serpent. This promised victory seems to imply that the effects of the fall will be overturned. Since humans were originally commanded to rule over a perfect environment, it would seem logical that God's redemption would restore mankind to some kind of restored paradise, over which man would again rule, this time perfectly. Furthermore, promises that God made to Abraham in Genesis 15 and 17 also imply a restored or new earth. Genesis 17:8 states that God is going to give a land to both Abraham and his offspring, yet Abraham himself never owned this land. Genesis 11:9-16 indicates that Abraham did not expect an immediate fulfillment of this promise, but he looked forward to the new Jerusalem, which will be found on the new earth.[31] Canaan, therefore, is a type, a foreshadowing, of the new earth. Just as Abraham's literal descendants actually inherited the land of Canaan, so Abraham and his spiritual heirs will fulfill the words of Jesus in Matthew 5:5, that the meek shall inherit the earth.

One important question that naturally arises is, Will the present universe be totally annihilated and replaced by a new and completely

31. Anthony Hoekema, The Bible and the Future, p. 278.

different universe, or will the new universe be essentially the same cosmos as present, only renewed and purified? Some Christians insist that passages such as Matthew 24:29 and II Peter 3:12 teach an annihilation of the present earth. There are, however, valid reasons for rejecting that thesis. (1) Matthew 24:29 and II Peter 3:12, in describing the sun being darkened, the stars falling from heaven, and the elements melting with fire, certainly point to cataclysmic events that will accompany the passing away of the present earth. However, these events can be understood as referring to purification of rather than the total annihilation of the earth. (2) In both II Peter 3:13 and Revelation 21:1, the Greek word used for new is *kainos*, not *neos*. Since *kainos* means new in nature or quality, not new in time or origin, it implies continuity between the old and new cosmos.[32] (3) Paul's argument in Romans 8 further supports this interpretation. In Romans 8:19-21 Paul describes how the cosmos eagerly longs to be set free from its bondage to decay, which will occur when the sons of God are revealed. This present creation will be liberated from corruption, not some totally different creation. (4) Finally, the analogy between the new earth and the resurrection bodies of believers is contrary to the annihilation thesis. Although our resurrection bodies will be significantly different from our present bodies, there will also be an element of continuity. So also the change from this marred, sin-infested cosmos to the new, perfected, and restored earth will be radical. However, continuity will remain; the new heavens and earth will be the present earth wondrously transformed.

What exactly will this new earth be like? Although many of our questions cannot be answered, Revelation 21 and 22 give us some guidance. The new heaven and earth will be populated by God and His people. God's dwelling with His people fulfills the promise of the covenant of grace (cf. Gen. 17:7; Jer. 31:33; II Cor. 6:16; I Pet. 2:9-10). On the new earth death, crying, pain, and mourning will be abolished. Cancer, car accidents, AIDS, or funerals will be no more; only everlasting, unbroken fellowship with God and His people will exist. Revelation 21:24, 26 ("The kings of the earth shall bring their glory into [the holy city]") may imply that somehow the unique

32. J. Behm, "kainos," *Theological Dictionary of the New Testament* (Grant Rapids: Eerdmans, 1965), 3:447-49.

contributions of each nation to the life of this present earth will enrich the life of the new earth.[33] Abraham Kuyper has expressed this thought very well:

> If an endless field of human knowledge and of human ability is now being formed by all that takes place in order to make the visible world and material nature subject to us, and if we know that this dominion of ours over nature will be complete in eternity, we may conclude that the knowledge and dominion we have gained over nature here can and will be of continued significance, even in the kingdom of glory.[34]

Therefore, biblical cosmology expresses great hope. It asserts that a sovereign Creator forms both the material creation and His people into a house that glorifies Him. Both the cosmos and human beings have been corrupted and perverted by sin. God intervenes, however, and, by the works of Jesus Christ, redeems the creation and all persons who put their faith in Him. Salvation gives us a new nature in the present and promises us a resurrection body in the future. God's renewal of the cosmos means that the best of our culture will be purified and preserved and utilized by God's redeemed humanity on a radically transformed earth. Biblical cosmology, therefore, is not only a cosmology of hope, but also one of victory.

For Further Reading

Anderson, Charles C. "The Place of Miracles," *The Historical Jesus: A Continuing Quest.* Grand Rapids: Eerdmans, 1972. Pp. 121-55.

Blocher, Henri. *In the Beginning.* Leicester: Inter-Varsity, 1984.

Bultmann, Rudolf. "New Testament and Mythology," *Kerygma and Myth.* London: SPCK, 1964. Pp. 1-44.

Clouse, Robert. *The Meaning of the Millennium.* Downers Grove, Ill.: Inter-Varsity Press, 1977.

---

33. Anthony Hoekema, *The Bible and the Future,* p. 286.
34. Abraham Kuyper, *De Gemeene Gratie,* vol. 1 (Amsterdam: Hoveker and Wormser, 1902), pp. 482-83.

Dyrness, William. *Themes in Old Testament Theology.* Downers Grove, Ill.: Inter-Varsity, 1979.

Eichrodt, Walter. *Theology of the Old Testament,* vol. 2. Philadelphia: Westminster Press, 1967. Pp. 93-230.

Erickson, Millard. *Christian Theology,* vol. 1. Grand Rapids: Baker, 1983, pp. 365-410, 433-52.

Geisler, Norman. *Miracles and Modern Thought.* Grand Rapids: Zondervan, 1982.

Hoekema, Anthony. *The Bible and the Future.* Grand Rapids: Eerdmans, 1979.

Kidner, Derek. *Genesis.* London: Inter-Varsity, 1967.

Kline, Meredith. G. "Architectural Model for Biblical Canon," *The Structure of Biblical Authority.* Grand Rapids: 1972. Pp. 76-88.

Lewis, C. S. *Miracles.* New York: Macmillan, 1947.

Von Rad, Gerhard. *Genesis.* London: SCM Press, 1963.

Young, Edward J. *Studies in Genesis One.* Grand Rapids: Baker, 1964.

III.
MODERN
WORLD VIEWS

4
The Cosmology of Modern Science

Alan W. Rice

> . . . the first and most important problem of philosophy is: To give a general description of the whole Universe.
>
> —G. E. Moore

Introduction

In the last four centuries, remarkable changes have occurred in what is taught in Western centers of learning about the motions of the heavens, elementary substances, and the creation of the heavens and the earth. New conceptions of the cosmos lead to new views concerning God the Creator and His relation with the world He has made.

In this chapter we will outline these changes in cosmology. We will first describe briefly the medieval cosmology, which scholars living during the Renaissance and the Reformation inherited from the Middle Ages, noting primarily the medieval conception of the material elements and the motions of the planets.

Next, we will analyze some of the principal discoveries that produced the modern view of the universe. Many of these changes in how we understand the cosmos resulted from persistent study and research in the fields of physics, chemistry, astronomy, and atomic theory, subjects we now classify as the "natural sciences." Our discussion will emphasize the "Big Bang" theory of the universe's origin and the theory of general evolution. We conclude by evaluating cosmological options available to contemporary Christians and the relationship between science and Christianity.

71

Medieval Cosmology

It is a giant step from the "natural science" that scholars studied in the Middle Ages to the "natural science" that contemporary students learn in primary and secondary schools. Even the name has changed. The physical sciences used to be called "natural philosophy" or "philosophy of nature" and were studied as part of the liberal arts curriculum, leading to a degree in philosophy. The aim has changed, too. In the Middle Ages natural science was studied (in the Classical or Greek tradition) as a way to gain knowledge of the inner structure (essence) of things, and beyond that (in the Christian tradition) as a way to gain knowledge of the Creator. Now, specialists in physics study the inner structure of matter using machines so expensive that only states and nations can afford them. Nations fund this research largely to increase their economic or military strength. Scientific knowledge is primarily valued because it may be useful, not because it explains the nature of the universe, and even less because it offers insights into the nature of the Creator.

Not only has the aim of science changed, but so also has its method of establishing and confirming its claims. Since science deals with the world around us, it has always been founded on observation. The ancient Greek philosophers, especially Aristotle, were able to record, classify, and explain in a satisfying way a great number of observations of nature made up to that time. Aristotle's writings were highly esteemed in Europe both before and after the Renaissance, and his understanding of the world was regarded as generally correct by philosophers and theologians. During the Middle Ages theology was developed in conformity with the prevailing philosophy. Serious scientific work therefore was also conducted within the Aristotelian framework, and the results were expected to confirm and perhaps extend it. If they did not, the conclusions were suspect on both philosophical and theological grounds. To be accepted and taught as true in the universities, a scientific statement needed the approval of the professors of theology and philosophy, whose world view was Aristotelian. Nowadays, a scientific statement still needs the approval of experts for general acceptance, but the acknowledged standard is whether the weight of experimental evidence is in its favor. Instead of appealing to Aristotle, scientists appeal to the published record of experiments. The opinion of philosophers and theologians is considered irrelevant.

Many great thinkers accepted the Aristotelian world view for nearly two thousand years (400 B.C. to A.D. 1600) because it was plausible, comprehensive, and internally consistent. Its dominance in Western philosophy was broken when Aristotle's theory of motion was reluctantly abandoned in favor of a new theory championed by Galileo and given precise formulation by Newton, a theory that proved superior in describing the motions of projectiles on earth and planets in the heavens.

Medieval Astronomy

The astronomical system in use during the Middle Ages was that of Claudius Ptolemy (c. A.D. 100-178), a Greek philosopher of Alexandria. Assuming the earth to be central and stationary, and the apparent paths of the planets to be the result of combinations of circular motions, he developed a procedure for calculating the position of the sun, moon, stars, and planets by using algebra and geometry.

The Ptolemaic scheme was widely accepted for about fourteen hundred years (until the sixteenth century). Although it was developed in a world without telescopes, it was fairly accurate. It enabled early astronomers to assist in the production of calendars, and to predict eclipses of the sun and moon years in advance.[1]

We noted in previous studies of the medieval world view (vol. 1, chaps. 6 and 12) that Thomas Aquinas attempted to synthesize Aristotelian and biblical elements. He believed that Aristotle's philosophy provided a rational basis for Christian thought. When biblical ideas clearly conflicted with Aristotle's views, Aquinas modified or altered them or simply affirmed biblical teaching on a subject. In theology, for example, Aquinas accepted Aristotle's rational proofs for the existence of the unmoved mover and adopted or "baptized" them by adding personal sovereignty and other attributes to make them applicable to the biblical God. Aquinas

1. As St. Augustine noted near the end of the fourth century in *Confessions*, bk. 5, chap. 3.

attempted the same synthetic approach in his cosmology. Philosophers call his rational arguments for the existence of God "cosmological proofs" because they were meant to prove God's existence from natural premises that assert a general fact about the world. Our experiences of motion, cause and effect, contingency, and design in the cosmos leads us to posit an unmoved mover, first cause, necessary being, and designer.

But Aquinas also accepted Christian teaching that went beyond what Aristotle taught about the origin of the cosmos. Whereas Aristotle taught that the cosmos was eternal (reflecting Greek interest in establishing only a rational order to the universe while leaving untouched the question of origins), Aquinas affirmed the biblical doctrine of creation. We learn from revelation that God created the universe out of nothing, and that He created it freely, not by necessity. God created the world as the arena in which He would achieve His good purposes. God also upholds the cosmos by His providence. The harmony, orderliness, and goodness of the creation is due to God's sovereign control. Thus Thomas constructed a cosmology in which he fused together Greek thinking (its emphasis on order, harmony, and rational demonstration) and biblical teaching (the doctrines of creation, providence, and redemption).

Summary

Medieval cosmology taught the following: Although earth is at the center of the rolling spheres, it is the densest, dullest, and lowest orb in the universe and is tiny in comparison with the sphere of fixed stars. The universe, the different species of plants and animals reproducing after their kind, and the human race were specially and purposefully created by God. Humans are the most advanced of the animals, but they are probably least in the hierarchy of intelligent divine beings arranged in the bright, light heavens beyond the moon's orbit. God was pictured as an unmoved mover; the universe moves because the intelligent beings in it (human, planets, stars) seek God as their supreme good. The predominant astronomical system was fairly accurate and based on earth as the physical center of the universe. Theologically and philosophically, however, the mind's eye pictured God as the intellectual sun, around which all other heavenly intellects revolve, with human intellects near the periphery.[2]

The Newtonian Cosmology

We now move forward three hundred years, from the time of Gutenberg, who invented movable type in 1450, to the time of the French philosopher Voltaire in the mid-eighteenth century. Voltaire published an essay in 1737 on Newton's major work (*Principia*, 1687), which helped to make the Newtonian scheme of the heavens much more widely known.

Other great (and related) changes in education, economics, government, and religion were transforming Europe during these three centuries, but we will focus on changes in the way the heavens were regarded. A new understanding of the universe resulted primarily from the studies of Nicholas Copernicus (1473-1543), Galileo Galilei (1564-1642), Tycho Brahe (1546-1601), Johannes Kepler (1571-1630), and Isaac Newton (1642-1727).

By Voltaire's time the Copernican picture of the heavens had replaced the Ptolemaic. The sun had replaced the earth as the focal point for plotting the orbits of the planets. The earth is now recognized as the third planet from the sun, following Mercury and Venus. The moon circles the earth, and from Mars outward the order is the same as in the Ptolemaic arrangement. Copernicus's geometric construction yielded the relative distances of the planets from the center of the system,[3] distances previously not calculable. It then became apparent that the further a planet was from the sun, the more time it required to complete its orbit.[4]

Tycho Brahe's accurate observations of the heavens led his assistant, Johannes Kepler, to doubt that the orbits of the planets are combinations of uniform circular motion. Instead, after prodigious calculations, Kepler found that orbits of the planets appear to be ellipses with the sun at one focus (Kepler's first law). He also

---

2. Dante, *Il Paradiso*, Canto 28, line 15ff., cited by C. S. Lewis *The Discarded Image* (New York: Cambridge University Press, 1967), p. 116.
3. The center was found to be near, but to one side of, the sun.
4. A relation Kepler was to quantify in his third law.

discovered that a planet's speed is not constant, but apparently varies according to a rule during its cycle.[5]

The work of Galileo and others greatly changed the understanding of the mechanics of motion and culminated in the synthesis of Isaac Newton, whose three principles of motion and postulate of universal gravitation cast decisive weight in support of Kepler's astronomical system, leading scientists to discard Aristotle's views of motion.

Newton's first principle, which stated that every body will remain in a state of uniform motion unless acted on by external forces, did away with the need for a mover to keep the heavens revolving at their steady pace. Further, his principle of universal gravitation explained the sun-centered orbits of the planets and did away with the need for transparent spheres to support them.

Newton's synthesis was powerful. Starting with four basic principles or axioms (universal gravitation and three principles of motion, including uniform motion) and using mathematical deduction, Newton could accurately account for all the known earthly examples of motion. With the same principles, he could explain the apparent motions of the heavens, including Kepler's three laws. And if the same principles of motion apply to the heavens as well as to the earth, should not heavenly objects be made of the same "heavy" stuff as we find on the earth? The principle of universal gravitation said as much, and Newton provided formulas that enable us to calculate the masses of the earth, the sun, and all the other planets in the solar system. Terrestrial and celestial motion and matter, both distinctly different in the Aristotelian view, appeared to be the same in the Newtonian cosmos.

Using Newtonian principles and mathematical deduction, scientists could accurately predict the paths of planets in the heavens and of projectiles on the earth. Enlightenment poet Alexander Pope expressed pleasure and wonder at the illuminating achievement in the memorable lines,

> Nature and Nature's Laws lay hid in night:
> God said, Let Newton be! and all was Light.

5. A line between it and the sun sweeps across equal areas of its ellipse in equal times (Kepler's second law).

The heavens are the work of the Creator's hands, and it now began to look as if the general principles of motion and gravitation, as well as each heavenly orb with its particular motion, were part of the Creator's original design. This beautifully coordinated system seemed to vindicate the belief that had sustained Kepler and other astronomers as they labored to bring order out of the apparently chaotic complexity of their observations. They assumed that God was a master designer and mathematician, and that clear signs of His skill could be traced in His work of creation.

At the same time, God's involvement in heavenly motions seemed to be pushed back from the present to the origin of the world. Because the solar system moved as regularly as a clock, God was increasingly viewed as a wise and skillful clockmaker, whose finished work needed no repairs, no adjustments, no intervention. As long as matter held together, the solar system would run like clockwork, sustained by impersonal forces called inertia and gravity.

As people began to compare the heavens to a well-designed machine, the regular movements of the heavens seemed less and less like manifestations of divine intelligence. No longer could humans look up and say, "A prime mover 'way up there' causes steady motion in the universe." For steady motion was now considered a property of all matter. Moreover, there was no longer a need for a set of transparent spheres to support the planets.[6]

Summary

We may summarize this partial sketch of Newtonian cosmology as follows:

Kepler's astronomical system was much more accurate than Ptolemy's in accounting for observations; it was sun-centered,

---

6. After the path of a comet was observed to cut unhindered through space where the spheres were supposed to be, Tycho Brahe declared that he thought the spheres did not exist. Nor was there reason to think that all the stars were affixed to a sphere, or that the heavens had a very distant spherical boundary. Was the extent of the heavens finite or infinite? And what kept the law of gravitation from pulling the matter in the universe together into larger lumps? The solution of one set of puzzles led to others.

described planetary orbits as ellipses, and explained motion by Newton's principles of motion and universal gravitation.

Earth is now seen as the third of seven planets orbiting the sun, which are no longer ethereal but massive. Some planets have greater mass than does the earth. The sun has a mass ten thousand times greater than all the planets combined.

Humans are still the most advanced of the animals, but do the heavens display a hierarchy of intelligent beings? Such beings are no longer needed to account for planetary motion. And planets themselves are weighty and probably made of matter similar to that found on earth.

God is more often considered a master clockmaker than previously; the universe moves because God set it in motion sometime in the past. Apparently unhindered, this original motion has persisted to the present. God still sustains the cosmos, but He is less directly involved in maintaining its movement than earlier views assumed.

Characteristics of the New Science

The Aristotelian world view was plausible, well-integrated and satisfying in many ways. Nevertheless, many astronomical observations made toward the end of the sixteenth century conflicted with the Aristotelian view and could not be long ignored.

Moreover, during the next century an increased emphasis on experimental investigation was combined with algebra, geometry, and the newly developed calculus so that the results of investigation of the universe could be expressed in mathematical form. This development shifted attention from Aristotle's formal and final causes to the efficient cause of an event, with some interest in the material cause.

A discernible shift also occurred in natural philosophy during the Renaissance of the fifteen and sixteenth centuries: In this period much of philosophical thought "represented . . . an attempt to see the whole of nature as a single self-explanatory system." Philosophers sought "to eliminate transcendental influences—the activity of spirits and demons working on the world from outside, or the capricious intervention of God himself—and to explain all phenomena within the actual system of nature." Nature was regarded as "self-sufficient and as working under the government of law."[7]

This motif has been present in most of the scientific work carried out from Newton's time to the present day. As a result, modern science generally and cosmology in particular have been almost exclusively preoccupied with the material world and with the world as a self-sufficient system.

Modern Natural Science

In the two centuries between Newton and Einstein (the eighteenth and nineteenth), more and more of the objects and events in the creation were found to have order and structure. Progress in physics and chemistry came in part as experimental studies were combined with mathematics. Quantitative relations were discovered between areas of research previously thought to be separate, supporting the concept that the creation is a consistently ordered whole. Thus we have seen that Newton, with help from Copernicus, Galileo, and Kepler, proposed a universal set of mathematical principles for analyzing and predicting motion, combining celestial with terrestrial mechanics.

This kind of unification continued in physics and chemistry for the next 250 years: in the subfields of thermodynamics; in electricity, magnetism, and optics; in atomic theory; and more recently, in Einsteinian relativity and quantum mechanics. This work has produced advanced technologies as well as an increasingly accurate and extensive correspondence between the mathematical equations, or "models," that scientists construct and the observed behavior of parts of the universe. The results of these studies are incorporated into modern cosmology. Space permits only a brief review of some of these developments.

Thermodynamics

Thermodynamics is the study of the relations of heat with mechanical work and power. A great variety of experiments concerning temperature, heat, and work were brought together and

7. Herbert Butterfield, *Origins of Modern Science (1300-1800)*, London: G. Bell and Sons, 1957, p. 34.

interpreted by proposing four axioms, now known as the Zeroth, First, Second, and Third Laws of Thermodynamics.

Especially important for cosmology is the Second Law. One form of it states that, while order may be increasing in a small part of the universe, examining the surroundings reveals that any ordering process always produces more disorder than it dispels. Thus total disorder in the observable universe is always increasing.

The Second Law imposes some restrictions on a cosmogony. For example, all the stars in the universe are slowly losing energy by radiating heat and light (heat flows spontaneously from hot objects to colder objects but never the reverse). Eventually they will all burn out. The Second Law says this loss of energy is an irreversible process. But many stars are still shining. Therefore it appears that the universe is not infinitely old; otherwise all the stars would have burned out by now. In addition, the Second Law indicates whether given chemicals will react at a given temperature. This enables biochemists to estimate whether the conditions required for the production of proteins from simpler chemicals existed at some time and place on the early earth.[8]

Chemistry

Physics was not the only area in which the order and coherence of the creation became ever more apparent. In chemistry, too, systematic experiments on the composition of matter eventually provided the evidence and concepts needed to replace the four elements of the ancients with a more elaborate, but beautifully ordered table of over ninety elements. In the twentieth century, physicists proposed that the atoms of all elements were various combinations of electrons, protons (1919), and neutrons (1932).

Organic and inorganic chemistry had also been joined in the nineteenth century. Until then, chemists thought that only plants and animals, because they had a "vital force," could produce

---

8. Some people have thought that the Second Law forbids a spontaneous increase in order and complexity of any sort, particularly of the kind proposed in the theory of general evolution. While many valid arguments oppose this theory, the Second Law, used in this way, is not one of them. Those who argue this point overlook the necessity, mentioned above, of including enough of the surroundings in a process for the law to be correctly applied.

organic compounds. But beginning in 1828 chemists began to produce them from inorganic chemicals.[9]

In 1860 the French chemist Louis Pasteur (1822-95), by an ingeniously devised experiment, demonstrated that spontaneous generation of living organisms in a sterile broth does not occur. This convinced him that only life produces life and led him on to propose the germ theory of disease. His contemporary, the German physician Rudolf Virchow (1821-1902) thoroughly studied diseased tissues and successfully defended the view that all cells, even diseased ones, come from previously existing cells.

Improved optics provided astronomers with better telescopes. The earlier idea of a sphere of fixed stars near the outer boundary of the heavens gave way in the eighteenth and nineteenth centuries to the concept of a three-dimensional distribution of stars and nebulae in an infinitely extended space.

Electromagnetism and Light

In 1864 James Clerk Maxwell did for electromagnetism what Newton had done for mechanics, and with consequences that were just as far-reaching. He proposed a unified and consistent set of four mathematical equations summarizing electromagnetic phenomena, and he showed that electricity, magnetism, and light were various manifestations of one kind of thing—an electromagnetic field. On the basis of his equations he correctly predicted that electromagnetic waves—now used to broadcast radio and television programs—should travel through space at a speed equal to that of light. The achievement of Maxwell has been praised as the most significant event of the nineteenth century. Not only did his formulations bring electricity, magnetism, and light together under one set of principles and open the door to electrical and electronic

---

9. In 1860 French chemist Marcellin Berthelot published his "Organic Chemistry Based on Synthesis," in which he showed the possibility of total synthesis of all classes of organic compounds from the elements carbon, hydrogen, oxygen, and nitrogen. After this, most chemists rejected the doctrine of vitalism. H. M. Leicester, *Historical Background of Chemistry* (New York: Dover Publications, 1971), p. 173.

technology, but they intrigued Albert Einstein, leading him to develop his theories of relativity.

Twentieth-Century Cosmology

Relativity

In the twentieth century the acceptance of new theories of relativity and quantum mechanics greatly changed scientists' concept of the structure of the universe.

During the nineteenth century physicists and chemists showed that the universe is very orderly. Many of the rules or "laws" they developed could be expressed exactly by the language of mathematics. Albert Einstein, for one, thought this close correspondence between the structure of the creation and the mathematical (rational) constructions of humans was remarkable.[10]

Einstein and other physicists questioned Maxwell's equations for electromagnetism, which contained a new term and had some surprising implications. The equations were thoroughly tested in experiments and were never found to be in error. Eventually Einstein concluded that, if Maxwell's equations were correct, the basic concepts of length, mass, and time would have to be modified and related. He showed how this could be done in a famous scientific paper on special relativity, published in 1905 and in his general theory, published eleven years later.

Einstein's two basic assumptions for special relativity were: (1) The laws of physics (especially Newton's principles and Maxwell's

10. He wrote to a friend, "You find it surprising that I think of the comprehensibility of the world (insofar as we are entitled to speak of such a world) as a miracle or an eternal mystery. But surely, a priori, one should expect the world to be chaotic, not to be grasped by thought in any way. One might (indeed one should) expect that the world evidence itself as lawful only so far as we grasp it in an orderly fashion. This would be a sort of order like the alphabetical order of words of a language. On the other hand, the kind of order created, for example, by Newton's gravitational theory is of a very different character. Even if the axioms of the theory are posited by man, the success of such a procedure supposes in the objective world a high degree of order which we are in no way entitled to expect a priori. Therein lies the "miracle" which becomes more and more evident as our knowledge develops." Albert Einstein, *Lettres à Maurice Solovine reproduits en facsimile et traduits en français*, (Paris: Gauthier-Villars, 1956), pp. 102-3; quoted in Stanley L. Jaki, *Cosmos and Creator* (Edinburgh: Scottish Academic Press, 1980), p. 53.

equations) are the same in all systems moving in a straight line at constant speed, and (2) light will always be found to travel at the same speed (in a vacuum), regardless of the motion of the source or of the observer. He worked out the consequences of these assumptions in a theory that has changed the way physicists look at the world.

The most famous consequence of Einstein's theory is probably that energy can be converted to mass, and mass to energy, according to the formula $E = mc^2$. Although this relation pointed to a source of the sun's energy, it was most dramatically illustrated by the exploding of an atomic bomb in 1943.

While Einstein's theory of special relativity referred only to objects moving at constant speeds in straight lines, his general theory, published in 1916, treated accelerated motion also and led to a new view of gravity. When an elevator in which we are riding begins to move upward, we seem to weigh more than usual, and when it comes to rest after moving upward, or begins to move downward, we seem to weigh less. If we were standing on a weighing scale at the time, the scale would confirm those impressions. One's normal weight is due to what physicists call "gravitational mass," and the changes in apparent weight caused by the accelerations of the elevator are due to one's "inertial mass." A basic postulate of Einstein's general theory of relativity is that an observer inside a closed laboratory, such as an elevator, with no knowledge of how the elevator is moving, has no way to distinguish between the effects of gravity and the effects of uniform acceleration, i.e., between gravitational and inertial mass. This is known as the principle of equivalence.

Einstein's general theory led to a new view of gravity and of spacetime. It correctly predicts that light rays are slightly bent by the gravitational fields of stars (such as the sun).[11] Two physicists summarize its effects on the concept of space:

> Since we normally think of light rays in a vacuum as traveling in "straight lines"—in fact, a straight line is commonly defined as the path a light ray would take—the finding that light is bent in a gravitational field might lead us to reexamine our notions of

11. It also accurately accounts for a slight but steady shift in the orbit of the planet Mercury, which Newton's laws leave unexplained.

the structure of space. It has proved a fruitful notion to regard gravity as an alteration in the configuration of space near a body of matter, so that moving bodies and light rays naturally pursue curved paths there instead of straight ones. What we think of as the force of gravity can thus be attributed to a warping of space. . . . the new point of view has led to a variety of unexpected discoveries that could not have come to light in the older way of thinking."[12]

The universe that Newton proposed may be thought of as an infinite space, to which Euclid's axioms of geometry apply, and in which only one (absolute) time exists. This time was considered the same for all objects in that space, regardless of their relative speeds. This is an extension of a common-sense view, applied to all visible space.

However, Einstein's principles of relativity assert that space and time cannot be considered separately; they are mathematically and apparently physically related, and technically should be referred to as space-time.[13] Moreover, Euclid's axioms of geometry do not seem to describe space-time as conveniently as axioms proposed by Bernhard Riemann. Einstein's theory pictures space as expandable, warped by gravitating masses, and time as appearing to pass at a slower rate on objects moving by us at great speeds. His theory also modified the concepts of length and mass. Galileo and Newton thought these properties of objects were the same for all observers; Einstein asserts that they are dependent on (relative) speed.

These examples illustrate how the universe, as seen through Einstein's principles, is in some fundamental ways very different in structure from the one envisioned by Galileo, Kepler, and Newton. Although for many practical purposes the differences are negligible, for the Big-Bang cosmogony the differences are essential, and relativistic equations are therefore used in it.

12. A. Beiser, and K. Krauskopf, *Introduction to Physics and Chemistry*, 2nd ed. (New York: McGraw-Hill, 1969), p. 304.

13. Objects fill Newton's space; intervals between them are calculated from the three spatial coordinates x, y, and z of each object. Events fill Einstein's space; intervals between events depend on the spatial coordinates *and* the time of each event; intervals can be either "time-like" or "space-like." Time thus is referred to as the "fourth dimension" in relativistic equations used to describe space-time.

Quantum Mechanics

Besides Einstein's theory of relativity, the other major contribution to twentieth-century cosmology is the development of quantum mechanics. This field deals with the nature of light and of subatomic "particles." To account for the frequency distribution of energy radiated by hot, glowing objects, and for the behavior of the photoelectric cell (used in the "electric eye"), physicists had to treat light, which they had previously regarded as continuous waves, as a stream of tiny packets of energy, made up of "quanta" or "photons."[14]

Conversely, in 1924 Louis deBroglie proposed that a stream of electrons, hitherto regarded as particles, could also be studied as a wave. His proposal was soon confirmed, and shortly thereafter the electron microscope was invented, which provided pictures at much higher magnifications than were possible with visible light. In a short while physicists were extending deBroglie's idea to all subatomic particles, and they found that particles, like photons, can be described with wave equations. In their work with electrons as with photons, physicists discovered that the wave equations accurately predicted what large numbers of electrons would do as a group, but gave only the probability of an event involving a single electron.

Physicists made many attempts to get beyond probability to certainty in describing events occurring on the atomic level, but none succeeded. Then Werner Heisenberg proposed, as a principle of nature, that an irreducible minimum uncertainty will always remain in our measurements of subatomic particles.[15] Although there are several interpretations of the principle, no one has ever figured out a way to show that Heisenberg was wrong.

14. Scientists found that they could, in effect, only predict the *probability* of events involving photons. As long as millions of photons were involved, the predictions of their combined behavior were accurately described in the wave equations they had been using before. But the wave equation provided only very accurate probabilities about an *individual* photon's location and speed.

15. He specified a formula to calculate the magnitude of the uncertainty. It is tiny by ordinary standards. It plays an important role in atomic and subatomic physics and therefore in the Big-Bang cosmogony. But it is insignificant when considering objects as large as or larger than molecules, where the relevant probabilities are practically certainties. (See Beiser and Krauskopf, *Introduction to Physics and Chemistry*, p. 328.)

So subatomic physics in the twentieth century has taken a new direction. Physicists had to abandon the earlier ideal of "classical" mechanics, which was to predict exactly what would occur in an experiment with individual units of matter. They adopted a new approach, the method of "wave" or "quantum" mechanics, which yields only accurate probabilities regarding individual events. As one of them noted, this "may be a backward step, but no one has seen a way to avoid it."[16]

Since Einstein's principles lead to predictions that agree with observations and experiments, they are thought to represent accurately the relations between space, time, length, mass, and velocity.[17] His principles have been confirmed by observations of stars by astronomers and of subatomic particles by physicists, and they are used in combination with equations from quantum mechanics in constructing theories about the origin of the universe.

Astronomical Observations

During the twentieth century two central astronomical observations have shaped modern cosmogonies: (1) the reddening of light from distant galaxies of stars (1919), and (2) the detection of faint microwave radiation coming from all directions in space (1965).

One way to study stars is to compare the spectrum of starlight with the spectrum obtained from glowing objects of known chemical composition. Each element, when incandescent, radiates (and absorbs) light only at its own set of frequencies, making a kind of "fingerprint" for identification when the light is fanned out by a prism into a spectrum of colors. Analyzing starlight in this way has shown that stars are made of familiar chemical elements. V. M. Slipher of the Lowell Observatory in Arizona had noticed by 1919 that the spectra of distant galaxies showed a shift of the "finger-

16. R. P. Feynman, R. B. Leighton, and M. Sands, *The Feynman Lectures on Physics*, vol. 3 (Reading, Mass.: Addison-Wesley Publishing Co., 1965), pp. 1-10

17. They imply equations for mechanics that include Newton's laws as a limiting case. Einstein proposed a new definition of mass, and this makes a measurable difference for objects moving at speeds greater than about one-fifth the speed of light.

prints" of familiar elements to lower frequencies, as if the galaxies were rushing away from us.[18]

This feature of light from distant galaxies is called a "red shift" in their spectra because red light has lower frequencies than blue; it is one of the experimental foundations of modern cosmology. By 1929 Edwin Hubble had extended Slipher's investigation to show that the more distant the galaxies are, the faster they are receding from us. Some of the galaxies at the limit of our telescopic vision appear to be moving away from our galaxy at 80 percent of the speed of light.

If galaxies are in fact receding, the universe is expanding. Let us imagine what would happen if we could reverse time the way we can reverse a motion picture film. All the galaxies would be moving closer to each other. The closer together they came, the stronger the attractive forces of gravity would be, pulling them all toward a central point. All the stars would pile up together, and gravity would crush them into a smaller and smaller volume. Calculations indicate that, at about 15 billion years ago, all the matter of the universe would have been gathered in a very hot and dense speck,[19] smaller than a pinhead. Calculated temperatures of the speck are so hot that atoms could not exist in it, but subatomic particles could.[20] If all of the universe were compressed to a point, all mathematical equations expressing natural laws would become inapplicable at that point. Currently there is no imaginable way to calculate a state of the universe at any earlier time. So this point becomes a beginning of the universe for "Big Bang" cosmogonists. Going forward in time from this beginning, the universe of space and time appears (according to the equations) to burst into existence from a point with enormous energy and then to continue expanding thereafter.

Mathematical physicists began working on the "Big Bang" model

18. An auto horn is lower in pitch as the auto moves away. This happens with light, too, and is known as the Doppler effect.

19. Temperature, about 10^{32} kelvins; density, about 10^{94} grams/cm^3.

20. Some nuclear physicists are studying experimentally the behavior of these elementary particles at high temperatures. But since the temperatures in the lump reach heights the experimenters cannot hope to achieve, its conditions at the highest temperatures have to be calculated by mathematical physicists using the equations of general relativity and quantum mechanics.

of cosmogenesis in the late 1920s. In 1949 three of them predicted mathematically that, if the model were correct, light radiation released when the expanding universe became transparent (about ten thousand years after the beginning) should exist now as low-level microwave radiation (with a particular pattern) bathing the universe. A sensitive radio telescope detected such radiation in 1965.[21] Because the radiation now observed matches almost exactly what is predicted by the mathematical model, many astronomers tend to think that the universe was once in the state described by the model.[22] Acceptable modern cosmogonies must explain both this faint microwave radiation coming from all directions in space and the reddening of light from distant galaxies.

Darwin's Theory of Evolution

One of the most important biological theories put forward in the nineteenth century was Charles Darwin's hypothesis that species change slowly with time.

Until publication of Darwin's *The Origin of Species* in 1859 most naturalists held that species did not change. They knew that animals could be bred for desired characteristics, but horses remained horses, and dogs remained dogs. Most of them assumed that God had specially created each kind of animal and plant at the beginning of the world some thousands of years in the past. As geologists proposed ever-earlier dates for fossil-bearing strata of the earth, biologists had to allow for the possibility that life-forms had existed on earth for millions (instead of thousands) of years, and that these forms had appeared over a period of millions of years in a discernible sequence. The fossil record seemed to indicate that, for example, sea corals preceded reptiles and reptiles preceded mammals.

Nineteenth-century naturalists, principally Darwin, advocated

21. Microwave detectors (MASERs) with the required sensitivity were invented in 1954. Penzias and Wilson found the radiation as unwanted noise in a Bell Laboratories radio telescope; they received the Nobel Prize in physics (1978).

22. The order of prediction and discovery is worth noting. In putting together a cosmogony, the order is often the reverse: new information is obtained in the present, and then a past event is proposed to account for it. In this case, postulating a past event led to a prediction about the present, which was subsequently verified by observation.

an alternate concept of the generation of plant and animal species. Rejecting the view that God created plants and animals separately about six thousand years ago in six days, these naturalists proposed that plants and animals developed through a process spanning millions of years. The interaction of genetic and environmental changes enabled simple forms of life to become more complex organisms step by step. When intelligent human beings appeared in the relatively recent past, social and cultural factors, rather than biological ones, became dominant in determining any further changes. The creation of the cosmos, once commonly thought of as a completed event, was viewed as a process in time with no clear ending.

Darwin described in detail the process by which he thought new forms of life were generated. He proposed that the changes in a species over a series of generations result from (1) variations in offspring that provide (2) relative advantages in survival of some offspring to adulthood (avoiding predation, obtaining food, water, and shelter), and (3) consequent reproduction of individuals with the advantageous characteristics.[23] The combination of factors 2 and 3 is referred to as "natural selection."

Darwin argued that the same factors account not only for the observed variations within a species, but also for the gradual development of all the diverse species of living forms, including humans, from simple one-celled organisms. Darwin's successors have modified this theory of macroevolution or general evolution. The weight of the evidence for the development of life forms from simple to complex has been and continues to be a subject of much debate. The normal genetic variations appear to be insufficient to account for the extensive changes in the genetic material proposed in this theory. Proponents contend that "mistakes" or "accidents" occur in the transcription of genetic material in the cells involved in reproduction. Some of these "mistakes" are supposed to be constructive in the sense that they produce individuals better suited to survive to

23. An important feature to note is how the variations in offspring are produced. Sometimes these variations are a normal consequence of genetics; sometimes a "mistake" occurs in the transcription of genetic material and a "mutant" offspring is produced.

adulthood and reproduce themselves. The effects of these constructive "accidents" are alleged to accumulate over many generations,
accounting for the changes in organisms required by the theory.
Biologists use the terms "mistake" or "accident" to describe the
genetic changes involved in producing variant or mutant offspring
to indicate that the changes came about through random or chance
processes, rather than by a deterministic biochemical mechanism.[24]
Thus, the concept of chance or random processes occupies an
important place in the theory of general evolution, and it warrants
additional comment later.

The theory of general evolution involves many assumptions. Too
often the theory "is extended from one animal to the rest of the animal kingdom with little or no further evidence." Biologist G. A.
Kerkut identifies the following assumptions:

> (1) Nonliving things gave rise to living material, i.e., spon-
> taneous generation occurred.
> (2) Spontaneous generation occurred only once.
> (3) Viruses, bacteria, plants, and animals are all interrelated.
> (4) The protozoa gave rise to the metazoa.
> (5) The various invertebrate phyla are interrelated.
> (6) The invertebrates gave rise to the vertebrates.
> (7) The vertebrates and fish gave rise to the amphibia, the
> amphibia to the reptiles, and the reptiles to the birds and mam-
> mals. Sometimes this is expressed in other words, i.e., that the
> modern amphibia and reptiles had a common ancestral stock,
> and so on.

He continues:

> Supporters of the theory of [general] evolution hold that all
> these seven assumptions are valid, and that these assumptions
> form the general theory of evolution. [These seven assump-
> tions, however,] by their nature are not capable of experimen-
> tal verification. They assume that a certain series of events has
> occurred in the past. Thus, though it may be possible to mimic
> some of these events under present-day conditions, this does
> not mean that these events *must* therefore have taken place in
> the past. All that it shows is that it is *possible* for such a change

24. A biochemical mechanism would presumably work in a predictable way and
could be demonstrated in the laboratory by biologists.

to take place. Thus, to change a present-day reptile into a mammal, though of great interest, would not show the way in which the mammals *did* arise. Unfortunately, we cannot bring about even this change; instead we have to depend upon limited circumstantial evidence for our assumptions.[25]

As we have seen, special evolution and general evolution are quite different even though their names give the impression that they are similar. Special evolution refers to changes in a species. These have been observed, and in the case of the pepper moth in England (at least) the proposed manner in which change is brought about has been confirmed.

The theory of general evolution, by contrast, refers to more fundamental changes involving taxonomic groupings higher than species and genera: families, orders, classes, and phyla. Such changes supposedly occurred long ago and therefore are not capable of experimental verification, which rests upon how things behave in the present. Moreover, even today's best breeders have not been able to make changes of the type necessary for general evolution to occur.

Failure to make and maintain this distinction between general and special evolution has resulted in much misunderstanding. Many biologists assert without qualification that "evolution is a fact." "Evolution," however, is too vague a term to be useful, especially in the current climate of controversy over teaching about origins in public schools. Natural selection is observable, and special evolution may be a demonstrable fact. Nevertheless, as one critic writes,

> In the case of [general] evolution, the observed facts are a variety of surviving vegetable, animal, and human remains, together with the observed results of any chemical or physical analyses to which we can subject them. That and no more. All beyond that is an unverifiable, however attractive, hypothesis.

---

25. G. A. Kerkut, "Implications of Evolution," *International Series of Monographs on Pure and Applied Biology*, vol. 4 (New York: Pergamon Press, 1960), p. 3, quoted in Paul E. Little, *Know Why You Believe*, rev. ed. (Chicago: Inter-Varsity Press, 1968), p. 76.

[Moreover can evolutionary theories] be tested, and have they been tested, by experiment? Here, of course, as in the case of any discipline that seeks to reconstruct *the past* hypothetically, the answer must be no. You cannot predict the behavior of the past and then verify your prediction by experiment.[26]

Theories about what happened in the past—not only to plants and animals, but also to the earth, to the solar system, to stars, and to galaxies—are not experimental science, but something else, which we may call speculative natural history or theoretical (or forensic) science.[27] Given this distinction, the restrictions discussed above regarding general evolution apply to any theory about the past, and therefore to any cosmogony built from these theories. Such theories are, and must remain, hypotheses, inherently incapable of experimental verification. Nevertheless, popular news magazines present an unproven general evolution, and other cosmogonical theories, as established facts not hypotheses.[28]

The terms "chance" or "random" when used in the theory of general evolution to describe events such as a genetic mutation are technical terms, indicating "lack of knowledge of causal connections between events"; ". . . for one reason or other no prior event is known by us to account for them in some particular."[29] Thus the use of the words "chance event" in a technical context is a confession of ignorance concerning its cause.[30]

26. Owen Barfield. *Speaker's Meaning* (Rudolph Steiner Press, 1967), p. 100.

27. This distinction is made by the terms "operation science" and "origin science," in N. Geisler and J. K. Anderson, *Origin Science* (Grand Rapids: Baker, 1987).

28. The recently discovered of bones in the Olduvai Gorge of Tanzania, for example, are said to be remains of Homo habilis, which is identified as an "ancestor" of Homo sapiens. Since no proof of the implied genetic relationship exists, however, "alleged ancestor" would be a more appropriate term.

29. D. M. Mackay, *The Clockwork Image* (Downers Grove: Inter-Varsity Press) p. 48 ff. Also compare: "Now the concept of chance is precisely what a hypothesis is devised to save us from. Chance, in fact, = no hypothesis." O. Barfield, *Saving the Appearances* (New York: Harcourt, Brace and World, n.d.), p. 64.

30. Donald McKay points out that the Bible has a doctrine of chance events: "The lot is cast into the lap, but its every decision is from the Lord." Some events, therefore, that appear to be chance events to humans, are declared to be controlled by the Creator and express His will. It therefore seems illogical for anyone to conclude that "chance" in the technical sense rules out the influence of the Creator (McKay, Ibid.).

A Contemporary Scientific View of Origins

Most scientists today use some form of the "Big Bang" theory to describe the generation of the universe of galaxies, and then a modified form of the nebular hypothesis to explain the generation of the solar system of planets around the sun. These postulated events supposedly produced an earth that is congenial to life. Scientists then use the theory of general evolution to explain biological progress up to the appearance of Homo sapiens. According to the current view, the universe and the earth could have arisen through the following general steps:

1. About 15 (plus or minus 5) billion years ago, proper amounts of matter and energy were generated with a high enough temperature, density, and pressure to produce, after about one million years, a universe of galaxies of stars. In the interior of stars, hydrogen nuclei combined by atomic fusion to form helium nuclei. Further nuclear fusion reactions produced all the heavier elements, which were blown into interstellar space as each star eventually exploded.

2. About 5 billion years ago, the system of planets revolving around the sun was formed, possibly from a rotating disk-like cloud of material ejected from earlier stellar explosions. About 4.5 billion years ago, the earth formed in orbit around the sun.[31]

3. By about 3 billion years ago, the planet earth had become capable of supporting life; that is, it had acquired sufficient water and a congenial atmosphere. Fossils of life-forms appear in rocks that today are dated from about these times, although some question the scientific correctness of the dating methods. They indicate the existence of the following life-forms at these approximate times:[32]

---

31. Many techniques (based on radioactive decay) for dating aggregation of elements into rocks point to this time in the past, if extrapolating the data that far back in time is reliable.

32. For a thorough discussion of these dating methods, see Davis A. Young, *Christianity and the Age of the Earth* (Grand Rapids: Zondervan, 1982), chap. 7.

3 billion years ago: rod-shaped cells
600 million years ago: corals, snails, and starfish
300 million years ago: reptiles
2.5 million years ago: earliest hominid forms appear

4. In geological strata now dated no earlier than about fifty thousand years ago, archaeologists find remnants of villages and human artifacts.

5. Extending current theories into the future, cosmogonists predict that the sun will expand, and about 6 billion years from now will become a red giant star. Having engulfed Mercury and Venus, its surface will reach nearly to the orbit of the earth. By then earth will have been burned up.

The Nature of Cosmogony

A cosmogony is an account of the generation of the cosmos. In the twentieth century such an account is made by weaving together many theories from various branches of modern science.[33] Almost all of what is called modern science has been done in the last four centuries on the planet earth, according to the modern scientific method. For the empirical sciences this method consists of observation, conceptual model building, prediction, and repetitive experimental testing to confirm or disprove predictions.

Cosmogony is an attempt to construct a history of the universe reaching as far as 15 billion light years away from earth and 15 billion years into the past, extending to places and times where no human has ever been. Thus it cannot use the empirical scientific method to any large degree.

Scientists construct modern cosmogonies from their present idea or "picture" of the universe. This picture is composed almost entirely of observations made relatively recently (that is, since A.D.

---

33. It is built from theories in astronomy, physics (including astrophysics, elementary particle physics, thermodynamics), chemistry (including organic, inorganic, physical, and biochemistry), biology, geology, archaeology, and paleontology. One writer (a biochemist) has referred to it as a story that extends "from Big Bang to behavior" because he thinks that some aspects of animal behavior are genetically determined. In that case other fields may have to be included as well.

1550). Observations made by earlier cultures are usually not considered. The present picture of the universe is incomplete, and details are constantly being added or modified as additional scientific work is completed and published. But cosmogonies are designed to conform to this current picture of the universe. Cosmogonists are like detectives trying to reconstruct past events without eyewitness testimony. They use whatever evidence is available in the present.

Moreover, any cosmogony, since it is a hypothesis about the past, cannot be tested by experiment and therefore must remain a conjecture. These two points were emphasized above in the discussion of general evolution, but they apply equally well to any theory about events in the prehistoric past.

Even though modern cosmogony makes use of scientific "laws," is developed and propounded by scientists, and is discussed in the scientific journals, it is not, strictly speaking, empirical science. The questions cosmogonists seek to answer are historical ones such as: What sequence of events in space and time preceded the universe as we know it? or, How much of what we see in the universe can be explained as the outcome of a process consistent with current "natural laws"? To the extent that a modern cosmogony is verified in the present, it describes what *could* have happened in the past (assuming the past was like the present). But it is logically impossible to show by experiment that any proposed cosmogony *must* have happened. This important distinction must not be forgotten.

Nevertheless, cosmogonists confidently describe objects and narrate events of long ago and far away. They devise mathematical and conceptual "models" based on the here and now and recommend their constructions as viable hypotheses—possible versions of the history of the universe.

How do cosmogonists construct their hypotheses? Using the observed universe as a basis, they work backwards in time as far as possible, employing "laws" and equations provided by science and engineering. If there are no forks in the road, no choices between alternatives, they might come to a single starting point for the cosmogony as they work backwards in time. This starting point would consist of the materials and conditions they need to begin the calculations. Then from these starting conditions, using scientific "laws" and equations, they retrace the sequence forward in time. This sequence shows how the universe, assuming it was once in the condition of the starting point, changed step by step according to "natural laws" until it came to match the present portrayal of the universe. We will now examine some of the important assumptions cosmogonists use to build a cosmogony in this way.

Assumptions for Scientific Model-Building

1. *The "laws" describing natural events in the universe are the same, yesterday, today, and forever.* (The "elements" and "laws" of the creation are uniform in time.) To construct models of the past or scenarios of the future it is convenient to assume that "natural laws" have operated the same way in the universe from its beginning and always will.

Cosmogonists push this assumption to the limits by extending their descriptions backward several billion years to the creation of matter and energy, and forward several billions of years past the time when the sun grows cold. To be accurate, they should present their descriptions as "if-then" statements: "*If* the laws of nature have remained the same, and *if* we (with our modern concepts) had somehow been present 4.5 billion years ago, *then* the following probably resembles what we would have seen." Such statements would show the imaginary character of their descriptions. But modern cosmogonists usually omit the *ifs*, possibly because they consider them unnecessary.[34]

---

34. Cosmogonists also study what might happen in some of their calculations if they do not make this assumption. For example, some physicists are studying the sometimes dramatic differences in their scenarios of the beginning and the future of the universe caused by slow changes in the universal gravitational coefficient G.

Some people who think modern estimates of the age of the earth (4.5 billion years) are much too great allege that geologists have adopted a "substantial uniformitarian" view in interpreting strata. That is, geologists assume that all processes that have affected the earth in its history are active now, or that they always proceed at the same rates. Whether or not this was true in the past, modern geologists do not adopt this view. They admit the possibility of catastrophies such as the flood recorded in Genesis, and expect that such a flood would leave a record of its

Are cosmogonists justified in extending their map of the present into the past? Evidence supporting this procedure will have to be obtained, if possible, from observations of past conditions. Astronomers can observe some conditions of the past directly because of the time it takes light to reach the earth. The light from the sun is over eight minutes old when it arrives on earth; light from the nearby star Sirius is over eight years old. The light from stars in the Milky Way, at the edge of our own galaxy, appears to be about 100,000 years old. Despite its apparent age, the light arriving from these distant stars displays the spectral lines familiar to scientists from the study of elements on the earth.

Past positions of the planets of our solar system can be calculated from equations for planetary motion, which have been proved accurate.[35] Even so, we cannot use these equations to extend the present pattern of planetary motion backwards into the past without (as LaPlace noted) tacitly neglecting "external" influences on the solar system such as those from comets, which are not included in the equations. We may consult the observations of ancient astronomers to confirm our calculations, but astronomical records consistent with the present pattern of planetary motion and eclipses apparently do not exist prior to 747 B.C. Therefore, any extension of the present planetary pattern to times earlier than 2750 years ago is currently a speculative construction, apparently without historical support.

Using the equations of physics to predict the future of the solar system—or anything else—is done in faith. Prediction is based upon trust that the universe will behave in the future as it has in the past. This is a central assumption on which all scientific work depends, and it is unprovable. Scientific research would be futile if it were not so;

occurrence somewhere in layers of flood deposits. They do, however, make the same assumption that proponents of a younger earth do, namely, that whenever past events are proposed as the causes of an observed geologic structure, the laws or equations describing the proposed events are the familiar "natural laws" they have observed and tested.

Assuming that natural laws are unchanged is called the "methodological uniformitarian" view. See Davis A. Young, *Christianity and the Age of the Earth*, chap. 10.

35. For example, in the calculation of trajectories for planets, comets, and picture-taking spacecraft traveling as far as the orbit of Saturn.

engineering design is based on it; we plan our lives expecting it, but no (noncircular) proof has been advanced to guarantee it.

Most of us make the assumption, then, that "natural laws" do not change with time. Using them to construct a history of the universe by extending observed patterns backward in time is a speculative matter unless historical, archaeological, or paleontological confirmation is obtained. Using them to predict the future is purely a matter of faith.

2. *Those parts of the universe beyond our grasp or out of sight are basically the same as those within sight and reach.* This assumes the uniformity of the "elements" and "laws" of creation in space.

Such an assumption enables cosmologists to study all the branches of physics and chemistry, and then use what they learn on earth to explain their observations of the most distant galaxies they can detect. So far, this hypothesis has not been disproved, but it is not always taken for granted.[36]

Some elementary subatomic particles, however, consistently behave differently when detectors are present; that is, when they are being "watched." Physicists explain this difference as caused by interference from the detector, and as a necessary effect if the wave viewpoint used in quantum mechanics is valid.[37]

3. *The universe is an isolated, interlocking system of cause and effect, closed to outside influence.* Scientists doing experiments in laboratories assume they are working with a closed system of cause and effect because they take special precautions to eliminate outside influences, and can repeat their experiments until all factors affecting the experiment are known. But contemporary cosmogonists are extending this assumption to cover the universe as a whole, which was not in a laboratory during the period of its formation. Moreover, its formation is an unrepeatable event. The possible

36. Since particle physicists accepted the concept of matter/antimatter, some have wondered if some stars or galaxies might be made of antimatter. That the Mars landing probe did not explode on contact with the red planet's surface was regarded by some physicists as positive proof that Mars was *not* made of antimatter.

37. The possible additional implications this may have for cosmology are still being evaluated.

influence of the universe's Creator on the sequence of events in a cosmogony or a history is usually excluded from consideration as "unscientific."

As pointed out earlier, a cosmogony is a history, or a prehistory, not science in the empirical sense. And, therefore, an appropriate question to ask is whether the Creator might have directly influenced some events in the universe in a process called creation. We assume that He did.

Nevertheless, modern cosmogonists have attempted to construct a speculative history of a universe "closed to outside influence," probably because this is the way scientists normally construct explanations, and it is of interest to see what such a cosmogony would be like. For them, the Creator's role, if any, was to provide the initial conditions that begin the sequence and to establish the form and constancy of the "natural laws" by which, most scientists assume, the universe developed.

4. *Matter-energy is the fundamental stuff*[38] *of the universe; consciousness is derivative.*

At first sight these may not appear to be important assumptions. Unproven, unargued, tacitly accepted, they fit the picture of general evolution taken over from nineteenth-century science. They concern the development of consciousness, and hence affect work in biology, anthropology, and psychology. Since they are latent in modern cosmogonies, it is appropriate to list them here. One student of this matter has written:

> . . . if the presuppositions of the evolutionists are to be accepted, the evolution of consciousness has always been a process of expansion only. The world began (according to them) with nonconsciousness—a kind of existential objectivity without a subject—then consciousness appeared at a point in space located in some physical organism, and then this consciousness progressively expanded, until, in the organism of

---

38. The view that matter-energy is the fundamental stuff of the universe is strikingly similar to the pre-Socratic search for the *arche* (see chap. 2). Some modern physicists say, "All is quarks," a quark being the latest fundamental unit of matter.

Homo sapiens, it took the form of human consciousness. Thereafter it continued to expand further and further throughout the phases of prehistory and ultimately of history and of modern civilization.[39]

Modern accounts of the "origin of the human race" simply adopt without discussion such assumptions.

5. *For scientific purposes, the universe is not thought to be animated by spirits at any time* (although other disciplines or cultures may perceive it as so animated). Spirits, if they exist and affect matter at all, are assumed not to affect either scientific experiments or the history of the natural world.[40] Intelligent beings other than humans are mostly ignored because modern cosmology or cosmogony is exclusively physical in scope. Medieval cosmology, by contrast, incorporated both upright and fallen angels.

Is the Current Cosmogony Adequate?

Having listed some assumptions of modern scientific cosmologies, we now analyze whether the three main parts of the current cosmogony adequately account for the details of the universe.

1. Concerning the "Big Bang" Theories of Cosmogenesis

The equations and initial conditions used to calculate a description of the expanding universe must apparently be precise if such an expansion is to produce a cosmos approximately resembling the one we observe. A single starting point might account for any number of universes differing from the one we observe. Beginning with the Big Bang, the expanding universe has apparently followed a very narrow

39. The same scholar writes: "It can be seen that the presuppositions on which this whole picture is based on twofold: a psychological or physiological one, and a historical or chronological one. . . .

"The first of the two presuppositions is that inwardness, subjectivity of any sort, is not merely *associated with,* but is always *the product of* a stimulated organism. The second, arising out of it, is the presupposition that in the history of the universe the presence of what is called matter preceded the presence of what is called mind" (Owen Barfield, *Speaker's Meaning,* p. 102).

40. A scientific experiment would be spoiled if a spirit affected it at all, because modern science aims at exploring the regular happenings of nature left to itself.

path[41] to arrive at its present state. Astronomer Sir Bernard Lovell has stated a striking example. "When the universe was one second from the beginning of the expansion, *if* the rate of expansion had been reduced by only one part in a thousand billion, then the universe would have collapsed after a few million years."[42] This is a reduction of only 0. 000 000 000 001 times its measured rate of expansion. Since the universe, according to this cosmogony, had to pass on several occasions through very narrow "windows" on a wide spectrum of possibilities to arrive at a habitable earth, the existence of life on earth seems miraculous. Cosmogonists have begun to refer to an "anthropic principle," one form of which is stated, "If the universe were different in any way from the way it is, we [the human race] would not be here."[43]

2. Concerning the Formation of the Solar System

Information about the sun and planets has greatly increased in recent decades, especially from data and pictures obtained through space vehicles. Nevertheless, scientists have no completely satisfactory theory of how our solar system was formed.[44] The theories proposed fall into two main classes.

1. Collisional or catastrophic theories posit a close encounter between the sun and a passing comet or star, capable of pulling out

41. A path whose direction is very sensitive to such things as the magnitude of the initial mass, the ratio of photons to baryons (incl. protons and neutrons) in it, and magnitudes of some fundamental constants of matter, such as the gravitational constant G, and the mass and charge of an electron. See Hugh Ross, "Cosmology Confronts the Creator," *Reasons to Believe,* P.O. Box 5978, Pasadena, CA 91107.

42. Sir Bernard Lovell, from a lecture entitled "A Contemporary View of Man's Relation to the Universe," given October 13, 1977 at St. Johns, Newfoundland. The quotation is contained in J. C. Eccles, *The Human Mystery* (New York: Springer International, 1979), p. 32. Cited in W. J. Neidhardt, "The Participatory Nature of Modern Science and Judaic-Christian Theism," *Journal of the American Scientific Affiliation* 36, 2 (June 1984): 103.

43. Parker, *Concepts of the Cosmos,* p. 454.

44. See W. H. McCrea, "Astronomer's Luck," *Quarterly Journal of the Royal Astronomical Society* 13 (1972): 506-19; cited in Jaki, *Cosmos and Creator,* p. 122.

of the sun a cigar-shaped lump of material, which then broke up and contracted into orbiting planets.

2. Developmental theories are mostly variations of the nebular hypothesis set forward by LaPlace. They teach that the sun and planets were formed from a contracting cloud of rotating interstellar material, which flattened somewhat into a disk. The center of the cloud contracted into the sun; the outer parts of the disk condensed into the planets.[45] A recent version of the developmental theory is considered to be the best explanation of much that is known, but it has been impossible, so far, to fit certain contrary facts about the solar system into any general scheme explaining its formation.[46]

3. Concerning the Appearance of Life on Planet Earth

The main assumptions regarding general evolution have already been listed above. A detailed discussion of the evidence supporting them can be found in graduate-level textbooks. Evolutionists acknowledge that large gaps still exist in the evolutionary tree of descent, however. For example, "The predicted transitional forms leading to marine invertebrate animals have not turned up in an

45. Improved variations of the nebular hypothesis have been presented by C. F. von Weizsacker (1944), G. Kuiper (1951), and H. Alfven. The most recent version proposed a disk that was hot at the center and cooled off toward the edge, which accounts in a general way for the variation in the materials of which the planets appear to be composed, with rock-like materials forming planets close to the sun, and gases that condense at low temperatures forming the outer planets. Water and argon are exceptional. Most of the earth's water, according to the theory, would have first condensed as ice in a region near the present orbit of Jupiter. Some ice lumps, deflected by the sun-Jupiter gravitational field out of their orbit, are said to have found their way to earth.

46. A promising mechanism for the transfer of angular momentum from the sun to the planets has been proposed (charged particles moving outward through the sun's magnetic field), alleviating a major difficulty. Some of the chief remaining unsolved problems for any theory, developmental or collisional, are the following anomalies: (1) Venus and Uranus, with its satellites, are rotating in a direction opposite to the remaining planets. (2) Four of Jupiter's twelve moons, one moon of Saturn, and one of Neptune revolve about their respective planets in a direction opposite to the one expected from a study of the system as a whole. (3) The density of the moon, which is about one-third that of the earth, is lower than expected. (4) Eccentricities and inclined orbits characterize Mercury, Pluto, asteroids, comets, and meteors.

otherwise abundant fossil record."[47] Moreover, there are no recognized African ape fossils for the entire 12-million-year period preceding the present.[48]

Some biochemists are working on a demonstration of how non-living chemicals can be transformed step by step into clumps of simple cells that are, in some sense, alive and able to reproduce. This proposed transformation is called chemical evolution. Biologists assume that chemical evolution occurred on the early earth, producing cells on which natural selection could act. From that point onward, biological evolution according to variation and natural selection is presumed to have occurred.

The steps of at least one possible path of chemical evolution have been described in detail, and researchers are seeking to demonstrate these steps in laboratory experiments.[49] Though biochemists acknowledge the very low probability that chemical evolution occurred by chance, they argue that the sequence of steps could have been a deterministic response of chemicals to changes in their environment. With a favorable sequence of environmental conditions, reactions (which involve stereochemical selection of molecules) can (they assert) produce the desired compounds. The environment needed for this synthesis is assumed to have existed at some time on the early earth. Researchers are optimistic that they

47. D. Price et al., *Teaching Science in a Climate of Controversy* (Ipswich, Mass: American Scientific Affiliation, 1986), p. 37.

48. No fossil record exists "of the stem or branch of the ancestral tree leading to the chimpanzee or gorilla, which are the living apes whose DNA sequences most closely resemble our own. Why should those modern apes lack fossil ancestors, making them appear to have sprung out of nowhere?" (Ibid., pp. 40, 41).

49. First, simple energy-rich chemicals react under certain conditions to produce amino acids, necessary as the building blocks for proteins. Then mixtures of amino acids have been shown to polymerize to form tiny proteinoid spheres, suggested as the basis of early cells. Special conditions presumed present in the early earth are required, such as a nearly neutral (pH) aqueous solution, and temperatures such as are found in a hydrothermal vent (like the hot springs in Yellowstone National Park). Basalt rock may be specified as a surface on which the spheres form.

As of 1976, an obstacle to overcome in this sequence was to explain the association of nucleic acids and proteins: "Thus there is a paradox. Both nucleic acids and proteins are required to function before selection can act at present, and yet the origin of this association is too improbable to have occurred without selection" (Dobzhansky, Ayala, Stebbins, and Valentine, *Evolution* [San Francisco: W. H. Freeman and Co., 1977], p. 359).

will soon be able to form a primitive cell that has rudimentary cell functions but admit that a modern cell is currently out of reach.[50]

Options for Christians

Modern cosmogonists strive to assemble a plausible sequence of natural processes to explain the cosmos from its origins to the present. The processes they put forth are either deterministic or random and are considered a constituent part of the universe. If scientists succeed in closing all the gaps in their proposed sequence of events, they may be able to say something like the following: using the rules for relativistic quantum mechanics and a specific initial mix of particles and energy, we can show how the universe could have unfolded from the beginning to the present (although it may have passed through some very narrow gates along the way).

Christians regard science as a good gift of the Creator and appreciate the benefits increased scientific knowledge has brought. We seek, however, to distinguish theories that have been experimentally tested from those which, like all cosmogonies, remain unverified hypotheses. Nevertheless, as long as a proposed cosmogony does not contradict any clear biblical teaching, we need not object to it on theological grounds. Understanding how God's providence operates helps us in developing our cosmology.

> The general theme of providence is the relation of God to his creation. It presupposes that the work of creation is finished, so that the creation stands over against the Creator with a relative but real independence. In creation God is the sole agent; he creates out of "nothing." But once the creation is finished, it is itself a source of activity, which has to be taken into account in the doctrine of providence. All the problems which arise in this field—and some of them are extremely difficult—are aspects of the basic problem of the relation between the action of God and the action of the creatures.[51]

50. Sidney W. Fox: "Creationism and Evolutionary Protobiogenesis" in A. Montagu, ed., *Science and Creationism* (New York: Oxford University Press, 1984), pp. 225ff. This informative article is well worth reading.

51. George S. Hendry, *The Westminster Confession for Today* (Richmond: John Knox Press, 1960), p. 68.

Reformation theology indicates that God, by His providence, orders events to happen according to secondary causes, which operate freely (human choice), necessarily (natural law), or contingently (chance). Natural law and chance events are thus included within the scope of God's providence. Furthermore, while God in His ordinary providence makes use of means, He is "free to work without, above, and against them."[52] Biblical testimony indicates that He has done so, not in an arbitrary or capricious manner, but to forward His plan of redemption for fallen humanity. Therefore, Christians also maintain that the cosmos is open to God, who, as the first cause, produces supernatural events. They expect such events, however, to be rare, and mostly concentrated near the great turning points of redemptive history.

Open and Closed Systems of Cause and Effect

Scientists normally study any natural event in space-time as an effect that is fully explainable by a set of preceding natural events (its causes). Conversely, going forward in time, each event may become a contributing cause to subsequent events. If we trace this pattern for a few events, the network of cause-and-effect may look something like figure 1. Events are symbolized by letters and occur in time from left to right in the order A, B, C, etc. The arrows indicate causation.

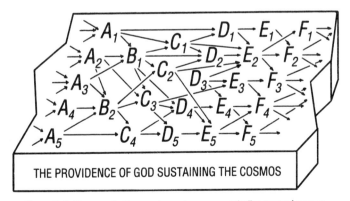

THE PROVIDENCE OF GOD SUSTAINING THE COSMOS

Figure I. Letters symbolize events, and arrows symbolize second causes.

52. Westminster Confession of Faith 5. 2. 3.

D—E—F extends this pattern, but shows an event that is not the result of preceding events. It is an event, symbolized by D_3, whose causes, if they are within the system of nature, are unknown.

Scientists try to ensure that the systems they study and seek to explain consist of events with cause-and-effect patterns as shown in the sequence A—B—C, and their work consists in determining the exact effect of each cause.

Christians assert that the creation can easily accommodate occasional events like D_3, where such events are understood as being caused by the Creator. The introduction of such events alters the normal pattern at the time, but then the reign of natural cause and effect is immediately re-established. This illustrates a nature that is "open" to occasional outside influence.

Twentieth-century cosmogonies present several major alternatives.[53] The first choice is between a universe closed or open to influences from God. If the universe is held to be closed in this sense, then what is observed is solely the outworkings of "natural laws" upon an initial deposit of matter and/or energy.[54] The proposed steps in any cosmogony will then have to follow one another either as necessary consequences or as chance events, with no additional intelligent guidance.

The other major alternative is that the universe is open to influences from God, which may be overt or very subtle. God created the universe and continually sustains it. The two main options under this alternative differ principally over how much additional direction God gave to parts of the universe during creation.

1. The *theistic general evolution* (theistic macroevolution) position holds that God originally created matter and its laws and later created man and woman in His image. Except for those two acts of

---

53. Dallas E. Cain: "Genesis One—The Family Tree of Interpretations, and a Best-Buy Analysis." Paper presented at the American Scientific Affiliation Convention (1986). Address: 18 Edmel Rd., Scotia, NY 12302.

54. Some physicists are attempting to show how, according to quantum mechanics, the required mixture of particles might pop into existence from a highly energized vacuum. I have not seen an attempt to explain where the principles of quantum mechanics come from.

creation, the universe has developed according to second causes as though it were a closed system in the interim periods.

2. *Progressive creation,* by contrast, holds that God produced and very subtly controlled the universe through all the steps of a cosmogony. In this view God with creative power continually directed the course of the cosmos while forming and filling it, making use of and guiding processes He created. This option provides a good framework within which to explore the relationship between biblical teaching about creation and the work of cosmogonists.[55]

The history of interpretation indicates that there are risks in attempting to harmonize scientific theories and biblical teaching concerning the earliest ages of the earth. Nevertheless, such attempts are being made, and we now mention two current views. The first holds that the long periods indicated by scientific cosmogonies are not excluded by biblical teaching. If this is so, then one way to avoid many of the problems that arise in correlating the fossil records with the Genesis narrative is to suppose that, while God spoke the creative words in six days, those words were fulfilled in subsequent ages that overlapped each other (rather than following each other).

According to this view, several different creative acts may have brought animals and plants into existence; many of the major transitions assumed in the theory of general evolution are ascribed to creative acts of God. God created Adam and Eve in His image perhaps around 10,000 B.C. (plus or minus five thousand years) as the crown of creation. This "old earth-recent Adam" view seems to be a satisfactory option for combining current scientific cosmogony with biblical theology.[56]

The other view seeking to show that science and Scripture are in harmony is a "young earth-recent Adam" view. Its proponents reject the very old dates and long times given for the formation of the

55. For a biblically based foundation study in Christian philosophy and science, see Vern S. Poythress, *Philosophy, Science, and the Sovereignty of God* (Nutley, N.J.: Presbyterian and Reformed, 1976).

56. The fact that it views physical death as present on the earth for ages before the fall may be a problem for some biblical interpretations. Young, *Christianity and the Age of the Earth,* reviews attempts at harmonization.

earth, calling attention to evidence that apparently does not fit the current scientific scenario.[57] The dispute concerning dating methods is being conducted on scientific grounds, with general agreement on the nature and technical interpretation of scientific evidence. The debate may thus help to clarify presuppositions into a cosmogony, and to emphasize that scientific methods yield ages of the earth and the universe only by chains of inference.

Conclusion

Our discussion has shown that a person's theology and cosmogony (or cosmology) are interrelated. If you believe the biblical teaching that God brought the universe into existence and that He has created and makes use of deterministic and seemingly random processes, then you will see "natural laws" as evidence of God's creative work. In working as a scientist to discover these patterns and see what they imply, you will be seeking to "think God's thoughts after Him." At the same time, you can hold that miracles, such as those recorded in the Bible, are revelatory events through which God is advancing His redemptive purpose, and that these enhance, rather than diminish, the value of His creation.[58]

On the other hand, if you hold that the universe was not created, then you must assume that it exists entirely "on its own." You might

57. Such as the unexpectedly thin layer of cosmic dust found on the moon's surface, and the halos left in granite by the decay of (presumably primordial) polonium 218, which has a half-life of three minutes. See R. V. Gentry, "Giant Radioactive Haloes: Indicators of Unknown Radioactivity," in *Science* 169 (1970): 670-73, and "Radiohalos in a Radiochronological and Cosmological Perspective," in *Science* 184 (1974): 62-66.

58. Your integrity as a "scientist," however, may be questioned because of your religious beliefs, especially if you are studying the theory of general evolution. Consider the following assertions of a biologist: The Judeo-Christian scientific tradition identifies God as the author of natural law, and as creating human beings in His image. "He has given us the opportunity to fathom His Law. But He remains aloof from Nature and refrains from capriciously intervening with its operation. It is possible to be a devout Jew or Christian and believe in miracles, i.e., in divine interferences with or contraventions of Natural Law, or even to believe literally in the biblical account of creation, but it is not possible to hold such beliefs and, at the same time, lay claim to being a scientist" (Gunther S. Stent, "Scientific Creationism: Nemesis of Sociobiology," in A. Montagu, ed., *Science and Creationism*, pp. 136ff.).

prefer a universe that has existed forever and thus does not have to "come into existence." The "Big Bang" cosmology, however, indicates that space and time had a beginning. And so you may assert that somehow the universe sprang into existence. Perhaps further work in quantum mechanics will show how it could have happened. You can view "natural laws," the patterns to which events normally conform, as characteristics of matter and energy, and you can presume that they account for all events without exception. The existence of life, and especially intelligent human life, is quite remarkable under these assumptions. Given the above, you will have to assume that something like general evolution occurred in order to account for the existence of human beings. Among other consequences, miracles, in the sense of exceptions to "natural law," will appear to be impossible, and therefore miraculous events recorded in the Bible will have to be regarded as illusions.

Many influential writers seem to hold this view. Carl Sagan, producer and narrator of the "Cosmos" series of science programs broadcast in the mid 1980s on American Public Television, has allegedly asserted, "The cosmos is all there is, all there was, all there ever will be."

Jacques Monod, a famous French biologist, writes that "pure chance, absolutely free but blind [is] at the very root of the stupendous edifice of evolution." Therefore, "man at last knows that he is alone in the unfeeling immensity of the universe. . . . Neither his destiny nor his duty has been written down."[59]

As we argued above, chance, in a technical sense, is an admission of ignorance concerning cause. Even if we grant Monod's premise about chance, his conclusions that God does not exist and has not revealed Himself to humanity do not follow. Monod improperly draws theological conclusions from a theory of biology.

German theologian Rudolf Bultmann argued that because most people today have accepted a scientific picture of the universe in which God does not produce extraordinary events, we must

---

59. *Chance and Necessity* (Collins, 1971), pp. 110, 167; quoted in MacKay, *The Clockwork Image*, p. 54.

"demythologize" the New Testament.[60] That is, we must remove or reinterpret all miracles in order to make the New Testament believable to modern man.[61]

The available materials for a cosmogony are generally the same for most communities and individuals who have an interest in constructing one. The way observations and natural laws are used and assembled, however, reflects beliefs about human life, the universe, and God that are beyond the purview of science. The cosmogony one adopts thus depends upon and expresses his philosophical or religious commitments.

Francis Crick, a molecular biologist who with J. D. Watson proposed the double-helix model of DNA (1953), argues that two cultures are vying for human allegiance today. An old and dying culture based on Christian values clashes with a new, dynamic, emerging scientific culture based on scientific values. Crick urges universities to champion the new scientific culture.[62] But this is to substitute a part for the whole. It is a misunderstanding to present science and Christianity as alternative bases of culture. Science is a method God has given us to investigate the built-in patterns of physical phenomena. It is not an adequate replacement for Christianity. A Christian world view gave birth to modern science. As Christianity addresses all aspects of life, science can fruitfully serve within that world view to help provide a better understood, more humane, and more prosperous world.

For Further Reading

Barbour, Ian. *Issues in Science and Religion.* New York: Harper and Row, 1966.

Barfield, Owen. *Saving the Appearances.* New York: Harcourt, Brace and World, n.d.

Butterfield, Herbert. *Origins of Modern Science (1300-1800).* London: G. Bell and Sons, 1957.

---

60. See our discussion of Bultmann's views in chap. 3.
61. But theologians find that when the miraculous is removed from the New Testament, no Savior remains.

Geisler, N. and J. K. Anderson. *Origins Science.* Grand Rapids: Baker, 1987.

Hummel, Charles E. *The Galileo Connection.* Downers Grove, Ill.: Inter-Varsity Press, 1986.

Lewis, C. S. *Miracles.* New York: Macmillan, 1947.

Mackay, D. M. *The Clockwork Image.* Downers Grove: Inter-Varsity Press, 1974.

Montagu, A., ed. *Science and Creationism.* New York: Oxford University Press, 1984.

Parker, Barry R. *Concepts of the Cosmos.* New York: Harcourt Brace Jovanovich, 1984.

Poythress, Vern S. *Philosophy, Science, and the Sovereignty of God.* Nutley, N.J.: Presbyterian and Reformed, 1976.

Price, D., J. L. Wiester, and W. R. Hearn. *Teaching Science in a Climate of Controversy.* Ipswich, Mass.: American Scientific Affiliation, 1986.

Trefil, James. *The Moment of Creation.* New York: Scribner, 1983.

Van Till, Howard J. *The Fourth Day.* Grand Rapids: Eerdmans, 1986.

Willis, David L., ed. *Origins and Change. Selected Readings From the Journal of the American Scientific Affiliation.* Ipswich, Mass: American Scientific Affiliation, 1978.

Young, Davis A. *Christianity and the Age of the Earth.* Grand Rapids: Zondervan, 1982.

62. F. Crick, *Of Molecules and Men,* (Seattle: University of Washington Press, 1966), p. 93.

PART TWO: SOCIETY

Introduction

W. Andrew Hoffecker

Our study of society is the largest unit in our analysis of the various components of a world view. Following the scheme proposed in the preface, in this part we analyze how our anthropological presuppositions determine our conception of the social order—its structure, institutions, and dominant ideals.

Our survey will examine the social views of Plato's *Republic*, the Old and New Testaments, Augustine's *City of God* and *De Trinitate*, Aquinas's synthesis of Aristotle and the Bible, the Reformers, America, Karl Marx's communism, and an example from dystopianism, Aldous Huxley's *Brave New World*. Each of these offers a different basis for order and harmony in public life. The most decisive issue in each example is how various thinkers have viewed human nature. Most have believed that all people share in a common human nature. But they have differed over what human nature is (moral, immoral, or amoral), whether people individually or collectively can change human nature or have it altered by some other force or being (the issue of perfectibility), and how, given human nature, we can form a more just political order.

Convictions about each of these ideas provide a basis for how we view the family, the state, the workplace, and the school—institutions God has established to promote peace, harmony, and justice in society. Are these institutions autonomous or subject to a higher moral law? Is the family the basic unit of society? If so, what is the family? Is it a divinely ordained covenant grouping that knits society together and the primary means of nurture and affection for instilling values into the young? Or is the family the basic economic unit whose task is to produce goods and services for the common good? Or is it a primitive, outmoded institution that no longer meets the needs of our technological society?

A second issue is political. What is the purpose and role of government? Our presuppositions concerning (1) the existence of human nature, (2) whether it can be altered or not, and (3) the best ways to organize social relationships exercise a marked influence on how we view the origin, structure, and duties of the state. Is the state a necessary institution or an artificial contrivance? Does it have limited responsibilities and powers commensurate with its duties, or should it regulate all kinds of human behavior? What is justice, and how can it be implemented in practical ways? Which takes precedence—the rights and responsibilities of citizens or the welfare of the community? How much freedom should individuals have? Upon what is freedom based, and to what areas of life does it extend? Finally, what is the relation between church and state? Does the separation of church and state require that religion be divorced from public life?

Economics is also an integral aspect of society. Should economics dominate all other institutions and social ideals and practices, or should it cooperate with and serve other social institutions? Do humans have an intrinsic right to own private property, or should all possessions be communally owned? Should individuals exercise stewardship over their property and use it to benefit others? How should we determine what is just and fair in the economic order, such as fair prices and whether the state can assess taxes and, if so, for what purposes? What provisions, if any, should society make to meet the needs of the poor and disadvantaged? Are these matters of individual or social or political concern?

Finally we consider the role of education in society. How do different presuppositions about human nature shape various understandings of the purpose of education? What assumptions about God, humanity, knowledge, cosmology, society, and ethics should guide schools' curricula, methodologies, and aims? Ought all citizens to be educated? Who should be responsible for educating the young—parents, the church, or the state? Can education reform individuals or society? How does a person discern and prepare for his or her vocation in life?

Such questions are not passing curiosities; they are rooted in concerns shared by many throughout the ages. Again our historical perspective serves us well by lifting our vision from a myopic preoccupation with today's ideas to a consideration of how earlier thinkers and societies responded to similar questions. Our evaluation of their views and the extent to which we believe the social order ought to be changed, if at all, will grow out of our total world view. Our world view will also determine whether we remain spectators or become participants in constructive change in our society.

In the following seven chapters we will explore these questions about the social order, the family, the state, economics, and education. Our purpose throughout this unit is to identify and analyze the underlying presuppositions and the historical or probable consequences of the various perspectives described above. We will begin with Plato's detailed examination of justice in his *Republic* (chap. 5). His purpose was to demonstrate that justice is a rational ideal capable of restructuring Greek society and eradicating its corruptions. It was Plato who gave the classic definition of justice, "Render to every man his due." A just society is possible only if philosophers come to power and form a society of three distinct classes: a ruling class that governs wisely, a class of guardians that protect society courageously, and a class of temperate workers that submit willingly to the authority of their superiors and produce the economic needs of society. Plato proposed a very structured educational system to train rulers to govern effectively and with absolute power over the state. In order to remove all temptations that might cause them to abuse their powers, rulers were not to have families or possessions. Plato assumed that perfect individuals and a perfect society can be achieved if the social order is properly modeled after immaterial, abstract ideals.

The biblical view of society (chap. 6) contrasts sharply with Plato's proposals for perfecting human nature. Old Testament society was a theocracy, a community under the rule of God. In social life as in private life people were to live in total dependence on God's sovereign grace by obeying God's covenantal will as revealed in Scripture. The structures and norms of Hebrew society presuppose not an autonomous, perfectible human nature, but the very opposite—that society is composed of sinful people who desperately need not only those structures and laws to point out and restrain sin, but also God's grace to free them from sin's binding power. His Word provides principles and laws for both individual and public life. To that end God created institutions such as the family, labor, and government to order and direct every dimension of social life. Social institutions structure how believers offer their worship and service to God. The covenant principles of justice, righteousness, grace, and stewardship reveal what is right and wrong in the economic, political, and social orders and how man can avoid and redress social evils.

In the New Testament Jesus has inaugurated a new covenant. Instead of working through a special covenant nation, the Jewish theocracy, God has established a church, a community of believers to be His ambassadors in the world. Christians are to plant the kingdom, or rule, of God in both their private and public lives, obeying scriptural teachings first in their individual conduct, and then also in the state, the marketplace, society, and the school. Christians should also continue to fulfill the cultural mandate of Genesis 1:26-28 and to undertake the new missionary mandate to preach the gospel to all nations (Matt. 28:18-20). God does not command believers to withdraw from society thus making Christianity a sect. Neither does He command Christians to form a state whose membership is coerced to profess Christian doctrine and worship in the Christian church. Instead New Testament writings stress that Christians in carrying out their vocations are conscientiously to promote righteousness and justice in all social institutions.

Among the very diverse medieval views of society (chap. 7) the teachings of Augustine and Aquinas have had the most enduring influence. Augustine's societal views are significant for several reasons. His *De Trinitate* was a self-conscious break with the classical social teaching of Plato and other Greek thinkers. Centuries later John Calvin attributed to Augustine the distinction of setting forth a clear biblical alternative to all of the other "philosophers." Augustine's famous trinitarian principle declared that the biblical

God establishes a foundation for society by providing in His very being a basis for personal values. God's plan of redemption, requiring conversion, is the only remedy for individual and collective sin. In *The City of God* Augustine defended the biblical world view in the aftermath of the fall of Rome in A.D. 410. The very title of that major work indicates his desire to model his views after Jesus' proclamation of the kingdom of God. The "City of God" and the "City of Man" are two spiritual kingdoms set over against each other. They imply the doctrine of the "two swords," or two spiritual authorities by which God orders society. The spiritual sword of the church works to bring people under the rule of the City of God, while God used the temporal sword of the state to restrain sin and keep order in society. Church and state are separate institutions and yet work together for the benefit of earthly order and welfare.

Eight hundred years later, in the thirteenth century, Thomas Aquinas expounded the view that characterized the high Middle Ages. His social perspective rested upon his anthropological synthesis of Aristotle's and biblical writings, which we examined in volume 1. He combined elements from Aristotle's view of the omnicompetent state with Augustine's biblical view of the City of God. The result was a dualism in which the church ruled Christian society. Aquinas revised Augustine's two-sword theory, replacing the understanding of church and state as separate yet cooperative institutions with a belief that medieval society was an organic unity, a Christian society hierarchically ordered, with the church as the supreme institution in society. The temporal authority of the state was to be subservient to the church's spiritual authority. Society conceived as a two-tiered hierarchy was consistent with other expressions of Thomas's dualism noted in volume 1:

SUPERNATURE	CLERGY	SACRAMENTS	CHURCH RULED BY POPE
NATURE	LAITY	DAILY LIFE	STATE RULED BY EMPEROR

The Reformation of the sixteenth century brought tumultuous changes to Western culture reflected not only in the formation of the Protestant church but also by radical changes in the social order—new conceptions of family and marriage, the rise of the middle class, development of a money based economy, and nationalistic struggles for political power. In chapter 8 we examine three distinct social views that emerged during this period. The Lutheran and the Reformed traditions both continued the medieval doctrine of the two swords, which called for a state church as the basis for social order. Martin Luther's teaching and example helped bring significant changes in marriage and family life. His social views, however, were conservative, especially in comparison with John Calvin's and the radical Reformers. In his attempt to implement a reformed Christian society in the city of Geneva, Switzerland, Calvin profoundly influenced the development of politics, economics, and education in Western civilization. The two Reformers agreed that a state church was indispensable for maintaining social peace and harmony. By contrast, the radical Reformers, or Anabaptists, demanded that the church and state be totally distinct. Moreover, they withdrew from the larger society in order to create a model community of believers, uncontaminated from the world's sin. These three views produced three distinct approaches to the relation between Christianity and culture. Whereas in the medieval era Thomas Aquinas argued that the church should rule over the state, Lutherans declared that a Christian's tasks are exclusively spiritual and only indirectly and partially capable of opposing social evil. Calvinists, however, believed that the social order can be transformed by means of biblical principles applied to all areas of life. But Anabaptists radically denied that Christians have any social mission at all. The gospel could reform individuals through conversion but could not transform society. Only the second coming of Christ would bring a renewed social order.

The underlying presuppositions of American society (chap. 9) are more difficult to distinguish than those of other individuals or groups in this unit. Current debates have emphasized that biblical principles strongly influenced the birth and founding precepts of our nation. However, no one individual or group can speak for the American social view. Our most important founding documents, the Declaration of Independence and the Constitution and the Bill of Rights, were composed by both deists (such as Thomas Jefferson, Benjamin Franklin, and James Madison) and Christians who wanted to infuse scriptural principles into our social life. Two social principles that are biblical in origin are basic to the American order: (1) human depravity requires checks and limits on government, and (2) despite our sinfulness, people are capable of much good. In addition the Bible has contributed to American belief that our laws must be rooted in a higher law and that society should allow significant individual liberty. The remainder of the chapter explores how secularism as a world view has permeated our society especially during the past hundred years and slowly eroded much of the Judeo-Christian foundations of such institutions as education, economics, and politics.

Sharply different from America's social principles is the Marxist world view. Because Marxist principles direct the social life of over one-third of the world's population, we consider them in detail in chapter 10. Examination of Marx's anthropological, theological, and epistemological presuppositions reveals that he advocated a naturalistic philosophy that reduced everything to modifications of the material. Despite his contempt for organized religion, which he called the opiate of the people, his world view is clearly religious because of the all-encompassing commitment it demands and values it expresses. But the irony goes still deeper. In many interpreters' opinions, Marxism is a secularization of Christianity. Instead of actually rejecting the principal ideas of Christianity, Marx recast them in secular form. The concepts of class struggle and alienation, for example, reinterpret the Christian doctrine of sin in secular terms. Like Christians, Marxists are guided by "sacred" writings (*The Communist Manifesto* and other writings by Marx), express ultimate devotion to a cause (the state), and have a missionary mandate to change the world. They also believe that heaven can be obtained—not in another realm but on earth through the revolution of the proletariat and the development of a new humanity. They claim all of this will be achieved in a classless society where wealth is evenly distributed.

Our final subject in society (chap. 11) projects us into the future by examining an example of a prominent contemporary literary genre, dystopianism. A dystopia (literally a "bad place") is the opposite of a utopia (an ideal community that has no real existence). Utopians promise that we can eliminate societal evils by jettisoning outmoded institutions, principles, and goals and restructuring society upon new and better ideals. Dystopian writers are most effective when they portray the striking disparity between utopian premises and the kind of society that would result if those ideas were actually implemented. Ironically, utopian ideals produce dystopias rather than utopias. We have chosen Aldous Huxley's *Brave New World* because he envisioned a future society born of the marriage of behaviorism—a prominent school of contemporary psychology—and technology. Huxley's view of society also lends itself to comparison and contrast with the societies of Plato, Augustine, and America.

Chapter 11 concludes by considering whether or not dystopian writers are "prophets." Writers such as Huxley are prophetic in the sense that they warn of a future calamity that may spell the abolition of society and human nature itself. But Huxley offers no constructive alternative to scientistic behaviorism. He simply urges man to choose to live sanely. In contrast to Huxley, biblical prophets such as Amos, who lived in the eighth century B.C., insist that people can remedy social ills only by developing society according to God's covenant revealed in Scripture. Thus our unit on society closes with the reminder that God's revelation provides a transcendent reference point to guide our analysis of social orders and our efforts to build a better world.

I.
CLASSICAL AND BIBLICAL
WORLD VIEWS

5

Plato's Republic: A Rational Society

W. Andrew Hoffecker

Introduction: Plato's Involvement in Greek Politics

Louisa May Alcott, author of *Little Women*, captures a popular conception in her definition of a philosopher as "a man up in a balloon, with his family and friends holding the ropes which confine him to earth and trying to haul him down." We often conceive of the great philosophers as so preoccupied with lofty thoughts that they are out of touch with everyday life.

Plato does not fit this caricature of the ivory-towered philosopher. Although his ideas may seem utopian or idealistic, he was very much entangled in Greek political life. In fact his life-consuming goal was to reshape Athenian society thoroughly according to his philosophic vision.

Socrates' famous pupil forged his social and political thought against the backdrop of a tumultuous struggle in Greece's history. Pericles' golden age of Hellenic democracy in Athens came to an end just before Plato's birth in 428 B.C. Athens had flourished under the Periclean democracy. The arts and literature prospered, the city was beautified, and wealth and commerce increased. Because it was the backbone of agriculture and industry, the family was one of the strongest institutions of Greek civilization. But even in the golden age of Pericles problems persisted. Prostitution was rampant in the great religious festivals. Greece's great playwrights lampooned the morality of everyday life in their comedies. Merchants, they claimed, used dishonest scales, while politicians regularly lined their pockets with bribes, and those who had power abused it. But all things considered, Periclean civilization was a period of relative prosperity, an era later remembered as one of Greece's finest hours.

Plato lived his youth, however, under the shadow of the Peloponnesian War between Sparta and Athens (431-404 B.C.), a conflict that brought an end to Athenian hegemony and marked the beginning of the decline of Greek civilization. During this long struggle between the two prominent city-states the Athenian government became increasingly demogogic.

Disastrous military setbacks precipitated an oligarchic revolution in 404 B.C. A governing body known as The Thirty, some of whom were Plato's relatives, seized control of Athenian government. They courted the young Plato's support of their regime, but he wisely waited to see what changes they would incorporate into public life. The schemes and violence of the oligarchy made the Periclean Athens appear to Plato a paradise in retrospect. He was particularly repulsed by The Thirty's attempt to implicate his esteemed teacher Socrates in a crime.

The oligarchy fell in 403 B.C., and Plato shared with many a hope that a restored democracy would heal the crippled city state. But in an injustice that Plato blamed on inherent weaknesses of democratic rule, a group of citizens brought his teacher Socrates to trial for the crime of impiety and corrupting the youth of Athens. Plato was appalled that Socrates—a man whom he considered "the most righteous man then living"—could be tried, condemned, and executed in his beloved Athens. Clearly society was coming apart at the seams. Rather than act rashly, however, Plato bided his time. Disillusioned by Socrates' death and in fear of his own safety, he fled from Athens and traveled as far as Egypt. But a dream lingered. Could not society, even one as transparently wicked as Athens, be reformed? Although all existing states displayed varying degrees of injustice, and many institutions were corrupt, was there no remedy for society? Plato believed that a transformation was possible, but the change he envisioned was based on a premise so radical that most people would scorn it as ridiculous. Either leaders must change their dispositions and take up the study of philosophy, or new leaders must arise from a totally unexpected source—the philosophic schools. Said Plato,

I was driven to affirm, in praise of true philosophy, that only from the standpoint of such philosophy was it possible to take correct view of public and private right, and that accordingly the human race would never see the end of trouble until true lovers of wisdom ["philosophy" is literally "love of wisdom"] should come to hold political power, or the holders of political power, should by some divine appointment, become true lovers of wisdom. [1]

Neither option seemed likely for Athens in the immediate future. In 367 B.C., however, while he was in his sixties, Plato received an opportunity to bring to fruition his dream of converting a ruler into a philosopher. And it came from an unexpected arena, the rival city-state of Syracuse in Sicily. Dion, counselor and relative of the new ruler, Dionysius II, had met Plato several years earlier and had immediately embraced his social vision. Dion summoned Plato to Syracuse with the expectation that Plato would transform the impressionable young prince into nothing less than a philosopher king. As an enlightened tyrant, Dionysius would enable Sicily to withstand Carthage's plans of Italian dominance. Plato and Dion hoped that this modest beginning in philosophic rule might revolutionize Greek politics and successfully break the recurring cycle of wars that debilitated Greek city-states.

Many factors frustrated Plato's best intentions. Sicily, a state of many parties, had a history of instability that provided a less-than-favorable environment for success. Also, in his enthusiasm for the project Plato was less than tactful in imposing a rigorous program of studies on the young ruler. Contrary to Dion's expectations, Dionysius proved unreceptive to instruction. He rebelled against Plato's plodding insistence that a thorough knowledge of mathematics was an indispensable prerequisite for philosophical studies. Dionysius impetuously favored action over intellectual study. Following in the footsteps of his merciless father, Dionysius I, he ruthlessly ruled Sicily and southern Italy, though with notably less success.

Plato's attempted reform of Sicilian politics involved two visits to

---

1. Cited by Francis Macdonald Cornford, *The Republic of Plato* (New York: Oxford University Press, 1945), p. xxv.

Syracuse, neither of which produced the desired results. During the second, in 361-360 B.C., Dionysius even held Plato hostage for a period and released him only after a mutual friend intervened. Further tragic consequences of the Syracuse affair were Dion's deposition of Dionysius, followed by Dion's assassination. Had Plato and Dion succeeded, Syracuse might have become a model for the rest of Greece to follow. Instead the Syracuse episode smacked of politics as usual, a struggle for and abuse of political power. As we shall see when we examine Plato's views, however, his involvement in Greek affairs reflects his carefully argued ideas in the *Republic*.

The Academy and the Republic

Because of his failure at Syracuse and the lack of opportunity in his native Athens, Plato made little contribution in the political arena itself. Rather he shaped a tradition of social and educational thinking through two vehicles, the Academy and his written dialogues. He considered his most important achievement to be the establishment of his school in 386 B.C. in a suburban grove of Athens, the Academy, named for a local deity. Plato devoted his last forty years to instructing students in his philosophical world view. His intellectual heirs used the Academy to disseminate Platonism in its various forms well into the Christian era.

None of Plato's closely reasoned and detailed lectures delivered at the Academy have survived; only his dialogues or philosophical conversations have. But we know some details of what Plato taught. A warning sign over the portal set the admissions criteria: "Let no one without geometry enter here." Plato's students in the fourth century made some of the most significant contributions to mathematics in ancient Greek history. But many other subjects received full treatment. Natural history, biology, astronomy, music, law, and, last and most important of all, philosophy constituted the curriculum. Students paid no tuition, but their middle-class families were expected to make generous donations toward the school's upkeep. Consistent with his teaching that all members of ability should receive an education, Plato admitted women among his students, a radical departure from ancient practice, which denied women opportunities for an education.

Plato made his most enduring and significant contribution to the history of world views through his famous dialogues. The *Republic*, Plato's most comprehensive dialogue, defends through philosophical conversation what he tried to implement in the curriculum of the Academy. His overarching goal was not to produce thinkers who would pursue their studies as ends in themselves, as mere intellectual disciplines. Rather his aim was ethical and political—to graduate morally disciplined leaders who could govern states justly. What he was unable to achieve directly either at Athens or in his abortive sojourns at Syracuse he attempted to accomplish indirectly through his *Republic*—to stimulate people gifted with wisdom to pursue an education designed to lead them to ultimate truth. After equipping them to fulfill their own inborn virtues and to discipline their wills, Plato planned to send them out into the world as philosophical kings to rid their respective states of corruption and injustice. They would accomplish this by direct rule, by administering political affairs through wisdom. Philosopher kings would not govern by adhering to and implementing a set of laws as the ultimate appeal in all political matters. The rulers themselves would be the ultimate source or authority because their education would prepare them to know what is good and how to apply that knowledge to daily affairs of state. Plato thus proposed the aristocratic state, rule by "the best," the most gifted and well-trained elite that Greece could produce.

In the *Republic* Plato discusses the many subjects that rulers of state would need to know. He draws together material on a multitude of subjects: metaphysics, education, moral philosophy, politics, epistemology, and others. Guided by right questions, the human mind can arrive at right answers. Yet, the final result is not so open-ended as it may first seem. His dialogues were anything but a serendipidity of stunning insights. Key to the Socratic method was asking the right questions. While Plato never inserts himself directly into the dialogue, his is the unseen hand directing the whole conversation. Just as a historian influences what a reader accepts as history by his choice and interpretation of events, so Plato controls every turn of his dialogue. He has participants, who were well known in contemporary Greece, put forward questions and answers appropriate to their philosophies. Though all positions are represented, Plato makes a case for his societal world view by probing, refining, and discarding certain answers as unfitting and carefully building on those appropriate to his purpose.

The Origins of States: the City of Pigs

Plato's basic premise in the *Republic* is that because society is man writ large (macrocosm) and man is society in miniature (microcosm), there is an inescapable relationship between the two. He ardently believed that both society and individuals can and ought to be reformed. Just as people are perfectible to the extent that reason assumes its rightful dominance over the spirited and appetitive parts of the soul, so society is reformable if it is restructured into three classes.

But how do states originate, and why must they be ordered? Plato does not describe the beginning of society in detail, nor does he claim his account is a historical narrative of real events. His is a rational statement of what states must be by nature. Though brief, his story is noteworthy because of the prominence he assigns to society's economic origin. States originate because individuals are not self-sufficient. We have so many needs that no person can meet them all: growing, harvesting and distributing food, building and maintaining houses, making and mending clothes and shoes, and other essential needs. Plato believed a state in its primitive condition resembles, of all things, a "community of pigs"—not that people live in sties of mud, but that communities at their inception have absolutely no luxuries. Citizens produce food, clothing, and other goods to meet the bare necessities of life. Such a society is so preoccupied with providing for people's minimal needs that it is totally lacking in creature comforts.

As communities grow, however, members become increasingly dissatisfied with their humble existence. Inflamed with desire, they want not just the minimum but every conceivable extravagance. An inordinant desire for luxuries is the root of social injustice. Unchecked appetites lead to theft, dishonesty, and finally wars. Swollen with abundance and lusting for more, the once simple "community of pigs" now needs swineherds and an army, kings and guardians, whose task is to purge the state of evil and institute justice in its place.

In Plato's idealistic view, a small, primitive society formed not to produce a political government—which was unnecessary because there was no injustice to control—but for the purpose of meeting physical needs. As the group grew into the luxurious state, far greater specialization of labor became necessary to meet people's whims for art, merchandise, and adornments. Desire grew in proportion to the increase in luxury, and with both came evil. Something was needed to curb the appetites, therefore, lest injustice continue unabated, and society collapse under the weight of its evil.

Three Classes of Society

Plato viewed society as subject to natural growth beyond meeting physical needs. His idea of the primitive community as morally innocent and thereby requiring no government reflects his anthropological perspective that human nature is only potentially evil. In individuals evil emerges as a disorder when appetite or desire usurps reason's rightful place of rule in the soul. Similarly in society evil arises when workers (artisans and farmers), who are fitted neither by nature nor by training to do so, and who ought instead to engage only in economic production, ambitiously seek political rule and power out of greed. As the largest class, workers are to produce goods and services society needs to subsist, not to exert political leadership. Thus Plato said little else about their role in society. After all, his purpose in the *Republic* is to describe how states may be reformed, not to tell farmers how to produce crops and carpenters their woodwork. Plato devotes far more attention to the upper two classes, whose specific task is to govern.

Guardians are the second class, a professional military corps fitted by nature to be fierce to the state's enemies and kind to its citizens. Plato likened them to watchdogs, who, guided by a philosophic instinct, challenge all strangers and welcome all whom they know. Their fierceness corresponds to the spirited part of the soul in Plato's anthropology. Strong in body and fearless in the face of danger, this courageous class protects society from external attack and preserves internal order. Since artisans and farmers are society's economic producers, and every person fulfills a single task in society, the lowest class readily submits to the guardians' rule. Free from economic concerns, guardians undergo a rigorous physical and intellectual training, which prepares them for their calling.

From the best of the guardian class, like the cream rising to the top, come the rulers, the philosopher kings. This highest and smallest class in Plato's ideal state corresponds to the rational part of the soul. The ideal man, whose head (reason) rules his body (appetites) through his chest (spirited) is a microcosm of society. Conversely society is a macrocosm of the tripartite soul. Philosopher kings, therefore, bear absolute rule in the ideal state. Guardians, whom Plato also called auxiliaries, are allies of the rulers. They execute and enforce the rulers' decisions. Ideally philosophers rule directly by making decisions in the day-to-day operation of the state. In the *Republic* Plato's express ideal is that education prepares its future rulers to know the Good through rational insight and embody its ideals by ruling directly over the social order.

At this point in the dialogue Plato interjected one of several striking illustrations, his allegory of the metals. Whenever he introduced a myth or allegory he acknowledged it as a "fiction." Not that it was a lie or a falsehood. Though his allegories or myths are neither historically nor literally true, they were intended to convey universal truth. Thus while Plato called the allegory of the metals a "convenient fiction . . . a single bold flight of invention"[2] describing the inborn nature of all people, it nevertheless manifests a truth about mankind that serves as a universal premise for his proposed Republic. Myths contain elements of truth, glimpses of transcendent reality that directly appeal to the imagination. While highly symbolic, myths and allegories become the means by which members of society pass their ideals and values to succeeding generations.

The allegory of the metals imaginatively portrays the birth of all the citizens of a country as the handiwork of the gods. Though

2. Here I follow F. M. Cornford, who comments, "This phrase is commonly rendered by 'noble lie,' a self-contradictory expression no more applicable to Plato's harmless allegory than to a New Testament parable or the Pilgrims Progress, and liable to suggest that he would countenance the lies, for the most part ignoble, now called propaganda" (Ibid., p. 106).

people are born from women, their real origin is the "womb" of the earth. Before birth the populace was in the bowels of its native land being fashioned by the gods. Because people have heard the story from their childhood, they think of their country not in terms of geography—i.e., a natural boundary, county, and street address— but as "mother earth" who nursed them to the light of day: "So now they must think of the land they dwell in as a mother and nurse, whom they must take thought for and defend against any attack, and of their fellow citizens as brothers born of the same soil." In a few lines, therefore, Plato inspires his readers' imagination to thoughts of patriotism and brotherhood as values absolutely indispensable to a nation. They are essential to a country's existence even though both may and have been horribly abused in world history.

In addition to instilling patriotism, Plato intended his allegory to teach his fellow citizens to think of their talents as inborn. Character, virtue, or gifts are not accidental to a person's nature, but innate. At birth the gods placed in everyone a spirit or soul with elements of the earth that form the body for the soul. Souls in bodies made with earthly soil containing gold result in children possessing the highest virtue, wisdom, which prepares them to become their country's rulers. People containing silver are gifted with courage as their characteristic virtue. They are fitted by nature to be society's guardians and are the natural allies of those who possess gold. Artisans and farmers, the third class, are born with iron and brass as their metal, representing temperance as their intrinsic character.

That all people possess metals symbolizing their own virtues is a key element in Plato's social theory. In his ingenius allegory Plato deftly combined theology, anthropology, cosmology, moral philosophy, and mankind's unique epistemological capacity to imagine. He admitted that the allegory might seem fantastic or even silly to people's rational minds. His purpose, however, was not so much to address our reasoning capacity as to appeal to our capacity to think in pictures or to dream. Allegories or myths invoke our imaginations. While reason might initially debunk this picture as too fanciful to accept, our imagination will grasp it as an ideal. Such ideals inspire and unify a people to perform the tasks for which they are most naturally fitted and thus help them to transform their social order.

By the allegory of the metals Plato hoped to motivate citizens in all three classes to see themselves as ordained by nature (or, what is the same thing, by divine appointment) to fulfill one particular calling in life. The very heart of Plato's social view is the specialization of labor. Each person can best perform not several tasks, or just any one at random, but one social function made possible by an innate capacity or virtue.

As we shall see, Plato opposed any political or social order that violates this principle. For example, he rejected democracy largely because it allows anyone to participate in government, not simply those naturally suited for rule. The outward performance of vocation is directly related to the inner constitution of the soul. Even though Plato advocated a rigorous educational curriculum to train citizens for their social task and carefully outlined the environment in which his guardians were to be trained, education only served to evoke the internal character of the soul. The justice and integrity of both individuals and the whole society was directly dependent upon a person's fulfilling his or her inner resources.

Plato's enumeration of the social virtues is one of the West's classic expositions of moral philosophy. These virtues, he believed, were the only sound basis for transforming individual life and the decaying Greek political order. What were they?

1. *Wisdom* is the insight of rulers (whom Plato called philosopher kings) about what is good for the whole community. Wisdom is not mere cognitive knowledge but moral prudence, which must characterize deliberative bodies of states. Philosophic rulers exercise wisdom because they possess it as a natural gift. Education only prepares them to use their virtue. Through philosophical schooling they advance from the world of appearances up the epistemological ladder to the transcendent world of forms. While the rest of society must be content with mere images, copies that are transient and subject to constant change, philosophers must rise above mere moral convention and discover absolute truth, moral certainty. Only then may they rule based upon Goodness itself.

Because wisdom is their unique character virtue, rulers choose what is prudent for the whole community. They are to seek not their own happiness but the happiness of the state. Since Plato also believed that once people know the Good, they will pursue it (no one sins on purpose), he was willing to invest rulers with absolute and unlimited political power. They would decide all matters by exercising their wisdom, not by framing laws and then passing judgment on cases according to law. Guardians were to be the natural allies of the ruling class, enforcing the leaders' decisions.

2. *Courage* is the peculiar virtue of the guardians, who must protect the community. Not only are they to defend against enemy attacks, but they are also to preserve the state's customs, ideals, and values. Guardians challenge strangers not in order to preserve ethnic or racial homogeneity but to insure the shared values of the state. Plato defines courage as "conviction, inculcated by lawfully established education, about the sort of thing which may rightly be feared." Courage, therefore, is more than bravery or fortitude, qualities demonstrated in the face of danger. Courage stands for a whole range of deeply held convictions undergirding the state, convictions so "indelibly fixed" that guardians will fiercely defend the state against any external attack and resolutely enforce its ideals among its citizens. They will not yield under any pressure but defend the chosen institutions and values of society as absolutely fixed.

3. While wisdom and courage are unique to their respective classes, *temperance* is relevant to the entire citizenry and is most appropriate to artisans and farmers. It is an orderliness, harmony, or control of one's desires and appetites. On the individual level people discipline themselves and become their own masters when "the part which is better by nature [reason] has the worse [appetites] under its control." Conversely, when a person allows his appetites full rein, he becomes intemperate, a disordered individual and thus a slave to himself. Temperance is evident when the inferior masses willingly submit themselves to the rule of their superiors.

An ideal society requires temperance throughout all its classes. Philosophers must be willing to exchange philosophical reflection, which they enjoy, for the wearisome duties of statecraft, which they dislike. Guardians must be willing to put their lives on the line to preserve the state. Lastly, artisans and farmers must recognize their calling to labor with their hands, not overstepping their bounds but submitting to the rule of their superiors. As a general principle, therefore, Plato defines temperance as the virtue most appropriate to the third class because lack of control over the appetitive part of society is the greatest danger to the social order. He defines temperance as "harmonious agreement between the naturally superior and inferior elements on the question which of the two should govern, whether in the state or in the individual." Only as people recognize their peculiar virtue will they acknowledge their specific function in the political order.

4. The four classic virtues culminate in *justice*. In the ideal state, whenever wisdom, courage, and temperance are practiced among the appropriate classes, a fourth virtue, justice, the grand theme of the whole *Republic*, will also be present. Plato defined justice as a "universal principle, that everyone ought to perform the one function in the community for which his nature best suited him." Justice may simply be "minding one's own business and not meddling with other men's concerns." The allegory of the metals finds its ultimate realization. People not only know their respective tasks but manifest their appropriate virtues by actually carrying them out in daily existence. Though no harm would occur if people were to change jobs in the third class (if a carpenter became a cobbler or farmer), great injustice would result if people attempted to move outside their class to usurp a position for which they were not naturally suited (if a soldier or cobbler should presume to rule).

Because the philosopher kings alone are trained to know the Good, they are uniquely responsible for bringing the ideal state into existence. Once they are educated in Plato's curriculum described below, they can actually reform evils that presently exist. Implementing justice in society requires prudence that can identify corruption and then decide upon an appropriate and practical remedy. To the philosopher kings therefore belong decisions affecting the justice of society as a whole.

Although the primary responsibility for justice in society lies in the hands of the ruling class, each class contributes to the justice of the state as a whole. The spirited class are the executors of justice and must support decisions of the ruling class by protecting the state from external attack and making sure that the classes remain distinct and that people remain in their respective places performing their appropriate responsibilities. They also must have a philosophic disposition, but their duties are more like those of a watchdog.

Finally members of the lowest class contribute to the justice of the state by submitting to the control of the superior classes. Artisans and farmers not only acknowledge their leaders' superiority but willingly take their place under their rule. They are content in their jobs as farmers, merchants, and craftsmen and are diligent in providing the physical and economic needs of society as a whole.

Justice is present in a state, therefore, if each class fulfills its primary virtue by assuming its role and actually carrying it out in society. Harmony is achieved by keeping the classes distinct and in their proper place. Justice is the fruit of an ordered society and should never be confused with temperance. Temperance is recognizing one's station in life, while justice consists of fulfilling your calling, doing well what you are born to do.

The following chart illustrates correspondences between human nature and social function, between Plato's anthropology and social views.

CORRESPONDENCES BETWEEN ANTHROPOLOGY AND SOCIAL RULE

	Wisdom	Courage	Temperance
VIRTUES:			
THREE PLACES OF SOUL (Anthropology):			
a. Physiological Location:	Head	Chest	Belly
b. Character Virtue:	Reason	Courage	Lust (a negative character)
c. Spiritual Trait:	Rational	Spirited	Appetitive

ALLEGORY OF METALS:	Gold	Silver	Iron-Brass
SOCIAL CLASS:	Philosopher Kings	Guardians	Artisans, production class
BODY OF GOVERNMENT:	Deliberative	Executive	Productive

Plato's allegory of the metals contains a distinctive provision in order to assure that each person find his or her place in the proper class. Plato believed that citizens will generally possess the same virtues and therefore serve in the same class as their parents. Exceptions do occur, however. Occasionally golden parents will bear a silver child and brass parents a golden offspring, and so on with all the other possible combinations. Therefore, to uphold justice in the state, rulers must examine meticulously the metals in the souls of children. Rulers should demote their own children to a lower class without any regret if their offspring do not prove themselves wise. Likewise leaders must immediately promote gifted children from lower classes. These injunctions were part of Plato's comprehensive educational program, which we examine in greater detail below.

In broad terms, therefore, Plato advocated a class society consisting of three distinct groups, each of which makes a unique contribution to society. Rank is not strictly determined by parentage and is not inflexibly fixed, as in a caste society. Movement between ranks is not only a possibility but an ethical responsibility entrusted to the ruling class. To safeguard his system, to insure that rulers fairly determined the metals of their citizens and thus their positions in the community, Plato created one of his most enduring institutions, his educational system.

Plato's System of Education

Plato did not leave the achievement of his ideal to chance. He was fully convinced that reformation of Athenian society was attainable only if its rulers adopted a system of education whose primary purpose was to produce philosopher kings. Only then would justice prevail in every segment of the political order.

The purpose of education was to create and sustain the Republic. Plato's founding of the Academy in Athens is testimony to the faith he vested in education. Society needed a state-supported educational institution to replace Athens's rampant individualism. Private or family-run education in Athens meant that many groups competed in the marketplace of ideas, including the Sophists. To Plato Sophists were often little more than adroit and slippery conversationalists. The itinerant lecturers of their age excelled in rhetorical flourish but lacked substance. Plato particularly resented their catering to upper-class youth. Educating only those who could afford to pay for instruction made wealth and not wisdom the chief prerequisite for political life. The Sophists' method of education would never produce a just social order. (See our discussion in vol. 1, chaps. 2 and 11.)

To counter the appeal of the Sophists, Plato advocated a state-run educational system that would take students in an orderly and systematic method to the highest level of knowledge. His Republic would establish a unified course of studies. Students were to pursue truth beyond mere opinion and conjecture, to rational discussion of the highest forms, to Goodness itself. Only then could rulers create and administer a truly just social order.

Some Western thinkers have highly praised Plato's views of education. Jean Jacques Rousseau, the famous French Enlightenment thinker, called it the "finest treatise on education that ever was written." Rudiments of his ideas are clearly visible in America's public educational system. Even though most modern educators now deny his belief in absolute moral values as the basis of instruction, public educators have adopted Plato's overall scheme. With Plato they believe that education is the primary tool by which the state can instruct and initiate the populace into its moral and spiritual life. The cream rises to the top as people ascend to the level of their competence.

In describing his curriculum, Plato rejected the Athenian tradition that each family choose its educational method according to individual preference. Plato believed such a model allowed too much diversity, and Athens paid dearly for its individualism by the presence of ignorant and morally unqualified public figures. Again the death of Socrates forever grated in his mind. No wonder the assembly condemned Greece's wisest philosopher! The Athenian democracy that sentenced Socrates to drink hemlock consisted of common, untrained people whose lack of character and education rendered them unfit to govern states. Despite its faults, however, Athens produced some gifted educators who taught a demanding curriculum.

Sparta, the traditional rival of Athens, had opposite strengths and weaknesses. Its greatest attribute was a demanding physical and military education controlled by the state. Sparta's curriculum, however, lacked intellectual breadth and depth. Plato therefore borrowed the best curriculum from Athens's private education and combined it with Sparta's state-run military and physical program. Such a program would produce soldiers and governors for his ideal state with well-developed bodies and enlightened minds.

Since Plato believed that learning consists of a series of mental conversions from ignorance to knowledge, he proposed a curriculum in which students progressed through courses commensurate with their capacity to learn. The physical and intellectual rigor of Plato's curriculum increased from level to level in order to stimulate students' inherent abilities.

In the child's early years, up to the age of eighteen, instruction consisted of gymnastics, which included nutrition and general care of the body, as well as studies in literature, music, and elementary mathematics. During this impressionable period society's rulers were to supervise closely what stories children read, the art they saw, and the music they heard. Specifically, tales of the gods were to portray what is good, noble, and beautiful. Plato strongly opposed traditional Homeric depictions of the gods as different from humans only in their power and not in virtue. Since children are naturally inclined to copy what is most readily at hand, if they learned that gods connive, cheat, and act in other immoral ways, they would mimic these behaviors. Plato, therefore, endorsed strict censorship of poetry and representational art. In a similar vein, he argued that music used in education should ennoble listeners by appealing to their rational and spirited soul and not pander to baser appetites. Were he alive today he would favor classical music for his philosopher kings and John Philip Sousa's marches for his guardians! Undoubtedly he would ban any contemporary music with a heavy back beat.

Plato believed that instruction should teach youth to appreciate the order not only of body and mind but also of the whole cosmos. If education is morally sound, as students progress to the highest forms at a later stage, their minds will greet wisdom, beauty, and all the other virtues as friends, not strangers. Children can apprehend the basic principles of morality even though they are not mature enough to articulate a rational understanding of what is good, noble, and beautiful. Education that builds character and fosters moral choice will enable children to be fully receptive to dialectical instruction when they reach the higher stages of education.

Plato proposed that during the late teens and early twenties, intellectual instruction give way to rigorous military skill and physical endurance that try one's courage. A person will manifest courage, however, only if he or she possesses it as an inward virtue. What we call "intestinal fortitude," or more popularly "guts," cannot be developed through exposure to difficult circumstances if a person does not possess it as an internal virtue. No amount of instruction can artificially implant what should be present as a gift of nature. Intensive physical and military training tests one's character; it shows who already has the "metal" to become not U.S. marines, but guardians and philosopher kings!

Students, both men and women, who successfully pass these first two stages are eligible for advanced studies. By this time their ranks have thinned out considerably. All who do not prove themselves are weeded out and assume a position in the artisan class. Only the most gifted remain, those capable of higher mathematics—plain and solid geometry. At last a selected few are ready to pass through the portal of Plato's Academy! They will spend their twenties engrossed in higher mathematics.

Only after completing their study in mathematics do a smaller minority continue the advanced training to become philosopher kings. They devote five years (from age thirty to thirty-five) to demonstrate whether they "can dispense with sight and the other senses and follow truth into the region of pure reality." While many of Plato's contemporaries, most notably the Sophists, advocated training in dialectic at an earlier age, Plato believed maturity an absolutely indispensable prerequisite. Students should not begin dialectical discussion of the great virtues such as honor and beauty until fully capable of defending them. He wanted to prevent the kind of intellectual immaturity (appropriately called "sophomoric" after the Sophists!) manifest in some young people who mistakenly think themselves possessors of all wisdom. Believing philosophy to be a kind of intellectual sport, they put on a show of arguments but cannot support them. Sophistic thinking is only sham dialectic. Rather than leading to truth, the goal of all reasoning, such intellectual chicanery discredits the noble field of philosophy.

In another of his ingenius illustrations, the allegory of the cave, Plato described how some gradually attain the heights of knowledge. By the age of thirty-five the young guardians are knowledgeable enough about the higher forms that they can put their learning to practical, i.e., political use. Leaving the classroom they enter public life. Their re-entry into society is nothing less than a descent from the lofty heights of intellectual reflection into the "cave" of military and subordinant political posts. Here guardians spend fifteen years not only gaining useful experience but also undergoing a further series of practical tests of their wisdom and courage. What they learned intellectually, they put into practice as public servants, and their metal is further tried by fire. The greatest danger in public service is that leaders will ignore wisdom and courage, abuse their political powers, and yield instead to their private desires and appetites. All previous education was not designed to train them in mere technical skills but to prepare them to use their skills morally.

Again, only the best survive this process. They prove themselves worthy of the ultimate position, philosopher king. Members of this highest class divide their time between further study of the Good and taking turns "at the troublesome duties of public life." True philosopher kings will regard public office not as a distinction but as a distraction from what philosophers love best, reflection on the Good. Thus Plato wanted to give political power not to those who seek it but to those who disdain it. Whoever seeks power is most likely to abuse it. True philosophers rightly despise the prestige and perks that usually attend political office. Instead they prize the right and honor of insuring social justice by carrying out the responsibilities of their office. Disinterested service alone would be their goal, since long before philosophers would have conquered any lust that might tempt them to defraud, extort, or misuse their considerable power.

Plato thus pays high tribute to education. From him springs the Western belief that proper education leads to the betterment of society. Schools that follow the appropriate curriculum will produce an elite corps of thoroughly disciplined rulers. They are fit to rule because under the eyes of their tutors they have developed physical skills, mastered morality, and attained the highest Good intellectually. Just as in his anthropology Plato argued that individuals can perfect themselves through the use of their natural endowment of reason, so society can reform itself through education. His faith that education could produce a class capable of ridding the state of its social ills parallels his belief in human perfectibility through reason.

Plato's twentieth-century heirs may even surpass his optimism by claiming that technology now exists to guarantee society's gradual perfection (see our chapter below on dystopianism). Even though Plato attempted to use education to achieve a moral purpose based on his concept of the Good, he tended to make education a technique. Some present-day pragmatists have gone beyond Plato to use educational techniques to achieve whatever ends they choose. Plato would have condemned such education as valueless and irresponsible. That difference notwithstanding, modern educators still share Plato's faith that humans can perfect themselves.

The Communism of the Guardians

Plato believed that just as individuals overcome evil and perfect themselves when they use wisdom to curb their appetites, in society philosopher kings control evil by curbing the appetites of the whole community. But what is to prevent these rulers from using their considerable power for personal aggrandizement? To forestall such an

144 Plato's Republic: A Rational Society

abuse of power, Plato conceived a built-in safeguard to keep the guardians from evil—a system of communism. In the ideal state only artisans and farmers possess property and participate in business and commerce. They alone maintain various degrees of wealth and an ordinary family life. Society's upper two classes live a more Spartan existence. They receive their rigorous physical and intellectual education while living in a kind of military communism. Plato idealistically believed that the life of reason is a life of unselfishness and that philosopher kings would be content without possessions and family. Those who have no wealth, property, or family will not be tempted to use power for personal or family gain.

Plato's communism bore little resemblance to what Karl Marx advocated in the nineteenth century. Whereas Marxists propose putting the means of production under the control of the state, Plato barely discussed the economic structure of his Republic, let alone make common ownership of the means of production the basis of society. Plato's primary purpose was to improve the soul by reforming the political order of the state. He always made material or economic matters subservient to moral virtue. Whatever guardians were to share communally, whether property or wives, was to accomplish an ethical end, not a material redistribution of wealth. The upper two classes were to be totally divested of any economic element because soldiers were totally preoccupied in the pursuit and practice of their character virtue, courage, and rulers were totally consumed in their quest for and implementation of reason. Thus while Marx constructed his communism on a naturalistic basis and made the material or external improvement of the state's citizens his primary goal, Plato clearly subordinated economic matters to moral purpose. Plato's priorities are evident in the fact that artisans and farmers did not practice communism. The lowest class retained private property and normal family life, albeit under strict state control.

Rulers assumed responsibility for assuring that each person fulfill the one task for which he or she was best fitted. Philosopher kings were (1) to maintain justice, (2) to supervise society directly so that citizens would do the work for which nature equipped them and would not interfere with others, (3) to enforce the principle that producers do not become too wealthy or too poor, and (4) to keep population roughly stable. Farmers and artisans in turn were to pay the salaries of the upper two classes for their wise guardianship.

Rather than establish specific laws or statutes that would bind the decisions of philosopher kings on such issues as the optimum level of wealth or population, Plato trusted education to prepare these leaders to make the most prudent decision as situations arise. In so doing, however, Plato did not espouse an ethic whereby the situation would dictate leaders' decisions. Rather he believed that rationally trained individuals would correctly perceive appropriate universal ideals and then apply them to political issues.

But would the lowest class accept direct rule, and would the upper two classes quietly accept his communistic restrictions? Plato acknowledged how radical his proposals were. Some would protest living in barracks and eating at common tables. But more would object to his abolition of marriage and family as society's basic institutions. In the most outlandish analogy of the dialogue, he compares breeding of sporting dogs and game birds in order to produce a "good stock" to rulers' management of breeding among the guardians. All mating arrangements should appear to result from a lottery system, while, in fact, rulers secretly control them to assure the best possible offspring and zero population growth!

Thus for Plato, the family and home are not the basic institutions of society but instead are significant obstacles to building a good social order. He proposed therefore that the state assume tasks formerly performed by parents. Public nurseries would care for the children from gold and silver couples, whose children would consider the state to be surrogate parents. All offspring born in the same months would believe themselves to be "brothers" and "sisters." To prohibit sexual promiscuity, Plato assigned to society's leaders the direct management of sexual unions and forbade any incestuous relationships.

Even more objectionable is Plato's proposal that the state dispose of inferior children. He was deliberately vague about exactly how leaders should carry out this policy. Some scholars believe that Plato would allow the Spartan practice of infanticide. Others contend that he would simply relegate "defective" children to the third class. Since public welfare was his overriding concern, a less comprehensive program may breed individualism, selfishness, and sedition.

To create Plato's ideal would require a rigorous system of education, censorship of the arts, communism of the upper two classes, and abolition of the family. Unfortunately, he never identified which if any of his proposals should take precedence. Indeed, if pressed, he probably would have argued that all factors were necessary to achieve the comprehensive reforms he sought. Nevertheless, the *Republic* discusses education much more than the abolition of the family or the communism of the upper two classes. Some defenders of Plato have argued that people can adopt some but not all of his ideas. Plato, however, considered all his ideas to be interrelated.

Corruption of the State

Plato devoted part 4 of his *Republic* to the decline of society. What kinds of states result when injustice is practiced? Similar to his earlier exposition of justice, Plato here explored how injustice corrupts both society (macrocosm) and the individual (microcosm). Injustice is a disorder or lack of harmony. Whenever one of the classes or an individual rejects temperance—the one virtue common to all three classes—the breakdown of society begins.

Plato did not simply juxtapose degenerate political order over against the ideal society. Instead he described how an ideal state gradually declines as it passes through various intermediate forms of government. He described the constitutions of corrupt states from his own observations of different Greek city-states. Beginning with the ideal state he proceeded down a hierarchy of corruption, all the way back to the cave—a condition of abject decay and deterioration. Each social evil springs from an absence of the harmony and order that ought to characterize states and people.

Identifying evil as merely a defect or an absence of some good quality is a consistent theme in Plato's world view. While that has much in its favor, the negative consequences become strikingly evident as he describes each stage of society's degeneration. Conceiving evil as merely a privation seriously underestimates the impact of both individual and social evil that results from willful, rebellious choice. If both individual and social sins are only deficiencies, then evil does not exist in either human nature or social institutions. Believing that no man sins on purpose, Plato thought that once a person knows what is right, nothing inhibits him or her from acting properly.

The first corruption in an ideal state occurs when the spirited class usurps the place of rule from the philosopher kings. The resultant state is a "timocracy" because guardians seize power for the wrong reason—for the "honor" (Greek, *timé*) it brings—rather than because they desire to implement justice. Plato has in mind the classic Spartan city state where reason was subject to avarice. A military state emerges, which, for neglect of Plato's hallowed system of education, lacks philosophically trained leaders. The communistic system begins to break down as leaders give up their quest for wisdom and instead seek to accumulate wealth and possessions. The leaders of a timocratic state are not single-minded in their pursuit of virtue; they serve society out of several motivations. Though not totally capitulating to their appetites, rulers let their spirited selves dominant reason. The courageous warrior replaces the philosopher as the hero of citizens. Such a society becomes ambitious and wages continuous war.

Oligarchy, literally "government of the few," is a further corruption of the state, resulting in greater social disunity. Instead of reason or courage, appetite dominates, manifesting itself in desire for wealth and property. Government resides not in the hands of intellectuals or the military but in the commercial class which has no natural capacity for rule. Worse yet is the loss of Plato's fundamental principle that each person should do the one task for which he or she is naturally suited.

The model for Plato's oligarchy was a corrupted Sparta, where citizenship was based on ownership of property. In this society the rich, because of their wealth, assumed rule. Their first priority was to dethrone wisdom and courage as primary virtues of the state. As order continued to deteriorate under the rule of mere appetite, criminals and beggers became prevalent. The disharmony of a timocracy leads to a greater disunity as two groups—the rich and poor—vie for supremacy within the one social order.

In an oligarchy, appetite for wealth dominates society. But a worse form of government than oligarchy can emerge, a democracy. Order breaks down as all the appetites, not just lust for wealth, receive ready expression in a democratic state. Restraint in all its forms—habit, discipline, custom, etc.—disappears. What follows, in Plato's opinion, is little less than anarchy, although he calls it democracy. Democracy brings a further debasement of justice as appetites are given free rein, instead of wisdom or prudence serving as the ruling virtue. Democracy's licentious freedom leads only to debauchery and widespread capitulation to individual preferences.

Plato's contempt for democracy stemmed in part from bitter remembrance of what Athenians did to his beloved teacher, Socrates. Whenever uneducated and undisciplined people exercise power, potential for great injustices exists. In contemporary terms, Plato foresaw democracies as run by morally ignorant, self-serving bureaucrats who corrupt government by preying on the middle class. Inevitably politicians appeal to the interests of the masses and revolution ensues.

Despotism or tyranny is the nadir of a government's decline. To prevent the impending threat of exploitation the people accept a leader as their "champion." By giving him blind allegiance citizens become like sheep in the hands of a wolf. The despot steadily accrues more powers, enslaves his people and provokes war with other peoples to divert attention from his evil acts. Eventually he must eliminate anyone who might oppose his brutal rule. Plato probably pictured here the policy of Dionysius I, tyrant of Syracuse. In its despotic form appetite goes beyond giving equal expression to all desires, as in a democracy. Tyranny produces lawlessness and vice. Because of the absence of virtues injustice reigns supreme and the state lacks all goodness.

Consistent with his view that the state reflects the character of its citizens, Plato's main point is that timocratic, oligarchic, democratic, and despotic states emerge as its citizens corrupt the ideal of justice. Plato believed that states take on the character of the individuals who are most dominant. Thus governments decline as power gradually leaves the hands of the wise and is taken up by those who are naturally inferior.

Summary and Evaluation of Plato's Social Views

The *Republic* is Plato's most representative dialogue, a classic of philosophical idealism. Plato believed his philosophy was practical, a cure for Athens's social ills. He conceived a philosopher's task to be the very opposite of being suspended in a balloon as in Louisa May Alcott's definition. If followed, the *Republic* would put philosophers' feet firmly on the ground where they belong. Plato would challenge philosophers first to be temperant—to recognize their true task as members of the upper class—and then to be just—to carry out their responsibilities of ruling the state. While philosophers might resist such compulsion, preferring instead the contemplative life of academics, society must not permit them this luxury.

How are we to assess Plato's social and political views? Are they compatible with the rest of his world view, for example his views of man, God, and knowledge? The *Republic* is remarkably consistent. Plato's society reflects his view of human nature inasmuch as society is but man writ large. The three classes of society are analogous to the three parts of the human soul. Ideally both society's classes and its individuals represent virtues appropriate to their function within the macrocosm and microcosm. A well-ordered and harmonious society reflects the moral status of its citizens. Few thinkers have stressed as consistently and as clearly as Plato that morality is indispensable in any consideration of human nature and society.

Plato deplored Athens's leaders' acceptance of the status quo and its many social evils. Not only was Athens's past glory fading, but the assembly refused to address obvious social injustice. But recognizing political evil is always relatively easy compared with the task of proposing a satisfying alternative. Effectively combating social injustice requires an accurate appraisal of human nature and identification of appropriate moral means to carry out reform. Plato failed in two ways. He seriously underestimated the basic flaws of human nature and he overestimated human capacity to correct individual and social deficiencies. He did not appreciate evil's radical impact on the human will. Plato's cosmic dualism led him to argue that evil affects primarily man's physical appetites. The mind and the will remain unscathed. Not only does the mind clearly apprehend moral goodness, but the human will (represented by the chest), being totally free, can perform morally good acts without any external assistance.

Because Plato believed that no man sins on purpose, sin is never the result of willful wickedness but only of ignorance, not knowing what is good. Individuals and society can avoid wrong by following the light of individual reason or the class gifted with prudence. At most, morally wrong behavior stems from a failure to choose the good, not perversity or wickedness of heart. In doing evil we fail to give priority to our rational selves or the wisdom of society's leaders. We never intentionally and with malice choose something we know to be wrong. Plato therefore defined evil as a privation, stressing that sins are exclusively acts of omission and never acts of commission.

Plato's view of human nature and evil differ sharply from the biblical perspective. In the Bible evil results not from man's metaphysical dualism, his choosing bodily appetites over spiritual ideals. Evil results from man's proud refusal to obey the commands of a rightful sovereign. Sin is man's rebellion against God, not a struggle within finite human nature. It includes acts of omission and commission that violate the law of God. The human mind, the heart, and the body are all alike corrupted by sin. Whereas Plato saw only the body as evil, the Bible describes the mind as "darkened" (Rom. 1:21), the heart as "deceitful above all things, and desperately wicked" (Jer. 17:9, KJV), and the body as "dead because of sin" (Rom. 8:10). Plato's contention that philosopher kings were innately more virtuous than the other two classes collides with the clear biblical and historical evidence of sinfulness throughout all classes and groups.

Biblical writers likewise differed with Plato on the subject of vocation. They stressed that all callings are of the same moral value. Vocations may demand different skills or gifts, all of which come from God, but each vocation requires people to use their gifts responsibly for the glory of God. No calling is innately inferior or superior. No task is without moral significance. Because God Himself worked in creating the earth, every legitimate job possesses dignity and value.

Our central criticism of Plato is his idealism—his belief in the perfectibility of man and by extension the perfectibility of society. In both instances perfection can be achieved by activating what is already inherent in human nature, the moral virtues. Plato's allegory of the metals thus is pivotal to his social vision. Society is perfectible because the soul is perfectible. The soul is perfectible because it is intrinsically immortal and possesses intrinsic virtues that if used correctly, can eradicate individual and social injustice. While some of his followers would deny the term, most critics argue that Plato's views are clearly utopian. He insisted that people and society could do more than gradually improve; they could actually approach perfection. Thus Plato believed that his ideal state would not be simply a construct or model in the human mind; it could be realized in Greek life.

Plato's faith in the inherent goodness of human nature and of man's innate ability to reform society clashes with biblical teaching. He proposed a class system produced by an educational curriculum and supported by a communalism of property, all of which, from a biblical perspective, dehumanize man.

First, Plato's class system, based on the allegory of the metals, superficially resembles the biblical view of vocation discussed above. But Plato artificially divided people into different classes, based upon their supposed moral virtues. In the Bible, king and cobbler alike are image bearers of God and as such are responsible to act morally within their respective vocations. The only difference between monarch and worker is their office, not their moral condition. Virtues are not assigned to special classes. Rather God graciously grants wisdom, courage, and temperance to all people. No class or group innately possesses superior moral qualities.

In addition, people do not live moral lives by their own rational, autonomous efforts. All persons, no matter what their vocations, need God's revealed moral guidelines governing their work. Scripture defines moral and spiritual responsibilities, and biblical characters are evaluated on the basis of God's righteousness revealed in His commandments. God does not stratify people by innate moral ability and assign them to qualitatively superior and inferior classes.

Second, the education Plato proposed tends to dehumanize man. Plato's educational system was built upon his rationalistic view of the virtues and tripartite division of the soul. By dividing learning into discrete segments Plato fragmented education. Even though his system provided for physical discipline and tested moral conviction, his primary emphasis, evident in every aspect of the curriculum, was to prepare students to apprehend rational ideals. The virtues Plato emphasized were primarily cognitive in content. They were also anthropocentric and autonomous, in that human beings achieve virtues by their own intellectualistic quests. Even though in Plato's view people can realize such virtues only if they are so disposed by nature, the actual achievement of virtue occurs as one gradually makes his way through the academic curriculum. Man's highest goal is intellectual or cognitive. From a biblical standpoint Plato never explained satisfactorily how this quest for impersonal and abstract ideals can ultimately fulfill *personal* beings. Therefore, Plato's attempt to understand reality through reason and his model society do not square with life as most people experience it. He tended to reserve to the smallest and brightest class the important moral tasks. While all people are to order themselves internally by allowing reason to restrain their appetites, their moral choices do not affect society. Plato thereby reduced the ordinary moral life of farmers and artisans to virtual insignificance. He implied that only choices made by those with social power (what we called in the preface to vol. 1 "historical power") are really significant.

By contrast, in the Bible no classes are especially equipped to achieve what Plato called the virtues. Moreover, wisdom, courage, temperance, and justice are not impersonal ideals to be reached by an autonomous rational quest. God commands us to live virtuous lives, but we do so by His power, not by our own strength. Because moral virtues are gifts of God, they are not in any sense of the term anthropocentric, but thoroughly theocentric.

Wisdom is a gift of God suited not just for political rule but for all callings in society. Even though King Solomon was especially blessed with wisdom (I Kings 3:1-3), in the book of Proverbs he enjoins all believers to seek wisdom in order to live a righteous life. Wisdom encompasses not only intelligence to make political choices but also skill and craft in all practical matters. For example, workers who were to build the tabernacle where Jews worshipped

God were "filled with ability, with intelligence, with knowledge, and with all craftsmanship to devise artistic designs, to work in gold and silver and bronze, in cutting stone for setting and in carving wood for work in every skilled craft" (Exod. 35:31-33). Similarly Isaiah 28:23-29 describes God's providing practical wisdom in farming.

Likewise the Bible declares courage to be a moral quality required of all people, not of only one class. In the Old Testament God commands Israel's leader Joshua to "be strong and very courageous" (Josh. 1:7); but God also commands all believers through the psalmist to "be strong, and let your heart take courage, all you who hope in the Lord" (Ps. 31:24); and Jesus commands His followers who may face persecution to "take courage" because "I have overcome the world" (John 16:33; see also Matt. 9:2, 22 where Jesus charges those whom He has healed to "take courage").

Moreover, temperance or self-control is expected of all Christians. Leaders of the church are required to exercise self-control (Titus 1:8), but so are all believers. II Peter 1:5-11 presents a list of qualities that are to characterize any believer: moral excellence (Greek: *arete*, "virtue"), knowledge (wisdom), self-control (temperance), perseverance, godliness, brotherly kindness, and love. Christians are to live virtuous lives, which only the sanctifying power of the Holy Spirit makes possible.[3]

In each of the preceding cases, virtue finds its meaning in the law of God, which reflects God's character. The virtues are thoroughly theocentric and personal in nature. God commands everyone to display His virtues because all of us, not just a special class of people, are His image bearers. Education in the virtues consists of instruction in God's commandments, a task enjoined upon all in the community of faith (see Deut. 4:1-8; 6:1-8).

Although Plato's views became the model for much of classical and modern education, his curriculum contains several defects. It exalts an impersonal absolute; it makes the human intellect autonomous (even though the Good illuminates all knowledge); and it limits instruction in the higher moral virtues to those who pass

---

3. Because justice is treated in great detail in the next chapter, we will not examine it here except to say that justice in the Bible is required of all believers and consists of righteous conduct as defined by the Word of God.

through all of the rigors of Plato's graduated curriculum. His intellectualism and elitism effectively dehumanized all classes of men, not just the lower classes. Plato's whole society from its leaders to its workers was based on an impersonal, abstract idealism, which fails to account for human beings' unique personal character as made in God's image.

Third, Plato's view of communal property and family has the opposite effect from what he intended. Instead of elevating the upper two classes his proposals tend only to dehumanize. If property is the gift of God and our stewardship over it is a reflection of our imaging God (that is, by virtue of our position, nature, and function), the denial of stewardship to the ruling class contradicts our calling to rule! Likewise, allowing artisans and farmers to own property assigns to them a moral responsibility in which they supposedly are not naturally gifted. In both instances Plato violated his basic principles. The negative consequences outweigh the positive benefits of removing a temptation for people in public office.

The effect of Plato's communism on the family is even worse. Biblically the family is one of God's creation ordinances, structured by God to help rule over what He created. Thus the family is neither a divine afterthought nor the invention of the human mind. The family is *the* basic institution of society. As a part of the cultural mandate God commands us to "be fruitful and multiply" in order that we may carry out the task of subduing and ruling over the created order (Gen. 1:28). The remainder of Scripture echoes the family's prominent role in God's design. In the New Testament, for example, one cannot be an elder or deacon unless first proving himself to be a good parent (assuming he is married and has children—I Tim. 3:4, 5, 12). Plato's suggestions that children be separated from their parents and be raised by the state as a kind of surrogate parent and that eugenic coupling should be used to produce better children directly contradict biblical norms. Marriage and family are not simply cultural mores that each succeeding generation can restructure at will, but sacred institutions carefully regulated by the commandments of God (see the next chapter for details).

Finally, Plato's *Republic* is too optimistic. History has demonstrated that man cannot perform through education alone all that

Plato sought to. Education has never produced an intellectual elite capable of exercising direct, unchecked rule over all institutions of the state without abusing it. Placing virtually unlimited power in the hands of philosopher kings is too dangerous. Plato's faith in human perfectibility and his conviction that no man sins on purpose are simply not borne out in history. Apparently Plato came to the same realization. He later amended his social views in his *Laws* by proposing a mixed constitution based on law, not simply on superior individuals. He also eliminated references to communism. But even his later proposal conflicts with the biblical conception of society. Because of the fact of original sin and countless historical examples where power has been abused, Christians in the modern period have been reluctant to assign direct power to any single individual or group without any checks and balances.

For Further Reading

Barker, Sir Ernest. *Greek Political Theory: Plato and His Predecessors.* London: Methuen, 1951.

Burnet, John. *Platonism.* Berkeley: University of California Press, 1928.

Copleston, Frederick C. *A History of Philosophy, vol. 1. Greece and Rome.* Westminster, Md.: The Newman Press, 1946.

Cornford, Francis Macdonald. *The Republic of Plato.* New York: Oxford University Press, 1945.

Guthrie, W. K. C. *A History of Greek Philosophy, vol. 4. Plato: The Man and His Dialogues.* New York: Cambridge University Press, 1975.

Morrow, Glenn R. *Plato's Cretan City: A Historical Interpretation of the Laws.* Princeton: Princeton University Press, 1960.

Murphy, N. R. *The Interpretation of Plato's Republic.* Oxford: Oxford University Press, 1951.

Passmore, John. *The Perfectibility of Man.* New York: Scribners, 1970.

6
Biblical Society: A Covenantal Society

Dale R. Bowne and John D. Currid

A Contrast: Greek Thought Versus Biblical

In sharp contrast to Greek thought, where man is the center of life and social relationships, the Bible presents God as the focal point of all cultural activities. The Greek view emphasized human efforts to build a society that embodies justice and goodness. Biblical theology argues that God's power, character, and norms should direct social development.

All the Greek thinkers discussed in other chapters declared man to be the center and focus of all activities and relationships. Plato, for example, maintained that man controls his own destiny and has the ability to achieve both individual and social perfection. Such perfection can be achieved if humans attain order and harmony within the universe. Thus Plato and other Greek philosophers regarded man as the internal unifying element of the cosmos.

In the Bible, however, all culture building and social progress depend on God, the Creator of all things. God is sovereign over the entire cosmos and nothing can exist or be understood except through Him. While God created and sustains the universe, He is totally self-sufficient and independent of it. Thus, in contrast to all Greek conceptions of the ultimate, God is both transcendent and immanent. For this reason, the Scriptures declare God to be the external unifying element of the universe and thus sovereign over the social dimension of life.

The Covenant as Foundational for Old Testament Society

The basis of all societal views in the Bible is the covenant treaty established by God with man. Within the covenant relationship God reveals who He is, what His purposes are, and, more importantly for this chapter, how His people are to live. Through the covenant God regulates biblical society, demanding obedience to His laws, statutes, and principles.

In the Old Testament there existed two phases to the covenant: the "covenant of creation," which applied to God's relationship with man prior to the fall and the "covenant of redemption," which is used to describe their relationship after the fall. Although these covenants have much in common (since all of God's dealings with humans possess a basic unity), a structural distinction must still be recognized. We focus in this chapter on the covenant of redemption.

Covenant Responsibility in the Old Testament

The most fully developed redemptive covenant in the Old Testament is the Mosaic covenant described in Exodus 19-23. This covenant provided the laws and ordinances by which Hebrew society was to function. It governed the relationship between God and the Hebrew people, and it determined the code of conduct within the Israelite society.

Specifically, the covenant community of Israel was required to submit to the laws God established and gave to Moses at Sinai. The statutes of the covenant of redemption, however, often changed depending upon the nation's immediate situation. When this occurred in Israelite history, the redemptive covenant between God and the nation was reconfirmed in order to take account of the changes in the law (e.g., Josh. 24). Although covenant law at times was altered, the basic principles upon which it rested were not changed. In the Old Testament, covenant statutes were based mainly upon four fundamental principles: justice, righteousness, *hesed*, and stewardship.

Justice

In the Old Testament, the term justice (*mishpat*) denotes the rights and duties of each party to fulfill their obligations under the covenantal law. Just individuals are those who satisfy God's demands and live according to the statutes established in the covenant. These laws and demands, however, refer not merely to the vertical relationship between God and man, but also to the horizontal relationship of man to man. Thus, under the covenant, people are obligated to fulfill their duties not only toward God but also to society as a whole.

A prime example of the concept of justice in ancient Israelite society is the covenantal demand that people maintain just relations with one another in all aspects of the economy. In the Old Testament economic framework, all economic dealings (selling, trading, etc.) were based on the weights and measures of certain valued items such as gold, silver, and grain; the Hebrews had no money or coin exchange system. God commanded the Israelites to maintain a consistent and fair system of weights and balances (Lev. 19:36; Deut. 25:13). Subjective or relative standards were forbidden in the economic system; all transactions were to be made according to objective measurements. As the writer of Proverbs points out, "A false balance is an abomination to the Lord, but a just weight is His delight" (11:1).

The Old Testament also clearly stipulated the administration of legal justice. The concept of *Lex Talionis* (Latin for "the law of retaliation") meant to the Israelites that what a person deserves, he should receive. This concept is a two-edged sword. On the one hand, those who pervert justice by breaking covenant law shall be punished according to their crime, and their punishment in some cases shall be the same as their crime (e.g., "Whoever strikes a man so that he dies shall be put to death"—Exod. 21:12, RSV). On the other hand, those who are victims of criminal acts shall receive restitution from the wrongdoer, that justice may be served not only on the criminal but on the victim as well. The *Lex Talionis* concept is summarized in Deuteronomy 19:19-21:

> So you shall purge the evil from the midst of you. And the rest shall hear, and fear, and shall never again commit any such evil

among you. Your eye shall not pity; it shall be life for life, eye for eye, tooth for tooth, hand for hand, foot for foot (RSV).

Righteousness

Whereas the Hebrew word for justice refers to the rights and duties of a covenant participant, the Hebrew word for righteousness (*zedek*) pertains to the conduct or attitude of the covenant parties (see Deut. 9:5; I Sam. 26:23; Prov. 21:21). It is often used of both God and man having the right and consistent conduct in all matters of the covenant agreement. God requires righteousness in all areas of existence: social, ethical, and religious. However, when *zedek* is used strictly in reference to either God or man the meaning of the word becomes much narrower.

Ultimately, righteousness is an attribute of God; it means that all He says and does is without flaw (Pss. 36:6; 89:16; Dan. 9:7). Specifically, the righteousness of God in the Old Testament expresses His perfection in all areas of covenantal conduct. In establishing the covenant, God set down the correct behavior for Himself and for society. God is the righteous judge who established the norms of the covenant and will decide right or wrong on the basis of His perfection.

Man, on the other hand, is not a righteous or perfect being, but a slave to sin and a covenant-breaker (Deut. 9:4-5; Job 25:4; Ps. 143:2). Thus, the Old Testament understands human righteousness not to be a human attribute but a human response. To be righteous, people must keep the law of God in accordance with His covenant terms. Noah "found favor in the eyes of the Lord" (Gen. 6:8) and Job was "blameless and upright" (Job 2:3) not because they were perfect but because their lives, in large part, conformed to and reflected the righteousness of God.

Hesed

If justice and righteousness were the only covenant principles, the relationship between God and man would be extremely impersonal. Concepts of attitude, conduct, duties, and rights evoke images of military regimen or court-room protocol, not of a loving and intimate relationship. The kind of behavior expected between the parties of God's treaty with man, however, goes well beyond impersonal "legal" and "moral" codes of covenant law and the principles of justice and righteousness. The most significant Hebrew concept in this context is *hesed*. The word is usually translated in English versions of the Bible as "loving-kindness": the covenant-makers are expected to love one another. *Hesed*, however, is not the main Hebrew word for love and, therefore, probably has a deeper meaning.

A story recorded in I Samuel 20 expresses the true understanding of *hesed*. In this episode David, who is fleeing from the vengeance of King Saul of Israel, makes a pact or covenant with Jonathan, the son of the king. They agree that Jonathan will tell David whether or not the king still wants to kill him. This is quite dangerous for the prince, for if the king finds out, Jonathan will be killed. Jonathan therefore says that if he informs David and survives, may David "show me the *hesed* of the Lord that I may not die, and do not cut off your *hesed* from my house forever."

What the word *hesed* means in this story is that David and Jonathan had made a covenant of loyalty with one another. Not only are they participants in an agreement, but they are comrades, loving and loyal to each other. When this term is used in specific reference to the covenant between God and man, knowing and practicing the statutes of the law are not enough. Both parties must have a deep love and loyalty for the other. As with the other principles discussed, however, human beings are to build a *hesed* relationship not only with God but with each other as well. (Because *hesed* shapes the relationship between man and God and among God's covenant people, it is no wonder that, when Jesus was asked which commandment or law was the greatest, He replied, "Hear O Israel: The Lord our God, the Lord is one; and you shall love the Lord your God with all your heart, and with all your soul, and with all your mind, and with all your strength" and "You shall love your neighbor as yourself"—Mark 12:29-31, RSV, quoting Deut. 6:4-5 and Lev. 19:18.)

Stewardship

Basic to the covenant of creation was the cultural mandate God gave to man whereby man was to be God's servant on earth. Even after man sinned, the cultural mandate continued in force as an integral part of the post-fall covenant of redemption. For instance, in Genesis 9:1 God makes a covenant with Noah and proclaims,

"Be fruitful and multiply, and fill the earth." The command clearly reiterates that given to Adam in the original covenant relationship and testifies to its continued requirements.

On this basis, under the covenant of redemption human beings are still responsible for culturally "subduing" the earth. They are to rule over creation as God's stewards. The requirements of vocation, devotion, and responsibility must be met.

Yet, because of sin's entrance into the created order, a new dimension is added to the covenant relationship. After the fall, God assigned a missionary mandate to individual Hebrews and to the Israelite society as a whole. The prophetic book of Jonah describes the responsibility of the individual. God tells Jonah to travel to Nineveh (a non-Israelite city) and preach repentance to its inhabitants. The communal responsibility of Israel for missionary work is attested to in Isaiah 49:6b where God speaks to Israel, "I will give you as a light to the nations, that my salvation may reach to the end of the earth" (RSV). Clearly, individually and collectively, the Israelites were to convey God's revelation to all nations.

The total concept of man realizing and acting upon his ordained position as royal servant and missionary is called "stewardship." Israelites were required to maintain a correct internal relationship with God and their fellow members of the chosen nation. But, also, they were to attain a right relationship with the external fallen world.

The Internal Covenant Society

The four principles of justice, righteousness, *hesed*, and stewardship provide the basis for the Old Testament redemption covenant. The Hebrews, both individually and communally, were to abide by these regulations and principles in order to maintain a correct relationship with God. Clearly, God and His law were to direct human activities in every area of life and were thus central to all cultural activity, serving as the foundation for Hebrew society. But how was this expressed in practical, everyday life? How does this theological basis affect specific Hebrew institutions of religion, government, society, and the economy?

The Cultus

The term "cultus" describes how the Israelites expressed their religious experience in concrete external actions performed within their covenant community. The cultic functions depicted in the Old Testament were given to Israel by God at Sinai, when Moses received all the laws of the covenant of redemption. The cultic system, therefore, was one aspect of the larger covenant. As such it came under the rulership of the great suzerain *Yahweh* (God's Hebrew name). It may be divided into five organizational parts:

1. *Cultic Sites.* In ancient Israel, specific sites such as the cities of Shechem, Jerusalem, and Samaria were designated for community worship. At these cultic sites priests of the holy nation performed religious rituals. These priests often lived in the cultic centers, and law required that the city's inhabitants provide for their material needs (Num. 18). Moreover, the entire nation was legally obligated to provide for the cultic centers and their priests; support of the cultic system was mandatory. Thus, all Israelites were involved in the cultus, which demonstrated the centrality of God for the whole covenant community.

2. *Cultic Objects.* In most ancient Near Eastern societies a temple (or temples) was the central place of worship. This became true for Israel only later in its history (after about 1000 B.C.). Prior to the Solomonic period, the central object within the cultus of Israel was the Ark of the Covenant, which was housed in the tabernacle (Exod. 25ff.). At Sinai Moses had been commanded to build a tabernacle, or a "mobile temple," a place where certain sacred objects such as the tablets containing the Ten Commandments and the rod of Aaron were stored. More importantly, the Israelites believed that God dwelled in the ark and individuals could meet Him there. This meant to the Jews that God was not remote from them, but was vitally present, indeed central to their entire existence.

3. *Cultic Seasons.* The Israelites observed many "religious" holidays rooted either in a historical event (such as the Passover, which commemorated the Exodus from Egypt) or in a natural event (such

as the Feast of Weeks, which celebrated the autumn harvest). Another example of a religious or cultic holiday was the Sabbath day. The Sabbath was much more than a day of worship. It was also a day of rest and relaxation (Exod. 23:12-13). Cultic rituals, therefore, permeated all aspects of society, commemorating how God was involved in all things. By no means a separate aspect of Hebrew society, a religious dimension and motivation underlay all of life.

4. *Cultic Actions.* The most important cultic actions practiced throughout the Old Testament period were offerings and sacrifices (Exod. 29ff.). More than mere rituals, these were acknowledgments that God owns and rules over all things. Offerings returned to God part of what He had given to the nation. Thus, for example, in the offering of firstfruits (Exod. 23:16), Israelite farmers gave to God the first portion of their harvests to acknowledge not only His presence but also His active involvement in all areas of the covenant society's existence.

5. *Cultic Administration.* Of the cultic offices in Israel the Levite or priest was the most important. In addition to administering the cultic laws to the people, the priest had duties in other areas of society as well. This offers further evidence that all parts of Israelite society were interrelated and under the covenant and rulership of God.

Our entire discussion of cultus illustrates the point that in ancient Israel the same devotion to God was expected in social, political, economic, and educational activities as was required in religious practices. God rules over all life through His covenant. Thus every aspect of Israelite society was religious.

Government

During its history, Israel experienced two stages or systems of government. The first, when Israel consisted of a group of tribes banded together by the covenant and their religious convictions (1200-1000 B.C.), is called a "theocracy," a government where God is king or ruler of the state. While in the Israelite theocracy God was the lawmaker and the judge, He used human agents to administer divine law. Thus, at Sinai, God commanded Israel to appoint national leaders. The early government of Israel consisted of three offices:

1. *Covenant Mediator.* This was the highest authoritative position in Israel. Its occupants mediated between God and His people in both secular and religious matters. Proclaiming the laws of the divine king, these men served as the voices of God. Leading examples of those who held this position, which was by divine appointment and not by democratic election, are Moses and Joshua.

2. *Judges.* At Sinai, God commanded the Israelites: "You shall appoint judges and officers in all your towns which the Lord your God gives you, according to your tribes; and they shall judge the people with righteous judgment" (Deut. 16:18, RSV). Judges were to administer the law of God to the people. Not limited to civic leadership, many of them also functioned as military leaders (see Judges). Then too, Samuel administered the law in both the secular and the religious realms. Again we see that the ancient Israelites did not separate religious convictions from governmental activities; all things existed under the covenant of God.

3. *Levites.* As mentioned above, Levites superintended Israel's specific religious rituals. They were the priests of this holy nation. Like judges, however, Levites had religious and secular responsibilities. For instance, Deuteronomy 17:8-9 states that "if any case arises requiring decision between one kind of homicide and another, one kind of legal right and another, . . . then you shall arise . . . and coming to the Levitical priests, and to the judge who is in office in those days, you shall consult them, and they shall declare to you the decision" (RSV). Levites thus administered secular law as well as religious law because to the Israelites no sharp line divided the one from the other. To the covenant nation, all of life was religion.

Israel's second stage or form of government developed after the Hebrews had settled in the land of Canaan. Because of external pressures (e.g., the invading Philistines) and internal chaos, the

Israelite people begged God to appoint a king rather than judges to rule over them. Thus the Hebrews discarded the original theocracy, as God declared to Samuel: "They have not rejected you, but they have rejected Me from being king over them" (I Sam. 8:7).

Nevertheless, Israel's kings were not to be absolute monarchs who lived above the law of the covenant. When God granted Israel's request to have a king, the form of government changed from a pure theocracy to a theocratic monarchy, wherein God was to rule through His agent, the king. The king was under God's command and was to perform the duties required of his office (Deut. 17:18ff.). While the king had civic and military responsibilities, his major function was religious. For instance, the king was expected not only to build administrative quarters but also to erect and maintain a temple.

Since in ancient Israel there was no separation of religion and civic rule, God's covenantal law directed all activities. Israel was to be a holy and religious nation, administered by God's agents through the law and its principles of justice, righteousness, stewardship, and *hesed*. Often throughout Hebrew history, however, the nation succumbed to differentiation (a form of secularization), where certain leaders attempted to separate civic practices from religious values. At these times, God raised up special men, prophets, to warn that such a policy would produce dire consequences. For example, the prophet Hosea proclaimed God's word against Israel:

> I will destroy you, O Israel; who can help you? Where now is your king to save you; where are all your princes to defend you—those of whom you said, "Give me a king and princes"? I have given you kings in my anger, and I have taken them away in my wrath (Hos. 13:9-11, RSV).

Israel could be a redeemed nation only if its people submitted to God's covenantal law in all areas of life and society.

Economics

God's covenant also provided principles intended to direct the economy of ancient Israel (the production, distribution, and consumption of wealth). Many provisions of the covenant are directly concerned with economic matters, from understandably important "property" laws to seemingly not so important "muzzle and yoke" laws. To comprehend the relationship of the Israelite economy to the covenant, however, one must first analyze the type of economy present in ancient Palestine.

For the most part, ancient Israel was an agrarian society. Cultivation and herding were the foundations of its economy. Specialized crafts such as pottery-making and metal-working made up only a small part of the overall labor force: the majority of workers were farmers. The main crops produced by the Israelites were those of the field and the vine, such as grain, wine, and olive oil (Deut. 7:13; Neh. 5:11; Hos. 2:8). The importance of land use in Israel can be seen from a limestone plaque found at the biblical site of Gezer from the ninth or tenth century B.C.:

> The two months of olive harvest;
> The two months of planting grain;
> The two months of late planting;
> The month of hoeing up flax;
> The month of barley harvest;
> The month of harvest and storage;
> The two months of vine-tending;
> The month of summer fruit.

This so-called "Gezer calendar" describes the agricultural year of the farmer. Israel's prosperity clearly depended upon the harvest its farmers produced. If the harvest was abundant, then the people survived and often thrived.

In addition to its natural agrarian economic base, Israel was a market economy. All major facets of an ancient market economy took place there: buying, selling, trading, bartering, hiring for wages, and slave ownership.

Ancient Israelites firmly believed that the produce of nature, that which allowed them to survive, came from God as Creator and source of universal life. In fact, Jews believed that all things belong to God, and people are merely allowed to use them. Thus stewardship—central in the covenant of creation—continued to provide the foundation for economic activity after the fall.

The concept of stewardship entails that, as God's image, we

reflect His concern for all of life. That includes using wealth and property for the benefit of the entire community. For example, the Old Testament covenant frequently stresses the welfare of the poor ("the fatherless, widow, and sojourner"). In Deuteronomy 24:19-22, God instructs Israel to harvest their fields only once a season; they are not to go back through the fields to pick up what was missed the first time. What remains in the field is reserved for the needy. Leviticus 23:22 commands farmers not to harvest their land to its very borders; they are to leave the produce of its edges for the poor. The covenantal stipulations providing for special social groups do not, however, indicate community ownership of property. For instance, when in I Kings 21 King Ahab and his infamous wife Jezebel murder Naboth and steal his vineyard, God condemns them not only for killing Naboth but also for seizing his private property: "Have you killed, and also taken possession? . . . In the place where dogs licked up the blood of Naboth shall dogs lick your own blood" (v. 19, RSV).

Concern for the poor and needy appears in other ways in the Old Testament as well. Deuteronomy 24:14-15 commands that the poor and needy worker be paid on the day he earns his hire. After all, he needs it to buy food for that day. Exodus 22:25-27 strictly regulates lending practices. A creditor may exact no interest from a poor man on money lent. If the collateral for the loan is a poor man's coat, he must have it back at the end of each day to use as his blanket each night. Exodus 22:21-24 warns the Hebrews to protect strangers and foreigners in their midst because God protected *them* while they were strangers in Egypt. Deuteronomy 16:18-20 provides for an impartial judicial process. Partiality and bribery are denounced: "Justice, and only justice, you shall follow, that you may live and inherit the land which the Lord your God gives you" (v. 20, RSV). The prophet Amos sharply attacks the judicial process in his day for its numerous violations of economic, social, and political justice.

God's concern to protect all of life within the covenant community is found in other regulations concerning the land. Leviticus 19:23-25 mandated that farmers who planted new orchards should not gather their fruit for three years. Such a command clearly shows God's regard for the land and for the community because by following this procedure the land would "yield more richly." Letting the land lie fallow every seven years, as a "solemn rest for the land" (the sabbatical year, see Lev. 25:1-7) expresses the same concern. By keeping the land out of production for certain periods, it would then provide abundantly at other times. Moreover, every fifty years there was to be a Jubilee during which the land lay fallow, slaves were freed, property was returned to rightful owners, and the poor and needy were aided.

Whenever the Israelites reflected God's concern and standards for all of life in the economic realm, they fulfilled the statutes and principles of the covenant. Often, however, greed drove individuals to violate God's rules for economic affairs (e.g., Ahab and Jezebel). The Old Testament strongly condemns such acts as a sinful breaking of the covenantal law, for they repudiate God's sovereignty over economic life. God and His law are the foundation for all economic matters.

Social Structure

Israelite society contained three major societal groups, which are as follows:

1. *Beth 'ab.* This Hebrew term literally means "house of the father" and pertains to the extended family. An extended family consisted of a series of close relatives living together as one unit. One Israelite family might thus be composed of grandparents, parents, children, spouses, and other relatives. The extended family was the most basic and stable social grouping in ancient Israel.

2. *Clan.* Within Israel, groups of extended families who often claimed descent from a common ancestor lived together in a particular community or region. Known as clans, these groups were ruled by a patriarch or chieftain such as Abraham. Thus when Abraham's nephew Lot was kidnapped, Abraham fielded a small army (of 318 clansmen) to rescue him (Gen. 14:11-16).

3. *Tribe.* The most complex social group in ancient Israel, a tribe was a group of clans descended from a common ancestor. Together

with its members, its slaves and its adopted strangers, these clans formed a community. Whereas the extended family and the clan were wholly ethnic in nature, the tribe was not. In Israel, there were twelve major tribes, all of which claimed descent from the sons of Jacob, namely Judah, Benjamin, Simeon, Asher, Dan, Issachar, Zebulon, Reuben, Gad, Naphtali, Manasseh, and Ephraim.

Central to all these societal groups and relationships stood one major institution: marriage. In ancient Israel, and among its neighbors, marriage was a religious affair, a transaction between two families bound by a covenant agreement and sealed with an exchange of gifts. To the Hebrews, the marriage covenant was a religious rite because God had ordained marriage at the creation ("Therefore a man leaves his father and his mother and cleaves to his wife, and they become one flesh"—Gen. 2:24, RSV) and had given numerous covenant laws to regulate it. Though the Israelite system of marriage recognized the practice of polygamy and in fact placed no restrictions on the number of wives a man could have (provided he could financially support them), the ideal was unmistakably monogamous marriage (Gen. 2:24). In addition, marriage was patriarchal, in that a woman left her own family and lived in the household of her husband.

Marriage in Israel began with betrothal. It was customary at that time for the bridegroom or his family to present gifts to the father-in-law and for the father of the bride to present a dowry to his daughter (I Sam. 25:42; Josh. 15:19). Betrothal could occur at anytime after a child's birth and was a family matter, arranged between the heads of the households. Both betrothal and marriage were covenant agreements, ordained by God, and thus required these ritual arrangements and seals.

The belief that marriage was ordained by God and existed under the redemptive covenant illustrates further the Hebrew conviction that all of life lies under God's sovereignty. Furthermore, the Old Testament upholds the sanctity of marriage as a religious ritual by frequently using marriage as a metaphor to depict the relationship between God and the Hebrew nation.

The family functioned as a religious community, which helped to perpetuate the faith in God, especially through education.

Predicated on a high regard for children as God's precious gift in fulfillment of the creation command to be fruitful and multiply, education was a family obligation. Three aims of education appear in the Old Testament. The first, and perhaps the most important, was *the transmission of the historical heritage of the Hebrew faith.* Joshua 4:21-24; Exodus 12:26-27; 13:8-10, 14; and Deuteronomy 4:9-10; 6:20-25; 32:7 all reveal the importance of passing down the covenant history and law of the people to each new generation of children. Teaching the theology on which society is based is necessary to maintain community stability within a changing environment. A second aim of education was *instruction in ethical conduct.* How shall people live with other people? What kind of behavior is right, and what kind is wrong? Deuteronomy 6:6-9, just one example of many, indicates God's command to provide such moral education. Closely related was the third goal of education, *instruction in the practical affairs of daily existence.* The book of Proverbs contains a wealth of practical aphorisms about such matters taught to each younger generation within the family unit.

The structure of Israelite society rested upon the centrality of God and His law. In all family relationships, from household to clan, tribe, and even nation, each social structure rested upon God as its foundation and guide.

Summary of Old Testament Society

God expected the Israelites to build their society upon an acknowledgment of His sovereignty and adherence to His laws. The covenant community was supposed to perform all its activities in such a way that it served and glorified God its ruler. The covenant God made with the Israelite people spelled out a society based upon the covenant law, which, in turn, rested upon the principles of justice, righteousness, *hesed,* and stewardship.

The Israelites' failure to live by these basic principles, however, is lamented by the prophet Jeremiah: "They have turned back to the iniquities of their forefathers, who refused to hear my words; they have gone after other gods to serve them; the house of Israel and the house of Judah have broken my covenant which I made with their fathers" (Jer. 11:10, RSV). Because the Jews broke the covenant with God, they were eventually conquered by an invading nation, Babylon, and were taken into exile.

But all hope was not lost for the people of God. In Jeremiah 31:31-33, the prophet announced that God would restore the people to a proper relationship:

> Behold, the days are coming, says the Lord, when I will make a new covenant with the house of Israel and the house of Judah, not like the covenant which I made with their fathers when I took them by the hand to bring them out of the land of Egypt, my covenant which they broke, though I was their husband, says the Lord. But this is the covenant which I will make with the house of Israel after those days, says the Lord: I will put my law within them, and I will write it upon their hearts; and I will be their God, and they shall be my people (RSV).

This new covenant which God established with His people is the foundation for the remainder of this chapter's discussion of biblical society.

New Testament Theology

New Testament guidance about society has the same theological basis as the Old Testament. The term "testament," which means covenant, indicates continuity of the Christian church with the Old Testament. Although the New Testament affirms the basic theology of the Old, several new factors have altered how the social order is to function under God's rule. The situation under the new covenant is different from that of the old in three significant ways.

First, Jesus' entrance into history was God's new and ultimate act to redeem mankind. God's repeated redemptive offers to the Hebrew people climaxed in Jesus Christ. God's offer was extended to all people, and the new covenant community that emerged was based no longer on birth and faith within the Hebrew families and nation, but rather on new birth into God's kingdom.

Second, at the time of Jesus' birth the Israelites no longer controlled Palestine politically. They continued to believe that God rules ultimately, sometimes even through foreign kings and generals who are pagan. Consequently, during the first century A.D., the Jews emphasized God's authority over the religious community and over people's lives and trusted that God would manifest that sovereignty in the political arena in His own way, in His own time. For the Christian community, this concept of God's rule came to focus more on members' individual lives, the church community as a whole, the future coming of the Lord, and God's ultimate dominion as Creator.

Third, the concept of collective or societal liability and the idea of stewardship and subduing the earth appeared in a new light. In the Old Testament, a person possessed identity because he or she belonged to an ethnically or religiously identifiable social group. Ordinarily, Jews were identified first and foremost by their association with the Hebrew community. In the New Testament, however, individuals gain identity by joining the community of believers in Jesus. In the Old Testament, blood, geography, and circumcision linked members of the Hebrew community so that mutual societal responsibilities grew from family as well as faith relations. After Christ's death, Jews and Gentiles from nations and cultures throughout the world joined in a common faith. Faith in Christ and baptism in His name replaced blood ties and geography as the connecting points. Accordingly, societal liability became more comprehensive. The new Christian covenant community included people from many different cultures and backgrounds. These people faced the need to live as a community of faith within a larger society of nonbelievers (a situation the Hebrews did not confront as a nation until after 587 B.C., and then never in quite the same way as did the early Christians). The question of how to live as a covenant community perplexed Christians persistently. According to the New Testament, what is a Christian society?

The Kingdom of God

Jesus began to preach His Good News by proclaiming the coming of the kingdom of God (Mark 1:15). This proclamation, in fact, summarizes much of His message. Many of Jesus' parables, for example, express and elucidate this very point; often they begin with the words, "The kingdom of God/Heaven is like . . . "

This ideal, the kingdom of God, is rooted in the old redemptive covenant. During Jesus' day many Jews expected a Messiah to appear, defeat the Romans who oppressed their country, and re-establish God's theocratic rule via charismatic rulers and kings. Hope of a return to the days of Davidic power and prestige provoked more than one military revolt in the first two centuries A.D. and inspired many Zealot revolutionaries.

In preaching about God's kingdom, however, Jesus rejected this theocratic concept of military revolt and political rule. Instead He stressed the sovereignty of the divine Creator before whom all creation lay subject. He urged all people to accept God's rule over their individual lives no matter under what political, economic, and social circumstances they lived.

Two important sayings from Jesus explain the meaning the kingdom had for His followers in their societal life. At the beginning of His ministry, Jesus quoted Isaiah 61:1-2a in the Nazareth synagogue on the Sabbath.

> The Spirit of the Lord is upon me, because He has anointed me to preach good news to the poor. He has sent me to proclaim release to the captives and recovering of sight to the blind, to set at liberty those who are oppressed, to proclaim the acceptable year of the Lord (Luke 4:18-19, RSV).

He then affirmed, "Today this Scripture has been fulfilled in your hearing" (Luke 4:21). Traditionally, Judaism had understood this passage to explain the work the long-expected Messiah would accomplish. Christians, however, insist that it explicitly describes how adherents to God's kingdom must serve God in society with Jesus as their model. Interpreted in both a literal and figurative way, these prophetic words of redemption provide the basis for Christian efforts to help the poor, the oppressed, the imprisoned, and the handicapped. Jesus came to do this, and therefore so should His followers. This is the Christian cultural mandate.

At the end of His ministry, Jesus gave His disciples a second important commission as kingdom workers, a missionary mandate: "Go therefore and make disciples of all nations, baptizing them in the name of the Father and of the Son and of the Holy Spirit, teaching them to observe all that I have commanded you; and lo, I am with you always, to the close of the age" (Matt. 28:19-20, RSV). To proclaim the good news of divine redemption, to urge people throughout the world to recognize God's sovereignty, and to teach people to carry out Jesus' commands is a huge task. It requires that Christians take the gospel to every society and culture, a mission that demands the concerted effort of all adherents to God's kingdom. This missionary call includes a concern for both individual and social redemption. To fulfill this commission today, Christians must help individuals to receive Christ as Lord and to work to base their societies and cultures upon biblical principles.

Other sayings of Jesus reinforce these two major themes. Matthew 5:13, "You are the salt of the earth," and Matthew 13:33 (with a parallel in Luke 13:20-21), the parable of the leaven, imply that Christians must live among the peoples of the world and are expected to affect and change the life of individuals and their societies. Similarly, in Matthew 5:14-16 Jesus calls His disciples the light of the world and argues that since such a light cannot be hidden, His followers will carry this light of the gospel into a world darkened by sin.

The Bible urges Christians to live as members of the kingdom of God within the societies and cultures of the world. The New Testament concept of the kingdom of God affirms the Old Testament idea that God rules; it does not, however, ever refer to a theocracy or a political entity or nation. The New Testament focuses on God's sovereignty over the entire creation. The question always to be asked, however, is How do those who are members of God's kingdom society relate to the societies and cultures in which they live? How do Christians carry out the social implications of the kingdom? How can they meet people's physical and material needs and win individuals to Christ? How are they to function as salt and leaven and light for the world? These questions lead us to consider again the same social areas addressed in the Old Testament: the church (cultus), the social structure of marriage and family, economics, and government.

Church

The Christian community is centered in the church. Although some parallels can be drawn with the ancient Hebrew cultus, the church in the New Testament takes quite a different form. It is more similar to the Jewish synagogue, a learning center, than to the temple and its cultic activities. The synagogue developed late in Hebrew society, arising after the historical period covered by the Old Testament (second century B.C.?). Most individual communities had synagogues where worshippers assembled to express their religious convictions, experience God's presence, and learn about their faith. The churches that developed during the first century A.D. also served believers in local communities.

The origin of the church lies in Jesus' choice of twelve disciples from among a larger following to serve as the inner circle of the new community He was building. Patterned on the twelve tribes of the old redemptive covenant, the new covenant had its twelve original fathers of the faith. The establishment of the church, which some church traditions trace to Matthew 16:18 ("And I tell you, you are Peter, and on this rock I will build my church, and the powers of death shall not prevail against it," RSV), becomes apparent in the book of Acts with the ascension and Pentecost. In Acts 1, Jesus ascended to heaven and left the eleven remaining disciples to choose a successor for Judas. In Acts 2, Peter's Pentecost sermon and the coming of the Holy Spirit sparked a rapid growth in the number of believers (Acts 2:41, 47; 4:4). This dramatic episode, combined with regular meetings of believers (Acts 2:46), the sharing of possessions (Acts 4:34-35), and the conflict these events provoked with the Jewish religious authorities (Acts 4 and 5), testified to the church's rapid growth from seed to sizable organization.

Comparing the church with the five aspects of the Old Testament cultic organization shows how different the church became. At first, homes of believers served as the cultic sites or places of worship; only later did Christians build church structures in local communities, comparable to Israel's community synagogues. The cross became the central cultic object. It served as a sign of Jesus' crucifixion and resurrection and symbolized the meaning of these events. The first day of the week (Sunday), which commemorated Jesus' resurrection, replaced the Jewish Sabbath, which had been celebrated on the last day of the week, as the primary cultic season. In addition to the regular activities of worship and education, which helped to integrate the new Christian community, the basic cultic actions were baptism and the Lord's Supper.

Such cultic actions did not emerge without problems, however (see I Cor. 11-14). Both worship practices and cultic administration evolved as the new covenant community struggled to express its faith experience. The apostles served as the nucleus of the church. The question of whether Hellenists could become members of the Christian church (Acts 6) and the references to elders, bishops, and deacons (I and II Tim. and Titus) provide a glimpse, not a detailed picture, of an emerging church administration. Unlike the Old Testament, which describes an already well-established cultus, the New Testament presents scenes depicting the life of a developing church with all the joys and problems involved in that development. (Despite these differences between the Old Testament cultus and New Testament church, some of the church's practices are rooted in Judaism and share significant continuities with Old Testament ways; for example, the foundations of the Lord's Supper are in the Passover.)

Because the Christian community took shape in the midst of a diverse group of cultures, it stands in marked contrast to the Judaism out of which it emerged. Along with their primary concern for the affairs within their faith community, Christians were also involved in the diverse cultural community to which they belonged. (Paul's admonitions to believers in Rom. and I Cor. affirm this view.) Since God ruled over all of life and His covenant through Jesus formed the basis for all societal relationships, both in and out of the church, the church community served as the base of support for Christian mission in the larger cultural context. Whereas the writers of the Old Testament, when discussing social issues, usually assumed that the culture Jews confronted was more or less homogeneous, the authors of the New Testament assumed that Christians must proclaim the gospel and live out their kingdom ethics in a heterogeneous culture. Nonetheless, both the Old and New Testaments presuppose that the faith community is the source of social unity. All life, whether politics, economics, education, or religion, stands under the covenant relation to God. Neither testament divides reality into sacred and secular spheres.

The early Christian church had two basic tasks in society. First, these believers felt compelled to evangelize, to tell other people about the deity and resurrection of Jesus Christ and to help them understand the nature and growth of the kingdom of God. Second, Christians wanted to live by the ethics of love and mercy that Jesus had taught. Since the new covenant was written upon their hearts rather than engraved on stone tablets, Christians sought constantly to respond to God's revelation as they interacted with fellow-believers within the Christian community and nonbelievers outside the covenant community.

In doing these two tasks, Christians were attempting to carry out Jesus' sayings in Luke 4:18-19 and Matthew 28:19-20, mentioned above. Because the citizens of the kingdom belong to a community of believers and are not isolated individuals, they are responsible to fulfill these mandates in both individual and communal efforts. The community is, after all, the locus within which the individual finds identity and power. That is why most of the New Testament letters are addressed to Christian congregations; and the letters addressed to individuals, such as Philemon, Timothy, and Titus, give evidence that they are for a larger audience as well. The many ethical-social injunctions in these writings, which elaborate the roles Christians are to play in church and society, were directed to church groups. The new community of kingdom citizens must carry out Jesus' mandates for both evangelism and the care of people's physical and material needs with the direction and support of the Christian body. Christians can significantly influence their societies as leaven, salt, and light only if they work together. No single grain of salt, no one lump of leaven, no solitary candle can have the impact that many grains, lumps, and candles can have. Only by functioning as a community can Christians be a city set on a hill (Matt. 5:14). Individual Christians derive their personal identity and their mission in the world from the body of Christ. The redeemed community makes known God's offer of redemption in Christ and attempts to show the world a community of loving, caring redeemed people (cf. Rom.; I Cor.; I Pet.).

Marriage and Family

The New Testament does not discuss marriage and the family as fully as does the Old Testament because the church includes people from many different cultures with varied customs. Much of New

Testament instruction on the subject does, however, rest upon Old Testament teaching because the church began within the Jewish community.

Jesus' comments about marriage and family are few but significant. On several occasions, as recorded in the Gospels, Jesus, following the example of the Hebrews, expressed deep care and concern for children. (In Luke 11:11-13 and Matt. 7:10-11, Jesus based this care for children on God's gift-giving care for those who ask.) In His references to divorce Jesus implied that a lasting and binding relation between a man and woman in marriage is always correct. On one occasion (mentioned in Matt. 12:46-50; Mark 3:31-35; and Luke 8:19-21) Jesus enlarged His family to include all who hear and do the Word of God. The kind of community concern noted in the Old Testament undergirds Jesus' comments, but the new community is built on faith, not genes.

In I Corinthians 7:1-2 Paul advocates celibacy but allows marriage for some "because of the temptation to immorality" (RSV). He provides a set of instructions about the relationship between man and wife and about marriage to and divorce from nonbelievers. Believing that the time is short until Christ returns, and therefore not wanting people to marry and become more anxious about worldly affairs, Paul encourages Christians not to wed.

Nevertheless, in Ephesians 5:21-33; Colossians 3:18-4:1; and I Peter 3:1-9, a *Haustafeln*, a table of household rules, appears. In Ephesians, Paul urges wives to be subject to their husbands and husbands to love and care for their wives. Such injunctions are based upon the relation of Christ to the church. Colossians concurs and adds that children should obey parents, that slaves should be obedient, and that masters should treat slaves justly and fairly. I Peter's instruction about the relation of husbands and wives is similar to Ephesians. Each of these *Haustafeln* orders the family and household relations under the sovereignty of God.

The New Testament words about marriage and family relations leave much unsaid. Moreover, the New Testament does not clarify some elements of the cultural situation as fully as we today might wish. Slavery, for example, was recognized as a cultural phenomenon that Christians were powerless to eliminate from the first century A.D. Roman Empire. Paul, in Galatians 3:28, stresses nonetheless the dignity of all people in Christ: "There is neither Jew nor Greek, there is neither slave nor free, there is neither male nor female; for you are all one in Christ Jesus." He also suggests that if a slave is given the opportunity to gain freedom, "avail yourself of the opportunity" (I Cor. 7:21). In whatever condition of life a person finds himself, he must always understand that God is sovereign. The Christian community constantly confronts the problem of recognizing God's rule in the changing circumstances of life.

Economics and Community Life

New Testament teaching on economic life is based on the Old Testament, but the new cultural context necessitates different emphases. Because the Christian church cuts across so many cultural boundaries, an agrarian economic base can no longer be assumed. Still, both testaments agree that what a person possesses must be used to glorify God, the Creator and giver of all. Uses of wealth and possessions that exclude concern for stewardship of the planet's resources and for the welfare of people are immoral. The ideals of the covenant must always be central in economic practice. Clearly, the private ownership of property is assumed as basic to the economic structure. Stewardship means that people must use their property for the glory of God.

The first century church wrestled with how to view money and wealth. When the church moved away from the Hebrew family situation into the varied cultures of the empire, it experienced the problem in even deeper ways. The teachings of Jesus nonetheless gave believers some guidelines for economic life. For example, Jesus instructed the rich young man who wanted to follow Him that he must sell all his possessions and give to the poor (Matt. 19:21; Mark 10:21; Luke 18:22). When the young man declined to do so, Jesus lamented to His disciples how hard it is for a rich man to enter the kingdom of God. On another occasion when a woman used costly ointment on Jesus, and some of His disciples complained that the money should have been given to the poor instead, Jesus rebuked them. He praised the woman for her overt display of love for Him. At the same time, He reminded His disciples that the poor are always there to be helped (Matt. 26:6-

13; Mark 14:3-9). When Jesus confronted Zacchaeus, a tax collector who had enriched himself at the expense of the poor, Zacchaeus responded by giving away half of his wealth to the poor (Luke 19:1-10). These various examples indicate that not all who followed Jesus were required to take a vow of poverty. And yet, helping the poor was not presented as optional for the Christian. Citizens of the kingdom were expected to use their wealth to benefit the needy. This theme is prominent in Acts (4:32-5:11; 6:13) and in I Timothy (6:17-19). Likewise James denounces Christians for failing to help those with physical needs (James 2; see also the Old Testament prophet Amos). Believers should aid the innocent poor, not blame them for their circumstances.

The apostle Paul displayed great concern for the poor by, for example, organizing collections among Greek Christians to help relieve famine and poverty among believers in Jerusalem (see Acts 11:27-30; Rom. 15:26; I Cor. 16:1; II Cor. 8-9; Gal. 2:10). Referring to the collection mentioned in his epistles, Paul wrote, "I do not mean that others should be eased and you burdened, but that as a matter of equality your abundance at the present time should supply their want, so that their abundance may supply your want, that there may be equality" (II Cor. 8:13-14, RSV). Thus he called for a balance among Christians through mutual help. To Paul, it is fair that Christians should assist each other according to their particular abilities (economic and noneconomic) whenever one group of individuals has abundant resources and another group or individual has great needs. Paul obviously considered the material aspect of life an important part of people's total welfare.

These ideas about economics expressed in the Gospels, Acts, and letters of the New Testament are rooted in the Old Testament's deep and abiding concern for the whole life and welfare of the community. The question is How ought Christians to use their possessions to help others? In other words, how can believers exercise stewardship over God's creation? And how should fellow believers and nonbelievers be treated in the economic realm? The New Testament does not answer these questions in detail, but it certainly urges Christians to engage in mutual sharing and to use their wealth responsibly. God's care for His creation obligates Christians to care for other people's economic needs, the resources God has provided to meet those needs, and the good earth itself.

Several biblical passages explain how this concept of stewardship should be carried out. The parable of the wicked tenants (Matt. 21:33-45; Mark 12:1-11; Luke 10:9-18) attacks the religious leadership of Judaism for its failure to exercise good stewardship over God's people, Israel. Similarly, the parables of the talents (Matt. 25:14-30) and pounds (Luke 19:12-27) praise good care of property and condemn misuse. From all these parables emerge three specific principles of stewardship. First, property is entrusted to people by God to be used to help others and glorify Him. Second, certain stipulations govern how these trusts are to be held. Third, stewards are accountable to God for what they do with the possessions entrusted to them. The extensive passages that discuss poverty and these stewardship principles underscore the church's mandate to care for people's material needs as well as their spiritual ones.

Concern for mutual welfare of Christians appears repeatedly in Acts and the epistles. Believers in Jerusalem sold their resources and used the proceeds to aid the needy in their midst (Acts 2:45; 4:34-37). The early church especially helped widows (Acts 6:1). Acts 5 tells the extraordinary story of Ananias and his wife Sapphira, who claimed to have given to the Jerusalem church all the proceeds from the sale of their property, but had actually conspired to keep some of it. For their lie, both were struck dead, the message being that God, and therefore the church, takes seriously societal liability.

Another difficult issue for any community and society is how to handle disputes among its members. Jesus teaches that anyone who has come to worship (who has brought his gift to the altar) and remembers a dispute with his brother should seek reconciliation before offering his gift and participating in the worship (Matt. 5:23-24). Paul in I Corinthians deals with a host of disputes: he confronts religious factions in the Corinthian church and argues for unity; he tells the congregation to expel the man who is living in sin with his father's wife; and he condemns the Christians who go to pagan law courts rather than settle their disputes in the church. For Paul, the church should be a community where believers draw together and find their unity. Societal liability covers community life in general, as well as economic life in particular, and must begin at home and then proceed outward to the world.

For the early church, education became the responsibility of the family of faith. In the Old Testament, the family of birth preserved the traditions of the religious community by teaching them to each new generation. The Christian family does the same, except now the family includes all believers, and blood kinship is not the center of relationships. The process of making disciples focuses upon educating believers about the new covenant kingdom of God. Jesus exemplified this by constantly teaching His disciples in the Gospels. Acts 2:42 describes early converts as devoting themselves to the teaching of the apostles. In I Corinthians 11:23-32 Paul teaches the Corinthians the tradition about the Lord's Supper. I Timothy 4:6-11 indicates that pastors have a responsibility to teach believers especially about correct doctrine.

Since God rules over both economic and social life, the new covenant relationship into which Christians have entered serves as the basis of all life, religious and secular. As under the old covenant, religious convictions are not separated from the everyday work world. All activity stands under the rule of the Creator and is subject to His will. Believers who acknowledge this sovereignty are guided by the ideal of stewardship as they relate to God's people and God's planet.

Government

In New Testament times, Rome ruled the nations in which the Christian church emerged. The contemporary political order and the particular circumstances of the church and its adherents in different geographical locations affected the Christian view of government. To be sure, God rules the whole world and the lives of believers; but how do Christians relate to governments controlled by those who are not members of the faith? Four samples demonstrate the common thread of God's rule while illustrating contrasting responses of God's people to their political masters.

As recorded in the Gospels (Matt. 22:15-22; Mark 12:13-17; Luke 20:20-26), Jesus responded to a question designed to ensnare

Him, "Is it lawful to pay taxes to Caesar or not?" with the classic response, "Render to Caesar the things that are Caesar's; and to God the things that are God's." Jesus' questioners tried to force Him into taking sides. If He advocated paying taxes, He would alienate His Zealot countrymen, who wanted to overthrow Roman rule and re-establish a theocracy. If He counseled against paying taxes, He would be guilty of treason against Rome. Jesus instead walked through the horns of this dilemma. Contrary to our common contemporary interpretation, which divides life into unconnected secular and religious compartments, Jesus echoed a fundamental Jewish sentiment familiar to His listeners. God rules life; God cannot be reduced to the level of Caesar. Although His followers must fulfill various social and legal obligations because they live under the political control of Caesar, God ultimately rules. As people carry out their various political obligations, they must consider God's will in making every decision.

In the same way, Paul wrote in Romans 13:1-2:

> Let every person be subject to the governing authorities. For there is no authority except from God, and those that exist have been instituted by God. Therefore he who resists the authorities resists what God has appointed, and those who resist will incur judgment (RSV).

Paul called for obedience to the political ruler on the ground that such rulers are appointed by and receive authority from God. While God rules ultimately, earthly rulers are to be obeyed as God's regents. As such, governors have both a positive duty to approve what is good and a negative obligation to punish what is bad.

In I Peter 2:13-17 civil government is called a human rather than a divinely appointed institution. Nonetheless, believers should be obedient to their political rulers and the emperor, "For it is God's will that by doing right you should put to silence the ignorance of foolish men" (RSV). In other words, the Christian is to obey the state in order to demonstrate to non-Christians that one's Christian faith commits him or her to living a morally and legally correct life.

The final book of the Bible, Revelation, also instructs believers how to relate to the political government. It describes Christians who confront the strong likelihood of persecution because they refuse to practice emperor worship. Actually such worship represented little more than a loyalty oath to the Roman Empire, but, to the author of Revelation, expressing allegiance to the emperor broke the first and most fundamental of all the commandments of the covenant by setting up another god alongside the Creator God. Revelation describes Rome and Caesar not as God's appointees but as the tools of evil and Satan, which must be withstood even if doing so means death for Christians! God rules, to be sure, and because God is the sovereign ruler, the state's authority is limited in the eyes of the Christian.

Both the old and new covenants provide social ideals to direct all the practical affairs of daily existence, whether government, economics, home and family matters, or ethical issues. All human relationships come under consideration in the divine-human covenant. Each new generation of those who adhere to the covenant tradition has this same foundation on which to build. God has acted to redeem His fallen people; He has offered a new relationship in the form of a covenant. Yet each new generation has to listen for God's will in its own contemporary situation. What does obedience to the covenant require of us today? What does it mean to be a citizen of God's kingdom while also being citizens of a national community? These are the kinds of questions that persist and require that we understand the biblical view of society as dynamic. The Bible calls people to live with God at the center of life as they are confronted with a world in constant change. Such a faith compels us to recognize the eternal contemporaneity of God's covenant.

For Further Reading

Bailey, Kenneth E. *Poet and Peasant*. Grand Rapids: Eerdmans, 1976.

———. *Through Peasant Eyes*. Grand Rapids: Eerdmans, 1980.

Bruce, F. F. *Israel and the Nations*. Exeter: Paternoster, 1969.

———. *New Testament History*. New York: Doubleday, 1972.

Cullmann, Oscar. *The State in the New Testament*. New York: Scribner's, 1956.

De Vaux, Roland. *Ancient Israel: Its Life and Institutions.* London: Darton, Longman, and Todd, 1961.

Eichrodt, Walter. *Theology of the Old Testament.* London: SCM Press, 1967.

Filson, Floyd V. *A New Testament History.* Philadelphia: Westminster, 1964.

Jeremias, Joachim. *Jerusalem in the Time of Jesus.* Philadelphia: Fortress, 1969.

Kitchen, K. A. *Ancient Orient and Old Testament.* London: Inter-Varsity Press, 1966.

_____ . *The Bible in Its World.* London: Inter-Varsity Press, 1977.

Richardson, Alan. *An Introductin to the Theology of the New Testament.* New York: Harper and Row, 1958.

Wiseman, D. J. *Peoples of Old Testament Times.* London: Oxford University Press, 1973.

Wright, C. J. H. *An Eye for an Eye.* London: Inter-Varsity Press, 1983.

II.
MEDIEVAL AND
REFORMATIONAL
WORLD VIEWS

7
Augustine's Trinitarian Ideal and Aquinas's Universal Christendom

Charles S. MacKenzie

Introduction

Augustine (A.D. 354-430) assembled noble insights of the ancient world, tested them against the teachings of Scripture, which he understood to be the infallible Word of God, and developed an evangelical but catholic world view that has deeply influenced Western culture to this very day. In his time, Augustine's thought represented the wave of the future. In our day, some believe that his influence upon the next thousand years may even be greater than it has been upon the last thousand.

When Augustine walked the stage of history, Rome had been declining for centuries. For a long time the Roman Empire had faced powerful enemies on her borders. Political instability and economic disintegration had been feeding on each other for generations. During one period of thirty-five years in the third century, thirty-seven different individuals served as emperor. Oppressive taxes collected to support Roman armies thwarted commerce. The struggle between rich and poor often erupted in violence. Inflation escalated unbelievably. Currency had been debased century after century. The alloy in a denarius rose from ten percent under Nero (37-68), to thirty percent under Commodus (161-192), to fifty percent under Septimus (146-211). By A.D. 260 the silver content of the denarius had sunk to five percent as government mints issued massive amounts of cheap, debased currency. Inflation, cheap currency, and the cost of big government were destroying the middle class by discouraging business, trade, and investment.

After years of anarchy, Diocletian (A.D. 284-305) came to power

189

and ruled in the style of Eastern despots. He openly abandoned the old ideals of the Roman Republic and developed a state socialism (like that which had long prevailed in Egypt), which sought to control even the minutest detail of every person's life. Roman citizens worshipped him as their emperor and regarded him as the earthly embodiment of Jupiter. Assuming paternalistic responsibility for the populace, he distributed food to the poor either free or at half the market price. His massive public work programs gave jobs to the unemployed. After using heavy taxation to crush private industry, he brought industry under state control. Despite Diocletian's attempts to halt inflation through wage and price controls, prices rose. Goods became scarce as the government strangled both production and distribution. Inefficiency and waste caused widespread discouragement in society. The 50 percent of the people who did not work for the government were being reduced to serfdom by oppressive taxation. Concurrently, accelerating moral decay ate away at the soul of the empire.

In the fourth century, Diocletian's successors inherited a demoralized, state-controlled empire where paganism, debauchery, and discouragement were rampant. Despotism and state socialism had destroyed people's sense of patriotism and civic pride. Paganism of the crudest sort crippled Roman society, leaving its citizens with no spiritual power to inspire moral behavior. Although the Emperor Constantine (A.D. 274-337) accepted Christianity, the Roman Empire was too weak to withstand its foes.[1] Consequently, when the Huns from northwestern Asia forced the battling Goths westward, the Romans lacked the will to resist. In 410, Visigoths conquered Rome. The mighty Roman Empire, which had for so long ruled the world, ended in smoking rubble. Thus was fulfilled the warning issued earlier by Gregory in one of his sermons, "Everywhere death, everywhere mourning, everywhere desolation."

The society that arose from the ashes to replace Rome (which lasted for more than a thousand years) to a significant degree was shaped in the fertile mind of Augustine, the genius saint. After a

1. Constantine is reported to have seen a vision of the cross and the words *in hoc signo vinces* ("conquer in this sign"). Shortly thereafter, in 313, he issued the Edict of Toleration, which stopped persecution of Christians.

life-changing conversion to Jesus Christ at Milan, Italy, in A.D. 387, Augustine had returned to Africa where the bishopric of Hippo was conferred upon him in 395. While in Hippo he combatted Manichaeism, Donatism, and Pelagianism, and he wrote two of his greatest works, *De Trinitate* (*On the Trinity*) and *Civitas Dei* (*City of God*). While Hippo was under seige by barbarian hordes, Augustine died on August 28, 430, having laid foundations for a new society and a new age.

On the Trinity (De Trinitate)

Every society is built upon distinctive principles. Graeco-Roman societies presupposed belief in the goodness and supremacy of man. Augustine, inspired by biblical teachings, taught instead that God should be the cornerstone for social development.

Augustine emphasized the triune nature of God. His important book *De Trinitate* accepted the church's Nicene understanding of God. He said, "Father, Son and Holy Ghost mean a divine unity of one and the same substance, and therefore are not three Gods but one God" (1. 7. 4). By writing about the Trinity he hoped to strengthen the faith of Catholics everywhere and to help them understand the God who was all-important to their present and future. He wanted to nurture their love and commitment to Father, Son, and Holy Spirit. The first four of *De Trinitate's* fifteen chapters focus on scriptural teaching about God. The next three teach both the unity of God and that the three persons exist as distinct from one another in their eternal being. The last eight, though appealing to the Bible, are creative, rational attempts to explain the Trinity.

Augustine's commitment to the Nicene Creed led him to oppose Arian teaching. In explaining why God sent Christ to save the world from sin, Augustine answered questions about Christ that later would be raised at the councils of Ephesus and Chalcedon. He brilliantly depicted man as created in the image of the Trinity, and he stated that the nature of the human soul is analogous to the Trinity. Man's mind remembers, understands, and wills (loves), yet he is one. Three are in one. Each is a distinct but indispensable part of man. They coexist and interrelate equally in the mind of man. Likewise, the Father, Son, and Holy Spirit are eternally three, yet eternally one. But Augustine also acknowledged that the Trinity is infinitely above and beyond the human capacity to understand (15, 27, 50).

The Greek wing of the Catholic Church, in speaking of God, had historically begun with the three (Father, Son, and Spirit) and then reconciled the threeness in God with the oneness of God by speaking of the consubstantiality of the three eternal persons, that each person of the Trinity shares in deity. Augustine began instead with the unity of God and then showed how in God's magnificent unity there is an eternal threeness—three equal and eternal persons who are eternally bound together in the oneness of eternal love. He used thirteen analogies to illustrate God's three-in-oneness. He spoke, for example, of a lover, of the beloved, and of love; the three are one in intense love.

In *De Trinitate* Augustine affirmed the glory of the one God who is eternally Father, Son, and Holy Spirit. In *Civitas Dei* (*City of God*), he related the Triune God to society. In *Civitas Dei* Augustine applied the trinitarian principle to the development of society, describing the future both in time and in eternity.

The City of God

Augustine's *Civitas Dei* was in part an answer to those who blamed Christianity for the fall of Rome in A.D 410. In 412 the pagan writer Volusianus accused Christianity of contributing to Rome's fall by weakening the empire. Augustine countered in books 1 through 10 of *Civitas Dei* that Rome's long-standing vices and pagan idolatries had brought about the empire's downfall. The healing power of Christianity had come too late.

In the last twelve books of *Civitas Dei* (bks. 11-22), Augustine traced both the history and the future of two cities, the City of God and the city of this world. In the City of God, Christ is the Creator, the head, the source, and the soul. By contrast, the devil rules and controls the city of this world.

Each of these cities is characterized by what its citizens love. All who belong to the City of God love the Triune God. Those whose allegiance is to the city of the world love the world or the flesh or the devil or self. They love that which is not God. Both cities are immortal. All citizens are predestined to live in one or the other. Citizens of the two cities intermingle in this life, but will be separated in eternity. Some members of the visible church belong to the City of God, but others do not. Augustine clearly taught that the church and the City of God are not synonymous or coterminous.

The two cities are essentially spiritual. The City of God exalts faith, order, righteousness, freedom, goodness, peace, unity, and justice. The earthly city rejects moral virtues and instead endorses sin, blindness, error, strife, and confusion. In *Civitas Dei* Augustine not only brilliantly analyzed weaknesses of the earthly city, but also offered a vision of what life could become if the trinitarian values of the City of God could be actualized in society.

Augustine's vision of society was profoundly affected by his theological, anthropological, and epistemological presuppositions. (1) The Scripture reveals God to be triune. (2) All people are fallen creatures (cf. Gen. 3; Rom. 3), unable to perfect themselves or society without God's grace. (3) God manifests Himself in nature (general revelation) and in Scripture (special revelation), which are received in turn by reason and by faith.

Graeco-Roman society had been based upon belief in the ultimacy either of impersonal being or of aloof, anthropomorphic deities. Rational and political means could be used to make man and society perfect. Disagreeing sharply, Augustine urged Christians to create a new society based upon a personal God who is a blessed Trinity. The redemptive trinitarian principle, which would be the source, inspiration, and basis of his new society, offered *hope* to a society of despairing people. Such a society could *unify* people divided into groups by ethnicity, language, culture, and custom. His vision could spark *creativity* in a society drugged by its own selfishness. It rested upon an understanding that persons were created in the image of a loving, powerful God rather than being nameless, insignificant pawns caught in the throes of chance or fate. Thus Augustine challenged Western civilization to revise radically its first principles and presuppositions, to change from classical, naturalistic, autonomous principles to tenets based upon the Trinity.

Augustine argued that, *the Trinity unifies all reality in a way that Greek and Roman philosophy could not.* For example, Plato maintained that being is ultimate. But Augustine insisted that God the Father is the divine essence. Plato spoke of becoming and the world of matter. Augustine stressed instead God the Holy Spirit who undergirds, supports, and sustains all creation. Plato taught that becoming "participated" in being. Augustine offered an alternative explanation: God the Son, in the unity of the Trinity, links together invisible and visible reality. By showing how all of reality was unified, Augustine encouraged Western society to seek the unity of mankind.

Augustine dug a great gulf between Greek and Roman values and Trinitarian ones:

1. The Greeks had sought to find the unifying principle, or first cause, of reality in nature. Thales thought he found it in water, Heraclitus in fiery motion, Parmenides in being. The Greeks considered nature to be sovereign over all things, affecting and influencing human affairs. Nature was an impersonal, powerful, closed system, which infused all of life with order. Yet the order of nature, as perceived by residents of the ancient world, was relentless, sometimes cruel, and always oppressive. Belief that nature was an all-powerful, self-sufficient, closed system operating under its own self-determined laws led to the dehumanization of persons.

2. Plato recognized impersonal being (the world of ideas) as the supreme first principle, which ordered all reality. But he also needed a second principle, which the first principle could order. That was the principle of motion and becoming, which undergirded the physical realm. The search for causes compelled Plato and other Greeks to develop a third principle to connect their first principle (impersonal being) and their second principle (material becoming). That third principle was intelligibility or mind.

3. The Greeks, however, were left with three independent and even contradictory first principles. Even the brilliant Plato could not adequately bring unity to the natural order since he could not unify three independent first principles. No necessary connection could be found to link being and becoming. The third principle was deficient and unable to unify them. Consequently, classical Greek philosophers could not explain

and unify nature, which nevertheless was believed to rule the affairs of men.

In contrast to these notions, Augustine viewed God as three uncreated personal beings: Father, Son, and Spirit. The Father is the creative principle; He brought all being into existence. The Holy Spirit is the principle of motion; He undergirds all things, sustaining all becoming. The Son or Logos is the principle of intelligence; He orders all things and serves as a bridge between the Father and Spirit. Father, Son, and Holy Spirit, operating within and beyond all nature, unify reality since the three are one. All of nature is undergirded with personality. All of nature is opened up to the order of God's love and will. Nature is not a closed system, impersonally tyrannizing humanity. It is an instrument in the hands of a loving, personal God. God's just, loving activity is displayed in the theater of nature.

Augustine's Trinitarian principle accomplished what Plato's philosophy could not. Plato had attempted to reconcile Parmenides' concept of unchanging being with Heraclitus's notion of constantly moving becoming. Material things in the realm of becoming "participated" in ideas belonging to the transcendent realm of being. Yet Plato never really succeeded in relating or unifying being and becoming.

Charles N. Cochrane in his monumental *Christianity and Classical Culture*,[2] speaking of Augustine's view of one God in three persons, wrote,

> In this formula the first hypostasis, Being, the creative principle properly so called is, strictly speaking, unknown and unknowable, except in so far as it manifests itself in the second and third; the second hypostasis, the principle of intelligence, reveals itself as the logos, ratio, or order of the universe; while the third, the hypostasis of spirit, is the principle of motion therein.

Cochrane in striking fashion showed how Augustine's Trinity unifies all reality in a way that Plato's notions of being, participation, and becoming could not. Augustine argued that the Trinity unifies

---

2. Charles N. Cochrane, *Christianity and Classical Culture* (New York: Oxford University Press, 1944), p. 410.

all reality while preserving a dynamic, creative sense of order in the universe. Plato failed because his ultimate (being) was transcendent but lacked immanence. Consequently, it could not unify the invisible and visible realms. The Trinity, because it is sublimely three-yet-one, is both transcendent and immanent, unifying and ordering all reality by the dynamic threeness-in-oneness that undergird the manyness (becoming) and oneness (being) of the universe. Augustine's trinitarian principle was to direct man's quest for social unity during the medieval period.

Augustine helped to convince many to consider nature not as a ruthless, impersonal brute force but rather as an arena in which people interact with nature's Creator. Nature is dependent upon God. Humans are to have dominion over it and to develop its potential. Human community in general and the City of God in particular are to be realized in nature.

Belief that the three-in-one God creates, sustains, permeates, and transcends nature provides a firm foundation for human solidarity and for the community of faith. Since God unifies nature, people, who collectively are the crown jewel of nature, also are one. Their solidarity is based on their common origin, worth, and responsibility in subduing nature. Therefore, obtaining human community has been a primary goal for Western culture ever since Augustine's time.

Augustine's teachings freed man from the Greek belief that nature operates by fixed, self-determined laws, which treat humans as mere cogs in either a cosmic machine or a cosmic system of ideas. Man is not forced to be part of an impersonal predetermined order. Nature is an instrument of God, who has endowed persons with freedom to choose their own destinies. Humans are not controlled by inexorable laws of nature; nature is simply a servant of the God, who rules over the world.

Charles Cochrane pointed out that Augustine discovered in the Trinity "a fresh foundation for what we have called the values of personality. And here the breach with Classicism [of the Greeks] was radical."[3] Plato believed that reality consists of impersonal form (being) and matter (becoming). Augustine, however, argued that

3. Ibid.

divine personality overarchs, undergirds, and permeates all reality. Because ultimate reality is personal, personal values are supreme and serve as the basis for society. Anything that dehumanizes and violates the sacredness of personality is evil.

The Trinity, which rules over nature, exalted man as God's image above nature. Belief in a personal God dethroned the classical, impersonal concepts of fortune and fate, which had led to the notion that the impersonal state was predestined to control human life and to monopolize physical and economic power. The trinitarian perspective presented a universe ruled by personality and a society in which human persons, made in the image of the divine persons, can live freely. By exalting human personality the divine personality helped to fulfill the classical dream of a just society. Thus, the Christian view of God provides a dynamic, philosophical basis for the fulfillment of the noblest ideals of humanity.

Augustine also maintained that the trinitarian principle is creative and comprehensive. It is the dynamic power that created, recreates, and redeems fallen humanity by grace. By meeting the needs of the whole person, God recreates the human personality. Heart and head are satisfied by faith and reason, which become instruments of God's revelation. Through faith individuals receive the special, saving revelation of God described in Scripture. Through reason people discern the general revelation of God in nature. Faith and reason work in magnificent interdependence and harmony with each other. By His redemptive power the Triune God recreates and unifies the whole person—body, mind, and spirit. In turn, whole, renewed people become the building blocks of a unified, redeemed society.

People who are regenerated by God's grace are capable of knowing and practicing love and justice in society. Greek notions of justice had permeated Roman society. Aristotle's notion of justice as the state's giving "to each his due" (*suum cuique*) had influenced Christian thought through Cicero and Stoic philosophers. Yet who is wise enough to render to each his due? Following the Scriptures, Augustine declared that justice (rendering to each his due) comes only when people have surrendered to God. "What fragment of justice can there be in a man who is not subject to God?" (*Civitas Dei*

19. 21). Justice comes only from God as He renders to each his due. Individuals act justly when they accept and obey God's will. Whatever the triune, sovereign God in His providence does is just.

Eternal law is God's reason ordering all things. Material law is man's intellectual grasp of God's eternal laws. Justice (God's just will) is to be worked out among human beings when people are related to God. Justice is realized in human nature. "Its origin proceeds from nature . . . it is not the product of man's personal opinion but something implanted by a certain innate power." Justice is understood as man's knowledge and practice of God's moral laws. Such a view of justice severely limits the power of the state and subordinates political power to the laws of God.

Apart from God's revealed justice and love, human justice and love have no content and drift on the sea of life, lacking absolute and unchanging authority. True absolutes are known only as the Triune God reveals what His absolute justice and love are. "True justice is not to be found save in that commonwealth . . . whose Founder and Ruler is Jesus Christ" (*Civitas Dei* 2. 21). The revelation of the Triune God in Scripture, received by faith seeking understanding, makes possible reliable and unchanging standards of justice and righteousness by which a Christian society can and must live.

Christ, the incarnate God, also revealed how society can be liberated from cyclically repeating the defeats and failures of the past. Christ, the second person of the Trinity, is both the revelation of how mankind is to live and the goal toward which history is to move. Augustine vigorously attacked the Greek notion of cyclical history: ". . . the infidel seeks to undermine our simple faith, dragging us from the straight road and compelling us to walk with him on the wheel" (*Civitas Dei* 12. 18). Augustine believed that the Greek view of history was cyclical because its proponents had been unable to grasp the notion of eternity or infinity. While Greek autonomous reason was earthbound, reason that is surrendered to God's wisdom not only can accept the idea that God is eternal but also can grasp the notion that human history had a beginning and is progressing in linear fashion toward a grand culmination in the future. Augustine contrasted scriptural linear history, which is a progressive revelation of the Triune God reaching its fullness in eternity, with the Greek theory of cycles. Christ is the incarnation of the love, the justice, and the purpose that are the goal of a truly just society.

Augustine also saw in the Trinity the power that can enable society to accomplish some measure of the good life (i.e., God's will) on earth. Cochrane declares, "The doctrine of sin and grace marks, in its most acute form, the breach between classicism and Christianity."[4] The Greeks believed in human self-perfectibility, which, because society is "man writ large," means the self-perfectibility of society. For the Greeks, autonomous man, through his own reason and intelligence, was clever enough to save and to perfect society. Yet facts contradicted theory. Society in Augustine's day was floundering. The state was crushing humanity by demanding and enforcing social conformity. Despair pervaded the Roman Empire as society disintegrated. People had proved that they were not capable of creating a perfect society.

Selfishness and sin have caused every society to destroy itself. The grace of the Triune God, Augustine said, is needed to free, to motivate, and to guide society. So Augustine sharply disagreed with Pelagius and the Greek tradition of self-perfectibility (Cf. *Civitas Dei* 19. 25). Only the grace of Christ can redeem people and empower them to form a Christian society. Only through grace can the classical ideals of justice, harmony, and beauty be realized. In Christianity's teaching of the fall Augustine found an answer to those who were asking why the Roman Empire fell. Lacking the cleansing, regenerating power of Christ, Rome had been overwhelmed by decay and corruption.

Augustine's Trinitarian understanding highlighted the two-edged principle of unity and division, which always has existed in human history. Christ's truth and values are not just for Jew or Roman or Scythian, but for all people since they arise from the will of the one universal God. They unite human beings in God. At the same time, Christ's truth and values divide the righteous from the unrighteous (*Civitas Dei* 19. 17).

The two societies or cities described in *Civitas Dei* amplify Augustine's understanding of the principles of unity and division. The City of God is peopled by those who love the Triune God, while

4. Ibid., p. 451.

the city of the world is peopled by those who love self, the world, or the devil. The City of God keeps the fleshly desires and appetites of the residents of the earthly city from destroying the world. The City of God is the "salt of the earth," preserving society even in the midst of human corruption and man's evil intentions. All who have ever lived belong either to God's kingdom or to the devil's. Yet the hope for social unity comes from the City of God, where love, freedom, and unity abound.

> That which animates secular society is the love of self to the point of contempt for God; that which animates divine society is the love of God to the point of contempt for self (*Civitas Dei* 14. 28).

Augustine's trinitarian principle has had a lasting impact upon history. Some of its most important influences for human society are the following:

1. Trinitarian teaching offers hope to a despairing society. Society is not trapped in endless cycles of hopelessness. Society, guided by the divine persons, is moving toward one far-off event—its culmination and fulfillment in Christ at the end of history. Through the grace of the Triune God, individuals can be transformed and raised to a quality of life that embodies love, freedom, truth, justice, and righteousness. Such a transformation empowers people to build the City of God to replace the fragmented, unjust, vicious cities of earth.

2. Trinitarian teaching liberates people from their imprisonment in a closed system of nature and their slavery to a dictatorial state. The Triune God is the sovereign Lord of nature. Nature, therefore, is the arena of God's purposes, which include redemption for humanity. God works in nature to implement the principles implanted there. Nature reveals God's loving power. Because it is part of the natural order, the state is subject to God's sovereign rule and judgment. Therefore, man, who is God's image bearer, has certain fundamental rights, which the state should recognize. The state has a legitimate but limited claim over man's life. Because both nature and the state are creatures of God, man can be free of their tyranny. Augustine's trinitarian understanding of freedom has grown from a stream, to a river, to a flood in Western culture.

3. Augustine's teaching also presents a unified view of reality. Being, becoming, and their ordered relations are infused with the personal presence of Father, Spirit and Son. A sense of cosmic unity and of cosmic personality pervade all things. Human beings no longer are orphans in the universe. Rather, in God, they participate in a universal, eternal community (the City of God) in which love and justice will prevail. Because each person bears the image of the Trinity, he or she is of infinite value. The value and sacredness of human personality, combined with a sense of human unity flowing from the divine unity in and beyond nature, provides the basis for a new vision and a new understanding of community. In our day, most who seek for true community continue to assume the value of each person and the unity of all things.

4. During the Middle Ages the Trinity undergirded political thought as the center and source of power in society. Trinitarian values powerfully influenced the development of the family, the church, education, the state, and the economic order in succeeding centuries.

In his vision of society Augustine placed the Trinity at the center of all things, which meant the divine power is present throughout society. The influence of the Trinity radiates outward, permeating all social institutions. As the trinitarian principle progressively saturates society, the City of God becomes a reality among humanity. Family, church, education, state, and the economic order are undergirded by God, and reflect His sovereign purposes.

The Family

Augustine insisted that the family, the basic unit of society, was based upon trinitarian values. Indeed, a basic teaching of Scripture is that God is our heavenly Father. His biblical view of the family led Augustine to decry the downfall of family life in the Roman Empire. Augustine believed that the sole legitimate purpose of human sexuality is to beget children. Sexual intercourse and procreation are only to be accomplished within the bonds of marriage. Marriage was a divinely ordained institution intended to perpetuate the human race.

Augustine maintained that the family, like the larger society around it, should be a "harmonious interplay of authority and obedience" (*Civitas Dei* 19. 14). A husband should have authority over his wife, and yet he must serve her. Likewise parents, who have authority over their children, should also serve them. Each member of the family should be concerned about the others' needs. All should be subject to God in Christ, who alone can make a family one.

The Church

Augustine's understanding of the church emerged with crystal clarity in his struggles with the Donatists. Donatists believed that since the church and its members must be pure and holy, no sinner could have a place in the church. A bishop especially must be free from sin. Consequently, they refused to accept the authority of bishops who, during the last bitter Roman persecution under Diocletian (A.D 303-5), had compromised with Roman authorities. The rest of the Catholic Church had forgiven and welcomed back these compromising bishops. The Donatists, however, elected new bishops, the first of whom was Donatus of Carthage. So the church in North Africa was split between congregations that had Donatist bishops and ones that had Catholic bishops. The outcome of this struggle determined the kind of church that would dominate Europe for over a thousand years.

Until Augustine's time, Donatists prevailed in Africa even though Emperor Constantine supported the Catholic position of tolerance for the collaborators. Augustine was aligned with the Catholic party, having grown up in Tagaste, which was a Catholic stronghold. He also had returned to Africa with strong Roman sentiments.

Donatists rested their case upon biblical teaching that Christians were chosen people who preserved their identity by refusing to compromise with an unclean world. They demanded bishops who were pure and who had refused to collaborate with Rome during the great persecution.

Augustine, however, believed that the Donatist schism was holding back the church's extension throughout the world. He chided, "The clouds roll with thunder, that the House of God shall be built throughout the earth: and these frogs sit in their marsh and croak."

Believing that Christians must coexist with sinners even in the church, Augustine argued that the church contained an inner core of truly dedicated members who were surrounded by a large group of weaker, sinful members. The inner core, or elect members, needed constantly to seek to correct their fellows, but they also needed to tolerate and love them. The Bishop of Hippo was committed to reforming the Catholic Church and worked vigorously to convince Christians in Hippo to live holy lives. But Augustine preferred an inclusive church, containing members of both the earthly and the heavenly cities, which some day might become coextensive with all of society, absorbing and transforming the whole social order.

Augustine's arguments and a wave of Donatist violence prompted the Roman emperor and the pope to condemn their heretical teaching, which led to the demise of Donatism. But the struggle had established in Augustine's mind, and in the minds of other theologians and priests living during the Middle Ages, that the church was to be inclusive—a hospital for sinners, not a show-case for the holy—and that the church was to work to transform all people and all human relations.

Education

In Augustine's day, formal education usually was under the jurisdiction of the civil government. Earlier, the emperor Julian had sought to purge schools in the Roman Empire of all Christian influence. Christian teachers and students had been persecuted. Consequently, in Augustine's time, schools generally were secular and humanistic. Education, following the example of ancient Greece, was viewed as training for service to society. Christian education had to be supplied both by Christian families and by the church, which provided catechetical instruction for Christians of all ages.

Christian education sought primarily to provide training in morality and righteousness.

Augustine supported education, even the secular education of the state. However, following the Hebrew (Old Testament) view, he saw God as the supreme teacher and education as leading to virtue, righteousness, and moral character. This was in sharp contrast to the Greek and Roman notion that education was for citizenship and service to the state. Education was also valuable, Augustine believed, because it reflected and promoted the awakening and the developing of a person's natural mental capacities. Education creatively enriched human life. "The arts of rhetoric and poetry have brought delight to men's spirits . . . ; musicians have solaced human ears . . . ; both theoretical and applied mathematics have made great progress" (*Civitas Dei* 22. 24). Considering the human mind to be the glory of this mortal life, Augustine encouraged its education, constantly noting that God is the Creator of the mind and urging individuals to submit their minds to the Triune God's illumination and wisdom.

The ancient Greek and Roman liberal arts included the trivium (grammar, dialectic, rhetoric) and the quadrivium (arithmetic, music, geometry, and astronomy). Augustine's educational ideals focused on the liberal arts and especially the trivium. The young Augustine was steeped in the classical tradition, especially Platonism. After his conversion, however, he became progressively more of a biblical thinker. In his mature years, he reached a strictly biblical outlook. Yet he never renounced the rich classical tradition of the past. He was not like Tertullian, who considered Greek thought useless and said, "What has Jerusalem to do with Athens?" Rather, Augustine thanked God for all he had learned because the questions raised by pagan writers had prepared him for Christianity and had made him more useful to God (*Confessions* 15. 24). A great teacher, Augustine guided his followers through the pagan liberal arts, using them as an introduction to Christian doctrine.

Augustine's influence upon education in the Middle Ages was significant. His dual emphasis on the Bible and on the pagan classics was carried into the schools of the scholastics. Also the great schoolmasters such as Boethius, Cassiodorus, Isadore, Bernard of

Chartres, and Hugh of St. Victor studied Augustine's works exten-
sively. Alcuin relied on Augustine when he composed his primers.
The Christian humanism of Augustine permeated great Cathedral
schools like Chartres, Lyon, Canterbury, and many others.
Augustine also helped to inspire the men who founded the great
European universities during the twelfth to fifteenth centuries.
Augustine's "De Doctrina Christiana," containing his educational
method and philosophy, provided educators with the basis for a
Christian humanism that utilized both the Scripture and the classi-
cal liberal arts.

The State

Augustine defined the state as a "group of rational beings, associated on the basis of a common tie in respect of those things which
they love" (*Civitas Dei* 19. 24). His analysis of the state focused on
the attitudes of the people of the two cities. Members of the secular
city are possessive and greedy. People's desire to possess arises from
their love of material things, which is based upon their love of self.
Selfishness produces an intense struggle for survival among members of the earthly city. "This world is a sea wherein men devour one
another in turn like fish." Full of fear, residents of this city long for
security. Fear of enemies outside the state induces a certain cohe-
sion within the state. Yet, Augustine pointed out, fear is an inevita-
ble element of life in the city of the world.

Belief in pagan gods, Augustine argued, sprang from people's
desire to justify their own self-love *and* to preserve society in the
midst of a dangerous world.

> It is the peculiarity of secularism that it worships a god or gods,
> by whose aid it may reign victorious in temporal peace, ani-
> mated not with the love of wise counsel but with the lust for
> possession. For the good use this world in order that they may
> enjoy God; but the evil use God in order that they may enjoy
> this world (*Civitas Dei* 15. 7).

Christians, however, as citizens of the City of God recognize the
Trinity as the only source of power. God alone reveals true love and
justice to the world. While the city of the world exalts the love of
power, the City of God exalts the power of love. Grace and love set

men free from selfishness and greed. The fragmented, warring secular city rests upon a naturalistic world view, which either considers the universe an autonomous machine (materialism) or one all-inclusive, autonomous idea (idealism). The City of God, in response to the revelation of the Triune God, describes the world as potentially unified, as finite, as created, and as sustained by the power of the living and true God upon whom it is wholly dependent.

Conversion, regeneration, and obedience to the Triune God restrain the sinfulness and selfishness of members of the City of God. To Augustine, the state is not the ultimate form of community (as Greeks and Romans believed), but merely an instrument for regulating the external relations of humanity. The state's purpose is to restrain evil, to encourage goodness, and to thwart the power of human sin. The state will never be able to eliminate evil. Only God can do that. Augustine condemned all efforts of the state to usurp the place of God by extending its power beyond its proper limits.

Augustine's view of the state differs sharply from those held by Diocletian and Constantine. Diocletian, with his totalitarian state socialism, viewed the state as supreme, autonomous, and destined by an impersonal fortune to save society. Constantine, even after embracing Christianity, maintained that the state has the sovereign right to rule over the church. Augustine, by contrast, insisted that the visible church participates in the life of the City of God. Therefore, he viewed the church as independent of the state. Ideally, they coexist, but neither rules the other. They should function as "two swords," both serving God's purposes. One sword (the state) wields material power for limited and temporary worldly purposes. God instituted it to restrain man's sinful condition and allows it to use coercion in fulfilling that purpose. Consequently, when rulers disregard God and assume prerogatives that do not properly belong to the state, the state violates its God-ordained role and becomes destructive. The other sword (the church) wields spiritual power on behalf of the City of God. Believing that the City of God is infinitely more valuable than the city of the world, Augustine assigned the church a much higher value than the state. Some used this teaching to support the church's domination over the state and all of European society, which lasted from the fifth to the sixteenth century. Because he thought that ruling authority should be rejected if it does not follow divine justice, Augustine would have deplored this development. He taught that the church and state *functionally* ought to balance one another in order to fulfill the roles assigned by God.[5]

The Economic Order

Augustine's vision of society did not call for a radical restructuring of society as much as for redirection. Like most early Christians he seems to have accepted the traditional, agrarian economic principles and structures of the ancient world. He accepted, as a divine right, ownership of private property, particularly for the purpose of consumption. However, he viewed ownership of property as carrying with it obligations of stewardship and charity. Whoever owns property is to use it for the glory of God and for the benefit of others, especially the less fortunate. All things exist to serve God and humanity. Augustine often counseled parishioners not to love material things more than God. He assured Christian merchants that God would bless them for dealing righteously in all transactions even if doing so reduced their profit. While defending traditional property rights, he encouraged a sense of stewardship and compassion in economic life.

The Trinitarian Principle and Society

The City of God is distinct from the visible church. Within the visible church are lovers of God as well as lovers of the world. The City of God includes only those who love God. It includes all who are part of the invisible church (all who truly love and serve God) whether they participate in the visible church or not. The heavenly city is a present, supernatural reality in the midst of humanity. It coexists in time with the naturalistic, autonomous earthly city. In present society citizens of the two cities intermingle. Only in eternity will they be completely and finally separated. Only then will the

---

5. Constantine believed the state should rule the church. Medieval Roman Catholics argued that the church should rule the state. Augustine advocated a *functional* balance and equality between church and state although he acknowledged the spiritual superiority of the church over the state.

City of God be perfected. Human sin, however, precludes the possibility that the city of the world ever will be perfected. Until Christ's second coming, the City of God and the city of the world will coexist and interpenetrate each other, "both alike enjoying temporal goods and suffering temporal evils, but with a faith that is different, a hope that is different, a love that is different" (*Civitas Dei* 18. 54). Until Christ returns, members of the City of God are commanded to promote the ascendancy of the good over the evil in society.

The Pelagian Challenge

Augustine's understanding of man and of society received its greatest challenge from a British monk named Pelagius. Pelagius had come to Rome from Britain about the time Augustine had arrived in Rome from Carthage (c. 383-84).

Watching nominal Christians living careless, lax lives greatly frustrated Pelagius. He was persuaded that God demanded more upright behavior from Christians; in fact, he expected Christians to obey perfectly all of God's commandments. Pelagius was convinced that all individuals had the power to obey God's laws and therefore could achieve perfection through their own strength.

Pelagius's crusade for moral purity enlisted many who were weary of the moral degradation of the day. Depressed by the widespread violence and brutality in their decadent society, many welcomed his exhortations to obey God's law rigorously.

Augustine, by contrast, did not expect perfect obedience to God from every believer. He believed that sin and selfishness were so deeply engrained in human nature that ordinary mortals could not expect to achieve perfection on earth even with God's help. Pelagius described sin as individual acts which people can keep from committing because they are essentially good. Augustine, however, maintained that sin was the common state of all human beings because they shared the same corrupted, selfish human nature. Pelagius rejected Augustine's teaching that sin is radical, deep, and pervasive and can be overcome only by God's powerful grace.

Augustine and Pelagius also differed in their understanding of human freedom. Pelagius assumed that human nature is free. Augustine argued instead that people are slaves to sin and must be liberated. Freedom is not a part of fallen human nature. Only God's grace can set people free.

Augustine's message of grace and freedom, developed from his understanding of the Triune God, spread like leaven across Europe, creating new persons who became the basis of a new society. Augustine believed that those healed and liberated by God's grace have a more acute sense of responsibility to God, to others, and to themselves. Only by God's grace can man make the choices Pelagius assumed he was free to make by his own power. In Augustine's free man, the grace of the Triune God has liberated and redirected a new humanity. Thus, freedom in Christ became a foundation stone for the society, which, through painful struggle, would emerge as a lighthouse of freedom for the whole world.

Pelagius's beliefs that sin is superficial and that man is essentially good, strong, and capable of achieving perfection led him to be optimistic about social improvement. Augustine's conviction that humanity must cast itself upon God's grace for healing seemed more plausible and comforting to those who felt helpless to prevent the imminent collapse of the Roman Empire. Convinced that the old, ethical ideals of human autonomy and self-perfectibility had failed, they were ready to rely upon God. Although Pelagius's views were widely accepted, most Christians embraced Augustine's teachings. Consequently his convictions that God's grace is absolutely necessary and that the Triune God is the center and source of human existence became cornerstones upon which Western civilization was built for the next thousand years.

From Augustine to Aquinas

The thinking of Augustine permeated the Western church and shaped much of Western Christendom. It influenced the thought of Pope Gregory the Great (540-604) who interpreted Augustine to medieval Roman Catholicism. Gregory's theology was Augustinian in that he emphasized, enlarged, and institutionalized the teaching of Augustine on the sacraments and afterlife (such as baptism, penance, and purgatory). Gregory was a powerful pope who strengthened the church institutionally and increased its commitment to Augustinianism.

In 496 Clovis, King of Gaul, converted to orthodox (Augustinian) Christianity. He began a close relation between the Roman church and the Frankish kingdoms. He was succeeded by Pippin of Heristal, "the duke of the Franks" and by Pippin's son Charles Martel who spread the Christian faith to large portions of West Germany and France. Power eventually passed to Charles the Great (Charlemagne) who greatly extended the dominion of the Franks and in A.D 800 was crowned emperor of the Holy Roman Empire. The kingdoms Charlemagne conquered accepted Roman (Augustinian) Christianity. During these years Charlemagne served as Christianity's chief patron, teacher, and protector. He was so devoted to Augustinianism that he slept with a copy of the *City of God* under his pillow. He sought to make the Holy Roman Empire into the City of God.

At the same time, powerful forces at work in medieval Europe made achieving the City of God very difficult. Feudalism arose in the latter years of the Roman Empire and dominated the earlier Middle Ages. This economic system devalued human personality and bred discontent and alienation. Because the number of slaves was declining, Roman landlords lured tenants or "coloni" to the land. In exchange for their housing, tenants were required to give a tenth of their produce and some free labor to their landlords. During the Middle Ages serfdom and a manorial, agricultural economy were common. The fragmentation of Charlemagne's empire after his death in 814 gave new impetus to feudalism as local and regional fiefdoms replaced strong, centralized rule. Scandinavian Normans invaded France. Saracens raided Italy. Hungarian marauders attacked Germany. With no national defense available, local nobles strengthened themselves to defend their lands. Thus, the center of power shifted to the local level after Charlemagne's death. Feudalism received new life. This produced intense local jealousies, power struggles, and divisiveness. Millions of people yearned for stability and order. They were prepared to accept, and even desired, a powerful papacy.

Amidst the near anarchy following Charlemagne's death, Pope

Leo IV and Nicholas I became the strongest leaders in Europe. In particular, Pope Nicholas I (858-67) made strong claims to papal authority. Though he sought to fulfill many of the ideals of Augustine's *City of God*, he went beyond Augustine to declare that the church's power is superior to all earthly powers. After Nicholas I, however, the authority of the papacy declined and confusion reigned. A crass feudalism, which nearly degenerated into tribalism, threatened Europe. Only the rise of great monastic movements (especially the Benedictines and the monastery of Cluny) prevented the complete degradation of human life under feudalism.

Hildebrand, who became Pope Gregory VII (1073-85), was educated in a Cluny monastery. He propounded extreme interpretations of Augustine's *City of God*. Believing he had the power to depose emperors, Gregory VII excommunicated and deposed Henry IV of Germany. Henry was forced to stand barefoot in the snow at Canossa and to plead penitently for pardon, which the pope granted in 1077. Gregory had humiliated the most powerful ruler in Europe. The victory of the papacy was complete—for a short while. The view that the church was superior to all other earthly powers reached its zenith in 1302. In that year Pope Boniface VII issued the famous edict, *Unam Sanctam,* which explicitly declared the papacy's supremacy over all civil powers. In this declaration a gross misinterpretation of Augustine's *City of God* reached its fullest expression. Augustine, unlike Gregory VII and Boniface VII, did not teach that the visible church was to be equated with the City of God, nor did he advocate its rule over the state.

Thomas Aquinas and Medieval Society

As the Middle Ages waned in the thirteenth through the fifteenth centuries, feudalism began to unravel. Commerce, industry, exploration, and the use of coins to replace barter all contributed to the emergence of new towns, trade, and the rise of capitalism. Renewed interest in Aristotle, largely stimulated by Arab thinkers in the twelfth century, began to alarm many who were concerned about a growing "secularization" of European life and thought.

Albertus Magnus, the philosopher and theologian who popularized Aristotle's work, and his brilliant student Thomas Aquinas

(1225-74) sought to reconcile Christian thought with the teachings of Aristotle. They accepted Aristotle's assumption that reason has priority in the natural order. By so doing, Albert and Thomas shifted the source of authority for the social order from God's revelation to autonomous man.

With the coming of the Renaissance and the revival of Greek notions of man's autonomy and power, semi-Pelagianism became a strong force in the church. Thomas Aquinas laid the foundation for this theological position. Dividing reality into two spheres, he assigned man's natural abilities to the natural realm and God's grace to the supernatural realm. By so doing he attempted to balance the power of man and the grace of God. In the natural world man was autonomous, while in the supernatural world God was sovereign. Natural law, discovered by autonomous reason, ruled in the natural order, which included society. The supernatural laws of God held sway in the supernatural realm, which included the church.

Aquinas saw a relationship between the eternal law of God, natural law, and human law. The eternal law of God is the rule of God throughout the universe. The natural law is that facet of eternal law which applies to humans. It is the participation of the eternal law in the rational creature. Human law of governments is derived from natural law. God reveals His divine law in the Scriptures, but the operation of human reason is able to discover eternal law in part. Natural law is built into the structure of the universe and therefore can be discerned by all persons. It teaches people to further their own good, fulfill their natural inclinations, and pursue the knowledge of God. Human law (or the law of nations) attempts to apply natural law to particular situations.

Thomas identified three groups of principles as constituting natural law. The highest group commanded individuals to love God, to follow the Golden Rule, and to perform good and avoid evil. The Ten Commandments constituted the second set of principles. The third group was made up of concrete rules of justice that people devised as they adapted the first two groups of principles to individual situations. Human beings, Aquinas taught, are naturally disposed to recognize the first two groups of principles but have trouble with understanding and using the third.

According to Aquinas, Genesis 3 taught that Adam lost only the gift of God's supernatural grace (*donum superadditum*) at the fall and that, therefore, he and his reasoning powers remained essentially autonomous and intact. With Pelagius, Thomas viewed human nature as essentially good. He maintained that although original sin was real and needed to be cleansed by the remission of sins in baptism, it did not seriously affect human nature. Thus, man was not totally fallen. Instead, Aquinas argued that man was capable of building a good society using his own reason. Like Aristotle, Aquinas held that the state existed to make possible human fulfillment. But whereas Aristotle believed the state could provide for *all* of people's needs, Aquinas held that the state could not meet humanity's spiritual or supernatural needs. Thus he rejected the absolute autonomy of the state. Although tainted by original sin, essentially good people were capable, in Aquinas's view, of building a relatively autonomous and good society if they would be guided by human reason to an understanding of the natural laws of the natural order.

The rediscovery of Aristotle in the thirteenth century profoundly affected both philosophy and political theory. Aquinas attempted to synthesize the Aristotelian and biblical conceptions of the origin and necessity of the state. His synthesis soon reshaped the medieval understanding of society. Before Aquinas, the state was considered by many to be an institution God appointed, but only because of man's fall into sin. Augustine, for example, stressed that the state existed primarily because sinful people need a coercive power to restrain their wicked tendencies and to punish their crimes.

Following Aristotle, Aquinas, however, derived the idea of the state from human nature. He accepted Aristotle's argument that "man is by nature a social animal." Therefore, even if men had not fallen, they would have lived in a society. The very nature of man requires and justifies political institutions. Man can best develop his potential and satisfy his physical and economic needs through an organized society. A common social life requires an authority to prescribe rules, settle disputes and promote the common good. That individuals cannot fully develop their talents without society demonstrates that God has willed the existence of civil society.[6]

Here again, Aquinas assumed that the natural and revealed orders harmoniously correspond. Aquinas accepted Aristotle's view that the state is a natural institution that can provide the fulfillment and goal for human nature. This assumption compromised the biblical emphasis on ultimate values that transcend both the human condition and human institutions. The Bible teaches that humans cannot attain ultimate values without divine assistance.

For Aquinas, government plays a very positive role in society. It is to preserve internal peace and order, defend the community, promote the moral well-being of its citizens, and ensure them a sufficient supply of material necessities (see *De regimine principum* 1.15). Aquinas taught that the state should actively work to produce conditions under which human beings can live full and prosperous lives.

Because he believed the state has a positive function of its own, Aquinas did not consider it a department of the church, or the ruler a representative of the pope. Like Augustine, he stressed that the state should manage material and temporal affairs, while the church directs spiritual affairs. Aquinas encouraged a close relationship between church and state, urging each to work in harmony and to respect each other's positions, rights, and responsibilities. Thomas insisted, however, that all power was necessarily and supremely unified in God. Because the aims of the church are superior to those of the state, spiritual authority should guide and direct civil authority.

Human positive law, the law of the states, according to Aquinas, should primarily serve to "define clearly and support by temporal sanction the natural law, in all cases . . . where this is required by the public good." Aquinas did not believe that "every precept and pro-

6. Thomas taught that political institutions are a part of natural morality. This suggests that even a pagan state serves a positive function, over against Augustine who insisted that the non-Christian state embodies the city of man and the work of sin. "Political authority has a value of its own, independent of religious belief"; it has such value for Aquinas because it expresses a natural and rational order. See Alexander P. D'Entreves, *The Medieval Contribution to Political Thought: Thomas Aquinas, Marsilius of Padua, Richard Hooker* (New York: The Humanities Press, 1959), p. 24.

hibition of the natural moral law should be embodied in legislation, "but he insisted that state should never pass legislation which was contrary to natural law."[7]

Citizens are obligated to obey all just laws but not any unjust ones. Both eternal law and natural law teach man's duty of obedience to authority. Human authority is limited by both divine and natural law, by ultimate standards of justice. Aquinas considered laws to be unjust if they impose duties on citizens not for the common good but rather to further legislators' ambitions, if they exceeded the powers committed to legislators, or if they impose burdens (such as taxes) unfairly and disproportionately.

While Aquinas did not believe that God had ordained any particular form of government for all people, he preferred a constitutional monarchy. That is, he thought that a king whose power was checked by popularly elected magistrates could best unify society and prevent tyranny. Moreover, because it was analogous to God's rule over creation, constitutional monarchy was the most "natural" form of government. Princes should be subject to the rule of law as the expression of the will of the community. Thomas insisted that people had the right to revolt against the state when it defied natural law and became tyrannical. He also believed that the pope could properly depose unjust rulers.

Although Thomas was deeply influenced by Aristotle and others, he still reaffirmed much of Augustine's social teaching. With Augustine he believed in the biblical teaching about the Trinity, the family, and the economic order. He argued that government should be limited and subordinate to God and to natural laws. He held that persons had a divine obligation to work. Thomas defended private ownership of property as warranted by natural law. He urged Christians, however, to use their possessions not "for purely private, egoistic ends" but rather for the good of their neighbors (*Summa Theologica* II-II, IXVI, 2). These social teachings, he believed, were rooted both in the Bible and in natural law.

Aquinas favored a society that was hierarchical, conservative, and based on a primarily agricultural economy mixed with an

7. Frederick C. Copleston, *Thomas Aquinas* (New York: Barnes and Noble Books, 1955, 1976), pp. 239, 240.

emerging technology. He pronounced trade to be legal but not virtuous. It must be governed by the principles of fair price, and Christians must abstain from usury. He departed from Augustine, however, by teaching that the church must be supreme over all civil authority and that humans are autonomous and capable of building a good society on earth apart from the grace of God.

Consistent with his dualism of the natural and supernatural realms, Aquinas maintained that the universal church incarnated supernatural grace. Aquinas exalted the church and invested it with the power of and control over the seven sacraments of grace. His teaching that there is no salvation apart from the church and the sacraments it controls encouraged multitudes of Christians to believe in the absolute supremacy of the church over all earthly powers. Along with Gregory VII, Aquinas extended the idea that the church alone dispenses God's saving grace. Through the seven sacraments the church controlled the flow of grace to all humans, including kings and princes. This power enabled the church to claim total supremacy over society.

Thomas argued that a unified Christendom subject to the institutional (universal) church should direct the state to fulfill the laws of nature in all areas of society. In Aquinas's hierarchical structure the church dominates all of life: culture, education, politics, the family, and religion. As the custodian of divine law, the church not only directs worship and the sacraments, it guides the state in ordering temporal life. The foundation for social life is both in God's revelation and in natural laws, which all reasonable persons can discern.[8] Perpetuating the feudal pattern, this view of the church made the pope and his bishops the new rulers of a new architectonic, feudal order. The notion of a Christian civilization emerged as state and society were seen fulfilling their natural and reasonable calling to be subservient to a universal church headed by a supreme pontiff. Thus, the Augustinian view of the twin swords in society

8. While the institutions of society are structured hierarchically with the church at the top, each institution has a degree of independence. Moreover, all social institutions are "so organically related to each other that while each serves a particular end, each also serves the others" (H. Richard Niebuhr, *Christ and Culture* [New York: Harper and Row, 1951], p. 136).

(state and church) was replaced by the view of a hierarchical society where the church ruled over the state.

Aquinas's attempt to reconcile the classical (Aristotelian) and Christian ideals of the state produced a deep and thorough reconstruction of medieval political thought.[9] Thomas's influence was enormous because he created a comprehensive, unified system of thought intended as the basis for the unity of Christendom. Guided by the insights of Aristotle, Thomas developed a synthetic world view based on reason. It provided the bewildered, confused citizens of the thirteenth century a vision of a good society and public justice. Thomism became the dominant philosophy in Roman Catholicism for over seven hundred years. Augustinianism, however, never died within the church, but it was eclipsed by Thomism and at times even was forced underground. Though Thomas's thought has been modified and updated by neo-Thomists and others, it has had an abiding influence in the Roman Catholic Church.

Conclusion

During the Middle Ages, Europe was overtly Christian. Art and literature embodied religious themes. Churches, monasteries, cathedrals, and cathedral schools dotted the landscape. They taught that man was dependent on the Triune God. Augustinian perspectives (usually reflecting biblical teaching) on the family, education, the church, the state, and the economic order were dominant until Thomas introduced a synthesis advocating at least a partial autonomy for man and society.

In the modern period of Western civilization, most people have accepted the ever-expanding notion of man's autonomy and have come to believe that individuals can save themselves and create the perfect society. In our day, a Pelagian view of man is widespread even among professed Christians. Having explored the heavens and conquered many diseases on earth, man seems capable of accomplishing anything. Even though human achievements such as nuclear

---

9. Aquinas's "revival of the classical conception of the state helped to destroy the medieval ideal of a universal community...; and it prepared the way for the modern idea of the particular and sovereign state" (D'Entrèves, *Medieval Contribution to Political Thought*, p. 35).

weapons and genetic engineering seem threatening, many today continue to consider man to be ultimate and technology to be savior.

The debate between Augustine and Pelagius continues to this day as does the tension between Augustinian and Thomist ideas. Is man autonomous and self-perfectible, or is something wrong at the core of his nature? Can man create a perfect society by his own efforts or are his attempts to build the City of God, even though often divinely inspired and empowered, always hindered by the powers of the city of the world?

The principles derived from Augustine's understanding of the Trinity provided the basis for a new social order in the Middle Ages. The persons of the Trinity, who rule over and sustain the universe, exemplify the priority of personhood in social relations and furnish a basis for justice, compassion, unity, and creativity in human society. At the same time, the Trinity provides the grace that can empower humanity to fulfill these ideals.

For over a thousand years Augustine's vision of the City of God influenced and inspired European thought. Charlemagne, Nicholas I, Gregory VII, and others sought to incarnate the City of God in the Holy Roman Empire. Toward the end of the Middle Ages, Thomas Aquinas attempted a bold new approach that differed from Augustine's view of the foundations of society. Aquinas envisioned a unified Christian society, but he based it on a synthesis of Aristotelian and biblical principles and held that the institutional church should guide all cultural activity. In addition, he posited an autonomy or independence of the state due to its foundation in man's social nature. In his hierarchical scheme of being, the state as an institution was subject to the authority of the visible church with the pope as its head. Practically, however, the state was largely independent from the church, rooted instead in natural law. Although Thomas did not intend to do so, by establishing the state on natural rather than revealed principles, he prepared the way for Renaissance and modern thinkers who would sever the state altogether from any accountability to God. As forces of nationalism and humanism grew, pressure mounted to consider the social order as an autonomous entity, subject to no authority other than its own immanent principles. Just as many cosmologists have come to claim the autonomy of the universe, many modern thinkers advocate an autonomous social order in which man devises governments that use human institutions to control people.

In the Reformation, Luther, Calvin, and others revived Augustinian social principles. They taught Augustine's understanding of God's sovereignty over society. Though they were unable to create the City of God on earth, they kept Augustine's vision of a godly society alive. As people today desperately seek a basis for peace and unity in a fragmented society, Augustine reminds us that there can be no peace without unity and that there can be no real unity apart from the Triune God.

For Further Reading

Augustine, A. *Augustine: Confessions and Enchridion.* Philadelphia: Library of Christian Classics, Westminster Press, 1955.

_____. *Augustine: Earlier Writings.* Philadelphia: Library of Christian Classics, Westminster Press, 1953.

_____. *Augustine: Later Works.* Philadelphia: Library of Christian Classics, Westminster Press, 1955.

Brown, Peter. *Augustine of Hippo.* Berkeley and Los Angeles: University of California Press, 1969.

Cochrane, Charles N. *Christianity and Classical Culture.* New York: Oxford University Press, 1944.

Copleston, Frederick C. *Aquinas.* Baltimore: Penguin Books, 1961.

D'Arcy, M. C. *Saint Augustine.* New York: Meridian Books, 1957.

_____. *Thomas Aquinas.* Westminster, Md.: Newman Bookshop, 1957.

Farrell, Walter. *A Companion to the Summa.* Sheed and Ward, 1939.

Gilson, Etienne. *The Spirit of Medieval Philosophy.* New York: Charles Scribner's Sons, 1949.

Neve, J. S. *A History of Christian Thought,* vol. 1. Philadelphia: Muhlenberg Press, 1946.

Niebuhr, Reinhold. *The Nature and Destiny of Man*, vol. 1. Philadelphia: Charles Scribner's Sons, 1949.

Payne, Robert. *The Fathers of the Western Church*. New York: Viking Press, 1951.

Regis, Anton. *Basic Writings of St. Thomas Aquinas*, 2 vols. New York: Random House, 1944.

Seeberg, Reinhold. *The History of Doctrines*, vol. 1. Grand Rapids: Baker Book House, 1954.

Troeltsch, Ernst. *The Social Teaching of the Christian Churches*, vol. 1. New York: The Macmillan Company, 1949.

Walker, Williston. *A History of the Christian Church*. New York: Charles Scribner's Sons, 1945.

8

The Reformation: Luther, Calvin, and the Anabaptists

Gary Scott Smith

Introduction

While the Reformation of the sixteenth century was above all else a religious revival, other factors—political, economic, social, and intellectual—contributed to its development and widespread impact. Martin Luther was its catalyst and the sale of indulgences its precipitating event, but without the particular combination of sociopolitical elements present in late medieval Europe, the Reformation would not have occurred.

Springing from these social conditions, the Reformation in turn produced many social changes of its own. In numerous ways the Reformation and the Renaissance, which accompanied it, were a cultural watershed. This complex tumultous movement in large part forged the foundation of the modern, pluralistic, culturally fragmented Western world.

This chapter explores the social consequences of the Reformation, focusing on the lives, teaching, and impact of Martin Luther, John Calvin, and the Anabaptists.

The Reformation occurred against a wide backdrop of social unrest and political turmoil in Europe. National states were emerging that challenged papal rule and other aspects of the old order. Exploited peasants increasingly expressed discontent. Trade revived between Europe and other parts of the world, cities grew, and a new socioeconomic class—the bourgeoisie—developed. Culture began to flourish under the Renaissance, and intellectual dissatisfaction intensified. The Renaissance helped to free "medieval man from the shackles of ignorance and superstition," one observer declares; "it introduced him to new worlds of art and literature," and enabled him to learn from the ancient Greek and Latin sources. Widespread clerical ignorance and abuse, disputes over who was pope, and the worldly lifestyles of the Roman pontifs weakened the church internally. Meanwhile, unrelenting pleas of Christian humanists for reform, challenges to medieval theology, and an outburst of popular piety battered the church from the outside.

Martin Luther

Few individuals are as colorful and complex as Martin Luther (1483-1546). Luther's attack upon medieval Catholicism and his rediscovery of the biblical doctrine of justification by faith in the early sixteenth century have powerfully affected theology, church polity, and worship ever since. At the same time, his views of the relationship between Christianity and culture, the nature of church and state, the sanctity of marriage and the family, and the importance of education strongly influenced the development of Western society. Teacher, orator, translator, theologian, composer, and family man, Luther symbolized much for which the Protestant Reformation stood. Contemporary Christian groups as diverse as Roman Catholics, Anabaptists, biblical fundamentalists, and ecumenical Protestants find support in Luther's teachings for particular convictions they espouse. Communist leaders in Luther's homeland, East Germany, today portray him as a vigorous critic of sixteenth-century capitalism and insist that their country's state socialism is fulfilling Luther's social vision. In both Europe and America Luther's pilgrimage of faith and his reformational teachings are attracting renewed interest.

After briefly examining Luther's life and ministry, we will analyze his views of society.

Although Luther often boasted that he sprang from peasant stock, his father was a burgher who provided Martin with a good university education, sent him to law school, and arranged for him a suitable marriage. A close escape from a bolt of lightning, however, drove Luther to an Augustinian monastery. There he struggled with sin and guilt. In his anguish he uttered such cries as "I see Christ as a stern Judge" and "To the gallows with Moses." Tormented by his sin,

Luther often remained in the confessional for hours, exhausting the patience of his confessors. An expert in the law, Luther felt the full force of standing disobedient and defenseless before the divine commandments.

Despite his inner turmoil, Luther was a very successful friar. By age thirty-three he was Professor of Scripture at the University of Wittenberg, preacher at the castle church, and priest in charge of the area monasteries. His doubt and despair persisted, however, until his famous tower conversion experience in 1516.

Luther's theological discovery, like Columbus's territorial one a quarter century earlier, transformed the course of the Western world. Study of the Scriptures led him to protest against numerous practices and procedures of the medieval Catholic Church. His ninety-five theses, now etched in bronze on the church door at Wittenberg where he first posted them in 1517, challenged the sale of indulgences (cash payments to remit sin) and many other medieval doctrines. Though Luther sought to reform the Catholic Church, not to separate from it, these theses, along with several tracts he wrote during the next few years led to his expulsion from the church and eventually to the formation of numerous Protestant ("protesting") groups.

Luther's 420 published works cover a wide range of topics, including commentaries on every book of the Bible, catechisms for children, scholarly debates with theological opponents, and tracts designed to reform the church, mobilize the nobility, and instruct the laity. Because of his outstanding gifts of oratory and biblical exposition, Luther's preaching was probably the principal work of his extremely productive life. His crowning literary achievement, however, was his translation of the Bible from Hebrew and Greek into the German vernacular. In so doing, Luther gave his countrymen a written language and significantly affected the development of German literature and dramatic arts. Moreover, for the first time God's printed Word penetrated everyday life.

Luther's impact upon the development of Western society is monumental. Especially significant are his views of Christianity and the social order, the relationship between church and state, marriage and family, and the purposes of education. Luther never expressed his theological or social ideas systematically, as did John Calvin. Nevertheless, we can identify several basic themes that underlay Luther's approach to culture.

Luther's influence on sixteenth-century political thought was even greater than that of his contemporary, Machiavelli. Repudiating the political understanding of the late medieval church, Luther advocated three principles that shaped Reformational political thinking. First, he argued that because God had instituted secular authority, rulers' authority came directly from God, not mediately through the pope. Consequently, God forbad rebellion against established authority under all circumstances. Finally, civil and ecclesiastical authority are completely distinct and must not be confused.

As in his teachings on justification by faith and the sacraments, so in his political views Luther sought to revive the teaching of Christ, as developed by the apostles and Augustine. His political ideas were a logical extension of his largely Augustinian view of the fall, of God's manner of governing the world, of man and society and of the unceasing warfare between the kingdoms of God and Satan. Although Luther's basic political principles sprang from his theology, they were significantly shaped by external events.

Luther's understanding of culture rested upon three pairs of dualisms, two of which represent parallels, and the third an antithesis.[1] First, God has established two realms or orders in the world, corresponding to man's two natures. In the spiritual realm, the order of salvation, individuals live solely in relation to God. By contrast, in the temporal realm, the natural order, man lives in relation to other people. The second dualism, which is closely connected with and at points overlaps the first one, asserts that God has instituted two forms of government, spiritual government of the Word and civil government of the sword. Cutting across the first two dualisms is the Augustinian doctrine of the opposing kingdoms of God and Satan.

1. How to interpret Luther's view of culture is one of the most hotly debated issues in scholarship about him today, and the dispute has produced an enormous amount of literature. In my discussion of this matter, I am indebted to W. D. J. Cargill Thompson, *The Political Thought of Martin Luther* (Totowa, N.J.: Barnes and Nobles, 1984), pp. 36-61.

Like Augustine, Luther taught that those two kingdoms are completely opposite in character. Members of God's kingdom of love hear His Word and are devoted to Him. Those without true faith belong to Satan's kingdom of lust and sin. All people are like a horse for which two masters compete. Either God or the devil rides people; no one can have two riders. The two forms of government (spiritual and civil) exist to retard and thwart Satan's work in the world.

Luther's idea of the two realms or two kingdoms underlies his mature social and political thought. Like Thomas Aquinas, Luther taught that two spheres exist: a spiritual and a temporal realm, or grace and nature. But unlike Aquinas and other medieval theologians, Luther did not believe that nature is below or inferior to grace, a lower tier in which people prepare themselves to ascend to the higher realm (through good works and indulgences.) Luther considered the two orders to be distinct and parallel (not hierarchical, higher/lower), corresponding to man's dual nature. In the spiritual realm individuals worship God and by faith believe in Him; in the temporal realm they live their natural life in the world.

The two realms are distinguished by their parallel (but different) features. Each order has its own form of righteousness or justice. That of the spiritual realm is essentially an inward, spiritual righteousness of the soul in relation to God. That of the temporal order is "a purely external righteousness, a righteousness of actions rather than of the spirit or of inner attitudes."

The kingdom of Christ possesses the power of God's Word; the kingdom of the world has the power of the sword. God rules over both realms, but His presence is hidden from the worldly or secular realm. Each sphere has its own justice and its own laws. As Karl Holl writes, for Luther "civilization always remains a secular aim beneath that of the true and highest kingdom of God. . . . Had one asked Luther if his gospel intended to advance civilization," Holl adds, "he would have replied with a resounding 'No.'"[2] Luther sharply distinguished between temporal life and spiritual life, between body and soul, between Christ and the world of culture. According to H. Richard Niebuhr, "He seems to have a double attitude toward

2. Karl Holl, *The Cultural Significance of the Reformation* (New York: Meridian Books, 1959), p. 25.

reason and philosophy, toward business and trade . . . [and] toward state and politics." These paradoxes suggest "that Luther divided life into compartments or taught that the Christian right hand should not know what a man's worldly left hand was doing."[3]

Three factors help explain Luther's paradoxical (some would say inconsistent) position toward culture. First, he fervently believed that the political and religious confusion in Germany signified God's wrath and foreshadowed the end of the world. Consequently, he argued that only the most urgent changes should be made in political structures and international relations.

Second, he asserted that God revealed His law to all individuals and that reason functioned to order human affairs. "God does not teach in Scripture how to build houses and make clothes, marry, make war and similar things. For these the natural light [of reason] is sufficient" (*Christmaspostill*, 1522). "In the state one must act on the basis of reason (the source of legal statutes) for God has subjected the government of this world and affairs of the body to reason" (*A Sermon on Keeping Children in School*, 1530).

Third, based upon Romans 12 and 13, Luther held that the church "serves the guidance and peace of the inner [spiritual] man and his concerns"; the government "serves that of the outward [earthly] man and his concerns." Christians ought to obey the temporal government because "whatever powers exist and flourish" do so "because God has ordained them." "These two kingdoms," Luther concluded, "must be sharply distinguished, and both be permitted to remain; the one to produce piety, the other to bring about eternal peace and prevent evil deeds; neither is sufficient without the other" (*Temporal Authority: To What Extent It Should Be Obeyed*, 1523). Positively, this doctrine led Luther to counsel toleration. "Let the Turk believe and live as he wishes, just as one permits the papacy and other false Christians to live. The sword of the Emperor has no business in matters of faith. It belongs to bodily and worldly affairs" (*On War Against the Turks*, 1529).[4]

Following Augustine, Luther considered life to be a continual

3. H. Richard Niebuhr, *Christ and Culture* (New York: Harper, 1951), p. 171.
4. Luther was not entirely consistent on this matter. In *Against the Robbing and Murdering Hordes of Peasants* (1525) he advocates no such toleration.

struggle between two cities or commonwealths—those who love and obey God and those who love self and are dominated by pride. Luther believed that both church and state are God's instruments for sustaining a world faced with sin, death, and evil. Individual Christians have to live in both the spiritual and temporal realms as members of the church and citizens of the state. God's two specific governments, secular and spiritual, battle against Satan, who continually tempts people to idolatry. The state fights Satan's kingdom with law and order; the church opposes it with Word and sacrament. God uses sword, Word, and reason to combat the devil's efforts through heretics and rebels to challenge the divinely ordained order. Marriage, family, and natural and civil laws are the pillars of God's orderly creation; by properly exercising their callings parents, educators, businessmen, jurists, and politicians promote justice and love in the world.

While Luther sharply distinguished between the two kingdoms or rules, he believed nevertheless that church and state should work closely together in performing complementary functions. The church governs spiritual life by the Word of God. Operating by love and humility, it seeks to help people receive Christ's righteousness so that they can attain eternal life. The state, by contrast, rules over temporal life by the power of the sword. Through use of coercion and force it restrains evildoers and preserves earthly peace. By so doing, civil government enables the church to minister to spiritual needs and to guide people toward eternal life. Luther argued (as John Calvin did later) that if everyone were a true Christian, government would be unnecessary. God ordained political structures to insure civil righteousness by regulating the behavior of sinful human beings who fail to heed His Word. Although Christians do not need government, they should serve in the state to promote justice and to help their neighbors.

While Luther maintained that government should not interfere with the everyday functioning of religion, he encouraged rulers to designate which religion would prevail within their boundaries. In order to avoid religious warfare in Germany, Luther argued that the religion of the ruler should determine the religion of the region.

Specifically his famous phrase *cujus regio ejus religio* ("whosever region, his religion") meant that those areas in Germany with Catholic rulers should permit only Catholic worship and those governed by Lutheran nobles should only allow Lutheran congregations to function. Luther charged civil authorities to maintain true religion and proper worship within their boundaries, but he forbad them to determine Christian doctrine or to interfere with anyone's conscience or belief.

Luther believed that a Christian commonwealth was impossible to create because the presence of sin in the world produced continual human rebellion against God. No state would ever be peopled by genuine Christians who do not need the law's restraint, "for the world and the masses are and always will be un-Christian, even if they are all baptized and Christian in name" (*Luther's Works*, 45:91). Christians therefore should not try to create a distinctly Christian state but must carefully distinguish between God's two governments, "the spiritual which produces inward righteousness and the temporal which creates external order." Luther was skeptical about the possibility of rulers being true Christians. "If a prince should happen to be wise, upright or a Christian," he wrote, "that is one of the great miracles" (*Temporal Authority: To What Extent It Should Be Obeyed*, 1523). Luther did not specify what form of civil government he thought to be best; but he encouraged Christians to participate in government because they best understand its limited role.

Luther firmly argued against rebellion. "Insurrection is an unprofitable method . . . and never results in the desired reformation. For insurrection is devoid of reason and generally hurts the innocent more than the guilty. Hence no insurrection is ever right no matter how good the cause in whose interest it is made. The harm resulting from it always exceeds the amount of reformation accomplished." Because government is divinely ordained and because it is very difficult to distinguish who is a tyrant, Christians should revolt only when the ruler becomes a madman (*An Earnest Exhortation*, 1522, WA 8, 676F). Luther did urge Christians not to obey rulers who forbad them to worship God or sought to restrict their conscience. Such resistance should be expressed through suffering, not violence.[5]

Because of such teachings Luther has frequently been criticized for supporting the status quo and encouraging passive submission to evil and injustice. Christians, he wrote, should submit "to the magistrates in love, even to their godless laws and all the burdens and dangers of this present life should the situation demand it" (*Lectures on Galatians*, 1535). Luther's social doctrines have been invoked under such German leaders as Frederick the Great, Otto von Bismarck, and Adolf Hitler to justify state authority and to crush opposition. Indeed, many blame the failure of German Lutheranism to resist Hitler's policies upon Luther's counsel of quietism.

Despite his belief that the church's mission in the world is exclusively spiritual, circumstances during the first half of the sixteenth century prompted Luther to participate in political debates and activities. Political issues were involved in Luther's denunciation of the sale of indulgences and the power of the papacy. Moreover, the nobility sought to increase their power at the expense of the papacy, and Charles V of Germany aimed to create a European empire. At the same time, Anabaptist peasants, inspired in part by Luther's writings, revolted against established authority in Munster, Germany, and the Turks threatened to invade Europe and crush Christendom. These developments led Luther to denounce the Peasant Rebellion, to discuss the theological implications of war with the Turks, and to use his influence to promote peace and justice. Luther urged rulers to revere God, to love and serve their subjects, to listen to their counselors, and to punish evildoers firmly. And he challenged all Christians to work to preserve peace, to seek to prevent evil, to pay taxes, to honor those in authority, and to further the aims of government.

Nevertheless, Luther always argued that the two governments should be kept distinct and not be confused. Satan's most potent

5. Luther provided three answers in regard to the question of civil disobedience or the right to armed resistance: (1) In order to protect oneself and one's neighbor, individual violent resistance is justified. (2) When a legitimate government uses violent political resistance, as in defensive war, capital punishment, and even revolution, it is justified. (3) In this world Christians should suffer political violence rather than forcefully resist it.

weapon in his perpetual conflict with God's kingdom is his effort to persuade either clergy or magistrates to ignore the distinction between the two rules and interfere with the authority of the other. Confusing the two rules violates God's order for the universe and leads to chaos. But although he counseled separation of roles, Luther, like Calvin after him, did frequently admonish magistrates when they ruled unjustly, and he urged other ministers to do the same.

Luther's two-kingdom ethic can be criticized for limiting the lordship of Christ by not encouraging Christians to reform the political and social order to make it conform to Christ's kingdom. Luther believed God worked primarily through persons or groups (parents, princes, fellowships), not in structures (family, government, economics). Nevertheless, Luther did try to overcome the confusion between the realm of Christ and the realm of the world created by medieval Catholicism's attempt to place all of life under ecclesiastical jurisdiction and by Anabaptist flight from cultural responsibility. While avoiding the extremes of church rule, separatism, and, later with the Puritans, theocracy, Luther "tended to separate the two kingdoms so sharply that their fundamental unity . . . was obscured."[6]

Luther's view of marriage and the home was as influential as his teaching on church and state. Ironically, a man who began his career as an Augustinian monk, committed to a life of celibacy and separated from worldly cares and concerns, helped to forge a new set of attitudes and ideals about marriage and the family. In 1525 Luther, aged forty-two, married Catherine von Bora, a former nun. Together they shared a happy home life and raised six children. Although generally paternalistic, Luther deeply admired his wife's leadership of their household where twenty people or more often gathered for meals. To Luther, marriage further testified to the Good News that God in Christ triumphs over sin, death, and evil. Luther's marriage led critics to produce a play depicting him as a whoring monk and to denounce him in print as the "most insane

6. I am indebted in this section to Eric W. Gritsch's and Robert W. Jenson's *Lutheranism; The Theological Movement and Its Confessional Writings* (Philadelphia: Fortress Press, 1976), from which this quotation comes (p. 183).

and libidinous of apostles" who had transformed Wittenberg into Sodom and Gomorrah by sleeping with a nun.

Luther's exegetical works and his lectures at the University of Wittenberg frequently discussed marriage. Several of his tracts answer specific questions about this God-ordained institution. In his writings, especially *The Estate of Marriage,* Luther challenged the commonly held medieval position that celibacy is the ideal state and that sexual relations in marriage are at best a concession to the weakness of the flesh. In the late medieval period manuals used for confessions frequently cited a memorable quotation incorrectly attributed to Saint Jerome: "Anyone who is too passionate a lover with his own wife is himself an adulterer." Over against such beliefs, Luther openly taught that sexual desire is natural and should be fulfilled in marriage. Sexual love and desire for one's spouse is a gift from God and therefore sexual intercourse within marriage is a positive good to both guard and enjoy. Making celibacy a higher state than matrimony, therefore, perverts God's established order. Because sexual desire is irresistible, God-given, and good, celibacy is contrary to God's natural laws. Moreover, Luther argued, few clergy were able to live the chaste life celibacy demanded.

Luther sought to make the home central to the Christian faith. Marriage, established by God in the Garden of Eden, preceded the two other foundational institutions of society—the church and the government—in both chronological order and importance. Luther urged husbands and wives to live together happily and peacefully and love each other devotedly. The children couples produce are a gift and blessing from God. By such teachings Luther elevated marriage and the home, thereby helping permanently to change Western attitudes toward them.

Luther's contribution to the development of education is also great. The German Reformer promoted education through his sermons, his catechisms for children, his treatises, and his teaching at the University of Wittenberg. He used his preaching to instruct lay people in religious doctrines. At Wittenberg he prepared teachers and ministers who carried Reformation doctrines across Europe. Even more important was Luther's expansion of the purposes and subjects of education. Arguing that both church and state required

trained personnel, Luther urged German towns to provide universal, compulsory education. Because pastors and parents were so
busy, Luther called upon nobles and city councils to establish and
maintain schools (see *To the Councilmen of All Cities of Germany
That They Establish Christian Schools*, 1524). He was the first person in modern times to stress the state's obligation to provide education for its people. Luther also expanded the scope of education,
advocating a board curriculum that emphasized both theology and
the humanities, which was designed to help students become committed Christians and cultured citizens. Moreover, Luther opposed
the use of rigid discipline and corporal punishment, which were
commonly employed in schools of the late Middle Ages. Instead, he
urged educators to use discussions, debates, and drama to appeal to
youth's natural inquisitiveness and desire to play. His emphasis on
education helped to raise the status of teachers in Germany. The
Lutheran Reformation thus replaced the narrow curriculum of
cathedral and monastery schools with community schools that had
much broader goals for education, thereby helping to establish educational institutions that served church, state, and society.

Luther's approach toward social issues was highly moralistic and
generally conservative. He was primarily concerned with the moral
questions raised by social problems. And he considered the existing
structures and institutions of society to be ordained by God and
therefore not in need of improvement. Since society's faults spring
not from institutional arrangements but from man's evil nature, the
way to correct social abuses is to curb individual vices and to convert
people to Christ. Luther continued the medieval practice of forbidding usury—receiving interest on loans—and denounced any commercial transaction that produced "excessive" profit. Luther also
shared the traditional medieval qualms about trade. While trade is
necessary, it often tempts merchants to be greedy and to charge
extortionate prices. Distrusting the "profit motive," Luther argued
for the medieval principle of "just price," which stated that the price
of a product should correspond to the cost of production. He preferred the long-standing medieval society of farmers, craftsmen,
and artisans over one resting on traders, bankers, and middlemen.

More positively, Luther, like Calvin, emphasized a doctrine of calling. Luther asserted that all callings are divinely ordained, that God places individuals in vocations, and that people should labor in their callings to the best of their abilities, themes later developed more fully by Calvin. Because all vocations can be used to serve human needs, they are of equal value to God. Although Luther believed that God has imposed labor on the sinful world as a discipline, he argued that through work Christians assist God in His ministry to the world. Consequently, he rejected the traditional medieval separation between clergy and laity, between an order of spiritual perfection whose members truly served God and a lower secular order whose members simply provided daily human necessities. All "stations" or "vocations," whether teaching, parenting, preaching, farming, or trading, should be "highly praised" because each of them could promote the righteousness and glory of God. "If you are a manual laborer," Luther stated, "you find that the Bible has been put into your workshop, into your hand, into your heart." As Calvin did in Geneva, Luther also organized relief for the poor. While Calvin and other Reformed theologians made poor relief a function of the church, led by deacons, Luther assigned the task to town councils. In his address, *To the Christian Nobility,* Luther encouraged each town to establish a common fund to assist the poor.

While Luther is best known for redirecting theological thinking and reforming church life, his teaching on political and social issues significantly shaped Western civilization. Studying his views helps us to understand religious life and vocation, education, and society in the modern Western world.

John Calvin

John Calvin (1509-64) was a second-generation Protestant Reformer, who like Martin Luther, played a wide variety of roles. Calvin was an educator, an apologist for the Christian faith, a champion of missions, an ecumenical church leader, a theologian, a pastor, and an international statesman. If Luther is remembered as the activist, the protestor, the explosive theological revolutionary, Calvin is known as the thinker, the dogmatician, the organizer. True, Calvin was the great theoretician, systematizer, and theologian of the Reformation. Yet he did even more than Luther to revolutionize the post-Reformation world. Luther rediscovered the biblical teaching on justification by faith and helped to restore apostolic Christianity. While also explaining and defending biblical orthodoxy, Calvin developed a scriptural world-and-life view that transformed medieval society. More strongly than Luther, Calvin sought to reorder all of life—school, marketplace, home, state, society, and the arts—according to the Scripture. Though Luther tended to depreciate the Christian's responsibility to promote civilization and culture, Calvin underscored this important duty. In Geneva, Switzerland, where Calvin spent the last twenty-three years of his life, he had an unusual opportunity to implement much of his vision for society.

Calvin studied literature at the University of Paris and law at Orleans. He was converted to Protestantism while studying in Paris and quickly became one of the Protestant leaders in that city. Persecuted because of his Protestant faith, Calvin travelled in France, Switzerland, and Italy for the next three years, frequently under assumed names and constantly on the move to avoid arrest.

In 1536, Calvin stopped at Geneva, Switzerland, on his way to Strasbourg, Germany. Under pressure Calvin consented to help Guillaumo Farel reform morality in Geneva. Their efforts to introduce strict standards of conduct and discipline into this profligate city produced many opponents who eventually succeeded in expelling them.

Calvin moved to Strasbourg and became pastor of a congregation of French refugees who had fled their native land to escape persecution for their Protestant faith. His pastoral work, his writing and his ecumenical activities gradually spread his reputation as a biblical scholar and theologian across Europe. Calvin's friends regained control of Geneva, and after resisting their exhortations for two years, Calvin finally agreed to return there in 1541.

Calvin was to spend the remainder of his life (1541-64) in that Swiss city. There he labored ardently to create a Christian commonwealth that later served as a model for Christians in many other locations. Although Calvin was a pastor and never held a government position in Geneva, he dramatically influenced not only the ecclesiastical but also the social, political, and educational life of the city. Geneva was strategically located at the crossroads of several important trade routes between northern Europe and Italy, and Protestant refugees flocked there from almost every country of Europe. Many of these refugees eventually returned to their own nations, spreading Calvin's views far beyond the borders of Geneva. Moreover, Calvin corresponded regularly with Reformed leaders in other countries, and his numerous books were widely read.

Before examining the specific programs and activities Calvin implemented in Geneva, we will consider the broader, theoretical principles upon which his view of culture rested. As Calvin began to devise his holy Christian city in the 1540s, three alternative understandings of culture confronted his own.

1. The Lutheran position, as we have seen, distinguished between the kingdom of the world and the kingdom of Christ and frequently depreciated cultural activity.

2. The Roman Catholic approach, described in the previous chapter, tended to equate the kingdom of God with the church. Following Aquinas, the Catholic Church of this period held that creation is divided into two realms—nature and grace. Faith guides the realm of grace, which includes religion, theology, ethics, the church, and spiritual life. Reason, however, governs the realm of nature, which includes culture. Through the fall, the world lost the supernatural gift of God's grace. Therefore, the church, which possesses the channels of grace, must supply this gift to the world. As the vehicle of God's grace and activity in the world, the church must seek to bring as much of life (economics, education, publications, politics, etc.) as possible under its control. All activities that did not come under the umbrella of the church were considered profane. Only monks and priests were thought to do the true work of God. The teaching that laity simply provide the mundane necessities of life—food, shelter, and clothing—depreciated the value of their work to God's kingdom.

3. Anabaptists, as we will see in more detail later, saw the kingdom of God as primarily a new order God would bring after Christ's second coming. Occasionally a group of Anabaptists sought to

bring this kingdom on earth immediately through political and social action as peasants did at Munster, Germany, in 1525. Most Anabaptists, however, separated themselves from the larger society, either arguing that Christians have no responsibility for cultural improvement in the present world or attempting to build a model Christian culture on a miniature scale.

In contrast to these three other views of culture, Calvin, following Augustine, believed that the gospel could and should transform cultural life. His understanding, which rested primarily upon three theological principles—the sovereignty of God, Christian vocation, and common grace—profoundly affected the subsequent development of Western civilization.

Because God is sovereign, He is Lord over all creation, not simply some parts of it. His kingdom pervades all of life. God created the world as a unity; it fell in its totality; and eventually the world will be renewed in its entirety. Consequently, reality is not divided into two compartments (nature and grace) or two kingdoms (Christ's and the world). The church plays a major role in advancing God's kingdom, but His kingdom, which is partially but not totally fulfilled, is much broader than the church. Christians must labor zealously to make all cultural life glorify God and promote His kingdom. Expanding upon Luther's understanding of Christian calling, Calvin criticized the sharp line the medieval church drew between clergy and laity. He insisted that God gives a vocation to every individual and thus "there can be no employment so mean and sordid as not to appear truly respectable, and be deemed highly important in the sight of God" (*Institutes* 3. 10. 6). The Scriptures assign human beings a cultural mandate to subdue the earth and have dominion over it (Gen. 1:28). An individual's vocation is the primary way by which he or she serves God.

Though Calvin did not use the phrase "common grace" itself, he argued that all people, despite the fall, still have both an urge and a duty to build a culture. God has given all human beings "excellent talents," which they should use to further His kingdom (*Institutes* 3. 2. 15). Common grace restrains sin and enables civilization to prosper. In God's providence, non-Christians often contribute very significantly to culture even though they do not seek to serve God by their activity.

This understanding of culture directed Calvin's attempts to restructure Geneva's political, economic, social, and educational life. In the mid sixteenth century most countries were governed by monarchs who claimed that God commanded them to rule with absolute power and authority. Influenced by his contact with the rising French middle class and his study of ancient classical thought, Calvin countered that religion, legal statutes, and the authority of parliaments and courts all limit royal power. Magistrates, Calvin wrote, are not "endued with unbridled power." They are responsible to God and men in their exercise of power (*Commentary on Romans*, 13:4). At bottom, Calvin's concept of the state rested upon his idea of covenant, which he derived primarily from the relationship God had with Old Testament Israel. Elizabeth I of England, James VI of Scotland, and many Lutheran princes complained that Calvin's teachings on government undermined royal authority.

Calvin argued that God had ordained civil government to fulfill a definite but limited role. Church and state were to be distinct, but they should work closely together to serve people's needs. The church's responsibilities were primarily spiritual; it should not attempt to prescribe civil laws. The state was to govern the external affairs of life; it should not interfere in the ministry of the church.

This position hardly sounds revolutionary in our day, but it was in Calvin's. The Genevan Reformer opposed the current practices of Germany, England, France, and Spain, where state leaders were trying to dominate the church. Calvin insisted that church members, not political rulers, have the right to choose their ministers, elders, and deacons. In Geneva civil rulers were allowed to intercede in ecclesiastical matters only in extreme cases and only at the church's request.

According to Calvin, the task of civil government is "to cherish and protect the outward worship of God, to defend sound doctrine, piety and the position of the church, to adjust our life to the society of man; to form our social behavior to civil righteousness, to reconcile us with one another, and to promote general peace and tranquility" (*Institutes* 4. 20. 2). First and fundamentally, magis-trates are God's servants, bound by His Law. "They have not ascended by their own power into this high station, but have been placed there by God's hand" (*Commentary on Romans*). In govern-ing, rulers should display "divine providence, protection, goodness, benevolence, and justice" (*Institutes* 4. 20. 6).

With regard to the state, the church should pray for political authorities, encourage the state to defend the poor and the weak, warn magistrates when they disobey God's Word, and urge rulers to help promote true religion and enforce church discipline. And citizens should honor and obey magistrates, pay their taxes, pray for rulers, and render military and other service as needed. To obey rulers is to obey God; to despise them is to despise God's providence.

Although Calvin never held a political position and did not even become a citizen of Geneva until 1559, his ministry of preaching and teaching and his prestige in the city enabled him to dominate the whole community. Calvin's political activities were not limited to Geneva. He labored unsuccessfully to organize a Franco-German alliance against Charles V, the Holy Roman emperor. He urged French Protestant princes to pressure their king to grant them toleration. And he helped devise a treaty of diplomacy between Bern and Geneva.

The impact of Calvin's political thought and practice is immense. To some extent Calvin confused the responsibilities of church and state by encouraging magistrates to enforce religious regulations. But he clearly separated the roles of church and state. Over against both popes and emperors, he maintained that leaders in one sphere (church or state) should not have power in the other sphere. He strongly asserted that civil magistrates are God's repre-sentatives, called to do His work and promote His justice. Unlike Luther, who stoutly discouraged revolt against a tyrant, Calvin per-mitted resistance to oppressive governors if the rebellion was engaged in cautiously, as a last resort, and was led by lower elected officials. This position encouraged the English revolution of 1643-48 under Oliver Cromwell and the American Revolution of 1776-81, military actions undertaken by predominantly Calvinist populations. Calvin's teaching that covenant or compact was at the heart of political life helped prepare the way for democratic government. John Knox carried many of Calvin's political views to Scotland where they have richly influenced that nation's government to this present day. The English Puritans who helped reorganize their country's government in the seventeenth century accepted most of Calvin's political tenets.

His insistence that human institutions err and fallible men need checks and balances contributed to the separation of powers in modern republics. Calvin's argument that the church should be independent from the state, not subservient to it, encouraged the development of a church free from political control. Finally, his distinguishing of the roles of church and state in Geneva without divorcing religious conviction from the government established a pattern many nations followed during the seventeenth through the nineteenth centuries.

Calvin's political theory has one serious defect. He was so influenced by the twelve centuries of unity between the two swords that he thought the state should help to enforce observance of the Christian faith and to punish sinners. Nowhere does the New Testament teach that the state should aid the church in this way. Calvin argued that "Holy Kings are greatly praised in Scripture because they restored the worship of God when it was corrupted or destroyed, or took care of religion that it might flourish pure and unblemished" (*Institutes* 4. 20. 9). Calvin did not distinguish sharply enough between the way God related to Israel in the Old Testament (especially through the theocracy) and the church in the New Testament. The New Testament does not teach Christians to create a state that abridges liberty of conscience and coerces people into attending church services. Instead, it directs believers to use persuasion in their attempt to win others to Christ.

By designating Calvin the "father of laissez-faire capitalism," in his widely heralded *The Protestant Ethic and the Spirit of Capitalism* German sociologist Max Weber has called considerable attention to the Genevan Reformer's influence upon economic development. In comparison to how much he wrote about other subjects, Calvin said little about economics. He was, however, significantly involved in the economic life of Geneva.

The Weber-Tawney thesis (R. H. Tawney, *Religion and the Rise of Capitalism*), which asserts that Calvinism inspired the development of modern capitalism, has been hotly debated. Without delving into the complexities of the debate, we will highlight several points upon which scholars agree. By attacking the medieval prohibition against usury (which disallowed interest on loans), by encouraging hard work and thrifty living, by accentuating the dignity and importance of labor, and by promoting commerce and industry, Calvin contributed greatly to the rise of capitalism. He repudiated the scholastic assumption that money is barren, established seven principles for lending funds, and in 1551 helped organize a city-owned bank in Geneva. These developments encouraged the pooling of money, which made business possible on a larger scale. Calvin's doctrine of calling and emphasis on thrift promoted productivity, which, in turn, led to increased wealth and reinvestment. Unlike Luther and the medieval theologians, Calvin encouraged commerce, seeing it as a natural way to enhance material well-being.

While agreeing that Calvin promoted capitalism in these ways, most scholars reject Weber's association of Calvinists' economic productivity with their belief in election. According to Weber, Calvinists worked so vigorously because they were convinced that material prosperity was the surest sign of divine election to eternal life. Calvin's writings contain no hint of such a notion. His followers worked energetically because they considered their labor to be important to God; they saw their work as cobblers, butchers, farmers, and merchants to be callings from God for the advancement of His kingdom. In addition, their status in many countries as a persecuted minority closed the options of government, law, and church to them and therefore channeled them into business.

Calvin's activities in Geneva dispute Weber's claim that he promoted "laissez-faire" capitalism. Calvin encouraged the government to regulate numerous aspects of the Swiss city's economic life. He contended that the state had the right to tax its citizens for public necessities, and he urged magistrates to use this revenue to support education, hospitals, refugees, and the poor. The great influx of refugees into Geneva during the mid-sixteenth century led Calvin to beseech the city's governors to provide public work for those in need. Moreover, Calvin encouraged the government to regulate prices, weights, measures, currency, wages, and employer-employee relationships; to prohibit monopolies and stimulate industry and commerce; and to promote social and economic stability through binding contracts. Rather than supporting laissez-faire capitalism, Calvin advocated a middle path between communalism and individualism. Private property belonged to individuals, not the state. But material wealth and prosperity were gifts of God, which individuals should use to aid the whole community. Calvin sought, therefore, to arrange social and economic life according to biblical principles of righteousness, *shalom*, and love.

As we have seen, Calvin strongly stressed the importance of vocation. "God has ordained that we work," he wrote. "But is work denied someone? Behold that man's life is stamped out" ("Sermon LXXXVII on Deuteronomy 24:1-6"). Christians must evaluate whether their work is socially useful. "It is not enough when one can say, 'Oh, I work, I have my trade. . . .' For one must be concerned whether it is good and profitable to the community and if it is able to serve our neighbors" ("Sermon XXXI on Ephesians 4:26-28"). Attributing such importance to work, Calvin frequently denounced oppression of workers and poor working conditions.

Calvin was also deeply involved in organizing social life in Geneva. To him the Ten Commandments, especially the last six, were the norm for all social activity. He agreed with Luther that God ordained marriage for human happiness and the propagation of the race. His marriage to Idelette de Bure while living in Strasbourg, like Luther's marriage, testified to his clear break with the Roman Catholic position of clerical celibacy. Calvin opposed the medieval custom of arranged marriages, insisting that individuals should choose spouses themselves.

Calvin was especially concerned that Geneva provide for the poor, weak, and defenseless. Under his direction, two hospitals were established in Geneva, one for the ill, the aged, widows, orphans, the poor, and travelers, and a second for victims of plagues. At the first hospital cloth-making, weaving, and jug-making businesses furnished work for some of the five thousand refugee families who streamed into Geneva between 1542 and 1560. In a form of social-ized medicine, doctors and surgeons at these hospitals were paid at the city's expense. To the diaconate Calvin gave the responsibility "to watch diligently that the public hospital is well-maintained and that this be so both for sick and old people unable to work, widowed women, [and] orphaned children . . ." (*Church Ordinances* 1541). Summarizing Calvin's passion for social justice, one scholar writes: "He lent the acumen of his mind and legal training to a codification of the city's laws and to the best adjustment of its taxes. The city's health was better for his aid in construction of sewers and erection of hospitals. He concerned himself with the methods of healing and protection against fires; through him the weaving industry was revived."

A major shortcoming of Calvin's social views was that the soci-ety he helped mold in Geneva was very protectionistic and pater-nalistic. In a zealous effort to insure proper conduct, extensive regulations governed behavior, and private life was under rigorous surveillance. The Christian discipline practiced in Geneva was often petty, frequently foolish, and occasionally even cruel. The emphasis on community welfare was so great that sometimes the rights of individuals were ignored. Authorities searched houses without due cause, peeping Toms informed on violators, and Ana-baptists and Catholics were banished or imprisoned. Liberty of conscience did not exist. Torture was threatened or used to pro-duce confessions. While these practices were not unusual in medi-eval society, they were perhaps even more intense in Geneva because of faulty interpretations of the Old Testament and fear of papist attacks.

Teaching at Johannes Strum's school in Strasbourg from 1538 to 1541 strongly affected Calvin's understanding of and interest in education. For Calvin the Word of God was the foundation of all learning. Without proper knowledge of both God and ourselves, true education is impossible. Educators should recognize that while people are created in God's image, they are fallen and their minds no longer distinguish reality clearly.

The primary aim of education is to help people accept Christ as their Lord and grow in their relationships with Him. Calvin wrote several catechisms for children to promote this goal. The Genevan Reformer insisted that proper training in the humanities and sciences is just as essential to the Christian life as sound instruction in religion. His curriculum came from two sources: knowledge of the Creator as revealed in Scripture and nature (the basis of theology and religious education) and knowledge of the creation evident from the way God formed and governs the world (the basis of the arts and sciences).

Calvin helped establish a universal system of education in Geneva that placed schools under the control of the church, not the state or the home. He urged parents to teach their children the basic principles of Christianity and to send them to school. Believing that the church should supervise the complete education of believers, he assigned the church the tasks of selecting teachers, overseeing the curriculum, and directing the school.

In 1559, Calvin founded the Genevan Academy, the crowning achievement in his attempt to build a Christian commonwealth. Drawing students from all over Europe, the academy maintained a very high standard of excellence in teaching religion, arts, and sciences. By Calvin's death in 1564, the school had grown to twelve hundred students. In most countries where Calvinism spread, similar institutions were founded, modeled on the academy.

John Calvin's influence on Western civilization and culture is immense. Like Luther's, Calvin's work schedule and accomplishments are truly staggering. Calvin promoted missions, worked vigorously to unify Christians all over Europe, and wrote numerous letters to monarchs, challenging them with the claims of the gospel and arguing for toleration of Protestants. His understanding of political, economic, social, and educational life, largely grounded in biblical ideas, has significantly shaped the Western world. While no religious body has ever born his name, the Reformed and Presbyterian denominations are his theological descendants, and his exposition of Scripture and view of culture have challenged and molded the thinking of countless Christians throughout the last 450 years.

The Anabaptists

While most Protestants were affiliated with the movements initiated by Martin Luther and John Calvin, a third major force arose in the 1520s that also sought to purify the church. Because they wished not simply to reform the Catholic Church but to reinstitute the church of the New Testament, this group has been called the "radical Reformers." Their practice of rebaptizing adult converts led opponents also to dub them Anabaptists.[7] Anabaptists contended that the magisterial Reformers (Lutheran and Reformed Protestant leaders) had not sufficiently purged the church of its unbiblical elements. They wanted to eliminate from the church all theological beliefs and liturgical practices not explicitly mandated in the New Testament. In contrast to Luther and Calvin, Anabaptists maintained that Christian congregations should consist only of believers who voluntarily chose to participate and who evidenced faith in and commitment to Christ.

Anabaptists produced no ministers who attained the stature and significance of Luther or Calvin. Moreover, none of their leaders was as important to their movement as Luther was to Lutheranism or Calvin was to the Reformed churches. This diverse reform movement, which stressed Christian discipleship, biblical literalism, and pacifism, sprang from a variety of reforming impulses in Continental Europe. Formally founded in 1525, Anabaptism spread quickly into almost all European countries, especially German and Dutch speaking areas.

The label "Anabaptist" has meant different things to different groups at different times. Its opponents in the sixteenth century regarded it as a dangerous movement bent on destroying Europe's religious and social institutions. Others have viewed Anabaptism as a curious social antiquity or as a tough, resilient Christian movement tied to the good earth and expressed in hard work and frugal

7. Actually there were three groups of radical Reformers—Anabaptists, Spiritualists, and Evangelical Rationalists. See George H. Williams, *The Radical Reformation* (Philadelphia: The Westminster Press, 1962).

living. Still others have considered Anabaptism the only true Protestantism, arguing that it alone eliminated all papist perversions and restored pure, primitive Christianity.

Fierce persecution, geographical barriers, and congregational autonomy slowed the movement's growth so that one century after Luther posted his ninety-five theses at Wittenberg, Anabaptists in central Europe numbered only thirty thousand. Typical of the strong measures taken to crush Anabaptism was an edict adopted in Zurich in 1529 that demanded that "every Anabaptist and rebaptized person, of whatever age or sex, be put to death by sword, fire, or otherwise. All preachers and those who abet or conceal them, all who persist in Anabaptism or relapse after retraction, must be put to death." Although no one leader was able to unify this diverse, fragmented movement, Anabaptists did hold several common convictions that were quite different from those espoused by other Protestants living in the sixteenth century.

Michael Sattler, previously a Benedictine monk from southern Germany, led the scattered Swiss Anabaptists to adopt seven articles that expressed their central convictions. This statement of faith, ratified in the Swiss-German border town of Schleitheim, is a typical formulation of Anabaptist beliefs and displays their disagreement with Luther, Calvin, Zwingli, and the other magisterial Reformers. The seven articles declare that: (1) Only those who repent, trust Christ as Savior, and demonstrate the fruit of Christian living should be baptized. Thus Anabaptists rejected Catholic and Protestant belief in infant baptism, "the greatest and first abomination of the pope." (2) The church should maintain believers' allegiance to God by banning disobedient members. (3) Repudiating the Catholic understanding of mass, Anabaptists considered the Lord's Supper to be simply a memorial to Christ's death meant only for true, repentant believers. (4) Believers should dissociate themselves from the Christ-rejecting world. Christians must avoid those who belong to the devil and therefore live in sin. (5) Pastors who meet New Testament qualifications should direct every congregation. Their role is to serve communion, preach, teach, exhort, and discipline members. (6) Christians cannot use the sword under any circumstances, neither to defeat evil nor to defend good. (7) While Christians should solemnly tell the truth, they must not swear an oath of any kind.

Their complete separation of church and state, defense of religious liberty, refusal to participate in government or take oaths or bear arms, and attitudes toward property differed sharply from the view of Calvin and Luther. Opponents contended that all these Anabaptist practices threatened the established political and social orders.

Luther and Calvin, as we have seen, argued that the leaders and functions of church and state should be distinct and separate. They insisted, however, that church and state work closely together. They maintained, moreover, that the state should promote true religion by punishing heretics, requiring church attendance, and enforcing religious regulations. Anabaptists, by contrast, contended that the church and state should be totally independent and separate. Challenging an assumption that had been practically unquestioned since Constantine forged an alliance between church and state in the fourth century, Anabaptists declared that magistrates should play absolutely no role in church affairs. The radical Reformers agreed with Catholics and other Protestants that sin's presence in the world makes government necessary. The state is God's agent to restrain those who have not accepted Christ's lordship. As such, the state uses the power of the sword to promote civil righteousness. Unlike Catholics and other Protestants, however, Anabaptists argued that government serves no worthwhile function for the Christian. In a truly Christian society, they contended, government is unnecessary; life is governed by the law of love. Christians are citizens of heaven, not of this world. Summing up Anabaptist convictions, one leader stated: "We grant that in the non-Christian world state authorities have a legitimate place to keep order, to punish the evil, and to protect good. But . . . Christians live according to the Gospel and our only authority and Lord is Jesus Christ."

Believing then that Christians have little responsibility to the state, most Anabaptists withdrew from society in order to build distinctive Christian communities free from the world's contamination. They maintained that Christians should not serve as magistrates. Arguing that Jesus' statements in the New Testament explicitly prohibited taking any oaths, they refused to swear an oath of allegiance to the state. Believing that the use of violence is contrary to biblical teachings and especially to the example of Christ, Anabaptists refused to serve in the army. No matter how much a particular situation might seem to demand fighting and killing, they regarded these actions as contradicting the law of love taught in the New Testament. As Menno Simons (1496-1561), founder of the Mennonites, the largest body of Anabaptists in Europe in the sixteenth century, and the major Anabaptist denomination in America today, wrote, "All Christians are commanded to love their enemies; to do good unto those who abuse and persecute them; to give the mantle when the cloak is taken, the other cheek when one is struck. Tell me, how can a Christian defend scripturally retaliation, rebellion, war, striking, slaying, torturing, stealing, robbing and plundering and burning cities, and conquering countries?"

Catholics and other Protestants considered Anabaptists' refusal to participate in warfare dangerous at a time when religious conflict was common and the Ottoman Turks threatened to attack Europe. Michael Sattler's declaration that he would not fight against the Turks was viewed the same way by sixteenth-century Europeans as Americans today respond to those who say they will not fight against communism. Most Anabaptists, especially Mennonites and Moravians, have continued to be pacifists to the present day.

At the same time, Anabaptists also challenged the ideal of a unified Christendom under a single religious authority, a view that had predominated for a thousand years. Catholic popes and magisterial Reformers alike maintained that the church encompassed all members of society, if not by conviction then by coercion. Dissent was not allowed, and heretics (false believers) were punished. Zwingli, Luther, and Calvin did not believe that individuals should have complete freedom of conscience to believe whatever they wished. Anabaptists, by contrast, renounced the idea that all members of a society belonged to the church simply by virtue of citizenship. They insisted instead that the church should be distinguished from the community at large and should include only those who have experienced the new birth and have committed their lives to Christ. No one should be compelled to join or worship in a church with which he does not agree. Whether they intended to or not, Anabaptists established a counterculture that challenged the "oneness of medieval society, in which church and empire, pope and emperor, bishop and king, priest and nobleman were united in their shared responsibility for maintaining wholeness, peace, and order."[8] Eventually through Roger Williams, Isaac Backus, James Madison, and others, their conception of religious liberty became widely accepted in America and incorporated into the First Amendment to the United States Constitution.

While Anabaptists agreed with other Protestants on the importance of justification by faith, they stressed more strongly than other groups the necessity of Christian discipleship, of a life of consistent commitment to Jesus Christ. They held to high standards of morality and expelled from their fellowship all who failed to live by their principles. Like medieval monks, Anabaptists sought Christian perfection in communities separate from the world.

Their view of discipleship and their sense of community prompted them to develop an attitude toward property unlike that of Catholics and other Protestants. Though individual Anabaptists were allowed to own property, their possessions were treated as common, as belonging to the entire community. Christians who owned property were morally obliged to help others so that no member of the Christian community was in need. As Anabaptist leader Balthasar Hubmaier declared, "Everyone should be concerned about the needs of others. . . . For we are not lords of our possessions, but stewards and distributors. There is certainly no one who says that another's goods may be seized and made common; rather, he would gladly give the coat in addition to the shirt." One group of Anabaptists, the Hutterites who first emerged in Moravia and today live primarily in South Dakota and southern central Canada, practiced a complete community of goods involving both production and consumption. They argued that Christians should reject private property because it prompts malice, envy, and greed, and produces quarrels, bloodshed, and war. Although Anabaptists did not

8. Walter Klaassen, "Anabaptism—Neither Catholic Nor Protestantism," *Christian History*, 4, 1:35.

expect others to adopt their understanding of possessions, opponents considered their position a threat to social stability.

Anabaptist arguments that the church should be a voluntary society of believers, that church and state should be completely separate, and that individuals should be free to choose any religion they wished seemed radical and dangerous to medieval minds, whose outlook was shaped by a millennium-long effort to build a unified Christian society. Eventually, however, Anabaptist ideas on these issues triumphed in Western culture, especially in America.

Contemporary Approaches to Culture

The approaches to culture developed or used by the major religious bodies of the sixteenth century have in large measure continued to direct Christian thinking to the present day. In his now classic book, *Christ and Culture*, H. Richard Niebuhr has identified several major positions on Christianity and cultural life that will structure our analysis in this section.[9] The limitations of space force us to simplify these positions and to ignore many of the subtleties of their arguments.

Many modern Anabaptists continue the cultural approach of their sixteenth-century forefathers, which Niebuhr calls "Christ Against Culture." They agree with Tertullian, the great church father of the third century, that Christians should withdraw as much as possible from cultural life. The "disciples of Greece," Tertullian exclaimed, have nothing in common with "the disciples of heaven." Because sin has corrupted politics, commerce, and the arts, Christians should shun them. Moreover, the believer's primary concern is to practice Christian piety and to prepare for the life to come. At best, Christians can establish their own havens from the world's contamination, which can model redeemed life; they cannot, however, expect to improve the world significantly.

Many contemporary followers of Martin Luther affirm his

9. In his book, Niebuhr discusses five approaches to culture. We will apply four of them to our groups: Christ Against Culture (Anabaptist), Christ Above Culture (Thomist), Christ and Culture in Paradox (Lutheran), and Christ the Transformer of Culture (Reformed). The fifth category, Christ of Culture, is most typical of liberal Protestantism as it developed in nineteenth-century Europe.

paradoxical or dualistic approach to culture. They maintain that the Christian's principal responsibility is to promote spiritual goals (evangelism, worship, Christian nurture, a pure church) rather than cultural ones. Believing that everything creaturely is sordid, that the whole cultural edifice is cracked and crooked, they argue that Christians may blunt the force of evil in the universe, but will never transform the world. Because selfishness and ungodliness are so pervasive, Christians cannot expect to bring Christ's rule of righteousness in this present world.

Most Catholics and many Anglicans have accepted Thomas Aquinas's approach to culture. While arguing that Christ transcends culture, Aquinas maintained that Christ and culture can be synthesized. That is, the church can have such a profound impact upon shaping social institutions and cultural activities that they become essentially Christian. The church directs individuals toward heaven, provides sacramental assistance, and as "custodian of the divine law" helps to order all temporal life. Thus the church "is the guardian of culture, the fosterer of learning, the judge of the nations, the protector of the family, the governor of social religion."[10] Since the law of God is inscribed in the individual heart and the structure of creation, people can use reason to apprehend and live by this law. While human reason is usually sufficient to determine how cultural life should be organized, it sometimes provides inadequate insights and must be supplemented by revelation. Critics protest that this view fails to recognize that God's kingdom is broader than the church, that it ignores the radical evil present in the world, and that it minimizes the extent to which sin has corrupted human reason.

In the twentieth century many Catholic leaders have departed from this Thomist approach to culture. The emergence of a pluralistic world and the brutal atrocities of the past fifty years have forced recent popes, especially John Paul II, to admit that the church no longer dominates cultural life and to assert that sin is pervasive in the world. Moreover, in Latin America, Africa, and Asia, many Catholic priests have espoused liberation theology, which stresses that Christ is decisively on the side of the poor and the oppressed in

10. *Christ and Culture*, p. 129.

their battle with the rich and powerful. This theology encourages Christians to make improving the lot of the poor their first priority. Its leaders urge Christians to use the political process to effect this result, and if that fails, to incite revolution.

Niebuhr describes the position of Augustine and Calvin as "Christ the Transformer of Culture." Their theological descendants argue that sin is deeply rooted in the human soul and pervades all human action. But these "conversionists" also assert that all human culture is under God's sovereign rule, and they maintain that Christians should seek to promote God's glory through all their cultural activity. Their attitude toward culture is positive and hopeful. Transformationists insist that God is the Lord of history and that He is building His kingdom on earth. This kingdom will be fully revealed at the consummation in a new heaven and new earth. Calvinists declare that Christ transforms culture by redirecting, reinvigorating, and regenerating human activity, which has become perverted and corrupted by sin. Jesus Christ heals and renews "what sin has infected with sickness unto death." They expect the gospel to permeate all of life. Calvin's followers today contend that individuals can express their faith and love and glorify God through their callings, that the state is God's minister for promoting justice, and that God is working to transform the world into His kingdom.

Within the transformation camp, two primary approaches to culture have developed in recent years. While the proponents of both positions agree that Christians should attempt to shape the institutions and values of their countries, they disagree over how and on what basis Christians should do so. One group of Christians argues that the United States was originally built upon a "Christian consensus," which informed and directed our nation's society and government.[11]

---

11. One variation of this approach, called "theonomy" ("God's law"), asserts that the moral and the civil law of the Old Testament is normative or binding for both Christians and non-Christians, who should obey all its regulations. Civil magistrates, therefore, should enforce all Old Testament laws, precepts, and penalties. Crimes such as adultery, sodomy, bestiality, rape, incest, kidnapping, persistent disobedience by children to their parents, Sabbath-breaking, apostasy, witchcraft, and blasphemy should be capital offenses. If our government enforced

Insisting that believers have a responsibility to make the nations in which they live thoroughly Christian, proponents of this view maintain that it is biblically correct and politically possible to rebuild America's Christian foundations so that the nation would become distinctively Christian. Denouncing the influence of secular humanism on America's public institutions and life, these Christians stress the church's cultural mandate to base society on biblical values. Groups that support this position such as the Moral Majority, Religious Roundtable, and Christian Voice, and Christian leaders such as the late Francis Schaeffer and attorney John W. Whitehead have had many laudable goals and have supported many good causes. Opponents contend, however, that several philosophical traditions, not simply biblical Christianity, shaped the development of American institutions and laws. Moreover, critics complain that this approach advocates using the power of the state in a coercive way that contradicts New Testament teachings and would impose Christian values on minorities.

Other Calvinists insist that the New Testament prescribes a radically different approach to culture, which they call cultural pluralism. Advocates of this view maintain that all groups with different world views should have equal opportunity under the law both to teach their understandings of life and to develop associations—schools, labor unions, political parties, businesses, voluntary organizations, and the like—to promote their convictions. According to this view, all ideologies should be recognized in public life, and public policies should be hammered out by compromise among various groups. All groups should not have to live under a public order controlled by one world view, as the Puritans sought to mandate in earlier American history and humanists and some Protestants strive to accomplish today. By trying to dominate public life in America, Protestants in the nineteenth century inadvertently encouraged Americans to develop a public order from which religion, narrowly

the civil laws of the Old Testament, America would become a consistently Christian nation, proponents maintain. Most Christians oppose theonomy, arguing that the position misunderstands the nature of God's relationship with the church, misinterprets the New Testament, and attributes unwarranted power to the state.

defined, became almost excluded and where one view of reality—secular humanism—has received a privileged position. Proponents of cultural pluralism find no warrant in the New Testament for supposing that a single, agreed-upon set of attitudes and values must control the public order. They argue that the laws of the land should not give any special blessings and benefits to Christians. Christians should not use law to coerce others into living by their views, and they should support the right of groups to espouse alternative perspectives and to argue for them in public life. Nevertheless, Christians should seek to convince others to accept the biblical world view and to support biblical values in the public arena. Opponents contend that the cultural pluralism approach underplays the effects of sin in the world, minimizes Christians' responsibility to bring all cultural life under God's dominion, underemphasizes evangelism, and promotes cultural relativism.

Conclusion

Having evaluated modern forms of the approaches to culture that crystallized during the Reformation, it remains only to summarize the diverse cultural consequences of this sixteenth-century movement.

Based upon their belief in God's sovereign control of all things, the Reformers introduced a new ideal of life. Its hero was not the monk who fled the world, but rather the artisan, merchant, magistrate, or pastor who served God within the world. The leaders of the Reformation stressed that commercial and civic activities contributed significantly to the kingdom God was building on earth. Through His growing kingdom God was working to leaven society, purify commerce, ennoble art, and improve social conditions. The Reformation gave a new sanctity and significance to marriage and the family. Its leaders accentuated the value and dignity of individuals. By declaring people to be ultimately responsible to God, not to the state, the Reformers advanced intellectual liberty. The Reformation fostered a spirit of democracy (all believers have equal access to God), revolutionized the concept of Christian charity (charity is for the welfare of the recipient, not the benefit of the donor), stimulated education, and played an important part in the development of the middle class. The half century from Luther's attack upon the sale of indulgences to Calvin's death introduced many ideas that have extensively altered Western civilization ever since.

For Further Reading

Luther

Brecht, Martin. *Martin Luther: His Road to Reformation, 1483-1521.* Translated by James L. Schaff. Philadelphia: Fortress Press, 1985.

Gritsch, Eric W. *Martin—God's Court Jester: Luther in Retrospect.* Philadelphia: Fortress Press, 1983.

Holl, Karl. *The Cultural Significance of the Reformation.* Translated by Karl and Barbara Hertz and John H. Lichtblau. New York: Meridian Books, 1959.

Schwiebert, E. G. *Luther and His Times.* St. Louis: Concordia, 1950.

Thompson, W. D. J. Cargill. *The Political Thought of Martin Luther.* Totowa, N.J.: Barnes and Nobles, 1984.

Calvin

Graham, W. Fred. *The Constructive Revolutionary; John Calvin and His Socio-Economic Impact.* Richmond: John Knox Press, 1971.

McNeill, John. *The History and Character of Calvinism.* New York: Oxford University, 1954.

Parker, T. H. L. *John Calvin: A Biography.* Philadelphia: Westminster Press, 1975.

Reid, W. Stanford, ed. *John Calvin. His Influence in the Western World.* Grand Rapids: Zondervan, 1982.

Anabaptists

Estep, William R. *The Anabaptist Story.* Grand Rapids: Eerdmans, 1975.

Klaassen, Walter. *Anabaptism: Neither Catholic nor Protestant.* Waterloo, Ont.: Conrad Press, 1973.

Littell, Franklin H. *The Sectarian Origins of Protestantism.* New York: Macmillan, 1964.

Moore, John Allen. *Anabaptist Portraits.* Scottdale, Pa.: Herald Press, 1984.

Williams, George H. *The Radical Reformation.* Philadelphia: Westminster Press, 1962.

Contemporary Approaches to Culture

Brown, Harold O. J. *The Reconstruction of the Republic.* New Rochelle, N.Y.: Arlington House, 1977.

Neuhaus, Richard. *The Naked Public Square: Religion and Democracy in America.* Grand Rapids: Eerdmans, 1984.

Niebuhr, H. Richard. *Christ and Culture.* New York: Harper, 1951.

Novak, Michael. *Will It Liberate? Questions About Liberation Theology.* Mahwah, N.J.: Paulist Press, 1986.

Schaeffer, Francis. *A Christian Manifesto.* Westchester, Ill.: Crossway Books, 1981.

Smith, Gary Scott. *The Seeds of Secularization. Calvinism, Culture and Pluralism in America, 1870-1915.* Grand Rapids: Eerdmans, 1985.

Spykman, Gordon et al. *Society, State, and Schools.* Grand Rapids: Eerdmans, 1981.

Walsh, Brian J. and Richard J. Middleton. *The Transforming Vision: Shaping a Christian World View.* Downers Grove, Ill.: InterVarsity Press, 1984.

Whitehead, John W. *The Second American Revolution.* Elgin, Ill.: David C. Cook, 1982.

III.
MODERN
WORLD VIEWS

9

America: A Free Society

Gary Scott Smith

Introduction

Throughout our study of world views we have argued that presuppositions determine actions. While people's presuppositions shape the social structures they develop, at the same time institutional arrangements in a particular society (types of government, economy, family, religion, and social systems) affect which ideologies and beliefs its people accept. In this reciprocal relationship presuppositions nevertheless remain primary. Especially important in influencing the type of society people build are their anthropological assumptions.

The American republic emerged not in an intellectual vacuum but out of philosophical principles rooted in a specific historical context. Our nation rests upon distinctive presuppositions about the nature, rights, responsibilities, and purposes of human beings and their societies.

In the second half of the eighteenth century several philosophical and theological traditions converged to form the emerging American understanding of government and society and to provide an ideological foundation for the new nation's institutions. In large measure, the United States represents the confluence of three streams—the Judeo-Christian tradition, the several varieties of the Enlightenment in Europe, and the ideas of the radical Whigs or Commonwealth men of early eighteenth-century England.[1]

1. The Whig political tradition, which transmitted the thought developed during the English Commonwealth of 1648-60, consisted of many different people and movements. While Puritans, especially John Milton, contributed to this tradition, so did Scottish and Irish nationalists who despised the rule of English

259

Because the European Enlightenment was so diverse, Americans were able to pick and choose among its principles and beliefs. Of special importance were the political theories of John Locke and Charles Montesquieu, which deeply influenced the founding fathers' understanding of natural rights, limited government, and liberty of conscience, and the empirical epistemology of the Scottish Enlightenment, which provided philosophical support for America's practical approach to problems. The radical skepticism of Scottish philosopher David Hume and the French philosophes had little impact in America. The Judeo-Christian heritage, which helped to contour American culture, had previously absorbed many ideas from the non-Christian classical world. Given these Christian, Enlightenment, and Whig roots, the American republic rests upon the broad Western humanist tradition, both Christian and secular. Nevertheless, because of the impact of the Reformation on Europe and the Puritan contribution to American settlement, the influence of Reformed Protestantism has been especially strong in our nation.

Because America's roots are so diverse, the frequently heard argument that the United States is a Christian nation cannot be supported historically. Many of our country's first settlers were devout Christians who sought to apply scriptural teaching to all areas of life; millions of other Americans have shared the same goal. Moreover, the English law tradition, which powerfully influenced the development of American society, had been molded in large part by Christian values. Nevertheless, America has never been nor is ever likely to be a uniformly, thoroughly, consistently, or even predominantly Christian nation. Since the arrival of the Puritans in the 1620s, the presuppositions of other world views have been mixed with Judeo-Christian ones in America, often by devout Christians. Neither the Puritans, nor the Revolutionary generation, nor any other group of American Christians has been able to create an essentially biblical society—that is, a nation where Christians "succeed reasonably well" in basing family, state, business and economics, and churches on scriptural norms, where justice and char-

monarchs, legal scholars who wished to protect the English Common Law, and philosophers John Locke and Francis Hutcheson.

ity are shown to the poor and outcast, upright morality prevails, and all cultural activity seeks to glorify God. Even the New England Puritans, who had great freedom in their attempt to build cultural life upon Christian values, fell short in many ways. Incorrectly interpreting Scripture, they regarded themselves as the new Israel, which produced among them pride and self-interest and led them to require church attendance, banish dissenters, limit the right to vote to church members, and execute those convicted of being witches.[2]

During the Revolutionary era, the values of both the Judeo-Christian tradition and Enlightenment deism helped to provide the foundation for the new republic. Though the American Revolution was not distinctively Christian, many of its underlying principles were compatible with biblical faith. Enlightenment teachings and the colonists' religious beliefs were merged into a political religion that stimulated Americans to revolt against England. Enlightenment principles linked Americans' social, political, and economic desires to the universal, transcendent principles of reason. Reformed Protestantism, Enlightenment reason, and radical Whig political ideology all converged in supporting the political, economic, and social goals of the Revolutionary era. During these years no distinctly Christian understanding of political thought, as opposed to Enlightenment rationalism, developed. This was so, explains George Marsden, because Christians had so thoroughly accepted natural law tradition that they no longer believed that reason led believers and nonbelievers to different conclusions.[3]

Principles drawn from both the Enlightenment and Christian world views, though rooted in very different assumptions, taught

2. For elaboration of this point, see George Marsden's "America's 'Christian' Origins: Puritan New England as a Case Study," in Mark A. Noll, Nathan O. Hatch, and George M. Marsden, *The Search for Christian America* (Westchester, Ill.: Crossway, 1983).

3. While Revolutionary thought had some harmony with Christian faith, it was not itself Christian. Christians identified "Revolutionary ideology, which grounded law and governmental institutions on nature, with the revealed will of God. In the eighteenth century . . . nature and God were linked together, but later on the culture's view of nature eliminated God." One hundred years later evangelicals had no "basis from which to analyze and combat the new secularism, for they too had agreed that a good politics and a just society could arise merely from the study of nature" (Noll, Hatch, Marsden, *The Search for Christian America*, p. 94).

that humans lust for power, that public virtue is possible, and that society should be built upon absolute norms. These convictions supported limited government, religious liberty, and the independence of religious and civic institutions from each other. Contemporary Christians often ignore or minimize the attachment of the founding fathers to the Enlightenment and picture them as much more Christian than they actually were. Among the fathers of our country only Patrick Henry, John Witherspoon, and Samuel Adams were orthodox Christians. Benjamin Franklin, Thomas Jefferson, James Madison, Alexander Hamilton, George Washington, John Adams, Thomas Paine, and many others drank deeply from the wells of the Enlightenment.

Although America has never been a thoroughly Christian nation, our public and private life has been richly informed by biblical presuppositions and values. During the last one hundred years, however, these scriptural principles have increasingly been challenged, rejected, or simply ignored.

Foundational American Assumptions

In large part proponents of the various traditions that helped to shape the American social order agreed on the two major assumptions about human nature held by members of the Revolutionary generation. During the first two hundred years of American history most Americans expressed a suspicion of human nature. Because people possess an innate propensity to crave power, prestige, and pleasure they must be controlled and restrained. American Christians have repeatedly traced this tendency to man's rebellion against and alienation from God. Rejecting divine revelation, exponents of various humanist philosophical traditions that have influenced American life have based their belief in depravity on observation of human behavior. Advocates of the Enlightenment and even many Christians, however, insisted that depravity affects man's will but not his reason.

A second widely held assumption about human beings, however, has tempered the first. Most Americans have asserted that people are not totally evil, but are capable of doing much good. Christians have argued that individuals can be redeemed; restoration to a proper relationship with their Creator makes people generally trust-worthy and obedient to law. Moreover, Christians have contended that God's common grace constrains human wickedness, making order and civilization possible. Proponents of Enlightenment phi-losophy, by contrast, have maintained that more education, better use of reason, and proper institutional checks and balances could improve individual behavior and produce a better society. During the last century, growing numbers of Americans, including many Christians, have moderated or even dismissed belief in human depravity, emphasizing, instead, that man is fundamentally good, self-reliant, and able to solve his own problems.

While several ideologies contributed to general American acceptance of these two convictions about humanity during the 1600s and 1700s, biblical Christianity was especially important. The English Puritans, who established the Massachusetts Bay Col-ony in 1630 and during the next several decades came in increasing numbers to New England, held biblical assumptions about human nature. Joining the Puritans (Presbyterians, Congregationalists, Reformed denominations, and some Baptists) in colonial America were four other major religious traditions—the Pietists (Lutheran and Brethren communions), the Wesleyans (Methodist), the Peace Church (Quakers and Mennonites) and the Established Church (Episcopalians). Through these groups biblical values, although sometimes synthesized with alien philosophical presuppositions and principles, strongly influenced the development of this nation. With the conversion of large numbers of blacks to Christianity dur-ing the hundred years prior to emancipation, and the arrival of many Catholics, Greek Orthodox, and Jews after 1850, American religion has become increasingly diverse in structure, ideology, and social values.

Because they constituted more than 75 percent of the colonial population and possessed a well-developed world view, Reformed Christians had more influence than other Christian bodies upon the early development of American social, political, economic, and educational life. Nevertheless, the American republic emerged on a foundation built both by disciples of the Enlightenment, like Thomas Jefferson and James Madison, and by evangelical

Protestant leaders. The remainder of this chapter will identify and analyze other underlying assumptions that have contributed to the formation and structure of American society.

America and "Higher Law"

Our colonial forefathers strongly believed that government and society are subject to a higher law. Christians insisted that God had revealed principles in Scripture and in nature that societies should seek to implement or models that they should seek to follow. Colonists sharply differed over how to organize the state, how to structure the church, how church and state should be related, and how citizens could be loyal to both the kingdom of God and their government. They generally agreed, however, that God's law (for Enlightenment rationalists, "natural law") provides the basis for answering these questions.

Many colonists derived their conviction that the American social order must rest upon transcendent ideals from their belief in God's sovereignty over the universe and their commitment to establishing His kingdom order on earth. Because God created, sustains, and rules the cosmos, divine norms rather than human preferences should guide social life. A republic, as much as any other form of government, is under God's authority and laws. Proponents of deism and rationalism maintained that natural law, which could be discerned by reason, not divine revelation, provided the foundation for American society. Advocates of Enlightenment philosophy such as Jefferson, Madison, and Franklin played a major role in shaping the Constitution and early American government. Nevertheless, almost all colonists agreed, despite their varied theological and philosophical commitments, that an objective body of truth, largely derived from Judeo-Christian principles, should serve as the basis for American institutions and laws.

The earliest Puritans came to America to establish a Christian commonwealth, a society built upon the Bible. In his famous sermon "A Model of Christian Charity," preached aboard the Arabella shortly before the Puritans landed at Massachusetts Bay in 1629, their leader, John Winthrop, declared that they sought to create a community that would be faithful to God and His law in all its actions. Although Roger Williams, who was evicted from Puritan Boston and founded Rhode Island in 1636, disagreed with the way Winthrop and the Puritans used the state to enforce religious belief, he concurred that scriptural principles should direct cultural life.

Succeeding generations of American Christians sought to construct, in the words of Samuel Adams, a "Christian Sparta," a nation peopled by disciplined, devoted followers of God. By the 1770s many colonists had become convinced that England's corruption was preventing them from creating a society modeled upon the Bible. This belief that there were ideal standards and patterns for social, political, economic, and religious life, divinely revealed norms for public institutions as well as private activities, continued to direct the labors of Cotton Mather, Jonathan Edwards, Lyman Beecher, Charles Finney, and countless other Christians who shaped American culture throughout the eighteenth and nineteenth centuries. Sinful patterns have been institutionalized and Christian and secular values have been mixed together in every period of American history. At the same time, biblical presuppositions about God, man, and society have deeply influenced our values, convictions, language, customs, and institutions, reaching a high point in the years from 1830 to 1870. After 1870, however, the methodologies of the new social sciences, linguistic and textual criticism, which damaged confidence in the Bible, and the penetration of various forms of relativistic humanism into American culture all began to erode belief that there are absolute standards to which American society should conform.

America, a Chosen Nation?

Closely associated with belief that American society should rest upon transcendent ideals was widespread conviction that this country had a special purpose, a peculiar destiny and mission. A century before America was settled, Martin Luther and John Calvin taught that Christians have both a cultural and a religious duty on earth. As we noted in the previous chapter, these Protestant Reformers rejected the common medieval idea that the monastery was the highest Christian calling. They insisted, instead, that believers should seek to glorify God by the cultural and religious tasks they perform in this world. For Calvin especially, the work of the laity is just as important as that of the clergy in advancing God's kingdom on earth. Building this kingdom requires teachers, doctors, lawyers, carpenters, farmers, merchants, and craftsmen as well as pastors. This idea of individual calling helped inspire tremendous efforts to construct flourishing civilizations in both Europe and America.

From William Bradford's *Of Plymouth Plantation* (1621) onward, many Americans have believed that not only do individuals have callings to serve god, but so do nations. Americans have assumed that our nation, more than other countries, plays a special role in fulfilling God's plans for the world. John Winthrop argued in "A Model of Christian Charity" that America was the new Israel; it had a unique relationship with God. In the American wilderness, God had made a fresh new start. He had reestablished His covenant with the Puritans, who would be blessed if they obeyed its stipulations and cursed if they did not. Other nations had suppressed the light of God; America would allow it to shine forth fully. Speaking for many colonists, Puritan pastor Cotton Mather began his *Magnalia Christi Americana* (1702) by declaring that the migration of thousands of God's servants to America was "one of the great and wonderful Works of God in this Last Age." Two generations later many ministers reemphasized America's divine mission during the Great Awakening (a series of colony-wide revivals in the 1740s).

Strongly asserted again during the 1770s, this conviction encouraged America's revolt against England. Hundreds of clergymen responded to the events of the decade by drawing analogies between America and ancient Israel. Many colonists insisted that the Revolution was a necessary antidote to moral decay. Religion would work hand in hand with republicanism to create frugality, honesty, self-denial, and benevolence among the American people. If Americans were to carry Christianity, morality, and liberty to the rest of the world, they must themselves enjoy both political and religious freedom. Colonists must sharply resist the oppressive policies of Parliament and the British king and prevent the establishment of Anglicanism as the national church. While Christian influence helped inspire the American struggle for independence, many colonists blended their political views and their Christian faith "thoroughly and indiscriminately," preaching, for example, that resistance to England was resistance to the Antichrist.[4]

This idea that America is a chosen nation with special duties has persisted throughout our history. President Woodrow Wilson, for example, stated, "America was born a Christian nation for the purpose of exemplifying to the nations of the world the principles of righteousness found in the word of God." This conviction helped inspire, and was further envigorated by, the rapid spread of settlers across the North American continent; America's military triumphs in 1848, 1898, 1918, and 1945; its brief ventures into colonization; its rise to the position of the world's greatest commercial and industrial power in the early twentieth century; and its high standard of living. Such accomplishments reinforced the widely held belief that America has a special place in world history. Events in recent decades, however, such as Vietnam and Watergate, have caused many to question America's calling and destiny.

Interpreted in this way, the chosen nation idea has been frequently used to justify military aggression and cultural imperialism abroad and to rationalize maltreatment of Indians, blacks, and other minorities at home. Belief that God has specially chosen America to fulfill His purposes in the world cannot be supported biblically. Only Israel in Old Testament times has had a unique relationship with God or special responsibilities before Him. God commands all nations to base their corporate life upon divine norms and to promote peace and justice. No country is His peculiar agent.

---

4. In *The Search for Christian America*, Noll, Hatch, and Marsden argue convincingly that Christian leaders during the Revolutionary era confused biblical categories with categories of political philosophy and patriotic nationalism, leading them to consider opposing Britain more important than Christian unity, to equate loyalty to America with loyalty to Christ, and to lose their ability to be self-critical. The failure of Christians during these years to develop a "new theology for applying Christianity in public life, prostituted the gospel, damaged the church and hindered the spread of Christian faith" (pp. 63-65). These authors point out that "explicit references to Scripture or Christian principles are conspicuously absent" in the political discussions of the Revolutionary and early national periods, in the Constitution, and in new state charters, as well as in the pamphlet literature supporting independence, in state debates over the Constitution, and in political disputes of the 1790s (p. 81).

In fact, the "chosen nation" idea perverts and undermines the gospel. It incorrectly considers the state rather than the church to be God's primary force in the world, and it discourages criticism of the state's actions. Moreover, conviction that our nation has a special mission became secularized in Enlightenment terms, as is evident in both the ideology of the Revolution and the concept of manifest destiny of the nineteenth century.

America, the Cradle of Liberty

As indicated earlier, widespread belief that America is the cradle of liberty has fueled its sense of mission. From Plymouth onward, colonists sought the freedom to worship God as they saw fit and to follow the religious practices that they believed were taught in the Bible. Most Americans opposed a national established church and insisted that political officials should not have any control over Christian congregations. While some colonies and states granted special privileges to certain denominations (establishing churches on that level), the ideal of religious liberty remained strong in America and was, after much struggle, eventually enshrined in the First Amendment to the Constitution, adopted in 1791.

The colonists firmly believed that religious freedom was directly tied to political freedom. Indeed, they insisted that the former was impossible without the latter; only those who enjoyed civil liberties would have the freedom to worship as they pleased. What the colonists desired was freedom from restraint, especially from that imposed by law. Their belief in human depravity led them to maintain that laws were necessary as guidelines for behavior, as embodiments of a people's morality and as constraints against crime. Law was a schoolmaster that taught people what was right. Yet, colonists were confident that Christianity's influence in America would produce the moral and upright citizens, the "public virtue" that a republic demands. God wrote His law upon the hearts of the redeemed, making them fit for liberty.

The desire for basic human rights, springing from both Enlightenment and biblical sources, was expressed in Jefferson's famous statement in the Declaration of Independence that men "are endowed by their Creator with certain unalienable rights; that among these are life, liberty and the pursuit of happiness." Human rights were firmly protected by the Bill of Rights, appended to the Constitution in 1791. The first Ten Amendments guarantee the right of citizens to participate in the political process and protect citizens against arbitrary police and court action.

It is important to understand that most Americans did not directly try to base their new nation upon scriptural revelation. They sought to rest government and public life upon general principles drawn from nature, which members of various faiths and non-believers accepted. Consequently, at some points, the government and public order they framed is consistent with biblical norms; at other points, it is not.

Colonists sought to create a political structure that would guard against humans' desire for power and would preserve individual liberties. The founding fathers believed that human sinfulness requires such a government. James Madison repeatedly warned about the "infirmities and depravities of the human character." Samuel Adams insisted that such is "the depravity of mankind that ambition and lust of power above the law are . . . predominant passions in the breasts of most men." Thomas Jefferson, although strongly influenced by Enlightenment philosophy, admitted that "free government is founded on jealousy, not in confidence; it is jealousy and not confidence which prescribes limited constitutions, to bind those we are obliged to trust with power." This same belief in human depravity underlies the *Federalist Papers* written in 1787 by Madison, Alexander Hamilton, and John Jay to help win ratification for the new constitution. As Richard Hofstadter put it, the architects of the Constitution "had a vivid [secularized] Calvinistic sense of human evil . . . and believed with [Thomas] Hobbes that men are selfish and contentious."

Their fear of human thirst for power led the founding fathers to construct a government that limited, distributed, and balanced power. Whether in the hands of a monarch, an elected legislature, or a state church, unchecked power is dangerous. The Constitution enumerated and thereby limited the powers of each governmental branch. The president, the congress, and the courts were given specified duties. Powers not explicitly mentioned belonged to the states and the people. By dividing the power of the federal government among three branches—the executive, the legislative, and the judicial—the Constitution established a system of checks and balances. The founders thought that this system would prevent any particular branch from gaining too much power and tyrannizing the citizenry. In addition, the Constitution balanced power by giving certain duties to the states and to local governments and other responsibilities to the federal government.

While most colonists thought human depravity required a government of checks and balances, they believed that the manifestations and effects of sin were limited. Christians argued that divine redemption and the restraining power of God's common grace arrest the power of sin. Virtually all leading political thinkers, whether Enlightenment rationalists or Christians, assumed, however, as historian George Marsden argues, "that the light of natural reason was strong enough to reveal the eternal principles of God's law to any unprejudiced right-thinking person." Though depravity has debilitated the human will, it has not blinded the human intellect. "Persons as diverse," Marsden continues, "as Thomas Jefferson and John Witherspoon, to pick the most 'Enlightened' and the most Calvinist of the major figures, agreed that humans naturally had essentially reliable innate abilities to apprehend the truth, both in the physical world and in the sphere of morality."[5] In short, while the American Constitution rests upon the Calvinist view of human nature, the eighteenth-century political theory underlying American government denies it. Although they provided controls for human nature, the founding fathers emphasized man's natural ability to design a just and healthy society. Madison, for example, acknowledged human depravity, but also insisted that other human qualities justify "a certain portion of esteem and confidence."[6] Republican government, he argued, presupposes "the existence of these qualities in a higher degree than any other form." Christians were confident that human beings, freed from slavery to sin by

5. Ibid., p. 62.
6. Madison represented the blend of ideological factors that shaped America. He was educated under Presbyterian clergyman John Witherspoon at Princeton, but was also schooled in Englightenment philosophy.

God's redeeming power, could effectively maintain a representative government, which required the honesty and civic virtue of the citizenry. Rationalists believed that natural rather than supernatural means—man's innate capacity to reason—could ensure both personal morality and social health.

Commitment to liberty was also expressed in American support of social equality and capitalism. Among the most famous phrases in American history is Jefferson's assertion in the Declaration of Independence that "all men are created equal." Jefferson did not mean by this statement that all people have equal talents or equal achievements. He meant that they should have equal opportunities in society and that they should be treated equally before the law. Laws must not discriminate against individuals because of economic, social, or religious (today we would add sexual and racial) factors. Biblical teaching that all persons are equal before God and the Enlightenment emphasis on natural rights possessed by all both contributed to colonists' belief in equality. And yet, the new American political system did not provide total equality. It restricted the rights of women, required men to own certain amounts of property in order to vote, and, most grievously, permitted slavery. Nonetheless, the American republic provided a wider range of freedoms for a wider group of people than the world had previously known. Since the ratification of the Bill of Rights, amended to the Constitution in 1791, America has slowly yet steadily extended fundamental human rights to various groups in society on the basis of values drawn from biblical, classical, and humanistic traditions. During the past two hundred years property restrictions on voting have been removed, slavery abolished, universal and free public education provided, legal segregation of races eliminated, asylum furnished for millions of immigrants, women's rights furthered, and original civil liberties expanded.

Most Americans have desired the same kind of freedom in the economic sphere that they have enjoyed in state, church, and society. Following the mercantilism of the seventeenth and eighteenth century in which America functioned as part of the British Empire, industrialization in the nineteenth century rapidly transformed the American economy. The capitalistic system that developed allowed the market to function freely according to certain basic "natural" laws with minimal involvement or interference of government. Its proponents argued that the pursuit of personal advantage produces public good. Participation in the marketplace and acquiring possessions, land, and other property has brought individual independence, social mobility, and a high standard of living and has protected people's right to exercise political power. Though greed, materialism, and exploitation have been common in America, the practice of free enterprise has often been combined with Christian ideals of cooperation, justice, and compassion for the less fortunate. This economic system has generally achieved high levels of productivity and quality and has helped make possible social, political, and religious advancement.

Secularization and American Society

Many minimize the role Reformed Protestantism has played in American society. From the Puritan settlement of New England until the Civil War biblical understandings of God, humanity, and ethics, though sometimes diluted or synthesized with alien world views, powerfully affected both public and private life in our nation. Convictions that God is sovereign over social arrangements and activities and that people are commanded to build a culture that glorifies Him were widely held. Scriptural teachings about human nature, sin, and society and the arguments of Locke, Montesquieu, and Adam Smith, derived from an Enlightenment commitment to natural rights and limited power, combined to persuade Americans to establish a republican government and adopt a system of free enterprise.

Despite the commitment of many founding fathers to Enlightenment rationalism, proceeding and following the Revolutionary period two Great Awakenings (1730s and 40s) and (1800-30) swept across America. These widespread revivals won thousands of converts to Christ, revitalized hundreds of congregations, and inspired the formation of numerous voluntary associations to promote a wide variety of benevolent causes. Collectively, these developments stamped Christian values deeply into American culture. The awakenings and the steady ministries of thousands of committed pastors and lay persons alike insured that biblical principles, generally expressed in evangelical Protestant terms, helped to define the new nation's values, ethos, and institutions. While Enlightenment rationalism and the classical (Greek and Roman) exposition of civic virtue molded the thinking of many American intellectuals, the Bible of the revivalists directed the understanding and behavior of most common people.[7]

Despite the many seeds of secularization planted during colonial, early national, and antebellum periods of American history, during these years biblical convictions were clearly evident in many Americans' attitudes toward work, social relationships, ethics, science, education, and government. During the nineteenth century, Christian congregations grew stronger, and evangelicals played a major role in government, social reform, and scientific investigation. Many Christians labored vigorously to rest social practices on divine norms, to provide education based on a biblical world view, and to win people to Christ and nurture them in the faith. Throughout the century, marriage, the family, entertainment, and the arts remained largely grounded upon biblical principles, and much of American private and public moral practice rested upon the Ten Commandments. Nevertheless, even during these years Enlightenment deism and humanistic principles strongly influenced our nation's life; then too, many social values were shaped as much by Victorianism and legalism as by historic Christianity.

After 1870, the assault upon Christian values in American culture intensified. Secular assumptions about ultimate reality, humanity, and social arrangements drawn from revitalized humanism and scientific naturalism increasingly challenged Judeo-Christian understandings. Religious institutions and norms became less influential in society, and biblical convictions about culture began slowly to erode. Unlike secularization on the European continent and in England, in America this process did not

7. As Noll, Hatch, and Marsden point out in *The Search for Christian America*, the leaders of the First Great Awakening "retained the Puritan conviction about the need for personal salvation, but largely abandoned the Puritan concern for a united commonwealth." Moreover, they did not develop a "biblically rooted framework for politics and society" to replace "the Puritan ideas they had rejected" (pp. 60-61).

usually involve overt attacks upon or indifference toward organized religion. Institutionally, in fact, in terms of members and finances, Christian denominations have prospered from 1870 to the present, experiencing small declines only in the 1930s and 1960s. Secularization in America has been a subtle process as gradually, and sometimes even imperceptibly, secular ideas have made inroads into our culture. Before 1930 only certain intellectual elites in education, journalism, science, and the professions embraced secularism as a naturalistic world-and-life view inimical to biblical ideas of God, humanity, and society. But many Americans, while continuing to espouse Christian values in their family and leisure activities, accepted secularism as the public philosophy required by a pluralistic culture. Though still worshipping God in their churches and homes, those who adopted a secular "public" philosophy considered God irrelevant in public, academic, political, and economic life. Many theists have contributed to and compromised with this growing secularization but other believers have staunchly resisted it. Several movements—naturalism in literature and science; pragmatism, positivism, and existentialism in philosophy; humanism in education; and utilitarianism in morality—combined to challenge the biblical values imbedded in American society before 1870.[8]

Secularism has its roots in ancient Greece and Rome, especially in the belief of Plato and Aristotle that humans can achieve their highest potential and society its fullest development solely through the use of human reason.[9] The secularism that challenged American culture in the late nineteenth and early twentieth centuries added few new principles to those it inherited from previous times. Its contribution, rather, was to use the new perspectives drawn from positivist paradigms in anthropology and psychology to develop a popular rationale for embracing naturalistic materialism. These new developments helped secular ideals appeal to a much broader section of society.

The systematic set of secular beliefs emerging fully only in the

8. These movements are described in *Building a Christian World View*, vol. 1, chaps. 8, 9, and 15.

9. For an extended discussion of the development of secularism, see *Building a Christian World View*, vol. 1, chaps. 8 and 9.

1920s offered a cosmology, anthropology, and epistemology that conflicted with the Christian world view. Its primary premise, taken from scientific naturalism, is that physical nature is the only knowable reality. Thus, supernatural entities either simply do not exist or, if they do, are unknowable. Humanity is a product of natural evolution. Human dignity and worth are rooted not in the created image of a personal, all-powerful, and loving God, but in man's position at the pinnacle of the evolutionary process. People can solve their own problems, unaided by any deity, through reliance upon reason and the scientific method. Human knowledge comes not from God's revelation but from what reason discovers through experimentation. Human rationality is the final judge not only of material facts, but of moral values as well. Society should be organized to serve people, not to glorify God. Ethics are grounded not in God's nature and revelation, but in pragmatic and utilitarian considerations.

Education

Shifts in educational philosophy and practices during the past one hundred years illustrate the change in the presuppositional basis of American society. During this period secular assumptions about God, humanity, knowledge, and society have in large measure replaced biblical ones as the foundation of American education.

Education in America sprang from the passionate Puritan quest for knowledge and wisdom. Within two decades after reaching the shores of Massachusetts, the Puritans founded both a public school system and a college. Like their counterparts in England, American Puritans attempted to establish schools that would equip every citizen with the necessary knowledge and skills to be a happy, useful member of society and a committed servant of God. A New Haven statute of 1656 succinctly states their primary educational aim: "Children and apprentices should be taught to read the Scripture and other good and profitable books . . . to understand the main grounds and principles of the Christian religion necessary to salvation."

Only by developing schools and colleges that promoted a biblical world view could Puritans build Winthrop's "city set on a hill." As one scholar put it, no Puritan "could envisage a Holy Common-

wealth without a reformed church and piously oriented schools."
These schools helped parents in their task in teaching piety, civility,
and knowledge to their children. Three themes underlay the Puritan
educational curriculum: creation, fall, and redemption. Human
beings are created in the image of a loving and holy God. His righteousness is the basis for justice and law, and His commandments
order all earthly life. Although created to have a relationship with
God, mankind chose to repudiate God and became alienated from
Him. Sin made people self-centered. But God brought redemption
and restoration to all who receive Christ as Lord and entered into
covenant relationship with Him. The influences of medieval Scho-
lasticism and Renaissance humanism, however, prevented Puritans
in both England and America from developing a holistic, integrated
curriculum that presented all subjects from a Christian world view.

Until about 1800, American education continued to follow the
Puritan pattern of denominationally based schools. After that date,
the lack of resources in newly settled areas west of the original thirteen colonies encouraged the various religious bodies to cooperate
in developing a nonsectarian Protestant school system there. Moreover, during the first half of the nineteenth century many Americans came to believe that only government or "public"—not
private, charitable, or religious—control could provide genuinely
free education for all children. By the 1840s, an evangelical consensus of faith and ethics was so firmly planted in America that a
majority of Protestants were willing to entrust the state with the task
of educating children, confident that this education would remain
rooted in Christian principles. During the antebellum years these
state-controlled schools used as their primary textbook the
McGuffey Readers, which taught the Protestant virtues that were
deeply engrained into American culture.

After the Civil War, however, Protestant dominance of the public
school system was increasingly attacked. By the 1870s, four parties
had emerged that held fundamentally different perspectives on the
proper nature and character of the schools. Protestants, who constituted the first party, continued to assert the long-standing argument that proper education must rest upon a biblical and, indeed,
thoroughly Christian foundation. Both parents and the state are

commanded by God to give children an education founded upon biblical values. Education based upon a secular world view, they contended, was incomplete and morally harmful. Such education was not neutral and did not present facts impartially; it rested upon naturalistic assumptions about ultimate reality, humanity, society, cosmology, and ethics.

Roman Catholics, who sometimes complained that the common schools were too Protestant and at other times that they were too secular, composed a second party; they desired denominational schools supported by the public treasury. Arriving in America in growing numbers after 1840, Catholics used most of the same arguments for basing the schools on biblical values as did Protestants described above. Because of their historic animosity and their theological differences, however, these coreligionists never once were able to work together to keep public education anchored to a distinctively Christian value system.

Members of a third group insisted that state schools should be impartial toward all specific forms or expressions of faith. Instead, common schools should teach general theistic principles common to Protestants, Catholics, and Jews. Advocates of this position argued either that Bible reading and prayer violated the rights of some taxpayers, or that these practices were so watered-down that they were detrimental. This third party drew together various Protestants, Unitarians, and Jews who believed that the separation of church and state and America's cultural and ethnic pluralism demanded a public school system based upon key moral principles agreed upon by all theists.

The fourth party in the debate over the proper nature of the public schools consisted of secularists, who argued that frankly humanistic and naturalistic rather than biblical values should underlie curriculum and instruction. The secular, or supposedly "neutral" approach, which dominated the public schools after 1930, was chiefly championed in the early twentieth century by philosopher John Dewey. He held that man is fundamentally good, that evil is merely a product of the environment, that application of the scientific method could solve all social ills and that careful consideration of consequences is the only proper foundation for ethics.

Given the strong historic influence of Christianity in America and the small band of secularists who advocated this fourth position before 1930, why was the biblical world view gradually removed as the foundation for our nation's education? Although the answer to this question is complex, four factors help explain the increasing secularization of American public schools after 1890. (1) By 1840 most Americans thought the state should provide education. Some who thereafter accepted the idea that the government should be functionally secular, logically concluded its education should also be impartial, not simply toward the distinctions among denominations but also toward differences between theism and atheism. (2) During the years between 1870 and 1930 many Protestants thought that American public schools were based more decisively on biblical values than they actually were. Thus, they either underestimated or misunderstood their opposition. (3) Although the first two parties constituted a large majority, their effectiveness was reduced by the inactivity of those who believed the schools were still solidly theistic and by the widely differing proposals they offered to keep Christian values prominent in public education. (4) Shifting American values, especially in colleges and universities, also promoted secularization of the common schools. Before the Civil War, Christians had largely dominated collegiate education. Six major religious bodies established 116 of the 182 long-enduring colleges founded by 1861, and the various denominations continued to control almost all American colleges. After 1870, significant changes occurred. Many state and urban universities were founded that had no explicit ties to religious denominations. Meanwhile, professors at some prestigious institutions established earlier by Christian denominations began to espouse and teach secular doctrines. Moreover, colleges began to de-emphasize liberal arts and stress vocational and technological subjects, areas in which Christian perspectives had not been fully developed. In the late nineteenth century, the rise of the social sciences as academic disciplines, rooted largely in naturalistic assumptions, also promoted a relativistic, humanistic world view. Especially in urban centers the pressures of a multi-religious community, the acceptance of humanistic perspectives by leading educational philosophers, policy-makers, and administrators, and the belief of many teachers that religion and education should be and could be kept separate led to the removal of Judeo-Christian values from the schools.

The convergence of these four factors in the years between 1890 and 1930, coupled with secularist arguments that liberty of conscience, the necessity of free inquiry, and America's growing cultural pluralism demanded "value free" education, helped convince many theists that schools should be based not upon a distinctively biblical world view but upon the American commitment to democracy and civil religion, the "common faith" John Dewey advocated. Only in 1962 when the Supreme Court prohibited prayer and Bible reading in the public schools did many Christians realize the extent of secularization there. The sheer presence of these practices in numerous public schools before 1962 led many to regard the educational system as still fundamentally Christian. But in their vision of life, as represented in their curricula and methods of instruction, most public schools had begun years earlier to teach an understanding of this world based upon naturalistic and humanistic assumptions. It was difficult for Protestants living in the late nineteenth century to realize that they erred in assuming they could keep public schools distinctively Christian. Their effort to do so clearly violated the First Amendment and obviously failed. Had these Christians instead supported a pluralistic approach to education where different faith communities rather than the state operated schools, our educational system might be radically different today.

In the 1980s Americans continue to debate how morality can be taught in the public schools and whether Bible reading and prayer should again be allowed. Some schools offer courses in world religions and "The Bible as Literature." Their rejection of explicitly biblical ethics and their attempt to teach from a "neutral, objective" perspective makes it very difficult for contemporary schools to find solid foundation for ethical instruction. Growing recognition of this humanistic orientation of today's public schools along with increased concerns about educational quality and, in some cases, racial integration, have led to a proliferation of private secular and Christian schools.

Economics

Enlightenment and Christian teachings influenced the development and operation of both mercantilism and capitalism in the United States. In general, however, as in education, secular values have increasingly replaced biblical ones as the foundation for America's economic principles and practices.

Contemporary American economic life has been heavily influenced by the industrial revolution and the rise of capitalism. According to Max Weber and R. H. Tawney, Calvinist doctrine, especially belief in God's sovereignty over the universe and the predestination of individuals to eternal life, produced the spirit that made capitalism possible. It did so, Weber and Tawney argued, by developing a distinctive ethical system that required people to labor arduously in order to achieve material prosperity and thus demonstrate their election. By promoting thrift, hard work, and careful provision for the future, Calvinism also supported a set of attitudes essential for productive capitalistic activity.

Calvinism did help produce the industrial revolution by rejecting the medieval prohibition against interest-taking, thus encouraging loans for business and making it possible to accumulate enough money to build factories and engage in commerce on a larger scale. It is also true that Calvinists taught industry and frugality. An accurate reading of Calvinist sources, however, reveals that they worked diligently not to demonstrate their election but rather to glorify God. John Calvin taught that all of life is sacred and that every individual's vocation is "a post assigned him by the Lord." Because people serve God and one another through work, they should labor energetically and enthusiastically. They should choose vocations that are satisfying and contribute to the good of society. Faithfulness to God's commandment to be responsible stewards of the good earth, Calvinists have maintained, usually brings material blessings.

The Puritans introduced this Reformed economic heritage to America, and it did much to shape our understandings of economic life. While the declared purpose for founding almost every colony was to promote Christianity, desire for trade and exploitation of natural resources also played a prominent role in the settling of

America. From 1620 to 1820 trade and agriculture formed the backbone of the American economy. As in Europe, land was considered the chief source of individual and national wealth. Owning land gave a person a place, position, and stake in society. The fluidity of the social order during the colonial period allowed many landless laborers to acquire and farm land, something that rarely happened in Europe. By 1776, slavery had become widespread in the colonies. Slaves played a major role in producing several profitable crops for international markets. Grievously, most Christian colonists endorsed or tolerated slavery. Nevertheless, many of them believed that economic activity was as directly under God's ordinances as were politics, religion, and the social order.

During the colonial period town legislatures passed laws carefully regulating the hours, standards, and obligations of the marketplace. Most colonists assumed that the community should control markets and trade by establishing fair prices and wages and reasonable profits to promote the corporate good. In the late seventeenth century, England developed "mercantilist" practices, which extended this tradition of market regulation to the larger commonwealth. Mercantilist laws governed all trade between England and her colonies and between British colonies and other European nations. Although these laws were made to benefit the British, for nearly a century after mercantilism was created, colonial merchants and magistrates also prospered. But the attempt of the British government to impose stricter market control on the colonies in the years between 1763 and 1776 fueled Revolutionary fires, already ablaze for political, social, and religious reasons, and provided a ready audience for Adam Smith's attack on mercantilism in *The Wealth of Nations*.

Like Jefferson's "Declaration of Independence," *Wealth of Nations* was issued in 1776 and had a revolutionary impact. During the next generation this book dramatically changed American thought about economics and the relationship between government and business. While the new American republic did not follow Smith's prescriptions exactly, for more than two centuries his ideas have significantly influenced our government's policy toward business. Smith accepted the argument of the French "physiocrats" that government should not interfere in the economy because its regulations always inhibit the increase of wealth (the "laissez faire" doctrine). Economic policy should enhance the well-being of citizens, not increase state power as mercantilism did. Smith argued that the "invisible hand" of the market, the unstructured system through which individuals exchanged goods and services, would regulate economic relationships much better than government edicts. Allowing the laws of supply and demand to determine the price and production of goods would produce a self-regulating economy and greater and greater wealth. Smith advocated the same notions of individualism and democracy in the marketplace as the American political revolution demanded in government.

During the years between the Revolution and the Civil War revolutions in transportation, agriculture, and industry; westward expansion; and large-scale immigration began to transform the shape, face, and character of American society. While most Americans continued to farm, the corporation arose as a new business organization. Though government at all levels tended to support business enterprise in general, during these years the growth of America's agriculture, industry, and commerce occurred without the oversight of the national government. By the early 1800s the well-ordered, cohesive colonial society had crumbled and fragmented. Individualism began to prevail. Seemingly limitless possibilities of advancement encouraged many to choose private gain over community responsibility. By the mid 1800s the self-made man of Horatio Alger's "rags to riches" stories had emerged. Despite their passionate pursuit of wealth and their exploitation of the environment, most speculators and entrepreneurs genuinely believed that such individualism provided the surest route to communal and national progress. Some of the businessmen who unfolded America's riches, such as the Brahmins of Boston and the Tappan brothers of New York, served responsibly as political and cultural leaders.

After the Civil War this extreme individualism contributed to many problems in a society undergoing massive changes. Rapid industrialization, urbanization, and immigration substantially altered the contour and character of America. Wealth became more and more concentrated so that by 1890 1 percent of American families owned more than 50 percent of the nation's wealth. Meanwhile, slums, sweat shops, illiteracy, immorality, bribery, and graft were commonplace. Disturbed by the hours, terms, and conditions of their employment and by the feeling that they were mere cogs in the giant industrial machine, many laborers began to organize unions, to strike to obtain better working conditions, and to advocate profit-sharing plans.

Their wedding of a laissez-faire understanding of economics to orthodox theology thwarted the efforts of religious bodies to help combat these massive social and economic problems. Many Christians assumed that if people avoided interfering with the principles God had embedded in the universe to undergird human relationships, everything would work out for the best. Reinforced by social Darwinism's doctrine of the survival of the fittest, proclaimed in America by Englishman Herbert Spencer and Yale professor William Graham Sumner, this laissez-faire approach encouraged an unrealistic optimism. Like Enlightenment philosophy, this view rejected the crucial biblical doctrines of the fall and sin, doctrines that underscore the necessity of regulation and restraint. During the "Gilded Age," as Mark Twain labelled it, the period of the so-called Robber Barons, most Protestants defended the social status quo and massive accumulation of private property, urged individuals to acquire wealth, and congratulated those who did. Leading clergymen like Phillips Brooks of Boston minimized the number and plight of the poor and told the indigent that they could pull themselves up by their own bootstraps if they only followed gospel teachings. In his famous sermon "Acres of Diamonds," delivered over six thousand times, Baptist pastor Russell Conwell, founder of Temple University in Philadelphia, instructed believers that it was their "duty to get rich." Many Protestants opposed all forms of state intervention to help the poor, advocated only modest charity for the indigent, and attacked the right of labor to organize and strike.

Other Christians responded to the massive problems of the late nineteenth century more humanely. Some, like evangelist Dwight L. Moody, insisted that revivals, individual conversion, philanthropy, and improvement of private morality would best help urban workers and the poor. Others created organizations such as the

Salvation Army, the YMCA, and the Knights of Columbus to promote these same goals. Still others argued that only redeeming society and changing social structures could alleviate the massive problems of this period. Washington Gladden and Walter Rauschenbusch developed a movement known as the Social Gospel, which attacked a variety of urban and industrial problems.

Some Christians living in late nineteenth-century America complained that currents flowing from naturalistic understandings of economics, from the rationalist notion that God is unconcerned about the universe, from social Darwinism's glorification of competition and progress, and from the Gospel of Wealth promoted by industrialist Andrew Carnegie and clergyman Russell Conwell, with its praise of acquisitiveness and material success, provided a complex and powerful rationale for excluding biblical principles from economic life. This view of economics challenged traditional belief that Christ is king over all of life and that economic activity cannot be independent from religious values. Many theists firmly resisted the idea, increasingly advanced in the late nineteenth and twentieth centuries, that the world of work, production, and exchange is a secular enterprise, removed from Judeo-Christian influence. Rather, they declared that biblical standards of justice, honesty, cooperation, and mutual love apply in business as much as in any other sphere of life.

In the twentieth century, American economic practice has frequently been divorced from biblical and ethical considerations. Instead of seeking first and foremost to glorify God and serve humanity through business enterprise, many companies have made pursuit of profit and benefit of stockholders their chief priorities. Many individuals choose careers based on salary, fringe benefits, and opportunity for promotion, not on how they can best fulfill the cultural mandate and meet pressing human needs. Leading Christians have protested against this approach to economics and have tried to provide alternative models of stewardship and compassion through their companies and vocations.

Today American Christians seek to implement biblical principles in economic life in two different ways. One group challenges convictions that individual selfishness leads to collective good, that continued economic growth will automatically help the poor, and that materialism and greed must be encouraged in order to stimulate economic growth. Pointing to finite supplies of such natural resources as oil, forests, fresh water, food production, key minerals, and space for solid wastes, these Christians call for a limited-growth economy built upon a new value system. They desire a global economic policy built upon a biblical foundation that seeks to give all the world's people a decent standard of living.

Other Christians, while also opposing materialism and exploitation of the environment, argue that the free operation of the market guarantees the highest level of productivity. This second group of Christians desires a benevolent or "enlightened" capitalism built upon ideas of the interdependence of the world community and shared responsibility. They believe that pursuing individual liberty rather than economic equality is more consistent with the Bible and will bring greater benefits to humanity. While strongly defending free enterprise, personal freedom, and individual initiative, they also insist that different groups within society and different nations are joint partners who should cooperate to help one another.

Politics

As we have seen, the American republic rests upon philosophical assumptions drawn from Enlightenment, Whig, and Judeo-Christian traditions. During the last century, the Christian aspect of that mixed heritage has been increasingly de-emphasized, and America's political ideals and practices have become increasingly secular. Three important developments will illustrate our argument: (1) changing interpretations of the meaning of the separation of church and state, (2) the steady erosion of belief that God is supreme over our nation and that our government and its legislation are subject to eternal law, and (3) shifting conceptions of the basis for our commitment to individual liberty.

America's most radical innovation was not its government or economy but the disestablishment of the church. For fourteen hundred years dating back to Constantine in the fourth century, all Christians (except Anabaptists and some sectarians in the post-Reformation period) had assumed that social order depended upon shared religious belief and that religion "was both a public good and a public responsibility." Americans clearly understood as they approved the First Amendment, which guaranteed the institutional separation of church and state and insured freedom of worship, that they were embarking on a new, uncharted course.

Religious liberty developed in America for both practical and ideological reasons. No one denomination or combination of religious bodies was powerful enough to establish a national church. The First Great Awakening of the 1730s and 40s convinced many that voluntarism in religion could produce great benefits. To be sure, some American states continued their colonial pattern of providing established churches to which all citizens belonged (except those dissenters who were excused) and which were supported by taxes (the last one was in Massachusetts and was abolished in 1833). The Awakening, the Revolutionary War, and the necessity of evangelizing large numbers of unchurched persons after the war ended prompted united Christian efforts and drew Americans together in a common commitment to evangelical religion, vital piety, and social concern.

Meanwhile, deist political leaders such as Thomas Jefferson and James Madison and pietist clergymen such as Isaac Backus and Samuel Davies presented an intellectual rationale for disestablishment, as Roger Williams and the Anabaptists had earlier. Both deists and pietists agreed that each person had the right of private judgment and should be free to pursue a personal relationship with God. No government, church, or other institution could properly interfere with that responsibility. In fact, their whole experience in America taught many colonists that the free, uncoerced consent of individuals was the only proper basis for all human organizations, civil and ecclesiastical.

While developing this understanding of the separation of church and state, however, most Americans continued to insist, as had their predecessors, that religious values should not be divorced from government. The state had no official religious commitment, all religious beliefs being equal before the law and freedom of worship protected. This did not mean, however, that the government should be hostile or even indifferent to the traditional religious beliefs of

Western civilization. Most Americans expected the state to reflect the ethical and spiritual principles of its citizens who were primarily Christians. Thus, while maintaining that church and state each had its own distinct sphere, many Christians argued that both were responsible to God. Moreover, political officials, as His servants, were to apply biblical principles to their administrations. During the twentieth century, however, the Supreme Court has repeatedly declared that our government cannot favor religion in general over atheism, although remnants of the Judeo-Christian influence remain in the provision of chaplains for the armed services, in the Pledge of Allegiance to our flag, and in the motto on our coins.

Convinced that the state was ultimately under God's authority and judgment, most American Christians during the first hundred years of the republic denounced the doctrines of both popular and state sovereignty. In repudiating "popular sovereignty," American Christians did not deny that government was based on a political compact between the ruler and the citizens and that government should represent the collective will of the people. What they rejected was the idea stemming from Jean Jacques Rousseau and the French Revolution that the state is "merely a human institution, a social contract, dissolvable at the will of the contracting parties" and in no sense a moral entity under God's sovereignty. Leading American Christians also attacked the concept of state sovereignty, a principle stemming from nineteenth-century German philosopher G. W. F. Hegel's philosophical pantheism. He assumed that ideas are immanent in reality and that the concept of the state is the highest idea of the relationship among human beings. In short, Christians rejected popular and state sovereignty because these philosophies renounced the Hebrew and Christian convictions both that government rests upon God's authority and that people must constantly test existing law by standards of eternal righteousness stemming from the nature and revelation of God.

After the Civil War, however, growing numbers of Americans accepted the notion that our government should be completely divorced from traditional religious ideals and principles. Some thought that increasing ethnic, religious, and ideological pluralism demanded such a government. Any other political arrangement would be unfair to unbelievers and would link church and state too closely together. Many came to regard government as beyond the concern of Christianity; religion and politics should not be mixed.

The question of how Christianity and government should relate is a difficult one. The Christian's ultimate allegiance is to Christ and His kingdom, which is first of all spiritual and not physical. Jesus does not encourage believers to create a separate political state, cut off from the rest of the world. Rather, Christians are to be light and salt in all the world's nations. Clearly, the Constantinian establishment, which fused church and state together and developed a cultural religion, has no support in the New Testament. Nor does Scripture teach Christians to withdraw from government and society as some Anabaptists have done. Instead, Christians are to be agents of God's advancing kingdom, which is penetrating the nations of the world. But in seeking first the kingdom and its righteousness, Christians are bound to affect the world in which they live. They are commanded to apply kingdom principles to all activities and to bring the world into subjection to God (Gen. 1:26-28; Matt. 25:14ff.).

The purposes of government as stated in Scripture and the existence of cultural pluralism in contemporary America raise important questions about the political process. How can Christians express their commitment to biblical ideals in the institutions, laws, and practices of society without infringing on the rights of other citizens who do not share the same religious convictions? In what ways and upon what foundation can Christians cooperate with citizens who belong to other religious faiths, and with secularists? Christians assert that nations are established to promote justice and morality. God instituted the state as well as the church to foster righteousness. To separate statecraft from the biblical ideals that should govern all human activity would rob the political order of its proper moral foundation.

While government policies should benefit all people and should not favor or discriminate against either Christians or non-Christians, the state is under God's authority and must be based upon some principles. All laws enshrine some moral convictions; the question is simply what moral values will underlie legislation. In making laws, legislators are obligated to see what the Bible teaches concerning each issue. The second table of the Ten Commandments, which deals with interpersonal relationships, provides guidelines for all legislation. Thus the Bible guides us in political affairs as well as in other matters. While the Old Testament does not superimpose its blueprint for the Hebrew theocracy on the pluralistic pattern of civil government, in the New Testament, God continues to judge nations and to command believers to promote justice and righteousness in public life.

In God's providence, the world is made up of a plurality of social spheres, institutions, and human interactions. Marriage and family, economics and work, social relationships, government, education, communications, and the church are all under God's authoritative norms and therefore should implement His will on earth. No one institution can properly dominate the others, as church and state have done at various times throughout history. While the state has the responsibility to regulate the relations among the various societal institutions so as to maintain order and harmony in society, it should not usurp the duties of the other spheres, as it often has done in modern times. Instead, the state should protect other institutions so that they can carry out their specific God-ordained functions. Denying that the state should be all-powerful, the Bible teaches that what sociologists Peter Berger and Richard Neuhaus call "mediating structures"—neighborhoods, families, churches, and voluntary associations—should intervene between private and public life. These intermediary institutions can curb the power of the state on the one hand and excessive individualism on the other.

Christian efforts once again to anchor American political life to a biblical foundation are only possible if we continue to defend the fundamental freedoms upon which our nation was established. The right of individual liberty is a cornerstone of the Declaration of Independence and is enshrined in the Bill of Rights. More than two hundred years of American history demonstrate that belief in individual freedom and responsibility promotes communal development. Christians must continually assert that freedom depends upon biblical presuppositions about God and humanity, not upon personal preference or utilitarian consequences. God is sovereign over all history and life, and human dignity and worth derive from being created in His image. These biblical truths compel us to recognize God's ultimate authority and the limited authority of all political rulers and all ideological systems. In the face of increased effort to regulate and regiment our life, we must continue to resist all efforts to abridge our liberty. And yet, liberty cannot become license. We are not simply free *from* various constraints and conventions (political, social, economic, and religious), but free *for* serving others and glorifying our Lord.

Conclusion

This chapter has examined the values that have shaped America's economic, educational, and political life. Because our public life rests upon the blending of several theological and philosophical traditions or world views—Judeo-Christian, Greco-Roman, Enlightenment humanism, and naturalistic materialism—a distinctively Christian public philosophy never developed in America. Sometimes these traditions have advocated the same values, based upon different presuppositions; at other times they have supported divergent principles and policies. On some issues American public life represents a compromise among these traditions, on others an amalgamation, and on still others a choice of one view over others. During the past one hundred years, however, conflict between Judeo-Christian ideals and relativistic, humanistic values has become more pronounced and intense, in many cases eroding biblical understandings of cultural activities and in some areas replacing them with secular ones. This causes some to rejoice but many others to lament the profound sense of the loss of the sacred, the deep feelings of the despair, disillusionment, and fragmentation, and the vast uncertainty about moral and social values that plague contemporary America. Some have even rekindled the old gospel fires, hoping that the Holy Spirit will again fan them into an awakening that will revitalize our nation.

From America's beginnings Christian and secular roots had been entwined and have grown together. For reasons described above, the secular roots have grown increasingly robust in the soil nurtured by Christianity so that today they threaten to choke the flowering of the gospel. Our task is to weed God's garden, preserving the good plants and fruit and discarding the bad. Such an assignment requires careful discernment.

America has never been, nor will it ever be, a Christian country. To claim that it is would be incorrect both theologically and historically. Our political system guarantees to all religions, including various kinds of secularized belief, the ability to influence public life. Accepting the pluralistic rules of the civic game provided by the Constitution, we should work to convince citizens to base their individual and corporate life upon biblical principles.

For Further Reading

Ahlstrom, Sydney. *A Religious History of the American People.* New Haven, Conn.: Yale University Press, 1971.

Brauer, Jerald C., Sidney E. Mead, and Robert Bellah. *Religion and the American Revolution.* Philadelphia: Fortress, 1976.

Brown, Harold O. J. *The Reconstruction of the Republic.* Milford, Mich.: Mott Media, 1981.

Cherry, Conrad, ed. *God's New Israel: Religious Interpretations of American Destiny.* Englewood Cliffs, N.J.: Prentice Hall, 1971.

Handy, Robert. *A Christian America: Protestant Hopes and Historical Realities.* New York: Oxford University Press, 1971.

Hatch, Nathan O. *The Sacred Cause of Liberty: Republican Thought and the Millennium in Revolutionary New England.* New Haven, Conn.: Yale University Press, 1977.

Hatch, Nathan O., and Mark A. Noll, eds. *The Bible in America. Essays in Cultural History.* New York: Oxford University Press, 1982.

Heimert, Alan E. *Religion and the American Mind: From the Great Awakening to the Revolution.* Cambridge: Harvard University Press, 1966.

Horwitz, Robert H., ed. *The Moral Foundations of the American Republic.* Charlotte, Va.: University Press of Virginia, 1982.

Linder, Robert D., and Richard V. Pierard. *Twilight of the Saints: Biblical Christianity and Civil Religion in America*. Downers Grove, Ill.: Inter-Varsity Press, 1978.

Marty, Martin. *Religion, Awakening and Revolution*. N.p.: A Consortium Book, 1977.

McLoughlin, William G. *Revivals, Awakenings and Reforms: An Essay on Religion and Social Change in America, 1607-1977*. Chicago: University of Chicago Press, 1978.

Mead, Sidney E. *Lively Experiment: The Shaping of Christianity in America*. New York: Harper and Row, 1963.

————. *The Nation With a Soul of a Church*. New York: Harper and Row, 1975.

Miller, William Lee. *The First Liberty. Religion and the American Republic*. New York: Alfred A. Knopf, 1986.

Noll, Mark A. *Christians in the American Revolution*. Grand Rapids: Eerdmans, 1977.

Noll, Mark A., Nathan O. Hatch, and George M. Marsden. *The Search for Christian America*. Westchester, Ill.: Crossway, 1983.

Novak, Michael. *The Spirit of Democratic Capitalism*. New York: Simon and Schuster, 1982.

Sider, Ronald. *Rich Christians in an Age of Hunger*. Downers Grove, Ill.: Inter-Varsity Press, 1977.

Smith, Gary Scott. *The Seeds of Secularization. Calvinism, Culture and Pluralism in America, 1870-1915*. Grand Rapids: Eerdmans, 1985.

Tuveson, Ernest Lee. *Redeemer Nation: The Idea of America's Millennial Role*. Chicago, Ill.: University of Chicago Press, 1980.

Weeks, Louis. *A New Christian Nation*. N.p.: A Consortium Book, 1977.

Wood, Gordon. *The Creation of the American Republic, 1776-1787*. Chapel Hill, N.C.: University of North Carolina Press, 1969.

10
Marxism: A Communist Society
Charles S. MacKenzie

Karl Marx and the Rise of the Modern Autonomous State
Throughout history, most societies have drawn inspiration from belief in some transcendent source of reality. Babylonians, Egyptians, Greeks, and Romans looked either to anthropomorphic deities or to overarching cosmic principles for guidance in structuring their societies and in conducting their lives. Ancient Israel and the Western Christendom during the Middle Ages sought to base social order on principles revealed by the God of the Bible, the Creator of the universe. By acknowledging a transcendent, external, uncontrollable, unpredictable power these societies expressed an openness to the unexpected. Societies in the East, most notably China, India, and Japan, have rested their common life upon principles inherent in the natural, spiritual order of the universe. None of these societies has considered the state to be either the ultimate reality or the creator of its own norms.

With the rise of Marxism in the nineteenth century, however, a new concept of the state and the basis of its authority emerged. Recognizing no transcendent reality and rejecting belief in anything nonmaterial, Marxism proposed a totally autonomous society, ruled by an autonomous state. According to Marx, the state has a life of its own; it is a law unto itself. The state is self-justifying, deriving its authority and sovereignty not from God or even from its citizens but from itself. An expression of the dialectic—an immanent, impersonal force that drives history—Marxist society is completely self-sufficient and closed to transcendent norms or influences. The coming Communist utopia will be a perfect classless society that needs no government. It will be ushered in by the autonomous dictatorial state, which then will wither away. Pure communism will have been brought about by an autonomous state, made up of autonomous people who will be the heart and soul of the autonomous Communist party. Karl Marx and his followers have offered the world the vision of a self-determined society freed of all transcendent, spiritual notions.

Karl Marx was born shortly after the French Revolution (1789) and during the early stages of the Industrial Revolution. Both developments produced large-scale social changes to which leaders in major social structures had difficulty adjusting. With millions of rural residents moving into cities, a massive shortage of housing, sanitation, schools, hospitals, and other social institutions resulted. In nineteenth-century Western Europe differences in lifestyle and income between the poor and the wealthy, workers and owners, were staggering. Into such a world, Karl Marx was born.

Marx grew up in European society when capitalism was the reigning economic philosophy. The product of many social, economic, and political forces, capitalism had become prominent in the seventeenth century. In the nineteenth century Europe was rapidly evolving from an agrarian to an urbanized society. Scientific curiosity and investigation had produced new manufacturing techniques. Calvinist and Puritan theology had exalted the value of work, of thrift, and of man's stewardship over God's creation. Capital was increasingly amassed; explorers and traders opened new markets; inventors continuously improved the manufacturing process; and new industries were created. Capitalism and industrialization dramatically changed the face of Western Europe.

Although the industrial revolution brought many benefits such as increased mobility and earnings to the masses, it also brought many problems. While many peasant farmers and wage laborers in the earlier agrarian culture had suffered greatly, the troubles of factory workers crowded together in urban centers were much more visible and notorious. Like many of their agrarian counterparts, who worked long hours each day to eke out a pitiful existence, industrial workers toiled seemingly endless days. A sixteen-hour work day was common, as many workers filed into the mills at six in the morning and trudged homeward at ten in the evening. Mill workers often lived in filth and despair. Many children as young as six worked long shifts in factories and mines and sometimes were subjected to whippings, sexual abuse, and other cruel treatment. As their problems became more and more visible, indignation and envy of the opulence of the rich began to build among the workers. Karl Marx hoped to channel this anger into a world-wide revolution.

The Life of Karl Marx

Karl Marx was born in Trier, Germany in 1818, the oldest son of a Jewish lawyer and the descendant of a line of Jewish rabbis. As a lad, he was fed an intellectual diet of Locke, Voltaire, and Diderot. He was raised as a Protestant after his Jewish father converted to Lutheranism largely for business reasons. He received his doctorate when he was twenty-three. While studying at the University of Berlin, Marx came under the influence of Georg Hegel and Ludwig Feuerbach, the leading thinkers of Germany in the mid-nineteenth century. Marx accepted key elements of both of their philosophies. When he was twenty-five, he left Berlin and went to Paris where he met Frederich Engels, an urbane, wealthy, aristocratic son of a textile manufacturer. Engels was to finance much of Marx's writing in the years that followed. The 1840s and 50s were turbulent times. Workers rioting in Paris suffered ten thousand casualties. In Berlin crowds stormed barricades. Mobs also roamed the streets in Vienna and Rome. While in Paris, Marx was influenced by French socialists, including Saint-Simon, Charles Fourier, and Louis Blanc whose writings described a utopian society where everyone owned everything in common.

After only a year in Paris, Marx was expelled from the city for participating in revolutionary activity. He spent the next five years in Brussels. Then in 1848, he and Engels issued *The Communist Manifesto*, a statement of socialist principles that sought to unite workers and inspire them to topple the existing order. The manifesto declared that Communist ends can be "attained only by the forcible overthrow of all existing social relations. Let the ruling classes tremble at the Communist revolution. The proletarians have nothing to lose but their chains. They have a world to win."

In 1849, at the age of thirty-one, Marx moved to London where he was to spend the rest of his life. There he spent his days from 10 a.m. to 7 p.m. studying and writing in the British Museum. He was deeply troubled by the extensive poverty all over Europe and by his own personal destitution. In a letter to Engels, Marx said:

> My wife is ill, little Jenny is ill, Lenchin has a sort of nervous fever and I can't call in the doctor because I have no money to pay him. For about eight or ten days we have all been living on bread or potatoes and it is now doubtful whether we shall be able to continue that. . . . During the past week or so I have borrowed a few shillings and even pence from workers. It was terrible but it was absolutely necessary or we should have starved.

His wife even had to beg money from a neighbor to buy a coffin to bury their dead child. Marx was trying to understand and explain why poverty, conflict, and desire for revolution were so prevalent in Europe. His answer appears in what is considered his major work, *Das Kapital*. While this book contains few new ideas, Marx arranged ideas he had borrowed from others in a forceful new synthesis. Disillusioned by squabbling among his followers, he died in London in 1883, declaring, "I am not a Marxist."

Marx's Teaching and Influence

What did Marx believe, and what do his hundreds of millions of followers believe today? Marx's philosophy is a comprehensive world view. Though he discerned all religion as invalid and harmful, he acknowledged that Christianity is the highest religion. In actuality, Marx sought to convert Christian doctrines, imagery, and hope for a better future into a new philosophy. Time replaced eternity. Matter replaced space. And his dialectic became the Redeemer. Because it proposes answers to life's basic questions about ultimate reality, humanity, knowledge, cosmology, society, and ethics, Marxism is a religious world view, even though its proponents consider religion to be the "opiate" of the people. Marxism's Bible is *Das Kapital*. Party members are the true believers. Its god is dialectical materialism. Its prophets, Marx and Lenin. All party members are to be missionaries of the new faith. The workers' revolution replaces Christ's second coming. And Marx's heaven is the classless society.

Marxism is thus a comprehensive world view resting upon certain central presuppositions. Marx rejected the biblical God, who created and sustains the universe. In the foreword to his doctoral dissertation, submitted to the University of Jena, Marx said, "I harbor hate against all the gods." And he rejected Jesus Christ as the life principle of the universe. What then did he consider ultimate?

While studying Hegel's philosophy at Berlin, Marx joined a group of young radical Hegelians there. Georg W. F. Hegel (1770-1831) was the most prominent German idealist in the modern period and was largely responsible for developing a philosophy of the autonomous state. Like Aristotle, Aquinas, and Kant before him, Hegel was a synthetic thinker. He attempted to construct a comprehensive system of philosophy composed of elements from preceding thinkers. He believed past philosophies were not so much alternatives from which people could pick and choose, as successive ideas in the development of the absolute, which he called spirit or mind. All of reality, whether it be nature, history, or thought, is the outworking of absolute spirit.[1] Hegel taught that the world of nature is all-important and that "God" or the absolute spirit-mind is the soul of nature. Hegel tended to identify God with human beings because people embody absolute spirit in a unique way. God is a spiritual ideal within nature. In fact, God is identical with nature. Nature can be known because its essence is the divine mind, which is in the process of unfolding from lower to higher degrees of perfection, by means of a dialectic (a process or dynamic pattern) moving from thesis to antithesis to synthesis (see below for more detail on Hegel's dialectic). History is the gradual self-realization of God in time. As a young man, Marx was impressed by Hegel's identification of God with nature, by his idea that reality is one, and by his view that history displays development in nature and in man's social, political, and economic thought. Marx borrowed from Hegel the notion that nature is all-encompassing, but his materialism led him to reject the idea that God is the inner being of nature.

Marx was also influenced by the German thinker Ludwig

---

1. Note that spirit for Hegel is not personal like the third person of the Christian Trinity. Spirit is more like Aristotle's unmoved mover. Unlike Aristotle's deity, however, Hegel's spirit is immanent and manifests itself in all things.

Feuerbach (see vol. 1 of *Building a Christian World View*, chap. 8, for our discussion of Feuerbach's ideas). Feuerbach, like Hegel, saw nature as pre-eminent. But for Feuerbach nature was totally and exclusively physical. Neither God nor anything spiritual existed. Accepting this view, Marx became a complete materialist, maintaining that everything is essentially matter, including nature, man, society, and human consciousness. Yet Marx did not attempt to specify a single form of matter as underlying all things. His followers see a wide diversity in the forms of matter and do not try to identify any one form as being essential matter.

Marx borrowed Hegel's idea of the dialectic and argued that the material world of nature is driven and moved by a principle of change woven into it. According to Hegel's dialectic *everything* is subject to a process of change described as a "passing into opposites." History is a dialectic process moving from one state (thesis) to its opposite (antithesis), which finally achieves a higher synthesis between the two. The synthesis then becomes a new thesis which is challenged by another antithesis as the dialectic process repeats itself again and again. This process of change underlies all reality and progressively brings about higher and higher stages of existence. Hegel considered the movement of reality into opposite states a necessary process whereby the divine spirit or ideal develops from lower to higher degrees of perfection.

According to Hegel, the rise and fall of civilizations displays the self-development of the absolute. The Greek, Roman, and medieval cultures emphasized individuals and their struggle for freedom (autonomy). Whereas Greek and Roman societies permitted slavery as one of its institutions, eventually under the influence of Christianity a limited human autonomy emerged. Individual autonomy, however, was not the ultimate ideal. Only in the Prussian military state has the absolute reached its climax. Since the German state developed after the family and civil society, the state is the highest expression of autonomy. Citizens view themselves not primarily as separate and autonomous individuals but as organic parts of a larger whole. The will of the state supercedes the will of individuals. Hegel made extraordinary claims for the state:

> The Universal [absolute] is to be found in the State. . . . The

State is the Divine Idea as it exists on earth. We must therefore worship the State as the manifestation of the Divine on earth and consider that if it is difficult to comprehend Nature, it is harder to grasp the Essence of the State. . . . the State is the march of God through the world.[2]

Marx used Hegel's dialectic to explain changes that take place in society. Most significantly, he contended that quantitative changes in the economic order produce qualitative changes in the structures of society. Thus he combined the materialism of Feuerbach with the dialectic of Hegel and created dialectical materialism.

Dialectical materialism took the place of God for Marxism. Lenin declared, "Atheism is a natural and inseparable portion of Marxism." Only physical nature exists. There is no soul, no spirit, no God, no afterlife—only nature. But nature contains a basic contradiction in its very essence. Within nature the dialectic moves reality relentlessly, absolutely, inexorably from one state to another. Marx asserted that the dialectic, not God, works immanently within the world and drives it toward its final destination. This necessary movement governs both nature and history. Nothing can stop it. As the inner being of the material order, the dialectic crushes everything in its path while moving toward its final goal of pure communism.

Dialectical materialism became Marx's primary interpretive principle for understanding the past and his blueprint for pursuing the future. He argued that the materialistic dialectic was moving history relentlessly through five stages. (1) In the primitive stage society was communal; people owned everything in common. Then the dialectic moved society progressively into (2) the slave stage, (3) the feudal stage, (4) the capitalist society, and finally and inevitably to (5) the socialist, or Communist stage. Marx was forced to

---

2. The quotations from Hegel were compiled by Karl Popper in *The Open Society and Its Enemies*, 4th ed., 2 vols. (Princeton: Princeton University Press, 1963), 2: 31 and are cited by Herbert Schlossberg, *Idols for Destruction* (Nashville: Thomas Nelson, 1983), p. 178. It is interesting to note Schlossberg's contention that few if any social theorists today would claim that "the state is God marching on earth." Nevertheless, Schlossberg continues, "at every turn we stumble over those who advocate actions that can be logical inferences only from such a position. For them the state is the only savior we can expect on earth" (Ibid.).

recognize, however, that retrogression or backward movement also occurs in history.

Marx emphasized that history is moving relentlessly and irresistibly from the capitalism of his day to communism. He defined capitalism as private individual or group ownership of the means of production (factories, tools, machinery) and distribution. The owners (capitalists) he called the bourgeoisie. Workers were the proletariat. During the nineteenth century, the bourgeoisie and the proletariat were locked in deadly combat for control of the means of production and distribution. However, the dialectic will eventually cause the proletariat to triumph.

Conflict usually is necessary, Marx said, to move history to a new stage. Therefore revolution is a positive good. V. I. Lenin, who led the 1917 revolution that introduced communism to Russia, added,

> The revolutionary dictatorship of the proletariat is violence against the bourgeoisie; and the necessity of such violence is particularly created, as Marx and Engles have repeatedly explained in detail, . . . by the existence of a military clique and a bureaucracy.

Many socialists have broken with Marx on this point. They believe that the change from capitalism to socialism can be brought about gradually without violence, through either legislation or the electoral process. Marx himself acknowledged that the change to communism might be accomplished in Britain and America without violence. But these countries would be exceptions to the general rule. Rejecting the biblical view that God creates and destroys empires, Marx declared that the dialectic, through revolutionary conflict, moves all history. The impersonal, materialistic dialectic will redeem humanity and perfect society.

Marx also taught that three "laws" govern the movement of dialectical materialism.

1. The first is "the law of the unity and struggle of opposites." Marx saw an inherent contradiction in all matter. Just as there are positive and negative charges of electricity, so there are opposing classes—the bourgeoisie and the proletariat—in society. Because of the contradictions within it, the universe is constantly being forced to progress toward a higher stage of

development. Thesis clashes with antithesis, compelling history to develop a new synthesis. Marx developed this law by applying Darwin's evolutionary theory to the social dimension of history.

2. The second law at work within dialectical materialism is "the law of negation." Matter is internally programmed to progress toward its opposite; thesis *must* move to its antithesis.

3. The third law of dialectical materialism is "the law of the sudden leap." Mao Tse-tung, leader of Red China from 1949 to 1976, used this phrase to describe China's great leap forward in the 1960s. This law teaches that a series of gradual, quantitative changes will be followed by a sudden qualitative advance, which will produce new social forms. This law parallels Darwin's belief that inanimate objects went through a series of quantitative changes and then by a sudden leap became living organisms. Similarly, organic life, Darwin contended, went through long eras of quantitative change and then periodically evolved upward by sudden leaps.

Marx believed that socialism represented the culmination of history. He acknowledged that in its early stages socialism necessarily would retain some vestiges of the capitalist past. Early socialist societies such as Russia might not be totally egalitarian. The needs of these societies might require that some have more power and privilege than others. But as the dialectic moved socialism forward, Marx argued, a completely egalitarian, totally classless society would eventually emerge as social forces and interests came into balance and equilibrium. Marx maintained that the development of a classless, egalitarian, socialist society would require a strong, centralized government.

Borrowing from the ancient Greeks, he believed that the state would achieve a pure, classless society by giving every person his due. He admitted that people would have to sacrifice their individual freedoms so that an authoritative state could create material and economic equality within society. The dialectic must produce the dictatorship of the proletariat before it could produce pure communism. But Marx hoped that as the state enforced equality, people would enjoy a new kind of corporate social freedom. Eventually the state would disappear as society grew accustomed to an egalitarian, classless society. In the final state—pure communism—equality and freedom, which had been enemies throughout history, would finally be reconciled. Neither Marx nor his followers, however, have ever been able to explain why the dialectical process ends when pure communism is achieved. What causes the dialectic to end? Why do things cease movement toward their opposites?

In the state of pure socialism, existing social structures will be radically transformed. All the means of production (factories, mills, laboratories, etc.) will be owned first by the state and then by the people collectively after the state disappears. Churches will be abolished. The state will totally control all education and all family life. Marriages will be arranged in order to produce the finest offspring. Marx predicted in the *Communist Manifesto* that "the bourgeois family will vanish as a matter of course . . . with the vanishing of capital."

Marx's understanding of history and society is related to his view of man. To Marx, human beings are not a special creation of God, made only a little lower than angels. People have no soul, no spirit; they are completely material. When they die they return to the ground from which they were made. Viewing man as a totally material, biological entity is one of the greatest weaknesses of Marxist philosophy, for Marxists cannot explain man's capacity and desire for self-transcendence. Moreover, the Marxist anthropology emphasizes the individual's subordination to the collective mass. Persons have value only as they contribute to the work of the Communist party. Marx argued that the dialectic changes human nature as it pushes history toward pure communism and that economic and social structures alienate man from himself in several ways. Religion oppresses people by subjecting them to the powers of others (i.e., clergy) and focusing their attention on another, fictitious world. Workers who don't share in the profits of an industry are alienated from the fruits of their labor by their oppressive employers. Competition for private property sets man against man and prevents cooperation and social solidarity. Eliminating religion and private property would remove the sources of man's alienation from himself and from his fellows. New social structures would enable people to realize and become reconciled with their own inner nature. Moreover, as pure socialist societies emerged, they would create a new type of person who would not be greedy or envious or warlike. Pure socialism, Marx insisted, would produce a new humanity.

Marx's epistemology follows directly from his materialism. Since human beings are totally material, thought is merely an electrochemical function taking place in the cerebral cortex, a physical by-product of the evolutionary process. Human thoughts are particularly influenced by the materialistic, economic order and flow of history. The economic order, especially the ownership and distribution of property and the structure of work in factories, mills, and mines, determines the content and direction of human thought.

Ideas and philosophies are superstructures that emerge from economic substructures. The ways in which people relate to each other as they produce and consume goods in the economic scheme shape the way they think and the ideas they hold. Consequently, ideas change as new material orders develop. For example, in a primitive society the economic system is based upon barter, by which people exchange possessions. In such a system the idea develops that people can offer God sacrifices in order to receive blessings. During feudal times when nobles had great wealth and power, God was pictured as an exalted, mighty, possessive sovereign. According to Marx, the slave, feudal, and capitalist economic systems led to the exploitation of the workers. Believing that the economic system affects and determines people's ideas, Marx sought to create a new economic order in which the state would own the means of production, thus changing the way people think and producing a new kind of human being.

Marx believed that in his day the dialectic was just beginning the revolutionary change from capitalism to socialism. The shift would come gradually through conflict or revolution, or both, first producing state socialism (sometimes called "state capitalism") similar to that of the Soviet Union today. Pure communism would emerge eventually from state socialism. One hundred years after Marx's death no society has yet achieved pure communism. Socialist countries have simply exchanged ownership of capitalists for that of party leaders who live as luxuriously and rule more absolutely than capitalists ever did. The classes exist; the classless society remains a dream of the distant future.

The Advance of Marxism

In one century these essential ideas of Marxism have become dogma to nearly half the world's people. In at least that respect Marxism has changed the course of history.

The translation of Marxist theory into practice gained momentum in the twentieth century. As the century began, the Social Democratic Labor Party, committed to Marxist philosophy, was organized in Russia. At its conference in Brussels, Belgium in 1903, Vladimir Ilyich Lenin declared that the party should be organized along military lines, employing firm discipline and demanding strict obedience. Denouncing Lenin's plan as too extreme, L. Martov argued for a more casual, loosely knit party organization. Lenin's position triumphed. His followers came to be known as "Bolsheviks" (related to the Russian word for majority), and the followers of Martov came to be known as "Mensheviks" (similar to the Russian word for minority). Consequently, communism came to be based upon a tightly knit, highly disciplined party.

The Communist party devised by Lenin sought to preside over the dialectical development from capitalism to communism. The proletariat (workers), though in sympathy with communism, rarely have been experts in Marxist thought and theory. Therefore, they were not (and are not) equipped to direct the socialist revolution. In changing society from capitalism to communism, a Marxist government cannot function as a representative democracy. Instead, a few leaders of the Communist party who have an in-depth understanding of Marxist thought must run the government. The leaders of the proletariat who control the party apparatus will rule over society through the party.

Consequently, Lenin maintained that the people could not be trusted to have a voice in their government since they are not skilled in Marxist theory. Party leaders must make all important decisions, whether or not the proletariat agrees. Communists call this form of government democratic centralism because the party supposedly knows the true interests of the people better than the people do themselves, and it therefore rules for their good. No wonder the Communist party has long been the center of power in Marxist societies.

At the time of Lenin's death, Josef Stalin expressed the following conviction about the party's role: "There is nothing greater than the title of member of the Party whose founder and leader was Comrade Lenin. . . . Comrade Lenin adjured us to hold high and guard the great title of member of the party." Similarly, the president of Communist China, Lio Shao-Chi, has declared:

> Whether or not a Communist Party member can absolutely and unconditionally subordinate his personal interests to the Party's interests under all circumstances is the criterion with which to extend his loyalty to the party. . . . To sacrifice one's personal interests and even one's life without the slightest hesitation and even with a feeling of happiness . . . is the highest manifestation of Communist ethics.

The party, at grassroots level, is made up of local units or cells organized in a neighborhood, a factory, or a school. Each local group elects a representative to a district council, whose decisions are binding on all members of the local units. Similarly, district councils elect representatives to ascending levels of higher committees, which are all subordinate to the Central Committee. The Central Committee elects a small core known as the Presidium or Politburo. This group is the ultimate authority. Its decisions, including the promotion or removal of members of lower councils and units, must be followed by all members of the party at all levels.

The party is the backbone of Communist society, with power concentrated at the top. The leaders of the party, from Lenin to Gorbachev, have had great power only as long as they have maintained the backing of the Presidium, which in turn controls the power of the party.

Lenin introduced Marxism into Russia. In February 1917, a non-Marxist revolution had deposed the Russian Czar. After a cruel reign of revolutionary terror by a weak democratic government, Lenin and his Communist followers seized control of Russia late in 1917. He gained power by promising to give poor peasants the land owned by the rich. Yet he did not deliver on this promise. Instead of taking land from the rich and dispensing it to the peasants, he usurped all property, even the peasants' harvest, which he gave to the state. No wonder his close ally, Leon Trotsky, complained that Lenin exploited the worst elements of the proletariat. Lenin developed a zealous group of Marxist revolutionaries who transferred farms and factories to state ownership. While Marx was the philosopher-architect of communism, Lenin was the ruthless engineer-builder who translated Marxist theories into reality.

When Lenin died in 1924 after seven years of autocratic rule, his comrade, Josef Stalin, took the reins of power. Stalin was not a theoretician but rather a ruthless dictator who forcefully continued to implement Marxist-Leninist ideas. He usurped the lands of millions of farmers. During the next two decades he forced twenty million people into slave labor battalions, and he imprisoned fourteen million citizens. As he did, he lauded the glories of the socialist state.

Another Marxist who attempted to translate Karl Marx's theories into practice was Mao Tse-tung. In 1949, Mao captured all of the Chinese mainland after an estimated fifty million people died during the revolution he led against Chiang Kai-shek. For twenty-five years Mao reorganized Chinese society in accordance with Marxist blueprints and forced millions of Chinese peasants to submit.

However, in recent times the Chinese have been liberated from the strict Marxism of Mao Tse-tung. Under the leadership of Deng Xiaoping, China's communism began to mix Marxist and capitalist ideas. Hu Yao-bang, the General Secretary of the Chinese Communist Party, asked a question on the minds of many Chinese when he said, "Since the October Revolution [of 1917 in Russia], more than 60 years have passed. How is it that many socialist countries have not been able to overtake capitalist ones in terms of development? What was it that did not work?" It was apparent to Deng and others that the working conditions and lifestyles of average Chinese workers had improved little in the years of Mao's reign (1949-76). Consequently, Deng changed course. His example has led others, even the Soviets, to experiment with some capitalist ideas. This new direction, however, should not be misunderstood. The Chinese commitment to Marxism remains staunch. Contemporary experiments with capitalist ideas are simply temporary means employed to achieve the final end—socialism. New York University Professor Bertell Ollman, a dedicated Marxist, has pointed out that "Marx had very little to say of a concrete nature about socialism," the transitional society that precedes the ultimate and final goal of an ideal, stateless, classless society. Since Marx said so little about the transitional socialistic period between capitalism and the ideal, Communist society, Marxist leaders are free to experiment with different structures as they seek to develop various temporary socialistic models for society. The Soviet Union followed Lenin's scheme for the intermediate society—the dictatorship of the proletariat. At present China seems to be opting for a mixture of Marxist and capitalist ideas. In both countries the Communist party is unchallenged. The commitment to the ultimate goal of Marxism remains firm. Therefore, simply because some Marxist nations may temporarily alter course does not mean that they have renounced Marxism. Until they do, free nations should remain alert to the dangers inherent in the Marxist ideology.

While some nations (i.e., the Soviet Union, China, and Eastern European countries) have accepted Marxism as a whole and have structured their societies accordingly, in many parts of the world, Marxist teaching has been accepted only in part. Such nations as Britain in the 1970s and Sweden have accepted in part or in whole the principle that the means of production should be state owned. But they have not completely embraced the total Marxist atheistic world view. They have accepted Marx's diagnosis of capitalism's inadequacies and consequently have transferred many industries to state ownership. But they reject Marx's anthropology, epistemology, and understanding of history.

Marx's Accomplishments

Among the accomplishments of Karl Marx are the following. He reminded nineteenth-century Christians (and us today as well) that economic conditions and people's physical needs are important. The church must preach salvation through Christ and aid the undernourished, overworked, and powerless in their struggle to improve their living and working conditions.

Second, Marx inspired an international workers' movement that adopted most of his teachings. In 1848 he helped to establish the Communist League of workers. In 1864 he participated in the founding of the First International Workingman's Association, which existed for ten years and spawned the second and third Internationals. The Soviet Union, China, and Eastern Europe have all accepted Marxism. Many nations in Western Europe, the Orient, Latin America, and Africa are embracing Marxism in whole or in part. Even in America there are considerable pressures to have the state take over the means of production. This international movement emerged from the diligent labors of Karl Marx.

Moreover, Marx stirred hope in the minds of millions of poor and powerless people. Marxism's greatest appeal has been to poor people in underdeveloped countries, even more than to the poor in industrialized nations. Those in underdeveloped nations generally see little hope for social improvement except through Marxist revolution. The poor in industrialized countries, by contrast, usually have other alternatives such as unions and government programs. Marxism's greatest growth in the future, therefore, seems likely to be among Third World peasants who hope that the dialectic will eventually bring them equality in the classless society of the future.

In addition, Marx's attack on capitalism forced owners and managers to analyze the nature and results of capitalism. It prodded capitalists to recognize and correct the weaknesses of their system. His writings particularly challenged capitalistic societies to make their economic system serve the welfare of all citizens. Faced with the criticisms of Marx and growing unrest among workers, capitalist nations sought ways to serve rather than to *rule* their people. Many capitalists became more committed to the Christian teaching on stewardship—that everything belongs to God and that we are accountable to God for how we use our possessions. Consequently, at their best capitalists sought to take proper care of the environment and the earth's resources, to treat workers and customers humanely, to produce useful and well-made products, to invest their profits wisely, and to give large sums to charities, such as hospitals, schools, and churches. For example, at one point in its history the Ford Motor Company gave 90 percent of its earnings to philanthropy.

The Weaknesses of Marxism

There are many weaknesses in Marx's thought, but the following stand out prominently.

His definitions of value are faulty. He defined the value of a product as the amount of labor required to produce it. The value of a shoe was the number of man-hours of labor involved in making it. He did not recognize that the value of the factory, of the tools and equipment necessary to manufacture the shoe, and the entrepreneurial and management skills of the capitalist must all be calculated in figuring the value of the shoe.

Marx defined the value of the worker as the wage he needs to exist, but he failed to devise an adequate formula for determining how much a subsistence wage is. For one person today it might mean $50 a week, for another $100 a week, for still another $200 a week. The wage one needs to live varies from person to person and from society to society. Yet Marx argued that one wage alone can supply everyone's needs. He ignored differences in ability, intelligence, competence, and need among workers.

Furthermore, he defined the profit of the capitalist as surplus value, which is everything over and above the cost of making or manufacturing an item. If it costs $25 to manufacture a shoe and the manufacturer sells the shoe for $30, there is $5 surplus value or profit. Is this surplus value justified? Is the businessman entitled to make a profit for the risk, investment in tools and factory, planning, and work he puts into his business? Is he entitled to reap a profit that he can put back into his business so that it can grow and prosper? Marx answered these questions negatively. Under his socialist scheme, the state takes all profit and distributes it as leaders see fit. All of Marx's definitions of value are questionable. Based upon materialism, they ignore human values.

Marx's understanding of the dialectic is even more problematic. His argument that the dialectic (thesis, antithesis, synthesis) has been moving relentlessly throughout all of history and will continue to move toward pure communism, the classless and stateless society of the future, ignores the retrogression that frequently occurs in history. He also failed to see that the negation of a thesis does not always lead to one single antithesis. More often it produces several possible antitheses from which society may choose to follow one or several concurrently. If one of these possible antitheses becomes dominant, then several possible syntheses usually emerge. But Marx seemed oblivious of these facts. He developed a rigidly determined dialectic that does not accord with the facts of history because it neglects the complex alternatives that are part of social history.

Still another glaring problem of Marxist philosophy is the inconsistency of its materialism. Marx's materialism focuses on a dialectic he identified with the development of economic structures in history. His obsession with class struggles led him to argue that the materialistic dialectic focuses on economic history, while he practically ignored the vast realm of nature. He did not adopt a consistent materialism, which emphasizes scientific verification and the actual processes of nature. Instead, he continued Hegel's mistake of fitting nature into a dialectic of culture and philosophy. In reality, nature and matter are subordinated to the dialectic. Consequently, Marx failed to address the philosophical problems arising out of scientists' study of the material world. He did not develop the consequences of his own materialistic assumptions because he myopically applied the dialectic only to economic history and not to the larger realm of nature. His materialism was not truly scientific because he blindly followed Hegel and Kant in saying that material objects must conform to the ideas and laws of the knowing mind. So the dialectic's development of culture in general and of economics in particular became all-important for Marx as he used the idea of the dialectic to explain all production relationships and as he reduced the empirical facts of material nature to merely incidental examples of the dialectical process. By so doing, he failed to develop an adequate foundation for modern science.

Yet another basic weakness of Marxism is its anthropology. Are human beings on the same level as animals? Is all reality simply material? Marx's anthropology especially fails to explain man's awareness of self-transcendence. People have consciences, aspirations, hopes, and feelings that are not explicable simply in terms of matter. Herbert Marcuse, a leading American Marxist theoretician, admitted that this shortcoming is Marx's Achilles' heel. Marxism cannot account for man's conscience, will power, creative impulses, prayers, worship, and ability to make decisions.

Similarly, Marx's analysis of history assumes that individuals and their societies can be analyzed in the same fashion as are the material objects of science. Treating human beings, the central actors in history, as no higher than animals led Marx to a deficient analysis of history itself. He maintained that history is driven by forces that people have no power to alter or redirect.

Marx's anthropology contains another glaring weakness. His teaching that man's self-alienation can be overcome by simply rearranging social and economic structures ignores the depth and true source of man's inner alienation. Changing people's external environment will not radically and permanently transform their inner drives and inherited characteristics. Man's self-alienation cannot be overcome simply by altering social structures. A higher, transcendent power is needed to make man whole because his alienation from his true self springs from his separation from his Creator. Man's separation from God results from his sinful rebellion against divine authority.

Marx's epistemology is also deficient. He argued that all ideas arise in response to and reflect the material order. However, his fundamental belief that history has a predetermined goal (the classless society) has no relation to the existing material order. The economic conditions of the nineteenth century logically could not have given rise to the idea of a classless society. Moreover, Marx's epistemology cannot account for the rise of the many erroneous ideas that have no basis in material reality.

Marxists also falsely reason that equality and freedom can eventually be reconciled in a classless society. A society where all people are completely equal would in fact be a slave society because it would disregard human nature and human differences. Free people who possess unequal talents, strengths, and weaknesses will inevitably have different levels of achievement. Freedom and total equality are enemies. Marxism's goal of complete equality inevitably destroys freedom (cf. the Soviet Union, Poland, Romania). Attempts to achieve an equality of possessions and power are invariably coercive as the state confiscates all the means of production and distribution and creates a huge bureaucracy to take over the role of the capitalists. Such a bureaucracy is necessary to enforce equality. Yet government coercion destroys freedom. Marx himself declared in *The Manifesto* that the Communist revolution aimed to abolish "bourgeois individuality, bourgeois independence and bourgeois freedom." In addition, the utopian notion of complete equality in a classless society defies the realities of human nature and experience. People with different levels of natural abilities will inevitably seek to fulfill their differing potentialities and hence will have different amounts of productivity and accomplishments. Human nature revolts against a classless society where all are compelled to adjust their goals and achievements to a common standard mandated by the state.

Moreover, in critiquing capitalism, Marx attacked a straw man, something that had never existed—pure unbridled, uncontrolled capitalism. "Pure" capitalism would have no checks or restraints upon it whatsoever, such as labor unions, churches, regulatory agencies, or even the restraint of the consciences of the capitalists.

Another shortcoming of Marx's thought is that his view of history is too simplistic. All history is not "the history of class struggle"; much of human history displays human cooperation and unity.

Marx also failed to recognize that a free society provides the flexibility that allows capitalism to adjust to meet the changed needs and the demands of society. Capitalism has frequently adapted to new situations. Such adaptations include the following:

1. Profit sharing plans whereby millions of workers share in the ownership of their companies.

2. Fringe benefits such as health insurance and pension plans, which give workers a share in a company's profits.

3. Philanthropy whereby businesses give away billions of dollars in profits to hospitals, colleges, art galleries, and other private nonprofit organizations.

4. The ownership of corporations, which in most cases, has passed from a few wealthy individuals to thousands of stockholders.

Karl Marx did not anticipate capitalism's dynamism and flexibility, which has allowed it to adjust and meet the needs of workers and society. So his analysis of capitalism's flaws and his prediction of its collapse have proved wrong, at least in free societies like the United States. If capitalism loses its freedom to adapt, if government takes over the regulation and virtual ownership of industry, however, then capitalism will no longer be able to adapt, and it may vanish as Marx predicted.

Such deficiencies in Marxism have been noted by scholars of many different world views. Those who accept the Judeo-Christian perspective point to additional problems with Marxist beliefs and practices.

First, they disagree with Marx's rejection of God and his exaltation of the materialistic dialectic as the ultimate. Such an exchange of ultimates fulfills Paul's diagnosis: "They exchanged the truth about God for a lie and worshiped and served the creature rather than the Creator" (Rom. 1:25, RSV).

Second, Christians argue that human beings are much more than the highest form of animal life, whose primary purpose is to advance communism. They insist instead that man is the crown jewel of creation, created in the image of God to glorify Him forever.

Third, Christians do not agree that all knowledge is derived from nature by man's autonomous scientific reasoning. God enables humans to know through their use of their senses, intellect, and faith.

Fourth, Marxism's collective ownership of property is to Christians unbiblical. Scripture affirms the right of individuals to own property: "Beware that thou forget not the Lord thy God. . . . it is he that giveth thee power to get wealth" (Deut. 8:11, 18, KJV). The Bible also teaches that people have the right to dispose of their property and the responsibility to use it wisely. The stewardship to which people are called by God presupposes that God gives them the right to possess and to share the fruits of their labor. By shifting the ownership of property from individuals to the state, Marxism destroys the possibility of stewardship. Marxism's forced redistribution of property violates the commandment "Thou shalt not steal" (Exod. 20:15, KJV).

Of course, people may voluntarily participate in a community wherein possessions are shared. Some in the early church in Jerusalem decided to pool their possessions. Some Anabaptists in the Reformation period and some today, as well as the Diggers in the time of Cromwell, also have voluntarily forsaken their right to own property. But ownership of property was indeed their right.

Fifth, Marxism destroys love in society. Its proponents advocate the use of violence toward capitalists and dissenters. Marxists authorize the impersonal state to use compulsion and coercion in its relations with people. Coercion is the enemy of love. The collective is exalted over the individual who can be used and even sacrificed for the well-being of society. Moreover, communism encourages the proletariat to envy those with material prosperity and to covet their goods. This philosophy of rebellion and protest demands the overturning of the material inequalities produced by unequal natural ability, intelligence, and ambition among people. Consequently, Marxism produces strife and alienation rather than love among people.

Sixth, Marxist philosophy absolutizes equality and ignores other biblical values such as love, freedom, and justice. When any of these virtues is subordinated to the ideal of material equality in a classless society, that virtue is destroyed because such equality can only be achieved by force and coercion in the hands of an all-powerful state. But when the biblical ideals of love, freedom, individual responsibility, and justice are given priority, moral equality results. As imperfectly demonstrated in American society, moral and spiritual equality increase the opportunities for the poor to improve significantly their standard of living. Economic freedom, guided by love and justice, has helped to bridge the gap between rich and poor. Today the vast majority of Americans have adequate food, shelter, and clothing.

Seventh, Marxism dehumanizes people. In societies where it is dominant, coercion and forced equality and inadequate incentives have caused many to lose their ambition, creativity, and love for others.

Eighth, Marxism ironically is not radical enough. Its goal of equality in a classless society is inadequate. The biblical ethic commands God's people to treat others not simply as equals but as *better* than themselves: "In humility count others better than yourselves" (Phil. 2:3, RSV). God's people are called to share with and work to improve the life of the underprivileged and the less fortunate.

Ninth, Marxism encourages dishonesty and alienation. In actual practice, forced equality of income leads people to use personal influence, bribery, and the black market to secure privileges they cannot afford. In socialist societies many citizens use these techniques to gain better apartments, automobiles, and educational opportunities. Two leading egalitarian economists, Assar Lindbeck and Gunnar Myrdal, have complained that the erosion of honesty is one of contemporary Sweden's most pressing problems.

According to professor Michael Voslensky of Moscow's Academy of Science, the *nomenklatura*, a group of Soviet bureaucrats who have special, elite privileges, has 750,000 members. Their governmental positions entitle them to nicer apartments; resort homes in the country; the use of better hospitals, schools, stores, and hairdressers; and even burial in special cemeteries when they die. Others obtain similar benefits through the black market and bribery, which are widespread in the Soviet Union. The Marxist attempt to create a classless society simply does not work because when people cannot gain what they want by their labor, many of them lose the incentive to do their work well and turn to dishonest means to fulfill their wants.

In summary, the Marxist world view is totally naturalistic. Marx's "one-dimensional" perspective on life repudiates the supernatural and considers man to be a part of nature, controlled by natural forces. Marxism is self-contradictory at this point. How can man experience, use, and organize nature while being nothing more than a part of nature? Does not his capability to subdue and direct nature imply that man is above nature? The idea that dialectical materialism moves history toward communism is another contradiction inherent in naturalistic Marxism. On the one hand, Marx argues that nature is completely materialistic (and hence impersonal); yet, on the other hand, he affirms a "purpose," a "direction" implicit in nature. How can nature be both totally materialistic and purposeful?

Marx insisted that society is self-perfectible. The perfect society (communism) is not merely possible, it is certain to appear in time and space as dialectical materialism reaches its final synthesis sometime in the future. But Marx's system ignores overwhelming evidence of people's natural selfishness and greed. Under capitalism these are kept in check both by the competition of the free market and by the restraints of church and state. Marx's argument that a Communist society would produce a "new man" totally unmotivated by desire for property, power, or prestige has been proved false. Contemporary Marxist societies manifest a wealthy class of Communist bureaucrats, who, by their greed, contradict and undermine Marx's communistic ideal.

Frenchman Andre Gide, a former Marxist, confessed that he was disillusioned after visiting the Soviet Union because the trip convinced him that Marxism does not work. He explained:

> The Soviet Union has deceived our fondest hopes and shown us tragically in what treacherous quicksand an honest revolution can founder. The same old capitalist society has been reestablished (with the party elite instead of capitalists at the top), a new and terrible despotism has been created, crushing and exploiting man, with all the abject and servile mentality of serfdom.

Marxism cannot deliver on its promises to create a classless society.

Conclusion

Will Marxism succeed in conquering the world? Soviet dissident and refugee Alexander Solzhenitsyn, who suffered terribly in that nation's concentration camps, offers some astute observations to the Soviet leaders, which contain three warnings:

1. He warns of war between Red China and the Soviet Union, a war that could kill hundreds of millions of people.

2. He warns that Soviet technology, based solely on materialistic presuppositions, could destroy the natural environment. Human and spiritual values are needed if man is to preserve the ecosystem in which he lives.

3. But most importantly he warns the Soviet leaders that the Marxist determination to conquer the world, to force the socialist ideal of state ownership of the means of production on all people, is dangerous. Marxist intentions to conquer the world, he argues, threaten the survival of freedom everywhere.

Solzhenitsyn's basic appeal to Soviet leaders is for freedom:

> Allow competition on an equal and honorable basis—not for power, but for truth—I myself see Christianity today as the only living spiritual force capable of undertaking the spiritual healing of Russia. . . . Allow us a free art and literature, the free publication of books . . . allow us philosophical, ethical, economic and social studies.

But the Soviet leaders are afraid to heed his advice. They know well that freedom is indivisible. If, for example, a society loses economic or business freedom, soon political and religious freedom will vanish. Or if it loses religious freedom, soon it will lose political and economic freedom. Destroy any facet of freedom and eventually you will destroy all freedom. By the same token, grant people one dimension of freedom, and soon they will want freedom in other dimensions. And so the Soviet leaders realize that if they grant religious or literary freedom, soon they will be forced to allow all other freedoms, because freedom is indivisible.

Yet some Marxists say that the Soviet people *are* free. They point to the Soviet Constitution, which guarantees citizens freedom of work, rest, education, speech, press, assembly, and religious worship. The Soviet Constitution, however, clearly states that such freedoms must be earned and are given only by the government. Freedom is not an individual right as in America, either divinely given or inherent in human nature. Rather, it is a reward for loyalty to Marxist ideals, a means to an end in Communist thought. Quoting Engels, Lenin said on this point, "The proletariat . . . does not use [its power] in the interests of freedom but in order to hold down its adversaries."

The Soviet Constitution further limits freedom in Article 131, where it declares that people who attack socialist doctrines "shall be regarded as enemies of the people." To criticize the Communist system is to be branded an enemy of the people. Many courageous individuals like Solzhenitsyn and Sakharov have been imprisoned or exiled for condemning the tactics of the Communist party. Soviet citizens are free only to speak or write about the glories of communism.

Marxist thought and many of its practices are antithetical to freedom. In Marxist societies individuals and their associations are not allowed free expression, particularly if they are critical of communism. In Poland, free labor unions such as Solidarity are forbidden. In the Soviet Union, the church and other religious organizations are not allowed either to spread their teachings openly or to challenge the principles or practices of Soviet society.

As mentioned in chapter 9, some have argued that God has ordained free, voluntary associations or "mediating structures" such as schools, churches, service agencies, labor unions to intercede between individuals, and the megastructures of society. These associations can protect the freedoms and rights of people and prevent their dehumanization by providing opportunities for people to worship, learn, organize their labor, and carry on other meaningful activities, which enrich both the individuals involved and the society as a whole. Such free associations are forbidden in Marxist societies, however, unless they are totally subservient to Communist leadership and committed to Marxist ideals. The autonomous society inevitably becomes the controlled or totalitarian society.

Nevertheless, people crave freedom. But freedom is impossible without transcendence. It is impossible in a state that claims to be completely autonomous and that suppresses individuals or groups that challenge its autonomy and the controls it inevitably must use. God has implanted an unquenchable desire for freedom within people, which cannot be thwarted forever. Therefore Marxism cannot succeed. It is blind to man's true nature because it has rejected the transcendent Lord. As an angry young man Karl Marx wrote:

"Then I will wander godlike and victorious through the ruins of the world. And giving my words an active force, I will feel equal to the creator." For many in the twentieth century Marx's thought has taken on godlike significance. The autonomous man (Marx) has created an autonomous society.

The tides of history ebb and flow. Until recently the tide of Marxism was rising rapidly. In recent years, however, Marxism has been receding as a host of people have sought freedom in Poland, China, Czechoslovakia, Yugoslavia, and other parts of the Communist world. It is imperative that lovers of freedom everywhere understand the strengths and weaknesses of Marxism, for the tide could turn again at any time. The challenge of Marxist thought and of the autonomous, closed society it has spawned will be with us for many years to come. As Engels, speaking at Marx's funeral in 1883, put it: "His name will endure through the ages, and so also will his work."

For Further Reading

Berlin, Isaiah. *Karl Marx: His Life and Environment.* London: Oxford University Press, 1959.

Cornforth, Maurice. *Introduction to Dialectical Materialism*, vol. 1, New York: International Publisher, 1953.

Hook, Sidney. *From Hegel to Marx.* Ann Arbor: University of Michigan Press, 1978.

_____ . *Towards the Understanding of Karl Marx.* John Day, 1933.

Lichtheim, George. *Marxism: An Historical and Critical Study.* New York: Frederick A. Praeger, 1961.

Lyon, David. *Karl Marx: A Christian Assessment of His Life and Thought.* Downers Grove, Ill.: Inter-Varsity Press, 1979.

Marx, Karl. *Capital*, vol. 1, Chicago: Charles H. Kerr and Company, 1919.

Marx, Karl and Friedrich Engels. *The Communist Manifesto.* Harmondsworth, England: Penguin, 1967.

McLellan, David. *Karl Marx: His Life and Thought.* New York: Harper and Row, 1973.

320 Marxism: A Communist Society

Sowell, Thomas, *Marxism: Philosophy and Economics*. New York: William Morrow and Company, 1985.

Tucker, Robert C. *Philosophy and Myth in Karl Marx*. Cambridge: University Press, 1961.

11
Dystopianism: Society Destroyed

W. Andrew Hoffecker

Introduction

This chapter concludes our historical survey of various views of society that have dominated Western thought. Terminating our study of society on a negative note marks a sharp contrast to the opening chapter in this section. We began with Plato's ideal—what many call his utopian dream. We conclude with dystopianism's horrendous nightmare. In this analysis of dystopianism, we shall see its exponents insightfully critique contemporary views of society, especially their underlying anthropological presuppositions. Interest in dystopianism as a novelistic genre flourishes in contemporary literature and in social science classes on college campuses. Works such as Aldous Huxley's *Brave New World* and George Orwell's *Nineteen Eighty-Four* are widely studied and considered classics in the brief history of dystopian literature. While many critics hail them as prescient of what society might become, few have analyzed dystopianism as occupying a critical position in the spectrum of world views. Dystopians criticize contemporary utopian writers for replacing major premises from world views we have studied throughout the history of ideas with their so-called "modern views."

Dystopian authors are far more than doomsday prophets, however. They warn that society might become a terrible place not so much from default or the absence of social planning, but from the success of societal plans that rest on false views of humanity. If utopian designs are actually implemented, dystopians argue, they will dehumanize people. One early and influential dystopian argument is Aldous Huxley's *Brave New World* (1932).[1] We will interpret *Brave New World* (1) as an explicit polemic against the behaviorism advocated by Johns Hopkins psychologist J. B. Watson and (2) as an implicit call for a return to more traditional philosophical premises regarding human nature, which have been pivotal in the development of Western culture until the modern period. Huxley's satirical presentation of a society resting upon behaviorist principles will be contrasted with the world views of three representative thinkers, one from each of the major periods of the history we have studied: ancient, medieval, and modern.

Before directly discussing Huxley's novel we must understand the history and assumptions of dystopianism. This movement did not arise in a literary vacuum. Rather, it developed as a critique of utopianism, especially its assumption of human perfectibility. In his excellent historical survey, *The Perfectibility of Man*, John Passmore perceptively traces the evolution of the modern view of perfectibility that became the underlying premise of contemporary utopias. As we have explained in previous chapters, modern world views are aggressively secular and very optimistic about human capabilities. Passmore cites Robert Owen's *The Book of the New Moral Order* (1836) as a turning point in nineteenth-century literature. Owen claimed that people could perfect themselves through the use of scientific methods. According to Owen, science gives man the capability of "endless progressive improvement, physical, intellectual and moral and of happiness, without the possibility of retrogression or assignable limit."[2] Owen, however, made no attempt to delineate a standard of perfection by which progress is to be judged. Retrogression is impossible and progress has no limits. No matter how perfection is defined, he argued that humans can attain it by applying scientific techniques.

What Owen in the nineteenth century envisioned as a future possibility, J. B. Watson in the twentieth century guaranteed as a scientific certainty. In his behaviorism Watson reiterated Owen's definition of perfectibility, adding that since humans are merely

---

1. All citations are from *Brave New World* (New York: Harper and Row, 1969).
2. Passmore, *The Perfectibility of Man* (New York: Charles Scribners Sons, 1970), p. 206.

conditionable animals, properly controlling their environment can eventually make them perfect. Behavioristic conditioning becomes synonymous with "improvement" and ultimately with "perfectibility." Such thinking epitomizes the widespread modern conviction that all development or evolution where man is the subject is for the better. Watson's faith in behavioristic technique knew no bounds:

> I wish I could picture for you what a rich and wonderful individual we should make of every healthy child if only we could let it shape itself properly and then provide for it a universe in which it could exercise that organization—a universe unshackled by legendary folk-lore of happenings of thousands of years ago; unhampered by disgraceful political history; free of foolish customs and conventions which have no significance in themselves, yet which hem the individual in like taut steel bands.[3]

Human nature according to Watson is not a fixed innate quality but infinitely malleable. While epistemological empiricists such as John Locke viewed the human mind as *tabula rasa*—a blank sheet that receives impressions and, through reflection, produces knowledge—behaviorists argue that man is *tabula rasa* in his total being: physical, mental, and moral dimensions. People possess no inner nature, only behavior traits and propensities conditioned into them through their environment.

Watson proposed that society as a whole could be planned and shaped just as people could be conditioned individually. The very word "utopia" involves a pun. Utopians have always described a "good place" (eu-topia) that is "no place" (u-topia), an ideal society that has no existence. Watson and others contended that by applying appropriate techniques, planners could condition members of society to be perfectly adjusted. In this view, individuals are amoral beings, mere pawns in the hands of their conditioners. Planners decide what values are important and condition their followers to accept them. Rejecting all absolute norms, this technologically trained elite (the planners) experimentally determine what techniques can best be used to structure and control human behavior to produce their desired ends.

Presuppositions such as these prompted Huxley to write *Brave*

3. Cited in ibid., p. 168.

New World. Dystopian writers present a fictionalized society of the future that shows the horrors springing from the utopian views of man and society. Instead of the world becoming a good place, the society envisioned by utopians like Watson would be a thoroughly "bad place" (dys-topia). Huxley wrote his novel in 1932, five years after Watson published his *Behaviorism* and twenty-four years after Henry Ford began mass-producing Model T Fords using assembly line technology. Huxley's novel portrays a future society born of the marriage of behavioristic philosophy and modern technology. The marriage is fruitful—it produces a wholly new social order. But that the marriage was "made in heaven" is open to serious challenge.

Interestingly, readers have not always recognized Huxley's novel to be dystopian. Many were the members of the 1960s "counterculture" who "grooved" on the idea of a Brave New World! They loved the uninhibited attitudes toward sex, drugs, and traditional values. But such an interpretation of Huxley ignores his clear intention. Huxley loathed the society he described—everything from Bokanovsky's Process to the feelies, soma, and Malthusian belts.

Huxley envisioned the Brave New World as the very antithesis of major conceptions of society proposed throughout Western history. It contrasts sharply with such diverse models as Plato's "Republic" in ancient Greece, Augustine's "City of God" in the Medieval period, and Roger Williams's "Providence Plantation" in America. The Brave New World society was based on presuppositions that deny fundamental assumptions about man and reality upon which past societies were constructed. Good has gone bad, Augustine's Heavenly City is perverted and secularized, and Roger Williams's liberty of conscience is imprisoned. Rejecting the ideas of Plato, Augustine, and Williams, leaders of Brave New World deliberately implement a behavioristic world view that denies any absolute good, relativizes all values, and rejects individual freedom. Developing the practical implications of behaviorism, Huxley envisioned a society that inverts traditional moral and spiritual values.

Plato's Good Gone Bad

At first glance, Brave New World appears consonant with Plato's Republic. Bokanovsky's Process seems to be the modern counterpart of Plato's allegory of the metals in which individuals possess three different types of soil. Distinct levels of ability and character (represented by gold, silver, and bronze) equip some to be philosopher kings who rule society, others to be guardians who preserve the ideals and values of society, and still others to be artisans who willingly submit to their rulers while doing the mundane labor of society. By performing its assigned task efficiently each class contributes its part to the harmony and order of the social whole. The genetic engineering of Brave New World appears to guarantee a perfectly ordered society. "Predestinators," those in control of the "Central London Hatchery and Conditioning Centre," not only determine what nature and skills individuals will have, but also actually give people their existence. Prenatal conditioning and hypnopaedia are used to complete this totally human-controlled social engineering. The hierarchical structure of society Plato proposed is also further refined. Instead of a three-tiered social order of philosopher kings, guardians, and artisans, Brave New World has a more complex stratification of classes from Alpha Pluses to Epsilon Minuses. The family is eliminated as the fundamental unit of society, as Plato suggested. Even the words "father" and "mother" are obscenities bringing a blush to the cheeks of those who hear them. The stable social structure of Brave New World is therefore achieved at the expense of individual mobility from class to class. Whereas Plato provided that leaders of the Republic elevate or demote people as their true "metal" became evident, no such provision is made in Huxley's novel. Behaviorism's genetic determinism and conditioning result in a caste society in which each person's position is permanently fixed not from "birth" but from technological "conception."

Despite some superficial similarities, Brave New World is not the futuristic embodiment of Plato's Republic. The resemblance is no deeper than the skin synthesized by "bokanovskification." Plato, in his allegory of the metals, presupposed a human nature common to everyone. All are fashioned by the god who mixed the metals in various proportions within each person. Human nature was common to society's three classes—all "brothers born of the same soil . . . all of one stock."[4] Social differentiation under the rule of philosopher kings was a hierarchy determined according to an absolute Good. In sharp contrast the Controller of Brave New World, Mustapha Mond, acknowledges no absolute values. Mond defines the good of society not in terms of transcendent norms but rather by using immanentistically determined group standards. As ruler of society, he justifies his reading of Shakespeare, a forbidden book, with the statement: "I'm one of the very few. But as I make the laws here, I can also break them."[5] No values exist except those decreed by the fiat law of the technological elite. Plato's philosopher king follows an absolute norm. Having emerged from the cave of ignorance and opinion, he is obliged to "climb the ascent to the vision of Goodness" and afterwards to descend and "ensure the welfare of the commonwealth as a whole."[6] Philosopher kings as well as guardians and artisans are bound by a transcendent ideal that they must follow diligently.

But the "Good" of Plato is not just eliminated in the Brave New World. Taking its place are the lesser ideals of stability and happiness, obtainable through genetic engineering. Bokanovsky Groups are the gyroscope that stabilizes the rocket plane of state. A technological process determines how many and what kind of people are made by artificially manipulating the genetic mix of the population. In the decanting process prior to "birth," all but the Alpha Pluses are deliberately stunted in their development to a greater or lesser extent, which insures that groups with various levels of ability will fulfill their predetermined roles in society.

One of Huxley's sharpest parodies is his depiction of happiness in Brave New World. Totally amoral in nature, it is a vapid contentment consistent with the absence of any spiritual or moral values. The Controller describes life as "childishly simple":

> No strain on the mind or muscles. Seven and a half hours of mild, unexhausting labor, and then the soma ration and games and unrestricted copulation and the feelies. What more can they ask for?[7]

4. Plato's *Republic* (New York: Oxford University Press, 1966), pp. 106-7.
5. *Brave New World*, p. 148.
6. *Republic*, pp. 233, 234.
7. *Brave New World*, p. 152.

Passages such as this have led some readers to think Huxley was actually writing a utopian novel. But this drug-induced, licentious hedonism is a pale substitute for the virtues of Plato's Republic. Leaders of Brave New World have rejected the four cardinal Greek virtues of wisdom, courage, temperance, and justice as outmoded and have replaced them with the "pleasant vices" mentioned above. Values are not self-evident absolutes commanding the respect of all rational people. Rather controllers choose values arbitrarily, their only criterion being whether or not they contribute to the stability and happiness of the hedonistic culture. All traces of traditional morality or virtue have been eliminated in Brave New World. To this total absence of virtue, Savage, a visitor to Brave New World from an Indian Reservation where a primitive way of living still prevails, speaking for Huxley, retorts: "But value dwells not in particular will. . . . It holds his estimate and dignity as well wherein 'tis precious of itself as in the prizer."[8]

But Mustapha Mond immediately reminds Savage that virtues such as love, self-denial, nobility, heroism, and chastity are impossible in their society. People do not esteem them as virtues because their controllers have not designed society to produce virtuous people. Under the new social order of stability and happiness, behavior traditionally considered immoral becomes acceptable, even commendable, as long as it promotes group stability and contentment. Among others we find the following "pleasant vices": rampant sexual promiscuity, drug-induced stupors such as a "half-holiday," "weekend," and "dark eternity on the moon," and unmitigated consumption of goods and services to satisfy every sensual desire. Old virtues are nonexistent because they are inconsistent with a technologically planned society.[9]

Thus Brave New World depicts Plato's Good gone bad. And Huxley pictures a society based on a world view antithetical to Plato's. Any similarities between them are superficial. Behaviorism seeks to create a society where an intellectual elite is above the law; where lesser ideals are substituted for an ultimate "Good"; and

8. Ibid., p. 160.
9. Ibid., p. 191.

finally where sensual vices replace virtues. Such a society stands Plato's Republic on its head. It is a perversion of goodness.

Augustine's City of God Turned Secular

A second model of society that behaviorists such as Watson repudiate is Augustine's medieval "City of God." *Brave New World* is a secular version of Augustine's Heavenly City. Carl Becker, in his classic work, *The Heavenly City of the Eighteenth Century Philosophers*, demonstrated that the first "modern" views of society advocated in the eighteenth century were earlier secularizations of Augustine's Christian vision. The secularism of behaviorism, however, exceeds that of Enlightenment philosophers, who were not atheists but primarily deists.

Augustine developed his Christian view of society to refute pagan charges that Rome fell to the barbarians in the early fifth century because her gods punished the Romans for accepting Christianity. He sought also to demonstrate the superiority of Christianity's view of society over the best conceptions of society that paganism had previously produced. Augustine argued that all mankind is divided into two "cities," each distinguished by its members' respective loves and the types of peace they seek. On the one hand, residents of the City of Man love self and the desires of the flesh and seek only an earthly peace between men and nations. Inhabitants of the City of God, on the other hand, love God, desire to be united with Him, and seek a higher, heavenly peace with God. Augustine believed that people have been created in the image of God "with a nature midway between angels and beasts, so that man, provided he should remain subject to his true Lord and Creator and dutifully obey His commandments, might pass into the company of the angels. . . ."[10] But mankind fell from that eminent position by rebellion and self-will. Ever since the fall and God's provision of redemption, two societies have existed within the human race.

Augustine's societal vision focuses more on the Christian's vocation in society than on a blueprint for a "Christian society." Given that context, "the pardoning of sins" is more important for the

10. *St. Augustine: The City of God* (New York: Doubleday, 1958), p. 262.

Christian than "any perfection of virtues."[11] Believers are to work for and use the peace of the City of Man, but the resident of the Heavenly City "knows and, by religious faith believes that he must adore one God alone and serve Him with . . . complete dedication."[12] In concluding his book, Augustine summarizes the all-encompassing salvation provided in the City of God:

> . . . in that final peace which is the end and purpose of all virtue here on earth, our nature, made whole by immortality and incorruption, will have no vices and experience no rebellion from within or without. There will be no need for reason to govern nonexistent evil inclinations. God will hold sway over man, the soul over the body; and the happiness in eternal life and law make obedience sweet and easy.[13]

The atoning death of Christ unites believers with God and makes their obedience to His law possible. While the Heavenly City uses the earthly peace sought by the city of man, such peace is subordinate to that of heaven. The ultimate peace, therefore, is "the perfectly ordered and harmonious communion of those who find their joy in God and in one another in God."[14]

The peace of Brave New World differs completely from Augustine's. The kind of peace and communion sought by the inhabitants of Huxley's society is evident in the Solidarity Service, which represents a secularization and perversion of the Christian sacrament of communion. Rejecting all transcendent ideals, Brave New World perverts the eucharist by substituting sensual gratification for spiritual communion with God. Orgiastic ritual performed under the influence of the drug soma engulfs participants in sexual pleasure, consummating their salvation here and now by indulgence in the flesh, not by obedience to the Spirit.

The Solidarity Service embodies the pleasures of Baal worship of the ancient Canaanites without their desire for fertility (cf. our treatment of Canaanite cosmology above, chap. 1). Twelve men and women (the number of the original Christian apostolate)

11. Ibid., p. 480.
12. Ibid., p. 464.
13. Ibid., p. 481.
14. Ibid., p. 465.

participate in the service. Members of the group seek to fuse their separate identities into the Greater Being. In order to become one they sing hymns, make signs of the T (a fusion of "sign of the cross" and Model T Ford technology) and share from a communion cup of soma. Even the second coming of Christ is symbolized in the service as the participants dance, chant, and shout phrases such as "He's coming, I hear him!" The incarnation of and synthesis into Greater Being occurs as the participants hear the words of the solidarity hymn:

> Orgy-porgy, Ford and fun,
> Kiss the girls and make them One.
> Boys at one with girls at peace;
> Orgy-porgy gives release.

A ceremony that for Augustine would exemplify the lusts of the flesh is transmuted by means of the dystopian vision into a stabilized equilibrium for everyone except Bernard Marx, a member of the most intelligent social group who questions many aspects of Brave New World society. Instead of being absorbed into the Greater Being, he remains isolated and empty. Even though he is locked in the embrace of a sensual woman, he feels more self-consciously alone than at any other time in his life.

Savage and the Controller discuss religion and philosophy further in a prolonged conversation. Mond defends Brave New World by articulating a philosophy that takes issue at every point with Augustine's. He shows the Savage books considered "pornographic" in his society—the Bible, Thomas à Kempis's *The Imitation of Christ*, and a book by Cardinal Newman, a prominent Anglican convert to Catholicism in the nineteenth century. The books are pornographic because they are old and contain outmoded ideas about God, which are not reconcilable with technology and happiness. Whereas previously belief in God helped to insure stability and order within society, now it does not. Now God paradoxically "manifests himself as an absence; as though he weren't there at all."[15] God and modern civilization are incompatible. Mond declares: "You must make your choice. Our civilization has chosen machinery and happiness. That's

---

15. *Brave New World*, p. 159.

why I have to keep these books locked up in the safe. They're smut."[16] Religious beliefs, like all other moral or spiritual values, are solely a result of environmental conditioning. Gone is Augustine's assumption that people are created by God and are restless until they find a relationship with Him. To the Savage's question, "Isn't it natural to feel there's a God?" the Controller retorts, "People believe in God because they've been conditioned to believe in God."[17] Those who believe in a theistic basis for society do so because they have been conditioned by teachers of the old morality. New morality proclaims instead that "[the god's] code of law is dictated in the last resort, by the people who organize society; Providence takes its cue from man."[18]

Brave New World's view of God as absent and of man as seeking salvation through sensual experience reflects a society motivated by principles diametrically opposed to Augustine's. Both Augustine's and Plato's ideals are inverted by behaviorist assumptions about God, man, and society.

Roger Williams's Freedom of Conscience Imprisoned

The final model for society that Brave New World rejects is one that has been realized only recently and only partially—freedom. Roger Williams, a seventeenth-century pastor, theologian, dissenter, and founder of Rhode Island, was a prominent defender of liberty of conscience. Belief that individuals have the right of such liberty, including freedom to worship God as they please, developed slowly and intermittently. In the biblical world view liberty is primarily freedom from the penalty of and indwelling power of sin and its effects on individuals and institutions. Through the Exodus, the Jews were liberated from their Egyptian taskmasters; their liberation as a nation reflected their liberation from sins associated with bondage—idolatry, rebellion, and pride. Freedom exists in the messianic promise of Isaiah 61:1, "The Lord has anointed me to . . . proclaim liberty to the captives . . ." (RSV); in the statement of Jesus, "The truth shall make you free" (John 8:32); and in Paul's words of

16. Ibid.
17. Ibid.
18. Ibid., p. 160.

salvation, "For freedom Christ has set us free; stand fast, therefore and do not submit again to a yoke of slavery" (Gal. 5:1, RSV). Freedom in these contexts also has a positive content—to love and serve God through righteous living as an expression of thanksgiving for a new, regenerated nature received from God's Spirit. But the biblical concept of liberty lay dormant until the Reformation and Puritan periods (sixteenth and seventeenth centuries), after which, nourished by both its biblical and Enlightenment heritages, it was revitalized and eventually incorporated in the First Amendment to the United States Constitution in 1791. As the spiritual and intellectual heir of the biblical and Augustinian tradition, Williams played an important part in this history. He was expelled from John Winthrop's Boston in 1636 because he rejected the long-standing Constantinian arrangement that united church and state. Laws in the Massachusetts Bay Colony compelled religious uniformity, forced public support of the church, enforced religious rules in civil life, and allowed no freedom of conscience. Williams founded his own colony, Providence Plantation (Rhode Island) in 1636, which separated church and state and permitted freedom of worship.

According to Williams, a good society must allow every individual to have liberty of conscience to stand before God on his own. Williams claimed that neither state nor church should interfere with this liberty. The state ought to remove "the civil bars, obstructions, hindrances . . . those yokes, that pinch the very souls and consciences of men." The state has the responsibility to provide liberty for all persons, not simply for Christians. Moving beyond John Milton's conception of religious liberty, Williams argued that a state ought to guarantee "a free and absolute permission of the consciences of all men, in what is merely spiritual." Freedom of worship would pertain not only to Christians but to all religious groups.[19]

Liberty of conscience reappeared in Western history first as the struggle for religious freedom. While Thomas Jefferson and James Madison did the most to incorporate religious liberty into fundamental American law, they and clergymen such as Samuel Davies and Isaac Backus, who fought alongside them, built upon the foun-

19. Cited in L. John Van Til, *Liberty of Conscience: The History of a Puritan Idea* (Nutley, N. J.: Craig Press, 1972), pp. 68-69.

dation laid by Roger Williams. Williams argued that man, because of his position in the created order, his nature as a moral and spiritual agent, and his function under God, was made to be a free and responsible individual. Williams claimed for all people what Martin Luther claimed for himself before both pope and emperor in the sixteenth century but denied to the German peasants when they revolted. Eventually in America and in other Western nations, religious liberty, the first liberty, helped to insure other freedoms in society—assembly, press, republican government, capitalism, and the family.

By comparison, what freedoms are there in the dystopian society? Only the freedom to give vent to every pleasurable impulse. All sensual desires can be gratified. But that is just the problem. Since man is considered merely a physical being, society panders only to those cravings. No other needs are even recognized. Liberty of conscience is denied because conscience itself is considered nonexistent. Thus Savage rampages his way through Park Lane Hospital for the dying ranting to the patients: "I come to bring you freedom. . . . Do you like being slaves? . . . Don't you want to be *free* and *men*? Don't you even understand what *manhood* and *freedom* are?"[20] Savage believes it self-evident that his freedom was rooted in his very personhood. But no such correlation is assumed in Brave New World. In fact, the opposite is assumed. Freedom and its correlative, dignity or intrinsic value, are inconsistent with the idea that man is conditioned by his environment.

Huxley exposed the startling and wide-ranging implications of the extinction of freedom. First, science is eliminated because it demands freedom as a prerequisite. Even Mustapha Mond began as a scientist but gave it up to become Controller. Society had to choose between scientific inquiry, the purpose of which is to know the world, and technology, the purpose of which is to control or change the world. At the point in history when science enabled a technological elite to manipulate society, science was discontinued, even "chained and muzzled,"[21] and technological control usurped its place, thereby holding society captively stagnant at that level of

20. *Brave New World*, pp. 146, 147 (emphasis added).
21. Ibid., p. 153.

development. While technology provided many advantages to society, not the least of which was the amelioration of many individual and collective ills, its main function was to control society and imprison its inhabitants at a carefully planned stage. Thus science in Brave New World is reckoned a "public danger," threatening to "undo its own good work in society."[22] Even Mond is tempted to dabble in science, and he admits that "happiness is a hard master ... a much harder master, if one isn't conditioned to accept it unquestioningly rather than [to accept] truth."[23]

Philosophy is also abolished in Brave New World because it too requires freedom of thought. Mond satirically defines philosophy as "finding bad reasons for what one believes for other bad reasons."[24] Before technology took control of Brave New World, everyone deemed knowledge the highest good and truth a supreme value. The human quest for knowledge progressed unabated until the horrendous Nine Years' War—a world-wide conflagration that threatened to destroy humanity—made the ancestors of Brave New World alter their priorities. The Controller contends that one cannot argue the point of truth and beauty when faced with extinction. Because humanity must survive, leaders chose to implement a totally planned society. Control leading to happiness became the supreme value. Mond rehearses the details:

> People were ready to have even their appetites controlled then. Anything for a quiet life. We've gone on controlling ever since. It hasn't been very good for truth, of course. But it's been very good for happiness. One can't have something for nothing. Happiness has got to be paid for.[25]

In his foreword to the 1946 edition Huxley called this transition from freedom to control the "ultimate, personal, really revolutionary revolution." It is the revolution whereby some (the controllers) make others (the rest of society) "love their servitude."[26]

Finally, religion and morality are extinct in a behavioristically

22. Ibid., p. 155.
23. Ibid., p. 154.
24. Ibid., p. 159.
25. Ibid., p. 155.
26. Ibid., p. x.

controlled society. Because freedom to believe no longer exists, the training of conscience and moral development, a long and arduous task in previous societies, is unnecessary and irrelevant. Moral training is replaced by soma, the all-purpose drug, and hypnopaedia, the constant repetition of aphorisms to inculcate ideas appropriate to each class in society. Religion as man's attempt to relate to God and provide comfort and consolation in the midst of the troubles of life is replaced by the Solidarity Service, which we have already examined, and soma. The most versatile drug ever devised, soma calms anger, makes people patient, and effects reconciliation between users and whatever troubles them. Whereas people in the past accomplished these tasks only with great moral and spiritual effort, now they need only take tablets. Extolling the benefits of soma, the Controller explains: "Anybody can be virtuous now. You can carry at least half your mortality about in a bottle. Christianity without tears—that's what soma is."[27] This mind-altering drug, when combined with other conditioning devices in society, effectively eliminates any need for conscience. Thus conscience, traditionally understood as basic to moral and spiritual understanding of right and wrong, is rendered unnecessary.

Hypnopaedia is the basic conditioning tool for social and moral education used after Bokanovsky's Process determines the genetic makeup of individuals. Hypnopaedia does not transmit "intellectual education," i.e., cognitive or factual data susceptible to logical or scientific demonstration. Instead it is a multi-purpose conditioner, instilling arbitrary social and moral values that the technological elite determine are best for each social class. Hypnopaedia tailors values to the demands of the situation since values conform to the current needs of society rather than vice versa. Like conscience, values are totally subjective, being created by the controllers for social efficiency and utility.

Since moral and social values have no objective basis, hypnopaedia is correctly described as "words without reason."[28] Hypnopaedia educates by repeating "truths" over and over again—sixty-two thousand times to be exact. This process directly and

27. Ibid., p. 162.
28. Ibid., p. 18.

unrelentingly instills in citizens the appropriate social values of their particular classes, from their sexual mores to their status, tasks, and clothing. Each child in the nursery is virtually "brain-washed" with this repetitive teaching until the "mind is these suggestions, and the sum of these suggestions is the child's mind." Truth is neither what the mind apprehends by dialectic (Plato) nor what it apprehends through experience (empiricists), nor what God reveals (Bible), but simply whatever comes over the omnipresent loud speakers. The mind apprehends what hypnopaedia teaches "not merely as true, but as axiomatic, self-evident, utterly indisputable."[29] The principle of the relativity of truth and the blatant manipulation of its content reach a zenith in Brave New World. The creed of human autonomy expressed succinctly in the biblical book of Judges (17:6), "Every man did what was right in his own eyes," (in ancient Hebrew culture) and echoed in the declaration of Sophist philosopher Protagoras, "Man is the measure" (in ancient Greek thought) reaches its climax in the Brave New World's denial of any truth save what is "created" and indelibly imprinted on people's minds by hypnopaedia.

There is no freedom in Brave New World, no choice between God and "happiness," science and "happiness," philosophy and "happiness," religion and "happiness," or conscience and "happiness." "Behavioristic freedom" alone exists; individuals are free to choose only what the technological elite has predetermined to be consistent with the ideals of society. Everyone chooses what he likes and likes what he chooses because he has been conditioned through physical and mental conditioning that absolutely guarantees the stability and happiness of society as a whole. The Controller cannot understand why anyone would wish to give up stability and happiness in exchange for God, science, philosophy, or religion.

Mond stands in amazement as Savage denounces Brave New World's loss of freedom by choosing instead not only God, science, religion, and philosophy, but the ability to "suffer" as well:

> I don't want comfort. I want God, I want poetry, I want real danger, I want freedom, I want goodness. I want sin. . . . Not to mention the right to grow old and ugly and impotent; the right

29. Ibid., p. 26.

to have syphilis and cancer; the right to have too little to eat; the right to be lousy. . . .[30]

Thus, by way of satire, Huxley reaffirmed traditional liberty as basic to man's very nature, the liberty Williams affirmed in the seventeenth century for all men. Freedom may result in certain ills to both individuals and society. But those ills are a small price to pay for a right as great as freedom. Williams advocated religious freedom—liberty of conscience—as the basis for the rest of human freedoms, whether political, economic, or social. Such liberties are denied in Brave New World with its behavioristic presuppositions about human nature. Human dignity is lost as people are considered no different from other species under mastery of the controllers. All thought and activity related to and dependent upon freedom are systematically eliminated from society. Thus Huxley's *Brave New World* projects a society void of freedom of conscience, an inversion of Roger Williams's Providence Plantation. Freedom, like Plato's Good and Augustine's Heavenly City, are banished from Brave New World.

Dystopianism and Biblical Prophetism

In addition to the historical models of society considered above, one more tradition distinctly resembles dystopian criticisms of society—Old Testament prophetic literature of the eighth century B.C. Like the Old Testament prophets, dystopian writers sharply criticize the cultures of their day by employing the various literary techniques of parody, sarcasm, parable, and polemic denunciation to convey their disapproval.

The prophet Amos illustrates this tradition. He excoriates the rich who oppress the poor because they "sell the righteous for silver, and the needy for a pair of shoes" (2:6, RSV). Leaders responsible for executing justice in society have perverted what they are responsible for upholding. They "turn aside the needy in the gate" (where cases were heard—5:12, RSV) and turn "justice into poison" (6:12). Rather than dispensing justice, in collusion with rich merchants they garner bribes and overlook the use of false weights to

---

30. Ibid., p. 163.

cheat the poor. The rich live in luxury, own summer and winter homes, lie on their ivory beds, and eat and drink excessively, amusing themselves with songs while showing no compassion to the poor who are in severe want (6:4-6).

Despite such callous indifference the rich and powerful hypocritically fulfill their religious obligations. Amos denounces their blasphemous self-righteousness and forewarns of a calamitous future—God will permit Israel's enemies to defeat her and lead her people into captivity.

Thus, both dystopian writers and the prophets attack present abuses and trends that will yield disastrous futures for society. Dystopians foresee a wholly new social order, the "bad place," while the prophets proclaim the end of the old age altogether. But both insist that widely held fallacious views of man and society will only bring ruin to society in the long run.

Still, the Old Testament prophetic tradition differs sharply from Huxley's view on certain crucial issues. Amos offers a clear alternative to the present course of events. He calls upon a transcendent source, which both society and its leaders must follow: "Let justice roll down like waters and righteousness like an everflowing stream" (5:24). The source of that justice is "the law of the Lord" and "His statutes" (2:4). All members of society alike must acknowledge that the prophet's words are not merely human wisdom but bear transcendent authority. Thus Amos boldly commands, "Now hear the word of the Lord" (7:16). He explicitly demands a return to God's objective standard of morality, the Mosaic covenant given through revelation.

Second, the biblical prophets assume that human evil is so radical that it goes to the root of our being, so that only the intervention of God's grace will effectively save individuals and society. Because all people sin, society is and will remain corrupt apart from God's grace. Thus the basis for hope is drastically different in the prophetic and dystopian views. Dystopian writers rarely present an explicit alternative. For example, only in a foreword to the 1946 edition does Huxley spell out a third choice of "sanity" for the Savage rather than simply giving him the possibilities of utopianism and primitivism, as in the novel. He proposed a form of government and economics, as well as the religion and philosophy that would undergird it:

> Religion would be the conscious and intelligent pursuit of man's Final End, the unitive knowledge of the immanent Tao or Logos, the transcendent Godhead or Brahman. And the prevailing philosophy of life would be a kind of Higher Utilitarianism, in which the Greatest Happiness principle would be secondary to the Final End principle.[31]

In the final analysis Huxley's hope springs from an almost unquestioned faith in human autonomy. Even as distorted philosophies such as behaviorism are increasingly accepted and implemented, humans can still choose to live sanely. The biblical writers, as we have seen consistently throughout our study, denounce efforts to live on any basis other than the authoritative Word of God. Human redemption is accomplished not by our own initiative but by God's gracious provision in Christ.

Thus, biblical writers present a counterproposal to utopias and dystopias—the kingdom of God. With the utopians the prophets extend hope of a better future. But they reject the utopian belief that man is either innately good or has no innate nature and thus any message can be "imprinted" on him. Perfectibility is based not on human potential for good, but rather on God's gracious provision. God's rule breaks into history as believers manifest righteousness and justice and implement biblical principles of everyday life.

Dystopian literature is "prophetic," therefore, in only a limited sense. Like the Old Testament prophets, it criticizes the present and predicts a dismal future if current trends are not radically altered. But that is where the similarity ends. Prophetic literature stresses God's revelation and grace, which preclude any belief that humans themselves can create a model society simply by making the right choices. Only the biblical world view provides a sound base for understanding human beings both individually and corporately. This perspective alone gives us the insight necessary to address such wide-ranging problems as individual and social justice and the application of technology to contemporary problems.

The Christian faith offers no simplistic solutions for today's

31. Ibid., pp. viii-ix.

complex problems. Nevertheless, as people created in the image of God, fallen, redeemable by God's grace, and under the sovereignty of God and His revelation, we can begin to remedy problems that threaten to destroy our humanity and dissolve our society. Only such a transcendent base as presented in the prophetic tradition and later developed by Augustine and Williams can provide an authority to form and shape society. At the same time, biblical ideals provide a criterion for judging leaders of society, thus helping to curb their violation of the law.

For Further Reading

Bellamy, Edward. *Looking Backward 2000-1887*. Boston: Houghton Mifflin, 1898.

Firchow, Peter Edgerly. *The End of Utopia: A Study of Aldous Huxley's Brave New World*. Lewisburg, Pa: Bucknell University Press, 1984.

Hillegas, Mark. *The Future as Nightmare: H. G. Wells and the Anti-Utopians*. New York: Oxford, 1967.

Huxley, Aldous. *Brave New World*. New York: Harper, 1932.

_____ . *Brave New World Revisited*. New York: Harper, 1958.

More, Thomas. *Utopia*. New York: E. P. Dutton, 1935.

Orwell, George. *Nineteen Eighty-Four, a Novel*. New York: Harcourt, 1949.

Passmore, John. *The Perfectibility of Man*. New York: Scribner, 1970.

Rabkin, Eric S., Martin H. Greenburg, Joseph D. Olander, eds. *No Place Else: Explorations in Utopian and Dystopian Fiction*. Carbondale, Ill.: Southern Illinois University Press, 1983.

Walsh, Chad. *From Utopia to Nightmare*. New York: Harper, 1962.

Watson, John B. *Behaviorism*. New York: Norton, 1930.

PART THREE: ETHICS

Introduction

W. Andrew Hoffecker

Ethics concludes our study of world views. Readers might be tempted to exclaim, "It's about time we got to something practical! Why the long delay in getting down to nitty-gritty ethical discussion?" The question is legitimate, and the exasperation understandable.

We remind the reader, however, of two ways in which our study has already addressed practical ethical issues: (1) Our unit on society included detailed examination of social moral obligation. From Plato's *Republic* to Huxley's *Brave New World* we emphasized principles of social justice, which demanded ethical behavior in family life, economic dealings, and the political order. To the extent that individual morality is a function of social obligations, the previous unit underscored many of our moral duties. (2) Our study of world views has stressed that explicit ethical discussion should rest upon the foundation laid in the first units. Ethical systems are not created *ex nihilo*. They are a function of theological, anthropological, cosmological, and social presuppositions. Along the way we referred to ethical implications for the ideas of Plato, the Bible, Augustine, Martin Luther, and many others.

Now, however, we are prepared to face ethical issues in a separate unit. Although the unit is short, we believe the reader will appreciate how a person's world view confronts him or her with inescapable moral obligations. The nature of one's ethical duty and the force with which we sense our accountability are directly tied to other elements in the world view. But strong or weak, simple or complex, every world view involves ethical responsibilities, and people feel bound to obey their deepest convictions.

343

We will focus special attention on the role of epistemology in ethics. How do we know what is right and wrong and how does our moral knowledge come to us? Is ethics merely a function of social and cultural mores or is there a transcendent reference point in morality? What is the basis for ethical decision-making: conscience, the Bible, or individual human experience? How do Christians and secularists differ in their evaluation of each of these sources? Should we distinguish, and if so how, between particular ethnic, national, religious, or other customs, on the one hand, and general norms that transcend societal groupings, on the other? What is the difference between objectively and subjectively based ethical systems? Does a truly objective and therefore universal ethic exist? Is belief in God necessary for such an objective ethic? All world views we have studied propose standards of authority. As ethical alternatives multiply in our pluralistic society, we note again that the basic alternatives are twofold. (1) Self-sufficient and self-governing individuals or social groups establish their own ethical system with little or no regard for deity as a basis for morality. (2) A transcendent, personal God reveals both Himself and His will for man who, as a dependent creature, is accountable to obey God's moral law.

When Christian thought dominated Western civilization, biblical answers to ethical questions were widely accepted. Even after the division of the Christian church into the Catholic, Orthodox, and Protestant groups, most considered the moral teaching of the Bible to be the primary source for ethical wisdom. But as Western thought has become more secular, especially in the nineteenth and twentieth centuries, traditional morality has been increasingly criticized and rejected. Scholars insist that secularization as well as innovations in technology and in evolving political, economic, and social institutions conclusively demonstrate that we are in a post-Christian age. Therefore they argue that the basis of morality must be changed so that our ethical principles reflect and keep pace with the secular shape of our culture.

As in the case of cosmology, we will not survey the history of Western ethical thinking. Instead we will focus on the essential differences between biblical and naturalistic ethics and conclude with a discussion of three contemporary ethical problems to highlight how the two positions lead to different moral reasoning and judgments.

The chapter on biblical ethics begins with the affirmation of God and His self-revelation as the only foundation for an objective moral order. Moral laws govern the cosmos and humans are accountable for their actions because God created and maintains all activities and events in the world according to His sovereign will. People know what is right and wrong through God's general revelation (most importantly in conscience), which is reinforced through special revelation (God's commandments in the Bible). Without an objective basis for morality in God's revelation, ethics is inescapably subjective and relative. Likewise the biblical view of human nature and redemption are indispensable to Christian morality. The Christian world view differs from all other philosophies by teaching that upright moral behavior does not produce a person's salvation, but results from salvation. Moral living is the believer's *response* to Christ's redemptive work on the cross, not the means by which a person establishes a relationship with God. Sinful human beings are unable without the regenerating power of the Holy Spirit to fulfill the demands of the moral law. Thus the work of the Holy Spirit provides the subjective element of Christian ethics. Jesus often reiterated and reinforced these presuppositions by stressing that God evaluates inward motivation and not just outward human behavior.

Finally we consider three faulty frameworks Christians have developed to direct ethical decision-making: legalism, situationism or contextualism, and intuitionism. While each system emphasizes an important aspect of biblical ethics (laws, situations, or intuition), none provides a comprehensive basis for biblical ethics. We therefore advocate a triadic approach that combines elements from all three perspectives. The transcendent God holds all three aspects together by providing norms, guiding history in which ethical decisions must be made, and motivating believers to follow Him in love and righteousness.

Our study of naturalistic ethics focuses on how philosophers who have not built upon a biblical foundation have stressed human autonomy in their ethical views. Though classical Greek thinkers

such as Plato and Aristotle did not deny the existence of metaphysical reality, they did lay the basis for naturalistic ethics. Plato did so
by subordinating God to the Good, an abstract philosophic ideal
regarded supreme in the realm of forms. Aristotle believed that
human beings have an intrinsic capacity for virtue. His view that virtue is a disposition of the soul or a habit a person creates by repeatedly doing what is morally correct is the exact opposite of Christian
moral teaching. Building upon Aristotle's teaching, Thomas
Aquinas affirmed a morality of natural law in which people can perform their moral duty without needing the Christian gospel.

The Enlightenment thought of Immanuel Kant thoroughly secularized modern morality. Kant reduced religion itself to morality by
making human reason the autonomous source of moral standards.
Any alternative ethic implies heteronomy, or "other law," which
modern minds find repugnant. Contemporary philosophers have
devised ethical systems that emphasize only one of the two elements
Kant tried to reconcile. Francis Crick and B. F. Skinner stressed
human determinism in the physical realm (Kant's phenomenal
realm). Existentialist Jean Paul Sartre exalted freedom in the realm
of the mind (Kant's noumenal realm). Influenced by these and
other naturalistic thinkers, secular theologians proclaim that man
has "come of age" and no longer needs a transcendent God as a
basis for ethics.

The naturalistic ethical triad differs vastly from the biblical one.
With God absent as a unifying factor, norms, contexts, and motivation do not complement each other. Rather, each ethicist proposes a different set of norms, a different view of history, and a
different motivation for ethical behavior based on his distinctive
anthropology or epistemology. Thus secular naturalists have further contributed to the fragmentation of our culture by providing
no unifying world view. Instead the prospects are for increased
conflict and tension.

Our concluding chapter on ethics examines three contemporary
problems—abortion, euthanasia, and homosexuality—and discusses how, based upon their world views, naturalists and Christians
have arrived at contrasting conclusions about what is morally right
and wrong. The main point in the debate over abortion is whether

the traditional Judeo-Christian presupposition guaranteeing the sanctity of life (for the fetus) is absolute and therefore supersedes the woman's right to choose whether or not to carry a baby to term. Other elements in the debate include when life actually begins, the personhood of the fetus, and the role of morality and law in a pluralistic society. The sanctity of life is central to the debate on euthanasia as well. Elements in the discussion include the difference between active and passive euthanasia, the relation between euthanasia and suicide and murder, and the potential for abuse of euthanasia laws. Finally the discussion of homosexuality focuses on two main issues: how a person becomes a homosexual and the civil rights of homosexuals.

Our discussion of these three ethical problems explains how Christians and naturalists differ radically on how to deal with them and other perplexing contemporary moral concerns. Only as Christians better understand the biblical world view and its unique triadic approach to ethics can they effectively advocate Christian positions on ethical issues and alter trends that are secularizing our culture.

I.
BIBLICAL
ETHICS

12
Ethics Revealed by God

W. Andrew Hoffecker

Introduction

Christians have pervasively shaped Western culture through their ethical teaching. From the fourth to the twentieth centuries morality in the West has been tied to Judaeo-Christian ethics. Biblical principles have directed both the private and public lives of many Christians, and they have developed political, economic, and social institutions on the basis of biblical morality.

All that we have considered in our study of world views has direct or indirect implications for Christian moral thinking. The various subjects we have covered provide the necessary foundation for moral reflection. Christian theological, anthropological, epistemological, cosmological, and social presuppositions have more than a theoretical content. They demand specific moral conduct, and our purpose in this chapter is to consider how the biblical world view in its totality provides the indispensable foundation for ethical thinking.

Theological and Cosmological Presuppositions: a Sovereign God and an Objective Moral Order

In its theological and cosmological presuppositions the Christian world view provides a consistently theistic basis for ethics, which can be stated both positively and negatively. By presupposing that God exists and that the cosmos has an ethical meaning, Christians state positively that specific ethical behavior is not only a possibility but an absolute necessity. If there is a sovereign, personal God who has created a morally significant universe, then we are obligated to discern its moral nature and obey His commandments, which support the moral character of our existence. No other system of ethics can provide a sufficient foundation for ethics, because it rejects God's transcendence and the moral cosmos that Christian teaching affirms. While other perspectives might affirm some of the same ethical principles as Christianity, these world views cannot fully justify their ethical demands; their foundations are false gods, who lack the personal yet transcendent moral attributes of the biblical God.

The Bible provides a transcendent reference point that is fixed and applicable to all particular ethical contexts and thus can demand absolute obedience from its followers. The Old and New Testament authors speak with a united voice that the personal, sovereign God provides such a point of departure. God alone is autonomous—the self-determined, self-sufficient Lord of all being. Everything else is totally dependent on Him for its existence. As creation's rightful Lord, He calls the world into existence by His powerful, lifegiving word and providentially maintains reality in its order. The clear implication is that if God were to withdraw His word from creation, the universe would fall into nonexistence and be discarded like a worn out garment (Ps. 102:26, 27).

But God's sovereignty is not exhausted by His creating and sustaining the universe. We must identify what kind of a world God has made. How has God manifested His sovereignty? Does the cosmos have any meaning beyond the mere fact that it exists? Do plants and vegetation, natural resources, wildlife, and human beings have any purpose or value other than the obvious fact that they are? How do we move from recognizing the world's ontological status, its real existence, to its moral value, which requires of us an appropriate ethical response? Unless the world has moral value, we are left with only an empty acknowledgment that whatever is, is right. But if that is the case, evil is either nonexistent or trivial. The Bible, however, clearly presents a different perspective of the cosmos. It affirms a transcendent God who assigns meaning to all that He made. God not only brought the vast diversity of the cosmos into existence—including the inanimate, animate, and human orders—but also appointed the various species to make their homes in the sky, on the earth, and in the ocean depths. In addition, God attributed to the cosmos as a whole and each being within it a purpose in accordance with His design or plan. In Genesis God repeatedly confirmed and approved the value of each element He had created: "And God saw that it was good." Light in the heavens, vegetation, creatures in the sea, animals on land and finally man as God's image bearer—everything has worth by virtue of God's creation and pronouncement that it is good.

Christian ethics, therefore, affirms that right and wrong are not finite, subjective values, originating by fiat from individuals as one of the latest elements emerging in an evolutionary process. All value resides originally and ultimately in God who defines righteousness and then rules the world in accordance with what He has prescribed. Ethical systems that do not begin with God must posit some other basis for ethical right and wrong or begin with the premise that no objective value exists. Those who do not begin with God as the basis for morality must create their own value system using various finite human resources such as reason or experience.

Many biblical passages build on this foundation of the objective value of creation. Nature psalms such as Psalm 104 teach that everything in nature was made to glorify God. God displayed His wisdom and power by ordering the creation, thereby making it beautiful and a fit habitation for His creatures. Even the forces of nature are not brute physical elements but servants of the living God (see Ps. 148). "Fire and hail, snow and frost" (v. 8, RSV) glorify God by their order, majesty, beauty, and power.

In addition, God issues moral commands to undergird and reinforce the objective value of creation. The cultural mandate in Genesis 1:28 to "be fruitful and multiply" and "fill the earth and subdue it" elevates the creation account above the level of a mere empirical report of meaningless origins. God distinguished Adam and Eve from the rest of the natural realm by assigning them an ethical task. Man and woman alone were God's image bearers and therefore fully moral creatures. God not only gave them dominion over the rest of the cosmos, but also made them morally accountable for the use of their power. God's commands concerning the earth and its many inhabitants indicate that the value of whatever exists to mankind should be the same as its value to God, who created it. Because God placed man in the garden "to cultivate it and keep it" (Gen. 2:15) and to name the animals (Gen. 2:19), human beings are neither passive inhabitants who live only by their instincts nor autonomous creatures left to use their considerable powers as they please. Human dominion is neither an amoral exercise of power nor limitless. God's commandments set the parameters of all human obligation. The cultural mandate, therefore, establishes the first moral context of human behavior. Both God's prescriptions and His prohibitions determine the quality and scope of all human activity.

Some critics of Christianity have argued that the cultural mandate does the exact opposite from what we have stated. Instead of directing people to unfold the earth's potential in a stewardly way, it invites us to plunder the creation. Not only does the Bible fail to establish a clear environmental ethic, these critics contend, but in ordering man to dominate the earth, it approves in advance all the damage that people have inflicted upon animals and the ecosystem.

Scripture, however, does not justify exploitation of nature. We must consider all parts of the Bible that clearly speak to a particular issue. Other biblical passages specifically teach our responsibilities to care for the morally valuable cosmos. Many psalms declare the objective value of the earth and explain how its inhabitants glorify their Creator. Even though God directs people to use plants and animals as food, the Old Testament established clear principles for the treatment of animals and the environment. Animals used in work were to enjoy the rest of the Sabbath (Exod. 20:10), and were to be helped when in distress (Deut. 22:4). Farmers were not to muzzle oxen that threshed grain but were to allow them to eat what their labor helped to produce (Deut. 25:4). Hunters were not to take mother animals for food but were to allow them to live to produce more young (Deut. 22:6). God gave clear principles for the Jews' use of forests and vegetation. In planning and constructing cities, builders were not to level forests indiscriminately (Deut. 20:19, 20). The earth itself was to lie fallow during the sabbath and Jubilee years (Lev. 25:2-7).

Old Testament prophets used these principles to castigate the people of Israel for despoiling the Promised Land. Before Israel's occupation Palestine was an abundant land, "flowing with milk and honey" (Exod. 3:8; Deut. 8:7-9), but toward the end of the Old Testament era, because of neglect and misuse, the earth was a barren wasteland (Mic. 7:13; Jer. 4:23-26). A supreme irony of the Old Testament is that the land, which the Israelites polluted with their sin by disobeying these covenant principles, "vomited" up the people into exile so that the land could have its appointed "Sabbath rest."

The objective value of creation is most evident in God's initial command regarding what man could and could not eat in the creation narrative: "You may freely eat of every tree of the garden; but of the tree of the knowledge of good and evil you shall not eat, for in the day that you eat of it you shall die" (Gen. 2:16-17, RSV). God's prohibition contains the most important ethical teaching of Scripture: God alone sovereignly determines through His commands what is right and wrong morally. What distinguished one tree from all others had to do with nothing inherent in the trees— their shape, color, size, or variety. God called one "the tree of the knowledge of good and evil." Its impropriety was due to God's command. And God's command implied that Adam had a fully developed moral character, which enabled him to apprehend its meaning and held him accountable for obeying that command. Humanity did not become moral by choice but was morally responsible from creation, prior to receiving God's prohibition. God's command (the cultural mandate) and prohibition demanded two things: discernment and obedience. The name "tree of the knowledge of good and evil" indicates that man's task essentially is moral. And God's Word is what establishes moral obligation and gives human activity meaning and purpose.

God's command was neither capricious nor arbitrary. Rather, God's command confirmed what was already implied by the cultural mandate, that He had created a moral realm, and our primary duty as His image bearers is to glorify Him by absolute obedience within that realm. Jesus confirmed this principle in the New Testament when Satan tempted Him to turn stones into bread. After forty days without food in the wilderness, why should the Son, who was the Father's agent in creation (John 1:1-5), not satisfy His hunger by such a miracle? Should it not be both possible and morally permissible for the Son of God to perform a miracle to satisfy His hunger? The only reason for Jesus' unwillingness to do so was the Father's revealed moral will that Jesus fast! Jesus, therefore, responded to Satan's temptation by reiterating the basis for God's ethical sovereignty: "Man shall not live on bread alone, but on every word that proceeds out of the mouth of God" (Matt. 4:4). In these words Jesus confirmed the foundation for Christian ethical obedience.

In the Old Testament the Ten Commandments and the ark of the covenant symbolized the objective nature of morality as based on God's sovereign self-disclosure. No one was to usurp the place of God's law and substitute his own laws. Only God could promulgate law, which He did through revelation to His chosen leaders (Deut. 17:8-13). Leviticus 19 illustrates how God is the source of value as He reveals various laws based on His moral attributes. God establishes the basis for what is right and wrong at the beginning of the chapter in the words "You shall be holy, for I the Lord your God am holy" (v. 2). Punctuating the thirty-seven verses of moral commands is the refrain "I am the Lord your God," which substantiates each command. Duties range from the familiar "Everyone shall reverence his mother and his father, and you shall keep my sabbath" (v. 3) to gleaning laws, which forbade farmers from stripping their fields bare at harvest time (v. 9). Because God is Lord, "You shall not curse a deaf man, nor place a stumbling block before the blind. . . ." (v.14). What gives force to each of these laws is not human acknowledgment of the justice of these commands but the moral sanction "I am the Lord." God's commandments in Leviticus 19 covered all phases of everyday life, not merely distinctively religious activities. In economic matters believers should not defraud their neighbors by taking what does not belong to them, and they should pay the wages of a hired man immediately (v. 13, RSV). Those exercising judicial powers should neither be "partial to the poor nor defer to the great" (v. 15). Specific prohibitions against immorality protected the integrity and sanctity of the family ("Do not profane your daughter by making her a harlot, so that the land may not fall to harlotry, and the land become full of lewdness" [v. 29]). Finally, general commands governed other social relationships ("You shall not take vengeance, nor bear any grudge against the sons of your people, but you shall love your neighbor as yourself. . . ." [v. 18]). Despite the vast diversity of human activity, one constant governed all situations: "I am the Lord" stood behind all moral obligations. Justifying every ethical injunction is the transcendent being of God, the great "I am who I am" of Exodus 3:14. Old Testament believers knew what was morally correct because the moral attributes of God established ethical commands governing all human behavior.

Anthropological and Societal Presuppositions: Fallen Man's Need for Law and Regeneration

Biblical teaching that God is the objective source of a moral cosmos relates directly to scriptural norms about man, God's image bearer, and human social institutions. As *imago dei*, human beings have a unique position, nature, and function. Our *position* is crown of creation; we are stewards over what God has made. By *nature* we are personal, rational, moral beings, fully capable of intimate relationship with our Creator. And our *function* is to rule the earth as faithful prophets (interpreting reality as God's world), priests (preserving or maintaining the world as God had intended), and kings (ruling and guiding the world to its final end in God).

Thus the Bible stresses the personal nature of ethics, as well as the objective basis for values. Biblical morality consists of a personal relationship between people and a personal, sovereign God. God framed His commands in the second person ("*You* shall . . ." "*You* shall not . . ."), not the less personal third person ("A person should . . ." or "One should not . . ."), thus holding us accountable to God Himself, not merely to an abstract legal code. Thus when David confessed his adultery with Bathsheba in his penitential psalm, he admitted that his sin was against God, not "commandment number seven": "Against thee, thee only, have I sinned and done that which is evil in thy sight, so that thou art justified in thy sentence and blameless in thy judgment" (51:4, RSV). David confessed breaking the covenant relationship with God, whose honor is the ultimate end of all moral relationships.

God's first moral injunctions are sometimes called "creation ordinances," ethical tasks originating from creation itself. They comprise several duties that have significantly formed our understandings of individual human activity and social institutions. Creation ordinances involve subduing and ruling over the earth and its various kingdoms (Gen. 1:26), marriage and procreation (Gen. 1:28; 2:18-25), labor (2:15), and Sabbath observance (2:1-3). We derive our primary cultural tasks and meaningful behavior from these ordinances. By fulfilling these commands mankind parallels the animal kingdom, and yet human activity is distinguished by its moral significance. God's command to multiply results in families and marriages based on promises of love, unlike animal procreation, which is based only on periodic instinct. Moreover God preserves the dignity of marriage and family by forbidding adultery and fornication. Through labor men and women enjoy the honor of finishing God's work begun in creation. Although many animals exemplify diligence in work (e.g., Prov. 6:6-11), cultivating the garden and naming the animals uniquely set man apart as a cultural agent capable of creatively developing the earth's potential and establishing the kingdom of God. Human families, labor, and creativity are fully meaningful and distinct from similar animal activities because people perform these rationally and under strict moral principles. By consciously obeying God's will we glorify God and find the meaning and happiness God meant us to have from the beginning. The creation ordinances shape our self-understanding and our views of the rest of creation so significantly that our lives would be empty without them. God created us to find our deepest satisfaction in submitting all activities to God's will. To attempt to live by any other standard or to define meaning independently of God's will is futile.

The fall into sin described in Genesis 3 radically altered man's ethical being. Previously Adam and Eve not only knew the will of God but also obeyed it freely and thus enjoyed intimate communion with God. But the fall affected each of these areas. While no dimension of human existence escaped the ravages of sin, damage to man's moral nature was most debilitating as evidenced by biblical metaphors describing the effects of sin. Sin "darkened" the heart

(Rom. 1:21) and mind (Eph. 4:18); human speculation became "futile" (Rom. 1:21); and man is now "dead in . . . trespasses and sin" (Eph. 2:1). Such descriptions stand in sharp contrast to the original integrity and righteousness that characterized human life at creation and served as the basis for the creation ordinances.[1]

The extent of human depravity illustrates the necessity of God's intervening grace if man is to be restored to a proper relationship with God. God established another moral covenant, this time a redemptive one. Through Christ's atoning death He has provided a way of salvation and He sent His regenerating Spirit to make holiness of life possible. Each of these anthropological elements has ethical significance.

God initially revealed His will in the covenant with Adam to establish the covenant pattern of morality. The Old Testament covenant given through Moses, however, is the heart of biblical morality. In all biblical covenants obedience brings life and other blessings from God, while disobedience brings separation from God, punishment, and ultimately death. Adam was to obey the cultural mandate and the internal promptings of his conscience.[2] But Adam's sin necessitated an additional external law by which God would hold all people morally accountable. God gave the law because sinful human nature after the fall required it. The law did not presuppose a perfectible human nature by which man could justify himself morally before God. It presupposed exactly the opposite—an ethically sinful nature passed down from Adam after the fall. Therefore the moral law revealed to Moses at Mount Sinai had three purposes; the first two are negative, the third is positive. Through the law God sought:

   1. *To restrain sinners* by commanding obedience to God's will. The external law confirms the content of man's internal conscience. Because sin so easily distorts conscience, rendering it ineffective as an absolute standard of righteousness, mankind needs an objective, external source to state clearly

---

1. Cainite culture in Gen. 4 is dramatic testimony to sin's effects: Cain murders Abel (v. 8); Lamech takes two wives instead of one (v. 19) and later kills a person who merely wounds him (v. 23).
2. See below for a detailed discussion of conscience.

what is right and wrong. Just as a magistrate is a terror to evil-doers (Rom. 13:3), so the law warns of the dire consequences of sin. In an unregenerate world, God's law is thus a detriment to sin. Individually we need the law to restrain our sinful impulses. The social order also needs laws to curb vices and thus maintain order in the political realm.

2. *To point unbelievers to Christ* by convicting them of their sin. The law establishes the guilt of unregenerate people by showing them their sin (Rom. 3:20). Paul graphically illustrates the law's pedagogic character by calling it a "tutor to lead us to Christ" (Gal. 3:24). The law performs a similar function in the social order by serving as a basis for conviction in a court of law. Those responsible for maintaining order in society must possess a standard to judge the behavior of the accused.

3. *To guide believers* by providing a standard they may imitate in everyday ethical decisions. While the previous two negative functions presuppose human depravity, the positive function of the law is to encourage those who have been converted to aspire to holy living. Theological differences divide Christians over this third use of the law. Martin Luther, for example, believed that sin is so pervasive, even in the Christian life, that the law can never serve a positive function; it can only restrain and convict of sin. Luther believed people are so prone to pride that a positive use of the law would incline them to use it as a means of self-justification, thus denying the necessity of God's grace in order for them to become righteous. John Calvin, however, while not minimizing God's grace as indispensable for salvation, believed that Scripture teaches the law is a guide to holy living for believers in passages such as Proverbs 6:23 ("For the commandment is a lamp, and the teaching is light...") and John 15:10 ("If you keep My commandments, you will abide in My love"). (See also Rom. 3:31 and 7:12.)

Christians have consistently maintained the absolute necessity of God's law for private and public morality.[3] In its verbal form in Scripture, the law illustrates God's revelation as indicative and

---

3. Those who have opposed the use of the law are called antinomians (literally "those who are against law"). Usually they affirm the law as necessary for unregenerate people but deny that the law serves any useful purpose for believers. See our discussion of the Anabaptists in chap. 8.

imperative. Not only does God tell us what is right and wrong based on His intrinsic character (addressed to our rational minds), but He also commands moral obedience consistent with the content of that revelation (stimulating heart or conscience and will to act appropriately).

God continues His gracious provision for man's needs begun in conscience and confirmed in the law with His redemptive activity. The Old Testament Exodus and Christ's victory on the cross epitomize the moral nature of redemption. The balance between God's justice and His love is integral to both testaments but is most prominent in the New Testament Gospels. At the center of redemption is the atonement in which Christ (the sinless Son of God) dies for the guilty (fallen human beings). God fully upholds moral justice and at the same time lovingly saves His people by sending His Son to die as an act of sovereign grace. We appropriate the benefits of Christ's death by faith.

Christ's vicarious atonement and justification by faith provide the objective and subjective basis for Christian ethics. Objectively, the work of Christ frees the believer from the demands of the law, which require that sin be punished by death. Because Christ paid the penalty for sin, He also freed believers from the burden of fulfilling the moral demands of the law on their own, which they could not do because of their sinful nature. The objective element of redemption provides the basis for the subjective change in believers who experience an inner release or freedom from the guilt of failing to live up to the law. Thus Christian ethics is the morality of the regenerate believer. The biblical ethics of regeneration stand in stark contrast to all naturalistic perspectives, which teach that ethics is the development of the innate human potential to be moral. Christianity claims that the natural man must be reborn or transformed in order for a person to follow the ethical teaching of the Bible.

The Bible underscores the ethics of regeneration by asserting that Christian morality can only by accomplished in the power of the Holy Spirit. Unless individuals are regenerated by God's Spirit, they are unable to perform consistently what the law requires. The "pneumatic" character of New Testament ethics (*pneuma* is the

Greek word for "Spirit") is clear from the fact that Pentecost, the event in which God dramatically gave the Holy Spirit to the church in the signs of tongues of fire from heaven (Acts 2), represents God's bestowing moral and spiritual power to the church. The remainder of the New Testament presupposes the Holy Spirit's presence in believers' lives as indispensable for righteous or holy living.

Paul describes the roles of the law and the Holy Spirit in the Christian life in Romans 7 and 8. In previous chapters Paul demonstrated that God justifies believers because of their faith in Christ, not on the basis of their perfectly obeying the law (Rom. 4 and 5). In chapter 7 he teaches that the effect of the moral law prior to their faith in Christ was to produce not life but death. Paul claims that he would have never known what coveting is had the law not convicted him of covetousness: "But sin, taking opportunity through the commandment, produced in me coveting of every kind; for apart from the Law sin is dead" (v. 8). Experience shows that we cannot be saved by following the moral law. Our moral inability only proves that although ethical commandments are "holy and righteous and good" (v. 12), unbelievers are totally unable of themselves to produce ethical behavior because of their sinful nature. It is in Romans 8 that we find the means by which righteousness is possible—the indwelling power of the Holy Spirit. When believers are converted by the regenerating power of God, they are empowered by God's Spirit to live in accordance with God's will. No longer are believers hostile to God, but their desire is to live obediently as adopted children (see vv. 14, 15). Rebirth by God's Holy Spirit brings a new moral freedom to Christian conscience. In Galatians, Paul describes the Christian life as being "led by the Spirit" (Gal. 5:18), which results in the fruit of the Spirit—love, joy, peace, patience, kindness, goodness, faithfulness, gentleness, and self-control (5:22, 23). He commands his readers to "be filled with the Spirit" (Eph. 5:18) as a daily requirement for Christian living. The Holy Spirit dwells in believers, empowering them to obey God's commandments consistently.

From our discussion above it is clear that ethics is not the means by which people initiate or earn a relationship with God. Rather, ethical goodness results from a relationship that can only be initiated by God. Ethical living is not the way to God but our response to a God who has made His way to us. In biblical ethics, we begin with what a person is (regenerated or unregenerated), not with what a person does. Christian ethics presupposes a redeemed nature. Paul states this principle in Colossians 2:6: "As you therefore have received Christ Jesus the Lord, so walk in Him" (see also Eph. 4:1). Christian ethics is impossible without a renewed nature.[4]

Epistemological Presuppositions

Christians maintain that morality must be thoroughly biblical in its orientation. Biblical revelation is authoritative in ethics because it is true to life. God, the standard of truth, stands behind biblical commandments, affirming their truthful content and establishing their undisputed authority. Belief in the authority of Scripture demands that we understand God's sovereignty as the foundation for all belief and practice.

Although a detailed examination of biblical hermeneutics (the study of how to interpret the Bible) is beyond the scope of our study, we must at least pause briefly to consider this basic question of the truthfulness of the biblical ethical teaching. God's Word is the final court of appeal for ethical issues. Even if the Bible does not explicitly speak to a particular issue, we must believe that God has not left us without a moral anchor by which we can evaluate life's ethical dilemmas. Our discussion of the characteristics of the Bible in the unit on biblical epistemology (its necessity, authority, perspicuity, and sufficiency) established that we must honor its teaching because it is true and God speaks to us through its pages. Nowhere are these principles more important practically than in the field of morality. We know what is right and wrong because of God's Word, the Bible.

Our discussion of the objective nature of morality above does not

---

4. Paul underscores the priority of character over conduct in Christian ethics when in his epistles he first establishes Christian teaching on redemption and then moves to matters of Christian conduct. The best illustrations are Eph. 1-3 and Rom. 1-11, where he discusses Christian teaching on redemption and then moves to specific ethical teaching in Eph. 4:1 (see above) and Rom. 12:1: "I urge you therefore, brethren, by the mercies of God, to present your bodies a living and holy sacrifice, acceptable to God, which is your spiritual service of worship."

mean morality has no subjective element. We saw in our study of biblical epistemology that God's self-revelation always demands a believing response—an obedient acknowledgment that His commands are binding religious obligations. The subjective element in biblical ethics is always a response and never creative or originating on our parts. At most it represents our heart's concurrence with God's will.

The subjective apprehension of morality, an internal acknowledgment of its truth, is a frequent theme of the Bible and takes many forms. Most obvious is the multitude of statements expressing religious devotion to God and His law. Psalm 119 records the psalmist's spontaneous delight in God's law. All of the 176 verses display a joyful and devout acceptance of God's moral law: "How can a young man keep his way pure? By keeping it according to Thy word. . . . Thy word have I treasured in my heart that I might not sin against Thee" (vv. 9, 11); "O how I love Thy law! It is my meditation all the day" (v. 97); "Righteous art Thou, O Lord, and upright are Thy judgments" (v. 137).

The objectivity of Christian morality reflects the biblical view that knowledge is based on God's revelation. Scripture reveals that all truth originates in God. Since God is transcendent yet personal, ultimate truth is not merely cognitive apprehension of abstract propositions, but knowing God and being in relation with Him. God has so constituted the universe and the human mind that as His image bearers we can know God, ourselves, and all other things in the cosmos. Undergirded by God's revelation human reason, sense experience, authorities, and intuition enable us to know what can be understood by using them as sources of knowledge in their appropriate fields. Reason is legitimate in knowledge requiring logic and common sense. Sense experience and scientific method, properly applied, yield knowledge of empirical reality. Similarly, we accept the claims of historians and other reporters when they research their subjects carefully and report their findings fairly. Finally, we have confidence that our intuitive awareness of self-existence and our trust in the integrity of our closest friends are also true sources of knowledge. People rightly depend on these sources of knowledge in everyday life. Disputes arise over which source or sources are primary or whether one source has a corner on the truth. In the Christian world view, reason, experience, authority, and intuition are only valid because God as the revealer of truth in its manifold forms substantiates them.

In addition to the sources of knowledge that enable us to know and understand the world, Christians have true moral knowledge revealed by God in general and special revelation. Paul describes the role of conscience in human experience:

> For when Gentiles who do not have the Law do instinctively the things of the Law, these, not having the Law are a law to themselves, in that they show the work of the Law written in their hearts, their conscience bearing witness, and their thoughts alternately accusing or else defending them" (Rom. 2:14, 15).

According to Paul, God has implanted conscience into every human being. Conscience is a moral awareness by which people distinguish between what is morally right and wrong. The root meaning of the Greek word for "conscience" includes two activities: knowledge of an act, thought, or motive, and an individual's reflective judgment of the morality of that activity. Conscience may function retrospectively by passing judgment on past behavior, or it may direct present or future action by prohibiting or urging specific acts consistent with its reflections. Some people call conscience a "moral organ," a monitor, or even "the voice of God" within man, which judges, warns, and encourages moral decisions. All activities of conscience presuppose our rational capacity for self-transcendence—that we can in a sense stand outside of ourselves and make our motives, thoughts, and actions objects of serious moral reflection. In two passages Paul actually calls on his conscience as a witness to what he affirms (Rom. 9:1; II Cor. 2:12). Although calling upon conscience to give verbal witness in a legal proceeding is obviously impossible, Paul's metaphor indicates the true function of conscience as an independent yet internal source of more knowledge residing in human consciousness.

In the New Testament "conscience" appears thirty-one times, most frequently in Paul's epistles. Earlier in this chapter we saw how conscience functions as a source of moral knowledge through general revelation. Conscience provides everyone with the inescapable demands of God's moral law. God holds all people accountable when they disobey the dictates of conscience.

But Paul also described a positive role for conscience in Christian living. A dispute arose at Corinth over whether Christians could eat meat after it had been sacrificed to idols and sold in the marketplace (I Cor. 8 and 10:23-33). Paul said that mature believers, Christians who had developed their consciences in accordance with God's moral law revealed in Scripture, knew that pagan idols are false gods and do not actually exist. With this knowledge in mind (which is the meaning of "conscience"), they could eat such meat "in good conscience," that is, eat without approving and therefore participating in the sacrifice. But "weak" believers, who were freshly converted out of paganism, did not have this knowledge; they had not yet developed an informed Christian conscience. Because the meat reminded them of their previous participation in pagan rites, they could not eat without their consciences being "defiled." Their eating was accompanied with a troubled awareness that by eating they were still involved in their former idolatry, which all men know from nature and conscience is morally wrong.[5] Therefore, Paul commanded mature Christians to defer to "weaker brethren" by abstaining from eating meat. Christians should never exercise even legitimate freedom of conscience if such action tempts weaker believers to violate their consciences.

Taken together the various biblical passages on conscience have several implications. God implants conscience in all people by

5. Paul also teaches the basic functioning of conscience in his description of pagan rejection of natural revelation in Rom. 1:18-23. All people who deny the existence of God violate conscience. Paul claims that all men know the true God but "suppress the truth in unrighteousness," that is, they know God exists from His clear self-disclosure in creation, but refuse to obey the ethical significance of that knowledge and worship false gods instead of the one true God. Not only do they deny the true God but they violate conscience, which condemns idolatrous worship. Because of their sinful rebellion, God gives unbelievers over to "a depraved mind" (i.e., a depraved conscience), which permits a host of gross sins such as sexual immorality, envy, greed, murder, etc. (vv. 24-31). Paul summarizes the pagan degeneration of conscience in v. 32: "Although they know the ordinance of God, that those who practice such things are worthy of death, they not only do the same, but also give hearty approval to those who practice them" (1:32).

creating them in His image. Since conscience reveals our moral duty, no one can claim ignorance of his or her moral responsibility. Sin, however, severely cripples conscience. While sin does not destroy conscience just as it does not eradicate our ability to reason or use other sources of knowledge, nevertheless, conscience is susceptible to sin's noetic effect. Conscience suffers from the "darkening" of the mind and the futility of thinking that Paul discusses in Romans 1:18-23. The effect of sin is progressive and cumulative. The more one sins, the greater the damage to conscience. If a person persistently violates conscience, Paul warns, he or she can experience "hardness of heart" and become "callous" (Eph. 4:19). In extreme cases conscience is "seared" as if by a branding iron (I Tim. 4:2) so that a person is no longer sensitive to warnings, urgings, and other moral promptings.

We conclude from these passages that although conscience is fallible, it is nevertheless inviolate. Therefore, one of our highest ethical responsibilities as Christians is to educate conscience. Despite conscience's limits, Christians possess in the Scripture an infallible moral standard of the sovereign will of God. A believer's individual responsibility is to conform his or her conscience to the revealed will of God. In addition God holds believers mutually accountable for each other's moral welfare including the development of conscience. Peter charges his readers to "keep a good conscience so that in the thing in which you are slandered, those who revile your good behavior in Christ may be put to shame" (I Pet. 3:16). Believers' behavior should be so exemplary that those who witness it are actually stricken by their conscience though they may outwardly ridicule moral rectitude. Paul affirms that the goal of Christian ministry is not simply to educate believers in doctrine but also to produce in believers "love from a pure heart and a good conscience and a sincere faith" (I Tim. 1:15). In several passages the apostle advocates keeping conscience in conjunction with maintaining the faith. He reinforces the ethical dimension of knowledge when he states that a qualification of deacons is that they hold "the mystery of the faith with a clear conscience" (I Tim. 3:9). Acting in good conscience means that a person attempts to live in conformity with his convictions as shaped by God's moral law. If believers will live ethical lives that conform to God's commandments, their witness will be positive.[6] Christians therefore know what is morally right and wrong from God's revelation. But sin and its effects mean that we need more than conscience. Thus in special revelation God reveals His moral law and also provides a covenant of redemption by which a fully Christian ethic is possible.

Jesus' Kingdom Ethics

Jesus' ethical teaching in the Gospels exemplify and reinforce these presuppositions. Many people have commented that what differentiates Jesus' teaching from those of other religions is not His ethical content. He did not propose a new list of commandments to replace Old Testament ethical teaching. The remarkable continuity between Jewish and Christian moral law has led to the phrase "the Judeo-Christian ethic," which describes traditional morality in the West.

Though Jesus' external demands were not unique, His ethical teaching was distinguished by its remarkable power and persuasiveness. Each of the gospel writers testifies to people's astonishment at the authority with which Jesus taught and the compelling nature of His teaching. Matthew reports that crowds "were amazed" at Jesus' teaching because He "taught them as one having authority and not as the scribes"; His words bore a kind of self-authenticating authority (7:28, 29). Moreover, unlike other great ethical teachers, Jesus sometimes performed miracles to authenticate His ethical authority. When Jesus healed the paralytic who was lowered through the roof (Matt. 9:2ff.), the multitudes who witnessed the miracle were "filled with awe and glorified God" not just because the paralytic was able to walk again, but because the healing confirmed Jesus' unique moral authority, to forgive sin (7:8). Although He did not always perform signs and wonders when teaching about ethics, that He occasionally did so indicates that we are to view His ethics in conjunction with His teaching about Himself. His ability to teach with authority on any subject is ultimately bound up with His being the Son of God. If Jesus claimed to be the Son of God and was mistaken in that claim, then we could hardly accept His ethical teach-

6. See also I Tim. 1:19; 3:9; Heb. 13:18; Acts 24:16.

ing. Therefore, the question of Jesus' ethical authority is intimately connected with His teaching about Himself.

Jesus expounded His ethics as part of His teaching on "the kingdom of God." The phrase is a new one on His lips even though the idea of God as king over the world occurs frequently in the Old Testament. As He began His public ministry, Jesus announced, "The time is fulfilled, and the kingdom of God is at hand; repent, and believe in the gospel" (Mark 1:15). God's kingdom is neither a geographical area nor a political state. Rather it is a spiritual reality wherever people acknowledge and follow God's authority or rule in everyday life. By making repentance the condition for entrance, Jesus established moral obedience as a sign of one's participation in the kingdom.

Jesus included several important ethical principles in the Sermon on the Mount. Over against traditional Judaism's demand for a mere physical or external obedience to the letter of the law, Jesus emphasized the spiritual motivation underlying an act. Jesus taught that a person breaks the sixth commandment not simply by overtly murdering another person but also by anger and hatred in the heart (Matt. 5:21, 22). Similarly adultery is not merely the physical act of intercourse but is also a lustful glance or internal thought (Matt. 5:27, 28). In each of these instances Jesus, far from negating the Old Testament commandments against murder and adultery, actually strengthened them. He internalized and intensified their meanings by locating obedience in the mind or heart (corresponding to intention or motivation) as well as in external action. Because traditional Jews of Jesus' day tended to focus exclusively on external matters of physical cleanliness or religious ritual, they missed the spiritual dimension of morality. Most of Jesus' contemporaries taught that of the original Ten Commandments, only coveting is an internal sin. If a person could refrain from actually stealing, lying, murdering, Sabbath breaking, etc., then he or she would be morally righteous.

By His reinterpretation of these two laws Jesus made obeying all of the commandments a matter of the same internal dimension of the heart as the last commandment of covetousness. People not only covet others' property in their hearts; they also break all of the other commandments in the privacy of their thoughts or imaginations. Thus Jesus rephrased the law in the spirit of Jeremiah 31:33, where the prophet foretold a "new covenant" that would be unlike the law code of Moses written on tablets of stone. Instead of morality focusing only on external behavior, the new covenant Jesus inaugurated judges inner motivation as well. His view reflects Jeremiah's words, "I will put my law within them, and on their heart I will write it . . ."

Jesus summarized His teaching on motivation by saying that unless His followers' righteousness "surpasses the righteousness of the scribes and the Pharisees," they would not enter the kingdom of heaven (Matt. 5:20). Christian ethics are to be a straightforward reflection of the heart, not performed to impress people outwardly, but to please God who sees the heart (Matt. 6:1-6).

The remainder of Jesus' ethical teaching is equally rigorous. He forbade the taking of oaths meant to circumvent telling the truth (Matt. 5:33-38; 16:16-22). He rejected the *lex talionis* (an eye for an eye) as a basis for individual behavior. Jesus' teaching requires a willingness to give of oneself even to those who will take advantage: "If any one wants to sue you, and take your shirt, let him have your coat also. . . . Give to him who asks of you, and do not turn away from him who wants to borrow from you. . . . Love your enemies, and pray for those who persecute you" (Matt. 5:40-44). Each of these radical reinterpretations establishes the highest standard for believers, a standard of love that exceeds the ordinary requirements of justice. Christians confess that only Christ Himself could meet them. And He fulfilled them in a life that led to suffering on the cross. Jesus summarized the Christian ethic in terms not of authority and power but of service:

> You know that those who are recognized as rulers of the Gentiles lord it over them; and their great men exercise authority over them. But it is not so among you, but whoever wishes to become great among you shall be your servant; and whoever wishes to be first among you shall be slave of all. . . . For even the Son of Man did not come to be served but to serve and to give his life a ransom for many (Mark 10:42-45).

In addition to His straightforward ethical teaching, Jesus also included moral teaching in His famous parables. His parabolic teaching also contradicts conventional ethical wisdom that people can secure their moral standing with others and in the sight of God by morally self-justifying acts. Two parables especially highlight the radical nature of Jesus' ethic: the parable of the vineyard owner and the parable of the good Samaritan. In the former (Matt. 20:1-16), the owner of the vineyard hires people at various times of the day to work at a given wage. But at the end of the day he chooses to show his generosity by paying those hired late in the day a full day's wage just as he had promised those who worked through the whole day. Members of the kingdom of God are to be just as generous in their dealing with other people for God set this example for us to follow.

The parable of the good Samaritan further confirms Jesus' radically new command to love even our enemies (Luke 10:25-37). When an expert in the law questioned Jesus about how one should inherit eternal life, Jesus responded with the commandment to love God and one's neighbor. When the lawyer pressed Jesus about who is one's neighbor, Jesus told the parable in which a Samaritan, a person of mixed ethnic background, whom the Jews despised, emerged as the ethical hero because he helped a Jew who had been beaten and robbed. Just as the Samaritan in helping a Jew aided someone who was totally undeserving of help, so His followers were to assist even their enemies.

Jesus' ethical teaching is an integral part of His teaching on the kingdom of God. He does not alter the ethical teaching of the Old Testament but rather strengthens it. His summary statement is that He did not come to annul or abolish the law, but to fulfill it (Matt. 5:17,18). Therefore, Christians support the moral teaching of the Bible in every way possible and seek to apply biblical norms to the cultures in which they live.

Misleading Ways of Applying Biblical Ethics

Only as we understand the presuppositions of biblical ethics will we be able to apply them in life. Simply memorizing isolated verses will not equip us to confront concrete ethical decisions wisely. We must develop an ethical framework for dealing with specific issues.

The Ten Commandments, by themselves, are just the beginning, the bare minimum of what God requires. Jesus' teaching in the Sermon on the Mount moves beyond a superficial adherence to individual regulations and proof-texts from the Bible. Since one of the basic principles of biblical interpretation is that we are to use Scripture to interpret Scripture, we must search God's Word in order to grasp the full extent of our responsibilities. The Bible is both necessary and sufficient for making ethical decisions, but doing so is not always a simple matter. For example, should a Christian couple who have been unable to have children use contemporary medical technology to conceive a child? If so, what methods may they use? Are all methods equally valid?

Legalism

Christians have proposed several approaches to answering such questions. Legalism assumes that identifying and obeying biblical commands is the exclusive means of resolving all ethical questions. Legalists consider the Bible to be essentially a book of rules, which they consult to find the appropriate command to fit the circumstance. The Bible is thus reduced to a legal directory to meet specific needs.

To their credit, legalists acknowledge that God's commandments reveal what is morally correct behavior. Not to take God's revelation seriously is tantamount to rebellion against the rightful authority of the Word of God. But legalism errs in its claim that rules are the only means by which we may understand the will of God. Legalism ignores, for example, that God reveals moral principles in Jesus' parables that shed light on how we understand God's moral law. People who are legalists also fail to recognize that the Bible cannot explicitly speak to every new situation that has arisen since it was written. Technology enables us to perform many tasks, such as organ transplants, that previously were impossible, forcing us to confront the question of what we should do when we find no direct biblical command. Also legalism fails to acknowledge that goodness consists of more than strict conformity to the letter of the law, as Jesus' teaching on inner motivation reveals. It is possible to do the legally or morally correct thing, but from the wrong motivation. A person might perform a "charitable" act such as giving to the poor because a list of contributors is printed in the local papers. Or a person might refrain from stealing but only because of the probability of being caught in the act. While legalism recognizes our accountability to biblical commandments, it treats only actions and their consequences as important.

Situationism

A second method of applying Christian morality, situationism (also called contextualism), begins not with rules but with the particular context in which the act occurs. Rather than attempting, as the legalist does, to identify which of the many commandments of the Bible applies to the particular issue at hand, the situationist accepts only one absolute moral command—Jesus' requirement to love —as the basis for ethical choice. The only question is What is the most loving thing to do in this context? Love alone is the fundamental element in moral choice.

The obvious strong point of contextualism is its commitment to the love commandment that all New Testament writers stressed in their ethical teaching. Who could possibly disagree that love is of primary importance in all decisions? The central thrust of the gospel ethic is that we are to love others because Christ first loved us. Loving our neighbor means going beyond what justice requires. Situationism thus assigns preeminence to people and our responsibility to demonstrate love to a world that desperately needs it. While situationists do not simply ignore the rest of the biblical commandments, they do assert that only one law is absolute. In essence, they are ready to treat any or even all the rest of biblical revelation as relative and therefore dispensable. They are prepared to view every other commandment as provisional if they cannot see it as the "most loving" action in a given context.

The cardinal difficulty is that contextualism fails to recognize the unity of Christian truth. All of God's commandments are interrelated. Situationalists say that love may ordinarily demand faithfulness and integrity in a relationship. On occasion, however, love may demand unfaithfulness and deceit. "Love" becomes exceedingly plastic and malleable in the hands of the contextualist. Just as legalists take a necessary and indispensable element of the biblical ethic and distort it by absolutizing it, so the situationist takes the valid principle that all decisions must be made in a particular context and then absolutizes that idea as the only important element in ethical behavior.

Love is not open to our manipulation. If God's commandment to love can be filled almost at whim by what the context demands, then "love" is but an empty word. Situationism ignores the valid claims of the legalist that we must obey all of God's biblical commands. The rest of the commandments are not irrelevant but actually define *how* we are to love—by not lying, by being faithful in marriage, by regarding others' property with respect, etc.

Situationism also does not fully appreciate how a person's motivation may thoroughly distort his decision. Can we be sure, for example, that our presumably loving act is not self-centered or motivated by personal concerns, a disguised expression of greed, malice, or vindictiveness? Just as in legalism, wrong motivation in contextualism may completely cancel any goodness in our action. Situationism is fraught with the problems that beset relativism. Without some fixed principles we have no way to distinguish between right and wrong. As we noted in our study of existentialism (vol. 1, chap. 15), situationism places an enormous burden on the individual. Though contextualism offers a liberty to individuals that at first blush appears attractive, increasing human autonomy almost inevitably heightens people's anxiety. Situationism burdens them with a responsibility they were not created to bear—a godlike task of determining what is right and wrong and carrying what is right to its completion. Even though some have claimed in the name of Christianity that people are fully able to decide what the ethical content of love is in any given situation, most have recognized that such a relativistic and individualistic approach is not consistent with biblical ethics.

Intuitionism

A final approach to applying biblical presuppositions is intuitionism, which holds that individuals immediately understand what is right and wrong. Intuitionism makes ethical knowledge an exclusively internal and subjective experience associated with conscience. The strength of intuitionism is its recognition that moral decisions must never be made without reference to our internal capacity for moral reflection. Conscience is absolutely indispensable in morality because moral responsibility is impossible unless people possess a subjective, internal element relating them to a personal God. If our intellect were not marred by sin, pure or theoretical reason would be sufficient as a basis for apprehending intellectual ideals as Plato taught. Because we are ultimately related not to abstractions but to a personal God, we must possess a quality that makes that relationship possible.

Intuitionism enjoys popularity today because many people make ethical decisions without reference to codes or the Bible. For them, ethics is no more than following their feelings. But intuitionism has severe limitations because it fails to recognize other important elements in ethics. Without a moral standard in the form of laws and principles, a person lacks the ability to distinguish between mere emotional feelings and the dictates of conscience. History contains numerous examples of people who have presumably based their actions on conscience when they have actually acted out of purely emotional impulse or self-interest. Rational ethical discussion is impossible when people uncritically appeal to their intuition. Christians should use biblical norms to examine their feelings so that they do not confuse their emotions with conscience.

Intuitionism also is a form of antinomianism. Antinomians believe that the indwelling of the Spirit in their lives makes the moral law superfluous because God deals with people directly through His Spirit, not through law. Groups such as the Anabaptists or radical Reformers in the sixteenth century relied not on the Scripture, which some considered a "dead letter," but on God's continuing internal revelation to individuals. Antinomianism rests on a misunderstanding of Paul's contention that the law is of no use in earning salvation from God. Its proponents incorrectly interpret Paul's teaching to mean that law serves no positive function for Christians. According to the third use of the law, however, Christians are sinners who still need the law as a guideline for holy living.

Legalism, situationism, and intuitionism fail to produce biblical obedience because each presents only an aspect of the Bible's holistic ethic. Each absolutizes a single element at the expense of other equally valid elements from the biblical world view. We must, however, find a way to combine valid elements from each of the perspectives into a coherent, unified view. Believing in the unity of truth, Christians seek to provide a balanced ethical perspective in which all elements receive the same emphasis the Bible accords them.

The Biblical Triad

The framework for Christian ethics can best be conceived as a triad in which valid elements from each of the three perspectives described above receive due emphasis.[7] In order to obey God, a person must apply the *norms* of Scripture to *himself* in his particular *situation*. That involves (1) recognizing which biblical norms or principles apply to the decision or situation at hand, (2) understanding how those norms translate into the terms of his experience in that situation, and (3) accepting and obeying God's norms as binding on himself. All three are necessary if we are to avoid the pitfalls of legalism, situationism, and intuitionism. In fact our response to God's norms addressed to our situation is one inseparable act of obedience. The three perspectives are interdependent—not isolated or autonomous—all held together by and expressing the lordship of God.

The normative standard presupposes God as our transcendent

7. The following material on the biblical triad is adapted from classroom material on Christian ethics by John M. Frame of Westminster Theological Seminary, Escondido, California.

authority. As Creator and sovereign Lord, God has established laws and revealed principles that tell us what is truly good. Earlier in this chapter we explained the significance of God's sovereignty for ethics and stressed Scripture as His revelation. Without God's divinely revealed norms for human behavior we would be left to the whims of man (our own impulses or others') and lost in a morass of subjectivism and relativism. Faced continually with an array of personal challenges, decisions, needs, and issues, each of us should at all times ask, What standards has God set down to enable me to respond properly to this situation?

There is more to obedience than knowing God's law in the abstract. A person may be able to recite the Ten Commandments without understanding or submitting to what the commandments say about him in his situation. He may, for example, know that stealing is wrong and yet (for whatever reason) fail to make the connection between stealing and his practice of embezzling funds. Despite his awareness of the norm "You shall not steal," he goes on stealing because he has yet to grasp the full meaning of the norm as it was meant to apply to him in his situation. A genuine appreciation and application of God's norms must take into view the other two corners of the triad as well.

We never make ethical choices in a vacuum. Every decision occurs in a complex historical context. Whereas the normative standard presupposes the transcendence of God, the second element of the triad, the situation, presupposes His immanence, His presence within the historical setting in which we live. God is concerned with the details of every situation we face. Not only does He control and direct history by His providential hand, but His Word sheds light to guide all our choices, either by explicit commands or by broad principles. The better we understand the intricacies of our various situations in life, the more pointedly we can apply God's laws to our experience. In a sense our understanding of our situations enhances our understanding of the biblical norms, and we are enabled more fully to bring our lives under the lordship of Christ. Our moral choices thus reflect our status as faithful stewards who seek for God's kingdom to come and His will to be done on earth as in heaven. We can apply God's norms to our situations with the underlying assurance that God sovereignly works to bring about good consequences to the lives of those who love Him. God's control of history insures that He is glorified not only by acts of obedience but also by the repercussions of those acts as His unfolding purposes are fulfilled. The norms of Scripture are designed to produce what is pleasing to God and good for us in every situation.

Because history progresses, we are confronted with many ethical choices unknown to previous generations. For example, present-day technologies of human fertilization were unimaginable in biblical times. It is not surprising that we find no explicit biblical commands regarding such things as in vitro (test tube) fertilization, artificial insemination, and surrogate motherhood. But that does not mean such issues are value-neutral or that we may think or do whatever we please in reference to them. Since God is Lord of all of life, all issues have moral components, and in every new situation we must ask What would glorify God? Decisions about contemporary fertilization technologies must be made in light of biblical principles and precedents even if no explicit commandments are addressed to them. For example, does Abraham's use of Hagar to produce an heir provide a biblical basis for surrogate motherhood? Would surrogacy represent an intrusion upon biblically mandated marital faithfulness? How would biblical principles about the preservation of life and health pertain to in vitro fertilization? Would surplus human embryos be destroyed? What might the risks be for birth defects? Raising questions such as these enables us to bring even the highly complex concerns of our modern situation under the authority of God's revealed norms.

A discussion of norms and situations would be empty without the third corner of the biblical triad, the existential self. The existential perspective focuses on a person's ethical responses. A righteous response presupposes the indwelling presence of God's Holy Spirit in the life of the individual. It is possible for someone to know what the norms are *and* how they apply to his situation *but still not obey God*. Unless God's Spirit is at work in a person's heart, he will not do even what he knows to be right. In some cases he will do what is apparently right but for the wrong motives. Or he will disobey out of ignorance of the divine norms, blinded by his sinful nature. Whatever the reason, an unethical response constitutes a failure to embrace and fulfill God's norms as binding upon oneself in one's particular situation.

God makes ethical goodness possible by giving sinners new hearts, indwelling them with His Holy Spirit, renewing their minds, and enabling them to love, which is the first fruit of the Spirit, against which there is no law. This inner working of God's Spirit enables men and women to act out of unselfish motives. The selfless love of a believer is the most compelling sign of Christian discipleship: "A new commandment I give to you, that you love one another; even as I have loved you, that you also love one another. By this all men will know that you are my disciples, if you have love for one another" (John 13:34, 35). Without such love, even an outwardly good act (such as giving all of one's possessions to feed the poor [I Cor. 13:3]) is of absolutely no ethical value, though it may be practically beneficial to others. Any act born out of a wrong motive dishonors God because good motives themselves are mandated by God's norms in Scripture. God is concerned that our inward self, as well as our outward behavior, be brought into conformity with Christ. Jesus' prayer, "Not My will, but Thine be done" (Luke 22:42) provides the ethical model for our existential response to God. Seen in this light ethics is an intensely personal matter between the individual and God. This personal concern distinguishes Christian ethics from systems that demand only normative or situational criteria for morality.

All three aspects of the triad are necessary for moral goodness, each implying the other two. None of them functions in abstraction or separately from the others. Each is a necessary and sufficient condition of good works because each involves the others. If (to complete an earlier example) the normative standard reveals that stealing is wrong, and in the situational setting I recognize that embezzling is stealing, then I must willingly apply that to myself by resolving never to embezzle. Instead, submitting to God's authority (normative) and trusting His good providence to meet my financial needs (situational), I must seek His work within me (existential) to enable me to work productively as a good and faithful steward.

Each perspective implies the others and the triad holds together because each angle is an expression that, as Lord, Jesus is the standard, controller, and motivator of ethical goodness. Obedience is nothing less than a full-bodied declaration of the lordship of God, who is central to biblical ethics. Or, to change the imagery, we might view biblical ethics not in terms of a two-dimensional triad but in terms of a three-dimensional pyramid with God at the apex. The Lord rules all three corners at the base. He has revealed His authority through His law; He demonstrates His sovereign control in any and every situation; and He manifests His indwelling presence by enabling believers to follow Him and thereby become Christ-like.

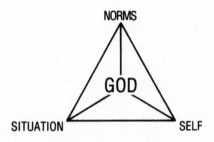

A mere diagram of Christian ethics such as the triad or the pyramid cannot by itself create Christian conduct. All of the systems of the world cannot establish righteousness. But in identifying the ethical components and implications of the biblical world view, we have attempted to illustrate the complexity of living out the Christian life as God's covenant people. God's covenantal stipulations call for behavior that best fulfills our humanity. Biblical ethics in no way stifles or hinders our unique identity as persons. Paradoxically, obedient service to God's law brings us ever-increasing freedom because we become like the One we serve. God's norms are given for the good of humanity. By following them we can realize contentment and purpose and can help to promote righteousness and justice in our world.

For Further Reading

Fletcher, Joseph. *Situation Ethics: The New Morality*. Philadelphia: Westminster Press, 1967.

Henry, Carl F. H. *Christian Personal Ethics*. Grand Rapids: Eerdmans, 1957.

Henry, Carl F. H., ed. *Dictionary of Christian Ethics*. Grand Rapids: Baker, 1973.

Kaiser, Walter C. *Classical Evangelical Essays in Old Testament Interpretation*. Grand Rapids: Baker, 1972.

_____ . *Toward Old Testament Ethics*. Grand Rapids: Zondervan, 1983.

Kline, Meredith. *The Structure of Biblical Authority*. Grand Rapids: Eerdmans, 1972.

Lewis, C. S. *The Abolition of Man*. New York: Macmillan, 1947.

Murray, John. *Principles of Conduct*. Grand Rapids: Eerdmans, 1957.

O'Donovan, M. T. "The Possibility of a Biblical Ethic." *Theological Students' Fellowship Bulletin* 67 (1973).

Ramsey, Paul. *Basic Christian Ethics*. New York: Scribner. 1950.

_____ . *Deeds and Rules in Christian Ethics*. New York: Scribner, 1967.

Van Til, Cornelius, *Christian Theistic Ethics*. Phillipsburg, N.J.: Presbyterian and Reformed, n.d.

White, R. E. O. *Biblical Ethics*. Atlanta: John Knox Press, 1979.

Wright, C. J. H. *An Eye for an Eye*. Downers Grove, Ill.: Inter-Varsity Press, 1983.

II.
NATURALISTIC
ETHICS

13
Ethics of Human Autonomy

W. Andrew Hoffecker

Introduction

Since within any given world view one assumption likely depends on another, we would expect to find an integral relationship between naturalistic ethics and other aspects of the naturalistic world-and-life view.

With that in mind, this chapter will (1) show how theological, anthropological, and epistemological presuppositions determine the foundation, method, and contents of naturalistic ethics; (2) present a brief historical survey of naturalistic ethics; (3) discuss several representative naturalistic ethical systems; and (4) analyze how naturalism inevitably results in autonomous humans' creating autonomous ethical systems.

Theological Presuppositions

Fundamental to naturalism is a denial of anything metaphysical. Reality is made up entirely of finite, natural entities perceived by our senses. In their cosmology, naturalists contend that nothing is beyond nature; nature is a self-contained, closed system of cause and effect. No transcendent person, force, or influence exists outside the realm of empirical objects. This view raises an ethical question voiced long ago by Plato: Is something ethically good because God designates it as such, or does God simply recognize and proclaim the moral goodness of what is intrinsically good. All forms of naturalism differ sharply from theism in answering this basic question.

If we answer as we discussed in chapter 12 that good is what God declares to be good, we affirm that God Himself is the source of all goodness and requires our conformity to it through His revealed moral law. In this view God is ultimate, and the source, explanation, and motivation for morality are found in a sovereign, transcendent being. Scripture teaches that good does not result from an irrational, arbitrary choice of a sovereign who could just as readily command us to murder as to love. Rather, good originates from God's very nature and has its meaning in Him. God determines the meaning and purpose of everything because He alone created out of nothing and providentially orders the entire universe.

Believing that theism rendered the existence and meaning of good arbitrary, Plato proposed that Goodness is not derived from God, but, as it were, exists beyond God and all being, a higher Goodness in itself. Plato's implicit naturalism maintained that God commands obedience to the moral law because it is intrinsically good. Plato's "God," the Demiurge, was subordinate to the Good, not the source of all goodness. In Plato's dialogue *Timaeus*, the Demiurge (as we have discussed in chap. 2) is described not as a transcendent creator but as a subordinate craftsman deity who constructs the universe following eternal forms or archetypes as blueprints. Transcendent, impersonal forms, not the Demiurge, are ultimate in Plato's philosophy, which paved the way for autonomous naturalistic systems, in which there is no use whatsoever for God.

Plato's writings on ethics, more than anything else, justify our claim that his system of thought was fundamentally naturalistic. That judgment may seem harsh given Plato's insistence on vigorous training in the moral virtues rooted in transcendent, absolute forms. Plato despised Protagoras's relativism, summarized by the Sophist philosopher's oft-quoted dictum, "Man is the measure of all things; of those that are, that they are and of those that are not, that they are not." Plato believed that an absolute moral truth exists which should be the foundation for all education. But in his critique of sophistic relativism Plato attributed a similar autonomy to human moral effort, akin to Protagoras's contention that "Man is the measure." Although Plato proposed a system of objective moral value in which virtues have their existence and meaning independent of man's assessment, he went beyond this and said that right and wrong are independent of the gods as well. The Good is uncreated, necessary, and absolute, but ultimately impersonal and abstract. Therefore, Plato denied the need for a personal deity who reveals His character and provides covenantal law that specifies right and wrong.

Plato may have believed that the Good simply resides on the other side of existence. His reason for separating morality from the gods is apparent. If he made the gods the source of morality, people would assume that he meant the deities of Greek tradition. We have already seen (vol. 1, chap. 2) how inadequate Homer's immoral, personal deities depicted in the *Iliad* and *Odyssey* were for Plato's purposes. Like his teacher Socrates, Plato despised these gods because only in their power, not in their morality, were they superior to mere mortals. But whatever Plato's reasons for making Goodness and not deity ultimate, in the final analysis Plato rested his ethical thought on a naturalistic foundation. His desire to refute ethical relativism and reform Athens's religious life by denouncing the foibles and immoralities of Olympian deities is commendable. But he replaced the gods with an autonomous and impersonal absolute and assumed that humans possess a godlike ability to perceive the Good apart from revelation and to perform moral good apart from divine grace.

Thus, Plato's theological presuppositions as they affect ethics are consistent with other forms of philosophical naturalism we have previously discussed. While not as polemic as Stephen Crane's or Francis Crick's atheism, Plato's system pointedly illustrates how foundational theological presuppositions are for ethical reflection. Relating God and the good is a watershed issue that sharply divides theists and all types of naturalists: Theists view morality as grounded in a transcendent source outside of human experience. Naturalists consider the moral law to be an impersonal, autonomous ideal or to be grounded in some finite base, usually human choice.

Anthropological and Epistemological Presuppositions

Since naturalists deny a transcendent being who reveals ethical right and wrong immanently in space and time, the source and meaning of morality must lie elsewhere. Various naturalists identify different sources. Karl Marx believed that the dialetic, an impersonal process that moves history to its predetermined conclusion, determines right and wrong. Existentialists such as Jean Paul Sartre have argued that morality is based upon human freedom, the free choice of autonomous individuals. B. F. Skinner, Francis Crick, and Jacques Monod have claimed that only trained specialists, a technological elite, possess experimental know-how to discover and teach moral principles conducive to human survival.

Contemporary naturalists assign man the task of determining right and wrong. The interrelatedness of naturalists' anthropological and epistemological assumptions is evident in the following quotation:

> We human beings select what we determine to be fact, by means of hypotheses that we design to answer our questions, allay our doubts, appease our curiosity, and augment our understanding. . . . We use the tools of logic to structure our concepts, to regulate our inquiry, to articulate our discourse, and to validate our inference. . . . We do all this as we guide our hands and brain, in order to describe and explain the world and make it finally more amenable to our ideals. Thus, there is an irreducibly anthropocentric surd [irrationality] in knowledge.[1]

Not all naturalists would concur completely with Abel's assertion, nor would all of them affirm human autonomy so blatantly. Nevertheless, the question of meaning is inescapable in philosophy, and even naturalists must provide some basis for meaning in their world view. A few philosophers have so despaired of this task that they call themselves nihilists (from Latin *nihil* which means "nothing"). Nihilists deny that reality, including ethics, has any justifiable meaning or purpose. Though a radical form of naturalism, nihilism correctly (though unintentionally) calls our attention to the futility of finding meaning apart from God.

Aristotle provided the classical anthropological and epistemological presuppositions for what has become naturalistic ethics.

1. Reuben Abel, *Man Is the Measure* (New York: The Free Press, 1976), pp. 272-73.

Although Aristotle affirmed an unmoved mover as the final cause of reality, in his ethics he attributed significant autonomy to the human soul. Foremost among the soul's powers is control of the appetites or desires. Moral virtue results when a wise person makes choices that produce habits of moral behavior. All people have a natural capacity for moral goodness, which must be developed through practice. Virtue is not an individual act but a habit resulting from doing repeatedly what reason knows to be right. For example, by telling the truth, a person builds honesty as a habit. Thus while all people begin with an inherent moral capacity, only those who continually tell the truth actually develop the virtue or habit of honesty.

Aristotle's guide for moral virtue was the golden mean, a median course that reason chooses between two extremes. The extremes are vices, one of defect, the other of excess. For example, courage is the mean between rashness, a foolhardy boldness, on the one hand, and cowardice, a shameful reticence to act, on the other. Courage is virtuous not simply because it is a mean that one can calculate mathematically between extremes but because courageous activity conforms with reason's demands.

Like Plato's before him, Aristotle's naturalism was not as radical as contemporary thinkers' in that Aristotle considered reason divine. Although for Aristotle reason was not a gift of a personal yet transcendent God, it was intrinsic to human nature. By thinking and ordering the moral life, human beings approximate the life of the unmoved mover, Aristotle's god.

Contemporary naturalists, as we have noted, recognize no such metaphysical basis for right and wrong. And yet actions are based on premises of one kind or another. Can finite creatures provide an adequate ethical base for all moral obligation or must value systems rest on some other foundation?

Consider, for example, a society's prohibition against stealing or its injunction to tell the truth. One way of justifying such behavior is to appeal to innate human dignity, which requires people to respect others' property and speak truthfully. Another rationale might be the pragmatic argument that society works best when governed by truthfulness and integrity. Still another tack would be to ground such moral regulations in the will of a transcendent God. All three approaches appeal to authorities. An interpretive principle explains the source of moral obligation and how and why stealing is wrong and truthtelling is right.

Having discussed naturalistic presuppositions we are now prepared to examine the historical roots of naturalistic ethics. We have contended that ethical systems are closely related to epistemological presuppositions. We will attempt to show how modern epistemology has directly affected the development of contemporary ethical naturalism.

Historical Roots of Naturalistic Ethics

Gradual, subtle shifts in epistemology have influenced ethics since the Middle Ages. In his view of reality, Thomas Aquinas (1225-74) distinguished between two metaphysical realms— nature and grace. "Nature" can be understood by means of rational categories as articulated in Aristotle's epistemology. Sensation and reason, constituting a kind of "common sense," enable us to know the physical world and objects in it. But beyond nature is a transcendent, spiritual reality (supernature or grace) known only through revelation. God dispenses grace by His eternal law and governs nature through natural law.

Thomas never delineated an explicit or absolute dualism between the physical and spiritual realms and their respective laws. But by distinguishing two spheres of nature and grace, which are known by two separate though complementary modes of knowing, Thomas introduced an important idea into Western thought. His view can be diagrammed thus:

GRACE – GOVERNED BY ETERNAL LAW– KNOWN BY REVELATION
NATURE – GOVERNED BY NATURAL LAW– KNOWN BY SENSATION AND REASON

In our earlier study of Thomas's theology and anthropology, we noted rudiments of his moral theory. According to Thomas's view of natural law, human reason is capable of directing individuals, whether Christians or not, to achieve their ethical end or goal in life. He believed that natural man is capable of performing Plato's natural virtues—wisdom, courage, temperance, and justice. Natural man, however, lacks the ability to act in faith, hope, and love because of his loss of the *donum superadditum* (supernatural gift) and the stain of original sin upon his soul. Reason played a crucial role in Thomas's natural law theory. We inhabit a temporal sphere governed by natural law, and God has given us reason as a means of living purposeful and meaningful lives within that sphere apart from the Christian gospel. People form institutions such as family and political and economic structures and order them morally according to reason.

> In the case of volitional activities, the proximate standard is human reason but the supreme standard is eternal law. Therefore, whenever a man's action proceeds to its end in accord with the order of reason and of eternal law, then the act is right; but when it is twisted away from this rightness, then it is called sin (*Summa Theologica* 1-2. 21. 1c).

Therefore, Thomas's distinction between nature and grace carried over into his ethics. He asserted the primacy of human reason in moral matters. Individuals may develop moral virtue exactly as Aristotle said. Revelation (as a means of knowing and as power to perform) is needed only to perform spiritual activities associated with theological virtues.

Other Christians, both before and after Aquinas, taught that the unity of truth or the organic nature of Christian thought militates against such distinctions between nature and grace, natural law and eternal law, reason and revelation, and natural virtues known by reason and performed by unaided will and supernatural virtues perceived by revelation and accomplished by an infusion of grace. Thomas did not hold that nature and human morality are autonomous. But building upon his distinction between natural and supernatural realms, later philosophers, no longer committed to a Christian world view, gravitated toward such autonomy.

Modern Science: Newton and Kant

Advocates of modern science four centuries later encouraged this direction. Sir Isaac Newton, the renowned English physicist and mathematician of the seventeenth century, formulated his three famous laws of motion, which became the basis for much of modern scientific endeavor. Although Newton did not personally hold to the naturalistic world view, many believed that his laws of motion produced a conception of the universe as a vast mechanism controlled by physical laws (which Newton believed described, not caused, natural processes). Thus many thought Newton's laws supported a deistic view of reality—that God may well have created the cosmos but abandoned it to operate on its own according to natural laws. A considerable advance beyond Thomas's views of natural laws, this idea had enormous consequences for ethics. Although Thomas distinguished between two realms, he maintained that God continues to control the world though natural law (that is, natural law mediates God's eternal law) and that humans freely use reason in making moral decisions. To consider the world a vast mechanism is to deny both God's providential control of the universe and human moral accountability.

Immanuel Kant recognized the implications Newton's laws of motion had upon man as a religious or moral being. Kant not only assumed that Newtonian physics accurately describe how physical reality works; he also proposed that Newton's three laws are deducible from three synthetic a priori categories of reason. If, for example, popular acceptance of Newton's laws led people to think of the universe as a machine susceptible to scientific investigation, that posed a particularly difficult problem for freedom of choice in ethics. If inexorable laws of cause and effect control all reality, how can human beings be held accountable for their choices? What about man's sense of duty—the categorical imperative that individual's *ought* always to choose so that their action could become a universal principle of human behavior? That people have an inner experience of "ought," said Kant, implies that they possess moral freedom to obey or not to obey that obligation. But if human beings are part of a "closed world," a physical universe governed by laws of cause and effect, how can this paradox be resolved?

Kant formulated a solution in which he thought he could recon-cile what many believed was the "Newtonian world machine" and human moral freedom. He transformed Thomas's distinction between nature and supernature into an explicit dualism. Reality consists of two totally separate realms. We discussed this revolu-tionary idea in our study of Kant's epistemology. But his "Copernican Revolution" had more than epistemological signifi-cance —it had radical ethical consequences as well. While the phe-nomenal (empirical) self is totally enmeshed in the determined physical realm of cause and effect, the noumenal self (the realm of the mind and disposition or will) is not. Because Kant limited knowledge to what can be perceived through the senses, we have no knowledge that the self (or "I") even exists as a nonphysical entity. For morality to be possible, however, we must postulate not only that there is an inner self, but that the noumenal self is free, not sub-ject to mechanical laws of nature. Thus, Kant argued that our moral experience demands the existence of the inner self, that the "I" is free, and that man is morally autonomous. People possess not merely freedom of choice but an innate moral rationality (a morally legislative reason) that enables them to determine right and wrong upon which the human will can act. Every person is accountable to his innate rational self.

Kant considered human reason autonomous, literally "self law," a self-governing power. Human rationality, consisting of both intel-lectual and moral aspects, not only determines what we know but also governs what we ought to do. Just as the human mind deter-mines what is a priori because the categories innate to reason make reality conform to the operation of the understanding's categories, so we also know our moral duty not from experience (a posteriori) but prior to experience (a priori) by the categorical imperative. Moral law is indelibly stamped, as it were, on reason. Moral law, therefore, is not external to our essential nature as rational beings (imposed on us from without) but rather internal (within us) and structures our entire moral experience, just as categories of the understanding structure what we know about physical reality. If morality were external, man would be *heteronomous*, subject to *another law* forcibly imposed on him, rather than the autonomous being that Kant strenuously defended. Kant explained man's moral autonomy in the following way:

> Since the law arises out of our own moral nature, man stands in awe of it. We impose law upon ourselves as self-conscious rational beings. Reverence for such a law throws us down in order to raise us up; if it makes our mortal nature tremble like a guilty thing surprised before the awful legislation of reason, it enables us at the same time to feel that our mortal nature is not our inmost self.

While others considered a "spark" within man the basis for human dignity, which meant for many a divine spark, Kant insisted instead that human dignity rests on the immanent moral law indwelling every person. Reason as conceived by Kant takes on the attributes of God. The language Kant used of our being thrown down "trembling" before the "awful legislation" of reason is strikingly similar to Isaiah's feeling of fear before a majestic and transcendent God in Isaiah 6:5: "Woe is me, for I am ruined! Because I am a man of unclean lips, and I live among a people of unclean lips; for my eyes have seen the King, the Lord of hosts." Kant expressed a reverence and awe, but it is a reverence before our immanent rationality, not Isaiah's transcendent God. Kant's reverence is an awe of law, not of God who ordains law.

Throughout preceding centuries, Christians maintained a high view of law as ordained of God, through both general revelation, known by means of conscience, and special revelation, communicated in the Bible. But they never deified the law, making it usurp the place belonging to God alone. Traditional Protestantism stressed a direct, personal relationship between God and man. Although God reveals Himself through covenant law and commands strict obedience to its stipulations, believers render submission to God, not to an impersonal law code. Christian ethicists do not confuse God with the law He commands, much less substitute reverence for an immanent sense of duty for worship of the Creator Himself.

We are not implying that Kant was an atheist. But his ideas were clearly deistic. Kant believed in God as a postulate of practical reason: while we cannot prove God exists, society's need for morality requires us to assume that He exists and that He rewards obedience and punishes disobedience to the moral law. But God in Kant's view is not the *basis* of our obligation to obey the law. Thus, God serves a morally functional role of connecting the phenomenal world of Newtonian physics with the inner noumenal self.

Kant's Mature Ethics

Kant articulated his mature religious and ethical ideas in *Religion Within the Limits of Reason Alone,* a classic eighteenth-century exposition of deism or natural religion, whose title succinctly expresses his understanding of Christianity. Kant transformed Christianity from the revelation of God's sovereign grace into a totally rational religion. Correct moral behavior replaced worship of God as man's primary objective in life. Since only the ethical dimension of religion is universal, Kant made the church into an organization to promote ethical behavior instead of a covenant community of worshipping believers.

Kant drew an absolute distinction between religious worship and ethical behavior, which has significantly affected how many modern thinkers view religious devotion and ethical behavior. He believed that traditional religious acts such as prayer, worship, and the sacraments are morally worthless. In his opinion piety is a false substitute—even a bribe to curry God's favor—for what alone is valuable in God's sight, morally good behavior. Kant strongly supported the idea that Old Testament religion, for example, consisted of two diametrically opposed traditions: (1) a priestly religion requiring atoning sacrifices, rituals, and prayers, which are of no value whatsoever and have no intrinsic connection and (2) a prophetic, moral tradition requiring obedience to moral law, which is the heart of true religion. The Jews, following precedents in other primitive religions, succumbed to the deceit of priests who taught that morally worthless religious rituals could atone or substitute for what is inescapable in genuine religion—performance of moral duty. Kant refused to unite worship and moral obligation into an organic unity. He proposed instead eliminating what he considered nonmoral elements and retaining only those practices which promote an exclusively moral religion. Some scholars consider Kant's extreme position a reaction to his attendance at a pietistic school in his youth, where teachers expected rigorous devotion as the primary element of Christian living. Reportedly, Kant never was able to appreciate religious devotion and dismissed it as not having any role within a rational religion. In so doing he made a lasting impact on modern thinkers who have followed his lead in reducing religion merely to moral duty.

Kant retained respect for some elements of traditional Christianity including the Bible's authority in moral matters. But he shared Enlightenment disdain of Old Testament morality as primitive and outmoded. Only in the modern period has mankind finally broken free of servile acceptance of ancient dogmas. When confronted with how he would resolve a conflict between his rational idea of moral behavior and scriptural teaching, he stated, "I should try to bring the [biblical] passage into conformity with my own self-subsistent moral principles." Authority for moral thinking and living lies not in sacred Scripture but in the categorical operation of human reason.

Consistent with the epistemological subjectivism of his Copernican revolution, Kant held conscience in high esteem. Many contemporary ethicists attribute to conscience only a minimal role in moral choice because it is very susceptible to environmental conditioning. But Kant assigned to conscience the primary role in determining and directing morality: "The question is not how conscience ought to be guided (for conscience needs no guide), but how it can serve as a guide in the most perplexing moral decisions."

Kant's faith in human rationality and his unstinting confidence in our ability to choose right over wrong supported his view of human autonomy. He believed that underlying individual choices is the human disposition or will, which when "converted" by rational choice from an evil to a good "maxim" or universal moral principle, enables a person to follow the categorical imperative in particular moral acts. Thus Kant transformed the biblical concept of regeneration by the power of the Holy Spirit into a natural ethical conversion within the human will. This belief underscores Kant's faith in human self-perfectibility. His moralistic version of religion led him to redefine grace. Whereas Christians traditionally have viewed grace as God's sovereign, unmerited favor, Kant defined it as a benefit we make ourselves worthy of receiving. Thus he twisted Christianity into a deistic religion based upon human ethical achievement. Good works or ethical conduct are not the signs of a converted soul but the means by which a person earns acceptance with God. Jesus Christ, whom Kant called "the Teacher," was not the incarnate Son of God who died an atoning death for our sins. The earthly Jesus was a moral example, and a superfluous one at that, because people already have the moral law resident in reason. In addition to setting the tone for liberal Protestant Christianity in the nineteenth century, Kant provided a foundation for naturalistic ethics by stressing human reason, will, and autonomy.

Contemporary Ethical Naturalism

Many contemporary figures we have previously studied are heirs of Kant's philosophy. In their ethical systems they have followed Kant in two different directions. Each of these two approaches stresses one aspect of Kant's dualism while ignoring or rejecting the other.

Existentialism

Atheistic existentialists emphasize human autonomy in ethics. The primary spokesman of this movement, Jean Paul Sartre, accentuated only one part of Kant's dualism. We might diagram his view as follows:

FREE NOUMENAL SELF

<del>DETERMINED PHENOMENAL SELF</del>

Man's essential self, his mind or will, is free. He is nothing (inauthentic) until he freely chooses. External physical reality has no significant impact on our essential being, and no universal essence or "humanity" exists that defines or determines the nature of individually existing people. Rather, we exist and freely define ourselves by choosing existentially, that is, in concrete situations, to become something. Sartre summarized his view in the oft-quoted statement, "Existence precedes essence." There is no essential "humanity"; there are only *existing* men and women. In his famous essay "Existentialism" Sartre wrote:

> . . . man exists, turns up, appears on the scene, and, only afterwards, defines himself. If man, as the existentialist conceives him, is indefinable, it is because at first he is nothing. Only afterward will he be something, and he himself will have made what he will be.

Based on this extreme subjectivism Sartre established a radically individualistic conception of ethical obligation. Because each person stands alone in his or her subjectivity, no appeal can be made to a transcendent God who legislates absolute laws. No God determines the meaning of human existence by declaring what is morally right and wrong conduct.

> The existentialist . . . thinks it very distressing that God does not exist, because all possibility of finding values in a heaven of ideas disappears along with Him; there can no longer be an *a priori* Good, since there is no infinite and perfect consciousness to think it. Nowhere is it written that the Good exists, that we must be honest, that we must not lie; because the fact is we are on a plane where there are only men.

Man alone exists with no transcendent being to guide or comfort him. All people are free to will and act, and by doing so they forge their own moral identities. But existential freedom can also lead individuals to anguish and despair because every choice is fraught with significance. In this respect, existentialists have stressed even more than Kant the loneliness of the subjective "I." Existential man stands alone, without excuses, in Sartre's words, "*condemned to be free.*"

Sartre's emphasis on freedom, individuality, and a total absence of external authority has led some critics to charge that existentialism has no basis to criticize any who choose to exercise their freedom (and define themselves) in hedonistic, selfish, or destructive behavior. Sartre vehemently denied these charges. In his later writings Sartre carefully explained the social implications of existentialism and answered criticisms lodged against its individualism. An individual's freedom to define himself does not allow him to infringe on other people's freedom:

> ... freedom as the definition of man does not depend on others, but as soon as there is involvement, I am obliged to want others to have freedom at the same time that I want my own freedom. I can take freedom as my goal only if I take that of others as a goal as well.

While his response might satisfy some critics, Sartre's assertion of human accountability raises an even more serious problem for his major premise. Sartre quite subtly yet undeniably affirmed a universal law, an ethical absolute, which he previously denied existed. Though negative, it is nevertheless an absolute. Paraphrased, Sartre has said "No one ought to exercise his freedom in a way that infringes on the freedom of another person."

To summarize, existentialists affirm Kantian autonomy as a starting point but deny Kant's physical determinism and his morally absolute, categorical imperative. Both determinism and duty contradict our essential freedom. But when critics complained that unlimited freedom can become a license for debased behavior, Sartre qualified his original position by affirming an absolute. Any naturalistic ethic that presupposes radical human freedom faces this same problem.

Determinism

Like existentialists, scientist Francis Crick and psychologist B. F. Skinner reject one part of Kant's dualism while accepting the other. But, opposite to existentialists, they either ignore or deny human freedom and stress instead environmental determinism. Their view is diagrammed thus:

~~FREE NOUMENAL SELF~~

DETERMINED PHENOMENAL SELF

For them, the free noumenal self (life of mind or will) does not exist. Physical reality, explainable in terms of physics and chemistry (Crick) or environmental conditioning (Skinner), exhaustively describes man's condition and culture. Although human beings are not qualitatively different from their surroundings, they alone have evolved to the point where they can ensure their survival. Survival is the basic premise and goal of Skinner's and Crick's naturalistic ethics.

Skinner's "Walden Code," which establishes the rules for living in his fictional utopia, *Walden Two*, summarizes his behavioristic ethical system. The "original sin" is self-interest, which produces conflict among people. The purpose of ethics is to mitigate this flaw by means of conditioning. Skinner seeks to solve this problem as he does every human problem by using a "totally experimental approach." He rejects all obligatory absolute norms, and he denies that humans have any innate good or evil human nature that would help or hinder them in living wisely. Two principles alone govern his method: (1) the human race ought to survive; (2) the social order (his emphasis is on society, not the individual or family) must promote survival by resolving clashes between people's interests as scientifically as possible.[2] What Skinner seeks are *techniques*, not values. Skinner has evaluated philosophies from Plato's to the present and incorporated the best into his Walden Code. In studying

2. Skinner repeatedly uses "science," and "scientific" to describe his behaviorism. However, as Albert H. Hobbs has convincingly argued in *Man Is Moral Choice* (New York: Arlington House, 1979), what passes as "scientific" in the contemporary "social sciences" and specifically in behaviorism is definitely not science and should not be accepted as such. Hobbs contends, "Claims of objective and permanent truths about human behavior do not evolve out of real scientific procedure (controlled observation; hypotheses which can be proved or disproved by controlled observation; and verification as evidenced by prediction), but they arise from false science, scientism, and only by rare chance do they happen to be correct" (p. 125). Social scientists use the term "science" to give credence to their naturalistic views of man. But such materialistic views fail to do justice to long-recognized human characteristics now dismissed by behaviorists. Hobbs writes: "Since the psychic and emotional parts of our lives, our inmost thoughts and deepest feelings, our fears and loves, our likes and dislikes, our preferences and prejudices, are qualitative rather than quantitative, and predictably variable rather than stable, the techniques of controlled observation cannot sensibly be used to collect data about them, to verify hypotheses or to rebut them. Nor can predictions be made from the conclusions we reach" (p. 122).

these philosophies, Skinner was not looking for absolute, unchanging moral principles that could be adapted to contemporary needs but rather for techniques that could be used to control behavior. From examining the teachings of Plato, Aristotle, Confucius, Jesus, the Puritans, Machiavelli, and others, the most useful technique he discovered was Jesus' insistence on "practicing the opposite emotion," summarized as "love your enemies."

For Skinner, however, "love your enemies" is not a morally obligating absolute, but a technique, a method of control, ultimately the self-control of practicing the opposite emotion when one person's interests conflict with another's. Responding in this way to a difficult situation helps individuals to develop a tolerance for frustration. In *Walden Two*, children are trained at the earliest possible age to practice the opposite emotion. They wear lollipops (dipped in powdered sugar to expose any licks taken secretly) around their necks like crucifixes. They may lick them only at specified times. This procedure helps children learn to tolerate frustration and to understand, even at the age of three and four, community standards for socially acceptable behavior. By practicing the opposite emotion children develop skills that enable them later in life to love even their enemies. In *Walden Two*, ethical training, all of which is based on experimental techniques, is complete by the age of six.

Skinner's naturalistic ethic is consistent with his behavioristic philosophy. Like any other human activity, ethics is a result of environmental conditioning. Writing on "values" in his book *Beyond Freedom and Dignity* Skinner states his view succinctly:

> The behaviors classified as good or bad and right or wrong are not due to goodness or badness, or a good or bad character, or a knowledge of right and wrong; they are due to contingencies involving a great variety of reinforcers.[3]

Skinner's view of human autonomy is slightly different from that of Kant. Skinner denies that there is an inner self free to choose between alternatives. "To [traditional] man *qua* man we readily say good riddance."[4] Yet, Skinner urges us to adopt his conditioning techniques as the only pragmatic and scientific way for us to survive.

3. B. F. Skinner, *Beyond Freedom and Dignity* (New York: Knopf, 1972), p. 113.
4. Ibid., p. 200.

Kant reminds us that commands presuppose that individuals are to respond. How can we choose to adopt this behavioristic conditioning if we are not free to act? Skinner's inconsistency is similar to Sartre's and likewise undermines his premises.

Francis Crick, who was a joint winner of the Nobel Prize in 1962 for his studies of the molecular structure of DNA, has also proposed a naturalistic philosophy and its implications. He claims in *Of Molecules and Men* that man is merely material—a physical collection of molecules with no inner self. In Crick's view, only contemporary biologists understand the implications of our essential materiality. By postulating natural selection as an all-encompassing interpretive principle, they are able to place all human problems (including ethics) in "a completely new light."[5] Since Crick assumes that technological changes must give birth to new moral systems to account for new developments, he believes scientists alone are equipped to deal with the ethical implications of today's technological explosion. As a trained elite they ought to decide what is best for humanity. Because of their insights and expertise, scientists must assume cultural leadership so that technology will be used to ensure, not destroy, our survival as a species. He charges university administrators to repudiate the older religious values of a dying Christianity and adopt instead curricula that will propagate the new scientific culture.

Crick and Skinner agree on an ultimate value—human survival. Ethical obligation must begin with that premise. Both claim that scientists, committed fervently to the value of human survival, can save the world from possible destruction due to either nuclear holocaust or massive starvation. They favor an alliance between the intellectual and scientific communities and the state, an alliance that would ultimately rule the world. Critics have pointed out dangers implicit in such a proposal. They question whether a single value (human survival), and such an anthropocentric one at that, is sufficient to guide mankind. Should this task be managed by either national or world leaders who are avowedly neutral toward traditional values that have directed human behavior for centuries? Those holding traditional values oppose making human survival the only concern. Are human beings the ultimate arbiters, authori-

5. *Of Molecules and Men* (Seattle: University of Washington Press, 1966), p. 93.

ties, and rulers in the universe? Further, they ask what qualifies scientists, intellectuals, and government leaders to handle such diverse moral problems? Who or what will control the controllers and condition the conditioners? Will it be possible to correct mistakes made by a technologically trained elite? Unless the elite were themselves under the authority of a higher law, would not this vast state eliminate individual liberties and produce Mustapha Mond of *Brave New World* or Big Brother of *1984*? Christians have long acknowledged a sovereign God who has established the basis for human morality. God has provided moral laws such as the Ten Commandments to direct our behavior. Can moral sovereignty be transferred to human beings who define the nature of their humanity and morally acceptable behavior according to a totally anthropocentric definition?

In addition to existentialists, behaviorists, and naturalistic scientists, contemporary secular humanists have emphasized ethics as a primary element in their writings. Humanists accept naturalistic tenets that God is nonexistent and that man is therefore autonomous. They deny all things metaphysical, argue that nature is self-contained, and believe that human beings are the standard of all aspects of life including morality. Nevertheless, humanists are much more optimistic about prospects for the human condition than are naturalistic materialists. Moreover, their concern about ethics is generally much greater. They write extensively about ethical issues and problems and seek to encourage responsible ethical decision-making. "Humanist Manifesto II," for example, issued by leading secular humanists in 1973 to summarize and expound their views, primarily focuses on morality.

Secular humanism has long roots that stretch back through the Enlightenment of the eighteenth century and the Renaissance of the fifteenth and sixteenth centuries to ancient Greece and Rome (see vol. 1, chap. 9). During the past one hundred years such prominent Americans as sociologist William Graham Sumner, jurist Oliver Wendell Holmes, trial lawyer Clarence Darrow, political commentator Walter Lippmann, and philosopher John Dewey have advanced humanistic principles and ideals. Today many Americans in journalism, the professions, and higher education espouse humanism and express their views through a variety of publications, especially *The Humanist.*

Disbelieving in God's existence, secular humanists insist that there are no ultimate or transcendent standards or norms for ethical systems or human behavior. Therefore, people must devise from experience their own ethical principles based upon their perceptions of human need and social good. Humanist Manifesto II states, "Ethics is autonomous and situational, needing no theological or ideological sanction."[6]

Secular humanists argue that Judeo-Christian ethics (and indirectly all ethics based on ultimate principles) is defective on four counts. (1) Judeo-Christian ethics rests upon a tottering foundation. Humanists claim that tying ethics to belief in God, which is at best inconclusive and more and more people are rejecting, weakens its basis. Developing ethical principles and practices from common human nature, interests, and needs is much more sensible and sound. (2) Judeo-Christian ethics assumes incorrectly that human beings are sinful and depraved, that they do not naturally desire to do good and help others. In fact, however, humanists contend, man's evolutionary development has built into him tendencies toward cooperation and altruism that are reinforced each generation by socialization and social pressure. Human beings' innate social instincts, not God, account for their sense of conscience and their feelings of morality, which encourage upright behavior. (3) Judeo-Christian faith over-emphasizes the afterlife and depreciates life on this earth. Secular humanists, by contrast, devote exclusive attention to improving human life and conduct here and now. "Promises of immortal salvation or fear of eternal damnation are both illusory and harmful. They distract humans from present concerns, from self-actualization, from rectifying social injustices."[7] (4) The Judeo-Christian tradition teaches people to be dependent upon God instead of themselves. Because "no deity will save us" or

---

6. Paul W. Kurtz, ed. *Humanist Manifestos One and Two* (Buffalo: Prometheus Books, 1973), p. 17. See also Kai Nielson, *Ethics Without God* (Buffalo: Prometheus Books, 1973).

7. Kurtz, *Humanist Manifestos One and Two*, p. 16.

motivate our performance of ethical good, "we must save ourselves" and rely on our own strength and insight to do what is morally beneficial.[8] "Dependence upon any external power," wrote John Dewey, "is the counterpart of surrender of human endeavor."[9] In short, secular humanists claim that Judeo-Christian ethics is built upon a faulty foundation, denies and discourages man's natural social tendencies and goodness, encourages a selfish preoccupation with one's own salvation and virtue, and hinders a person's efforts to appreciate and develop his own potentialities and responsibilities.

Secular humanists argue that their love and care for human beings and their sensitivity to human need, not any divinely given rules and regulations, prompt their deep commitment to morality and human welfare. Frankly eclectic, the ethics of humanism accepts whatever principles or practices seem relevant and helpful from other philosophies or religions.[10] Leading spokesman Corliss Lamont urges firm allegiance to the second table of the Ten Commandments (the last six). He maintains that Jesus repeatedly taught such broad humanist ideals as social equality, human interdependence and community, and peace on earth. Nevertheless, because humanists have no faith in God, divine revelation, or prayer, they rely on autonomous reason and an autonomous scientific method to prescribe ethical rules. Reason, balanced with compassion and empathy, is considered the most effective instrument humans possess in their effort to promote the common good and solve human problems.[11]

Christians welcome secular humanism's emphasis on specific biblical norms such as honesty, respect, fidelity, love, justice, freedom, and the "preciousness and dignity of the individual" and on its attempt to build a "more peaceful and prosperous world."[12] By rejecting God's character and revelation as the transcendent foundation for ethics, however, humanism produces an arbitrary and rel-

---

8. Ibid.
9. Quoted in Alfred Braunthal, *Salvation and the Perfect Society: The Eternal Quest* (Amherst, Mass.: University of Massachusetts Press, 1979), p. 328.
10. See Corliss Lamont, "The Affirmative Ethics of Humanism," *The Humanist* (March/April, 1980), p. 6.
11. See *Humanist Manifestos One and Two*, pp. 17-18.
12. Ibid., p. 18, 23.

ative ethical system. Such ethical teaching leads to confusion, skepticism, hedonism, justification of one's own interests, and even nihilism. It fails to offer a purpose worth striving for. Made in God's image and likeness, human beings are commanded to respond obediently to God's norms for morality as taught in the Bible and through conscience. Because of sin in both individuals and social structures, people cannot and will not consistently do what is ethically correct. Only redemption in Jesus Christ and the empowering of the Holy Spirit enable people to follow God's norms faithfully. Whatever good features humanists have parasitically drawn from Judeo-Christian faith have been emptied of their power as humanists have severed them from their divine source.

A final form of naturalistic ethics requires brief mention. Some radical theologians recently have redefined Christianity in a way that is similar to the naturalistic ethics considered above. These theologians, building upon the "God is dead" theology of the 1960s, have argued that in order to speak to the contemporary world, Christianity must be recast in secular terms. With God eliminated, Christianity is virtually reduced to ethics. When these theologians deny that God ever existed or else declare that God has "died," they mean that the idea of "transcendence" as a working premise no longer helps people to understand reality. Since secular man has "come of age," he no longer needs "God"—the concept of transcendence—as an intellectual, psychological, or moral crutch to function effectively in the world. Gradually, human beings have become autonomous, not just in theory but in actual fact. The success of modern technology leads secular theologians to argue that we not only *can* but *must* proceed without God as a working hypothesis. If we can conquer disease, control our environment, and constrict population growth using scientific technology, then we can also achieve good ethical behavior without divine sanctions or guidance.

Radical theologians have joined forces with advocates of naturalistic ethics, claiming that only such an alliance will enable Christianity to gain a hearing in future debates about human destiny. Though secular theologians do not advocate human survival as the only goal or world control by a neutral state, they deny that God is the source of ethics and thus strengthen the hold of secularism in our society.

The adherents of contemporary ethical naturalism are many and hold diverse convictions. Only by understanding the various forms naturalism takes in the latter part of our century can culturally concerned Christians respond appropriately and effectively.

The Naturalistic Triad

As we noted in our study of biblical ethics, all ethical decisions involve three factors: (1) a normative standard or authority; (2) a situation or context in which an ethical choice is made; and (3) a personal, existential response to God's norm addressed to the situation at hand. The distinctive feature of the biblical triad is that the transcendent God is Lord over the whole triad and that all three elements are necessary and complementary. Because God is at the apex of the pyramid, the parts of the triad never conflict with one another even though tension may seem evident among them at times.

The naturalist triad, however, differs radically because it presupposes, as it were, a mere two-dimensional context in which all ethical choices are made. We exist in a closed universe of natural objects and processes. No transcendency overarches and influences the three elements of an ethical act. There are no transcendent norms either revealed by God or discovered in nature, no absolutes to prescribe what is morally right or wrong. Only human standards, determined corporately or individually, can direct conduct. While pragmatic, hedonistic, utilitarian, benevolent, financial, and other considerations may apply, no one factor is universal so that it could encompass or supersede all others. No absolute standard transcends our particular situation in a relative universe. Instead we find ourselves enmeshed in a world of competing, finite, and often antagonistic particulars. From a Christian perspective, a naturalistic triad is faulty because it denies any transcendent reference point. Though naturalists do not want to reject all standards, they can appeal only to an immanent, finite authority, open to continual questioning and adjustment.

At the second corner of the naturalistic triad, every ethical situation is detached, brute, cut off from any purposeful flow in history

because no metaphysical power, force, or influence directs historical events. Naturalistic ethics requires purposeful decisions in situations thought to occur by purposeless chance. No teleological force
governs human affairs or natural occurrences such as earthquakes.
Acts and events take on purpose or meaning only as we assign them
such meaning or purpose. Natural laws of cause and effect are the
sole determinants of all that happens. Reflecting no design or
intention, these laws leave us without direction in a bewilderingly
valueless cosmos.

Finally in the naturalistic triad, motives for ethical acts originate
in men, either coming from the individual or imposed by larger
groups. Motives range from disinterested "humanitarian" or "phil-
anthropic" concerns to selfish desires for power and prestige. For
lack of transcendent norms contextual and motivational aspects
become decisive in producing various behaviors.

Ultimately, the three elements of the naturalistic triad work at
cross purposes, as diagrammed below:

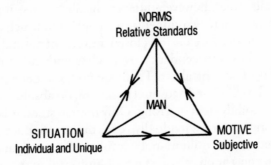

Whereas God created man so that various elements of the ethical
triad could be complementary, no such unifying factor holds the naturalistic triad together. Relativistic standards, individually unique
contexts, and different subjective motivations share no common
bond. Instead, each of the three elements of the triad claims its own
autonomy and vies with the other two for supremacy. Among the various naturalistic views the only constant is man. But competing philosophies describe man so differently that even "man" becomes a
meaningless concept. We have seen that Kant, Sartre, Skinner, Crick,
and secular humanists, though sharing naturalistic presuppositions,

have postulated radically different ethical systems. Both Kant and Sartre advocated individual ethics, but Kant stressed following innate moral reason, which Sartre replaced with radically individual choice. Marx argued for social revolution because only the elimination of the bourgeoisie will allow a fully Communist ethic to emerge. And Crick and Skinner maintain that only a scientifically trained elite make sane choices to ensure human survival.

No clear consensus has emerged from the secularist community. Contemporary man faces a bewildering cacophany of claims. Although naturalists have gained prominence in the marketplace of ideas, they possess no mandate from society and have done anything but manifest a united front with a clearly defined ethical system. Despite their frequent emphasis on human significance and survival, they can find no lasting purpose or meaning for mankind beyond the present moment. Naturalistic ethicists do not explain how we can resolve conflicts between competing anthropocentric authorities and assumptions such as existentialist, Marxist, and behaviorist ethics.

Theists have often likened autonomous humanistic ethics to a person's attempt to lift himself by his own bootstraps. Today's naturalists gladly assume such a challenge and condemn traditional moralists for underestimating man's ability. Throughout history, they argue, people have timidly refused to be responsible for their destiny and to affirm their own meaning. Some claim that even if in the end we jettison the traditional ethical categories of honor, integrity, love, dignity, faithfulness, and justice, no deity or any supposedly revealed ethical commands will save us. Other naturalists are more conservative. They support traditional moral values, but justify them on the basis of community opinion and pragmatic consequences, not divine sanction.

The fundamental difference between naturalistic and biblical ethics is evident in the Old Testament distinction between those who "did what was right in their own eyes" and others who "walked in the ways of the Lord." This issue continues to divide men today, and human destiny depends on which moral position people affirm and live by in the future.

For Further Reading

Braunthal, Alfred. *Salvation and the Perfect Society: The Eternal Quest.* Amherst, Mass.: University of Massachusetts Press, 1979.

Copleston, Frederick C. *Aquinas.* Baltimore: Penguin, 1955.

_____ . *A History of Philosophy,* vol. 1. New York: Doubleday, 1962.

Crick, Francis. *Of Molecules and Men.* Seattle: University of Washington Press, 1966.

Edwards, Paul. "Ethics, History of," and "Ethics, Problems of." *The Encyclopedia of Philosophy,* vol. 3. New York: Macmillan, 1967.

Geisler, Norman. *Is Man the Measure?: An Evaluation of Contemporary Humanism.* Grand Rapids: Baker, 1983.

Gundry, Stanley and Alan F. Johnson. *Tensions in Contemporary Theology.* Grand Rapids: Baker, 1983.

Kant, Immanuel. *Religion Within the Limits of Reason Alone.* Translated by Theodore M. Greene. LaSalle, Ill.: Open Court, 1934.

Kurtz, Paul W. *Humanist Manifestos One and Two.* Buffalo: Prometheus Books, 1973.

Lamont, Corliss. *Humanism as a Philosophy.* New York: Philosophical Library, 1957.

Nielson, Kai. *Ethics Without God.* Buffalo: Prometheus Books, 1973.

Packer, J. I. and Thomas Howard. *Christianity, the True Humanism.* Waco, Tex. Word Books, 1985.

Sartre, Jean Paul. *Essays in Existentialism.* New York: The Citadel Press, 1970.

Skinner, B. F. *Beyond Freedom and Dignity.* New York: Alfred A. Knopf. 1971.

_____ . *Walden Two.* New York: Macmillan, 1948.

Thomson, J. A. K., trans. *The Ethics of Aristotle.* Baltimore: Penguin, 1953.

Van Buren, Paul M. *The Secular Meaning of the Gospel.* New York: Macmillan, 1963.

III.
ETHICAL
PROBLEMS

14

Abortion, Euthanasia, and Homosexuality

Gary Scott Smith

Having analyzed the Christian and naturalistic ethical traditions, we now turn to a discussion of specific ethical problems. In this chapter we will examine abortion, euthanasia, and homosexuality in light of theological, anthropological, and epistemological presuppositions and the two triads described in previous chapters.

Abortion

Introduction

As recently as twenty-five years ago abortion was not an important public issue anywhere in the world. Almost every nation considered abortion, except under the rarest of circumstances, to be a criminal act. Since 1960 nation after nation has revised its abortion laws with astonishing swiftness. Today the United States, Canada, Great Britain, India, Japan, China, the Soviet Union, and the Eastern European and most Western European countries have policies allowing millions of legal abortions to be performed each year.

In the United States two landmark Supreme Court decisions in 1973, *Roe v. Wade* and *Doe v. Bolton*, struck down laws in thirty-one states that restricted abortions. In *Roe v. Wade* the justices decided (7-2) that abortion may be legally performed at any time of pregnancy up to birth. In 1969, 22,670 fetuses were aborted in America. By 1974 the number mushroomed to 900,000, and by 1985 the total had leveled off at 1,500,000. In all, 16.5 million legal abortions were performed between 1973 and 1985. During the past decade about 80 percent of women receiving abortions have been unmarried, and teen-agers have had more than 25 percent of all abortions. Today one of every four pregnancies ends in abortion, totaling about four-thousand each day. Each year in New York State the number of abortions equals the number of live births, and in Washington D.C. and several other major cities abortions outnumber live births.

In America, abortion has become an explosive political and moral issue. Legislatures wrestle with it; religious bodies are divided over it; citizens' organizations campaign to win public support and lobby to influence public policy on abortion.

Debate over abortion involves several major questions. When does human life begin? Should the law treat the unborn as "persons" having full human rights? When considering abortion, does the age or condition of the fetus make any difference? Should the risk to a woman's life, health, career, economic standing, or ability to meet other obligations play any role in determining whether a pregnancy may be terminated? Does how the woman became pregnant matter? Should public funds be used to finance abortions desired by poor women? Would reinstating stricter abortion laws be imposing morality through legislation? These and many other important questions underlie heated discussion of abortion today.

In the popular press, positions toward abortion are usually narrowed to two: pro-choice and pro-life. In actuality there is a continuum on the issue ranging from those who believe that abortion is never wrong under an circumstances to those who insist that abortion is right only when it saves the life of a pregnant woman. In between are several intermediate positions. Nevertheless, the issue is easiest to discuss by identifying the arguments of these two major camps and considering other positions as variations of them. Arguing that abortion is a medical matter between a woman and her doctor or else a matter of individual conscience, pro-choice proponents applaud the court's liberalizing of abortion laws in 1973. Their position emphasizes the right of individuals to control their own bodies and reproduction, and the quality of life. Pro-life advocates, by contrast, seek to reestablish stringent abortion laws. Their view rests upon a transcendent morality that exalts the right to life of both the born and the unborn, and considers abortion to be murder.[1]

Pro-Choice

Advocates of situation ethics, philosophical naturalism, and feminism (including some Christian feminists), as well as several major Protestant denominations support the pro-choice position. Among its strongest proponents are the Planned Parenthood Association of America and the National Organization of Women.[2]

Central to the pro-choice argument is the conviction that no absolute norms protect the life of the fetus when the baby is not desired by his or her parent(s) for a variety of possible reasons. Consequently, whether governed by the presuppositions of naturalism or situational ethics or by their understanding of the Scriptures, pro-choice proponents concur that the developing fetus does not possess full human rights until some point after which abortion is typically performed (such as viability or birth). Any rights the fetus does have as a potential human being are clearly subordinate to those of the mother, an actual human being.

The most radical pro-choice supporters declare that abortion is not a crime because the act lacks a victim. The pregnant woman is the only party whose interests or rights are at stake; the fetus has no standing whatsoever. Consequently, abortion is morally and legally equivalent to an appendectomy. As the American Medical Association declared in 1970 and the Supreme Court confirmed in 1973, abortion is simply "a medical procedure" related to the "preservation and protection of maternal health" (*Roe v. Wade*). Religious and philosophical objections to abortion, therefore, are as irrelevant as similar objections to blood transfusions or to certain types of surgery.

Underlying many feminists' support of abortion is their convic-

1. As will be explained later, many pro-lifers oppose all abortions except those necessary to save a mother's life. Other pro-lifers are willing to permit abortion in cases involving rape, incest, suspected severe retardation, and extremely trying sociological, psychological, and economic circumstances.

2. According to one recent study, the typical pro-choice activist is a forty-four-year-old woman who works outside the home, has a college degree, two children, and a family income of $50,000.

tion that women have "the right to control their own bodies." As one of them writes, "All the excellent supporting reasons [for abortion] . . .—improved health, lower birth and death rates, freer medical practice, the separation of church and state, happier families, sexual privacy, lower welfare expenditures—are only embroidery on the basic fabric: woman's right to limit her own reproduction."[3] In a world where women are still oppressed, leading feminists contend that the decisive consideration when a woman contemplates abortion must be her right to choose. Thus "the act of abortion is sometimes, even frequently, a positive moral good for women."[4] Strict abortion laws, feminists declare, prevent women from ending unwanted pregnancies that would hamper their careers and prohibit them from competing successfully with men.

Some feminists describe pregnancy as a parasitic relationship. While the mother supplies essential nutrients to the fetus and disposes of its wastes, the fetus contributes nothing to her wellbeing. Pregnancy produces weight gain, nausea, fatigue, and depression; it damages muscle tone and can cause dangerous complications. As one feminist declares, "Childbirth hurts. And it isn't good for you."[5]

Judith Thompson maintains that if parents "have taken all reasonable precautions against having a child," then their mere biological relationship to the child does not give them "special responsibility for it." The woman's prior ownership of her body and her right to control its use imply that she is not morally obligated to continue her pregnancy even though abortion will kill the fetus. This parasite has "invaded" her body; her right to control her body includes the right to resist such an invasion.[6] Similar reasoning leads other feminists to conclude that abortion can never be wrong, no matter what circumstances are involved. "As long as an individual is completely

3. Lucinda Cisler, *Sisterhood Is Powerful* (New York: Random House, 1970).

4. Beverly Harrison, *Our Right to Choose; Toward a New Ethic of Abortion* (Boston: Beacon Press, 1983), p. 16.

5. Shulamith Firestone, *The Dialectic of Sex: The Case for Feminist Revolution* (New York: Bantam Books, 1972).

6. See Judith Jarvis Thompson, "A Defense of Abortion" and "Rights and Deaths" in Marshall Cohen et al., eds., *The Rights and Wrongs of Abortion* (Princeton: Princeton University Press, 1974), pp. 21ff.

dependent upon the mother," declares Virginia Abernethy, "it's not a person." The claim that fetuses, like infants and defective children and adults, have on persons, she declares, "is compassion, not a moral right to life."[7]

Like many other pro-choice advocates, Joseph Fletcher, famous for his *Situation Ethics* (1966), argues that abortion is simply a technological tool for controlling natural processes such as procreation. In *The Ethics of Genetic Control*, Fletcher writes, "There are in the end only two ways of deciding what is right. Either we obey a rule (or a ruler) of conscience, which is the a priori or prejudiced approach, or we will look as reasonably as we can at the facts and calculate the consequences, the human costs and benefits—the pragmatic way."[8] Believing that only rationality bestows human personhood, Fletcher argues that we become human only at birth. In this approach, the pregnant woman has complete personal status and the developing fetus has none. Consequently, abortion is justifiable whenever the cost-benefit calculation indicates this act is in the woman's own interest, no matter what stage of pregnancy she is in. No woman should be forced to remain pregnant; the unborn is human if wanted, subhuman if not.

A key plank in the pro-choice argument asserts that it is impossible to prove that the fetus is a human being. Biologist Garrett Hardin argues: "Whether the fetus is or is not a human being is a matter of definition, not fact, and we can define any way we wish." Hardin compares the unborn and adult to a blueprint and a house. Neither the blueprint nor the embryo is very valuable, he maintains, because each can quickly be replaced by another copy.[9] These assessments of the fetus's value ignore long-standing arguments that God or an absolute norm assigns worth to the unborn.

While most pro-choice proponents believe that birth bestows human rights upon babies, the argument that rights rest upon rationality leads some of them to advocate infanticide under certain

7. Virginia Abernethy, quoted in *Newsweek* (January 14, 1985), p. 29.

8. Joseph Fletcher, *The Ethics of Genetic Control* (New York: Anchor Press, 1974), p. 119.

9. Garrett Hardin, "Abortion—Or Compulsory Pregnancy?" *Journal of Marriage and Family* (May 1968), p. 250.

conditions. For Michael Tooley, infants do not have a right to life until they reach a threshold of awareness. Tooley contends that we should choose "some short period of time, such as a week after birth, as the interval during which infanticide will be permitted."[10]

The pro-choice argument, then, rests primarily upon supporters' contentions that the fetus is not a "person" and that women have the right to control their own reproduction. These assumptions, in turn, are based upon belief that the rights of the unborn are clearly subordinate to the desires of potential parent(s) and that God has not declared abortion to be morally reprehensible. Pro-choice forces also insist that several practical factors justify liberal abortion laws. They stress that in the United States legalizing abortion has made the procedure much safer. Prior to 1973, rich women had access to safe abortions; poor ones often suffered at the hands of back alley practitioners or mutilated themselves with coat hangers. Each year during the 1960s, they argue, thousands of women died from abortions and many more were seriously injured. And if strict abortion laws are restored, the same pattern will prevail.

Pro-choice proponents argue further that the majority of Americans favor abortion on demand and thus it should remain the law of the land.[11] They characterize the pro-life effort as a maneuver by Roman Catholics and the Religious Right (fundamentalist Protestants) to impose religious dogma through legislation. Abortion is at heart a moral matter, they contend, and Americans should not use law to regulate morality. The state should not coerce individuals from engaging in private acts like abortion. The basic question underlying the abortion controversy is a philosophical one (whether the unborn are peers with humans and therefore should

10. Michael Tooley, "A Defense of Abortion and Infanticide" in Joel Feinberg, ed., *The Problem of Abortion* (Belmont, Calif.: Wadsworth, 1973). See also Michael Tooley, *Abortion and Infanticide* (Clarendon Press, 1983).

11. Pro-life advocates counter this argument by maintaining that growing numbers of Americans oppose abortion on demand. (A *Newsweek* poll in early 1985, for example, showed that 58 percent of Americans support a ban on legalized abortions except in cases of rape, incest, and danger to the mother's life.) They emphasize that their movement has mustered significant popular support for the Hyde Amendment of 1976, which prohibited the use of federal money to pay for abortions, and for a proposed Human Life Amendment to the Constitution, which would ban all abortions except those to save the mother's life.

be protected by the law) and therefore cannot be resolved by civil law alone.

In addition, pro-choice advocates maintain that abortion is psychologically therapeutic. It releases women from the stress, strain, and anguish of unwanted pregnancies. Abortions free them from physical discomfort and economic uncertainty and allow them to continue their careers uninterrupted.

Finally, supporters of abortion on demand maintain that it prevents many unwanted children from being born. As one of them writes, "Without legal and affordable abortion, many lives in progress are hopelessly ruined; the unwanted children often grow up unloved, battered, conscienceless, trapped and criminal."[12] Moreover, in an overcrowded world it makes no sense to compel women to complete unwanted pregnancies.

The official position of the Presbyterian Church, USA, in the 1980s typifies that of many pro-choice Protestant denominations and individuals. While sharing some affinities with the pro-choice arguments discussed above, Presbyterian recommendations on abortion (such as the Covenant to Life issued in 1983) are based upon what its proponents call "covenantal biblical faith." With other pro-choice forces, these Presbyterian policy statements argue that the right to choose abortion is guaranteed constitutionally and must "remain with the individual to be made on the basis of conscience and personal religious principles." While asserting that "abortion is not the only solution for unintended or problematic pregnancies," the Covenant to Life contends that "it may at times be the most responsible decision." The choice to abort in some cases is consistent with humans' obligation to accept the limits of the earth's resources. When the unborn is suspected of having serious genetic problems or when the family does not have adequate provisions to care for the child properly, then abortion can "be considered a responsible choice within a Christian ethical framework." With most other advocates of the pro-choice position, these Presbyterian statements argue that only at the point of viability does the developing child have any rights. Prior to viability, potential parents should make their decisions about abortion prayerfully in order to

12. Lance Morrow, *Time* (August 1, 1977), p. 49.

be good stewards over creation. Presbyterian leaders urge religious bodies to support enthusiastically family planning, sex education, adoption, and care for unwed mothers and to work to reduce the incidence of abortion.[13]

Deemphasizing the traditional Judeo-Christian and classical humanist commitment to the sanctity of all human life, the pro-choice position elevates the woman's right of choice as its absolute (or at least its highest) norm. That in effect moves God outside the picture and reduces the abortion question to a decision based on contextual and motivational factors in the ethical triad described in previous chapters. For many pro-choice proponents human dignity rests not upon being created in God's image but upon possessing certain attributes such as awareness, rationality, viability, and the potential to contribute to society. Long-standing theological, anthropological, and epistemological assumptions have given way to pragmatic concerns and unbounded freedom of choice. The woman's right to control her own body has become a central value replacing traditional commitments to divine law and the human community. Even the concerns of traditional humanism seem to have been rejected in favor of blatant self-centeredness. Ostensibly justifiable economic, sociological, and personal reasons for abortion have led to the large-scale sacrifice of lives (and, consequently, of the sanctity of human life) in the name of a woman's freedom to control her own body.

Pro-Life

Leading supporters of the pro-life or "Right to Life" position are Roman Catholics and conservative Protestants. Major pro-life organizations include the National Right to Life Committee, established in 1973, and the Christian Action Council, created in 1975.[14]

The pro-life position rests fundamentally upon the conviction

---

13. Quotations from "Covenant and Creation: Theological Reflections on Contraception and Abortion" (1983), pp. 368-69.

14. The typical pro-life activist, according to one recent study, is a forty-four-year-old married woman with three or more children and a family income of $30,000 who does not work outside the home.

that a fetus is an unborn human being who should be fully protected under the law. While disagreeing about whether life begins with conception or implantation and whether the fetus has a soul, pro-lifers are united by their belief that abortion kills a developing human being and therefore should be performed only in very unusual circumstances. Many pro-lifers want to limit abortions to cases necessary to save the life of the mother. Such cases, involving a tubal pregnancy or a cancerous uterus, are extremely rare (less than 1 percent of all abortions), and technological advances will make them even rarer in the future.

Christians who support this position insist that the Bible establishes the personhood of the fetus. In *Abortion and the Christian* John Jefferson Davis describes the biblical emphasis on the sanctity of human life.[15] Davis rejects Joseph Fletcher's suggestion that "humanness be defined in terms of such criteria as self-awareness, memory, a sense of futurity and time and a certain minimum IQ." In the Judeo-Christian tradition, human worth rests not in man's innate capacities or faculties, whether intellectual, moral, or spiritual, but in his unique ability to have a relationship with his transcendent Creator.

Davis maintains further that five types of biblical texts clearly imply the personhood of the unborn and thus obligate Christians to protect the unborn by using education, moral exhortation, and legislative action. (1) Several texts apply personal pronouns and proper names to the unborn (see Pss. 51:5; 139:13-16). Luke 1:44 declares that John the Baptist leaped for joy in his mother's womb. The term *brephos*, used to describe John here, elsewhere in the New Testament refers to the newly born and to infants (see Luke 18:15; Acts 7:19; I Pet. 2:2). (2) The Bible indicates that God has a personal relationship with the unborn (see Job 10:8-12 and Rom. 9:10-13, which discusses Jacob and Esau). (3) One Old Testament scholar writes, "It was so unthinkable that an Israelite woman should desire an abortion that there was no need to mention this offense in the criminal code."[16] Many scholars do believe, however,

15. Phillipsburg, N.J.: Presbyterian and Reformed, 1984.
16. Meredith G. Kline, "Lex Talionis and the Human Fetus," *Journal of the Evangelical Theological Society* 20, 3 (1977): 193-202.

that provisions in the Mosaic law, especially Exodus 21:22-25, provided protection for the unborn. (4) Scores of biblical passages presuppose the psycho-physical unity of human beings created in God's image. The Old Testament describes man as "flesh-animated-by-soul." The New Testament also stresses man's fundamental unity (see Rom. 8:6; I Cor. 3:3; and 6:13, 19-20; and Gal. 5:19ff.). (5) Passages such as Luke 1:26-45 include the prediction not only of Christ's birth but also of His conception. Summarizing the argument, one scholar concludes, "It is abundantly evident from Scripture that God relates to us and is personally concerned for us *before* birth."[17] Another adds, "The fetus is described by the psalmist in vivid pictoral language as being shaped, fashioned, molded and woven together by the personal activity of God."[18]

Advocates of the pro-life position also argue that scientific facts indicate life begins at conception. The unborn child is not simply a "mass of tissue" or a "part of the woman's body," but a unique human being. In Davis's words, "the newly fertilized egg contains a staggering amount of genetic information, sufficient to control the individual's growth and development for an entire lifetime."[19] U. S. Surgeon General C. Everett Koop and other Christian leaders contend that the burden of proof rests with those who maintain the fetus is not human. Simply because the unborn cannot be shown conclusively to be peers of human beings does not justify aborting them. Western civilization has long defended the weak and vulnerable.

Opponents of abortion attack a second lynch pin of the pro-choice argument. They insist that women do not have an unlimited right to control their own bodies. Bernard Nathanson, a Jewish agnostic physician who once directed the world's largest abortion clinic and helped lead the fight to repeal restrictive abortion laws, has become a leading advocate of the pro-life position. In *Aborting America* he argues that Western civilization has never allowed women to have absolute control over their own bodies. Western

17. Harold O. J. Brown, *Death Before Birth* (Nashville: Thomas Nelson, 1977), p. 126.
18. Ronald B. Allen, *In Celebrating Love and Life* (Western Baptist, 1977), p. 6.
19. Davis, *Abortion and the Christian*, p. 23.

societies have not sanctioned drug abuse, self-mutilation, prostitution, or suicide.[20] Moreover, woman have other available options to control their reproduction: abstinence, contraceptives, and sterilization of themselves or their sexual partners. By discussing the abortion issue solely in terms of the woman's personal rights, pro-choice supporters have "absolutized the principle of freedom at the expense of the principle of obligation and the reality of human interdependence."[21] Christians add that women are responsible first and foremost to God.

The pro-life argument rests upon conviction that the fetus is an unborn human being and that abortion is therefore murder. Nevertheless, pro-life proponents maintain that even when "benefit-cost calculations" alone are considered, their position is still superior to that of pro-choice. Pro-lifers contend that their opponents have greatly exaggerated the number of women who died from illegal abortions in the two decades prior to 1973; in reality few women died from abortions during these years. Studies indicate that before 1973 most (56 to 94 percent) "illegal abortions" were performed by doctors of the same qualifications as those who direct abortion clinics legally today, under conditions no less sanitary than those in today's clinics.[22] In short, as one Catholic priest concludes, "No reliable case has yet been made that legalization has made safer for American mothers the abortions they would in any case have."[23]

Pro-life forces also challenge the claim that strict abortion laws are unfair to the poor. They point out that most women who seek abortions are not poor blacks with large families on welfare but unmarried white teen-agers and professional women. Blacks argue principally for better employment, housing, and educational opportunities, not for permissive abortion legislation.

Pro-life proponents contest the pro-choice claim that the anti-

20. (New York: Pinnacle Books, 1979), pp. 195-96.
21. Kenneth Woodward, "The Hardest Questions," *Newsweek* (January 14, 1985), p. 29.
22. Pro-lifers also point out that after federal medicaid funds for abortion were cut off, 80 percent of the women who would have been eligible for this money paid for abortions themselves with no significant increase in maternal mortality.
23. James T. Burtchaell, *Rachel Weeping: The Case Against Abortion* (San Francisco: Harper and Row, 1984), p. 96.

abortion stand is essentially religious and should not be legislated in a pluralistic society. Such a charge displays confusion about the relationship between law and morality. The sanctity of human life, far from a sectarian position, is deeply embedded in Judeo-Christian tradition and Western civilization and has only recently been extensively challenged with regard to abortion. Moreover, because they embody a community's sense of justice and righteousness, all laws rest upon moral convictions. Laws will always express some moral point of view; the question is simply whose perspective will they represent. The First Amendment to the Constitution sought to separate church and state as institutions, not to prohibit Christians from influencing public policies.

Pro-life advocates maintain, further, that abortion is rarely, if ever, psychologically therapeutic. According to one investigator, "Studies indicate that women who display the most severe stress symptoms during unwanted pregnancy seem to develop the most psychiatric complications after abortion."[24] Davis adds that psychiatrists agree that "there are no known psychiatric diseases that can be cured or predictably improved by abortion."[25] Growing numbers of pro-lifers seek to provide good mental health care and emotional and spiritual support needed by pregnant women in difficult circumstances. Since 1980 more than three hundred programs furnishing maternity care for women with unwanted pregnancies have been established in the United States.

Pro-lifers frequently accuse pro-choice proponents of perpetuating a "conspiracy of silence" by ignoring the physiological and psychological effects of abortion on women and the scientific evidence of fetal development. By minimizing the side-effects of abortion and by overlooking the human character of the fetus, pro-choice advocates deprive women of important facts they need to make informed decisions.

Opponents of abortion also repudiate the argument that abortions should be performed to prevent unwanted children from being born. Simply because a woman does not want to be pregnant does not mean that she and (if married) her husband will not love

24. Ibid. See also pp. 68-72.
25. Davis, *Abortion and the Christian*, p. 30.

the child who is born. Before the advent of legalized abortion many parents who did not want to carry their children to term later professed to be satisfied as parents of those children. No research has documented that many children originally unwanted are victims of child abuse. Furthermore, adoption is an excellent option for parents who feel ill-equipped to raise their child. Millions of Americans today wish to adopt infants, and the present shortage of babies is due in large measure to the number of legal abortions in our nation.

Finally, many pro-life supporters contend that the widespread practice of abortion cheapens all life and encourages infanticide and euthanasia. Permissive attitudes toward abortion, C. Everett Koop and Francis Schaeffer have argued, diminish respect for all human life, especially the aged, the mentally retarded, the handicapped, and the unwanted. The leap from abortion to other forms of "mercy-killing" is short, and pro-lifers remind Americans that some pro-abortionists advocate this leap. Moreover, denying full personhood to fetuses opens the way to denying such status to other groups. After all, at times in our history, blacks, Native Americans, Jews, and women have not been considered "whole persons."[26]

Some of those who support the pro-life position want to permit abortions in such extenuating circumstances as pregnancies due to rape and incest, expected severe birth defects, grave threats to mental health, extreme socioeconomic distress, and some teen-age pregnancies out of wedlock. A relatively new medical procedure called amniocentesis makes it possible to detect Tay-Sachs disease, sickle-cell anemia, and Mongolism in developing fetuses. In addition, some families have a history of genetic abnormality, and some pregnant women are inadvertently exposed to dangerous drugs or radiation. Some pro-lifers believe that such conditions may require the sacrifice of the potential life of a child. Norman Geisler of Dallas Theological Seminary argues that the many valid moral norms can be arranged in a hierarchical fashion so that some take precedence over others. To Geisler, the "rights to life, health, and self-determination" are superior to those "of the potentially human embryo." His view, however, does not justify abortion simply

26. See Curt Young, *The Least of These* (Chicago: Moody Press, 1983), pp. 1-32.

because a baby is unplanned and unwanted.[27] While trying to prevent as many abortions as possible, Christians such as Geisler also want to preserve abortion as an option in certain trying situations.

Recognizing the hardships involved in such cases, other pro-lifers argue that these circumstances still do not constitute grounds for abortion. They stress that pregnancies resulting from confirmed cases of rape are extremely rare because the psychological trauma involved tends to inhibit the woman's normal ovulation. Moreover, when a rape or incest victim is promptly treated with a spermicidal agent, conception will not result. If a woman does become pregnant through rape or incest, the newly conceived life in her womb takes precedence over whatever difficulties the woman may endure. Many pro-life supporters also argue that fetuses should not be aborted no matter what the expected physical problems. The diagnosis may be incorrect. If a child is born with significant physical or mental handicaps, he or she can be a blessing and draw the parents closer to God. If the parents are unable to handle the child, other families are willing to adopt such children. Moreover, many pro-lifers contend that no possible psychological, emotional, or financial problems justify abortion. Pregnant women undergoing such strains need to have support, love, and encouragement, not abortions.

Conclusion

Underlying the two major perspectives on abortion in America are contrasting beliefs about the nature and moral standing of the fetus. Philosophical presuppositions and medical considerations have led pro-choice proponents to argue that the fetus becomes human only at viability or birth or some later point (rationality or awareness) and that, therefore, abortion is a medical matter, not a moral one. The right of the pregnant woman to control her body and the particular circumstances of her life justify aborting a fetus, which, for lack of personhood, has no (or only subordinate) rights. Advocates of this position assume that no ultimate being or absolute norms compel us to protect unwanted fetuses. Pro-life support-

27. Norman Geisler, *Ethics: Issues and Alternatives.* (Grand Rapids: Zondervan, 1971), pp. 218ff.

ers, however, maintain on philosophical, religious, and medical grounds that the developing embryo is a person possessing the right to life. Consequently, abortion is murder. Christian pro-life advocates are convinced that the biblical norm of the sanctity of human life applies as much to the unborn as to other human beings. Linking that revealed norm to the abortion situation is the scriptural and medical evidence for the personhood of the human fetus. Because abortion deprives a developing human being of life, we must take to heart (in our existential response) our obligation to oppose such killing and to defend the unborn.

Abortion is one of the thorniest issues facing our nation today. Unlike many other issues, there is no possibility of compromise between these two basic views. A fetus cannot be partially aborted any more than a woman can be somewhat pregnant. And the controversy is likely to be even more perplexing in the future because of new technological developments. Technology is making it safer for women to have abortions much later in their pregnancies, and yet it is also pushing viability back to earlier and earlier stages. Doctors are able to determine increasing numbers of crippling physical disorders before birth, and medical technologists are inventing new abortion techniques. Sperm banks, frozen embryos, artificial placentas, and surrogate motherhood introduce a whole new set of ethical dilemmas. Some experts predict that a low-priced suppository or pill that can induce abortion in the early weeks of pregnancy will soon be on the market. Such a product could make abortion seem like a completely private and commercial act. These potential developments require Christians to increase their commitment to protecting the unborn, to aid pregnant women undergoing difficulties, and to assist families struggling to support their children.

Euthanasia

Introduction

Like abortion, euthanasia is a complex and controversial issue, involving many perplexing questions. Under what conditions, if any, is euthanasia morally justified? Do individuals have the "right" to die? Are those who help the terminally ill end their lives morally or legally guilty of murder? Are comatose individuals or those mechanically kept alive still "persons"? Do doctors have a moral obligation to use every possible medical procedure to keep suffering terminal patients alive?

Euthanasia is derived from a Greek word meaning "good death." Often called "mercy killing," euthanasia means ending the life of someone terminally ill, so as to bring relief from suffering. There are two forms of euthanasia. In passive euthanasia no steps are taken to prolong the life of the terminal patient through the use of machines, surgery, or unusual medications. Active euthanasia, by contrast, involves human intervention to shorten life, such as by injecting drugs into a suffering patient, which actually kill him.

A second distinction is frequently made between voluntary and involuntary euthanasia. In some instances the terminally ill person has expressed a desire to die, either earlier through a "living will" or, if alert and aware, at the time of his illness. In other cases, the dying individual has not consented to euthanasia, either because his mental condition or physical state (coma) makes that impossible or because even in his suffering he wants to live as long as possible. The following diagram illustrates the possible types of euthanasia cases:

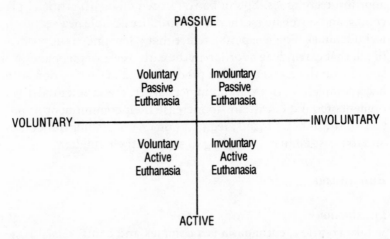

Today in Western nations euthanasia is vociferously advanced and widely supported. Recent polls reveal that majorities in both England and the United States support this practice. With 80 percent of Americans dying in hospitals and nursing homes, usually while receiving some medical treatment that could be withheld, questions about euthanasia take on great importance and urgency. State legislatures discuss how to define death and debate right-to-life bills. On both sides of the Atlantic "living wills," which specify certain cases under which individuals do not want to have their lives prolonged medically, and "suicide manuals," which offer foolproof methods for taking one's own life, have become popular. Sermons, best-selling books, and television talk shows discuss how to cope with the reality of death. In both high schools and colleges students flock to courses on death and dying. Hundreds of American and British communities have established "hospices" that provide medical care, companionship, and relief from pain for persons with terminal illnesses.

In the United States several cases have focused national concern on euthanasia. Most notable is that of Karen Ann Quinlan, who as a teen-ager in 1975 overdosed on drugs and slipped into a comatose state. A local judge denied her parents' request to have her removed from a respirator. In 1976 the New Jersey Supreme Court overturned this decision, and Karen Ann was removed from the respirator. She lived for nine more years, however, dying in 1985. In a second widely publicized case, two California physicians were charged with murder in 1982 for complying with a family's request to remove feeding tubes from a comatose, brain-damaged patient. Although the indictment was dismissed, the case raised thorny questions about physicians' responsibilities and liabilities. Another celebrated case in 1982 involved "Infant Doe," who had Down's syndrome and a deformed esophagus that prevented him from eating and drinking normally. When his parents decided against surgery to repair the esophagus (which was the only way to prevent the infant from starving to death), doctors sought a judicial order to allow the operation. A lower court decided in the parents' favor, the Indiana Supreme Court refused to intervene, and before the Supreme Court had a chance to act, the week-old infant died. In a final case, courts refused to allow cerebral-palsy victim Elizabeth Bouvia to leave a hospital in 1983 so that she could starve herself to death. Bouvia, a resident of California who has a bachelor's degree in social work, argued that her physical limitations deprived her life of quality. These and other cases have called attention to the difficult medical, moral, and legal question involved in euthanasia.

Part of the contemporary debate over euthanasia focuses on passive euthanasia. Many ethicists, religious authorities, and health professionals see this practice as simply "letting nature take its course." Most Protestant, Catholic, and Jewish leaders support passive euthanasia in cases where there is little hope of recovery. United Methodist leaders declare that physicians should not "prolong terminal illness merely because the technology is available to do so." Pope John Paul II judges withholding "heroic measures" from people about to die to be "morally justifiable." Contemporary interpreters of Jewish law maintain that sparing the family of an individual with irreversible brain damage the suffering of watching this life prolonged artificially is often "an act of compassion." A few Protestant fundamentalists do consider passive euthanasia morally objectionable, and some physicians fight to the end to keep all their patients alive, arguing that "incurability must not be equated with hopelessness." Moreover, in some cases, judges have refused to permit passive euthanasia. While doctors are divided over the issue of whether they should do everything possible to keep their patients "alive," a substantial proportion of the residents of the United States and other Western nations endorse passive euthanasia.

The most heated debate over mercy killing, then, centers on active euthanasia. A significant problem, which adds immensely to the complexity of this issue, is that the line between passive and active euthanasia is sometimes blurred, and it is difficult to distinguish where the former stops and the latter begins. Nevertheless, as with the abortion controversy, two major positions are taken on active euthanasia.

Pro-Euthanasia

Supporters of active euthanasia, who include many proponents of philosophical naturalism, insist that five principal arguments based upon individual liberty, quality of life, biological considerations, prevention of cruelty, and the needs of society justify their position. The London based organization, EXIT, (The Society for the Right to Die with Dignity), established in 1935 and today claiming 120,000 members, leads the crusade to legalize euthanasia. Academicians, ethicists, and lawyers on both sides of the Atlantic provide considerable support for the movement. Their fundamental contention is that individuals have a right "to die with dignity." Each person should be able to decide whether and under what circumstances he wishes to live or die. In its report entitled, "Deciding to Forego Life-Sustaining Treatment," the Presidential Committee for the Study of Ethical Problems in Medicine and Biomedical and Behavioral Research, composed of a panel of distinguished doctors, lawyers, theologians, and others, declared that a patient who is "able to understand treatment choices and their consequences, has all but an absolute right to decide his own fate." Whenever possible, the fundamental moral principle of the right of free choice should be incorporated into the law. An individual's decision to terminate his life does not harm others and therefore the law should not thwart his liberty to do so.

A second, closely related argument contends that life is not worth living under certain circumstances and consequently victims of these conditions should be allowed to choose death. For persons to die, as Joseph Fletcher puts it, "comatose and . . . tubed and sedated and aerated and glucosed" seems undignified.[28] Because such a life is subnormal, we should prevent individuals from sinking into such a state. Moreover, allowing the terminally ill to experience intense abiding pain and to watch themselves slowly deteriorate and become an increasing burden on others is "uncivilized and uncompassionate."

Supporters of active euthanasia insist further that certain biological conditions justify termination of life. Of what value is keeping alive those who are clinically dead or hopelessly injured physically or mentally? Such persons survive only because they are connected to sophisticated life-support machinery. They are "dead bodies with artificially induced life" and therefore are beyond ordinary moral considerations. Society has no moral obligation to use machines to sustain the life of the mentally debilitated. To count as a person, an individual must meet certain criteria: he must display some evi-

28. Quoted in "When Doctors Play God," *Newsweek* (August 31, 1981), p. 53.

dence of rationality, free will, capability of choice and self-determination, and self-awareness. Since the severely retarded have none of these, society has the same right to kill them as it does "to kill a debilitated, comatose and otherwise unresponsive dog." "What is definitive," writes Joseph Fletcher, "is the absence of cerebration of 'mind' even though other brain functions continue. A human vegetable is not a person."[29] Here we see similarities with the pro-abortion argument that asserts that because the unborn are not persons, they do not have a right to life.

Supporters of active euthanasia also stress that this practice prevents cruelty. Mercy killing brings relief to those whose suffering is prolonged and unendurable. Persons in such states cause constant anguish for loved ones and health professionals. The death of the incurably ill spares them, their relatives, and their attendants pain and grief.

Finally, proponents of mercy killing argue that social needs justify this practice. Society has both the right and the duty to terminate the lives of those who become hopelessly comatose. Such individuals serve no useful purpose and tie up productive resources that could be better employed elsewhere. The aged ill have already enjoyed the most pleasant aspects of life. Supporters of mercy killing emphasize that each new medical miracle—organ transplants, sophisticated diagnostic tools, dialysis machines—has sharply raised the cost of health care, causing greater competition for finite resources. In a statement to the Colorado Health Lawyers Association in 1984 that generated much controversy, Colorado Governor Richard Lamm summarized this argument succinctly. "Like the leaves which fall off a tree forming the humus in which other plants can grow, we've [the aged who become terminally ill] got a duty to die and get out of the way with all our machines and artificial hearts, so that our kids can build a reasonable life."[30]

As did much of the pro-choice argument for abortion, the pro-euthanasia argument, particularly as advanced by proponents of naturalism, rests largely upon conviction that people have the right

29. Ibid. See also his *The Ethics of Genetic Control.*
30. "Question: Who Will Play God?" *Time* (April 9, 1984), p. 68. See also Richard Lamm, "Long Time Dying," *New Republic* (August 27, 1984), pp. 20-23.

to determine their own fate. They are not seen as dependent upon and responsible to God, who demands their obedient service, or to absolute norms that direct their conduct. In the above arguments, either individuals or society, on the basis of either personal preference or social expediency, decide whether the terminally ill should live or die.

Many of those who advocate active euthanasia, especially philosophical naturalists, pay no serious attention to traditional Judeo-Christian teaching on the value of human life. Absent is any appreciation that individuals are created in the image and likeness of God and derive their worth from their relationship with Him rather than from their social usefulness. God's sovereignty in creating and sustaining life is also rejected. Human autonomy replaces dependence upon and responsibility to God, and man becomes the final arbiter of his own (or another's) life. Once again situational and motivational factors are divorced from biblical norms.

Anti-Euthanasia

Opponents of active euthanasia deny that individuals have a right "to die with dignity" by means of mercy killing. Their understanding of the sanctity of all human life leads them to contend that active euthanasia is tantamount to murder (in involuntary cases) or assisted suicide (in voluntary cases). Commitment to the sanctity of life in Anglo-American societies rests upon several pillars: Judeo-Christian teachings, belief that this principle is a basis of social order, and historical analysis displaying the dangers involved in not protecting all innocent life. Christians argue that God has categorically forbidden people to take innocent human life. God's commandments declare killing such persons deliberately to be morally wrong. God alone should determine when a person's life on earth is over. We do not have absolute ownership of our own lives. Our lives belong to God, the author of all life.

Old Testament scholar Douglas Stuart points out that in the Bible euthanasia is "not condoned or encouraged even when suggested or requested." In the one explicit case involving active euthanasia, the death of King Saul, disapproval is clearly expressed. Mortally injured in battle against the Philistines, Saul begged his armor bearer to kill him, but he refused. After trying and failing to take his own life, Saul beseeched an Amalekite bystander to kill him. Certain that Saul would not live long anyway, the Amalekite obliged Saul's wishes. David denounced the Amalekite's act as assassination and had him executed. Because the Scripture does not comment further on this episode, and no prophet condemns David's action, Stuart concludes correctly that David's action expresses God's disdain for active euthanasia.[31] In addition, many Old Testament psalms entreat God to restore individuals to full, productive lives; they never ask God to end life quickly.

Opponents of active euthanasia also reject the argument that the so-called diminished or inferior quality of life of the terminally ill or comatose justifies mercy killing. Who, they ask, has the right to judge the quality of another person's life? Worse yet, if the argument from dignity were accepted, it would allow elimination of all who lead an "undignified" existence. Permitting the mercy killing of consenting patients would erode other strictures against taking human life, and could allow unwanted infants, the mentally retarded, and even the socially deviant, not simply the incurably ill, to be annihilated. Spelling out additional implications, C. Everett Koop argues that such policies could lead to the termination of life considered unworthy because of a person's "ethnic origin, economic capacity, political activity, productivity potential, or any other undesirable form or function."[32]

Those who oppose active euthanasia argue further that any laws designed to give medical practitioners wide discretion in terminating life could easily be abused. In fact, the risk of abuse is so great that it outweighs all possible benefits. Such legislation could easily make wealth, social status, and age the determining factors in who lives and who dies.

Anti-euthanasia forces also sharply criticize the argument that mercy killing ends suffering and therefore prevents cruelty. Christians insist that God is sovereign over both the universe as a whole

---

31. Douglas Stuart, "'Mercy Killing'—Is It Biblical?" *Christianity Today* (February 27, 1976), p. 11.

32. C. Everett Koop, *The Right to Live: the Right to Die* (Wheaton, Ill.: Tyndale, 1976), p. 91.

and the lives of individuals. Consequently, any suffering a person endures is permitted by God for some purpose (examine the life of Job, the apostle Paul, and Heb. 2:18). While the Bible describes many individuals who suffer from prolonged fatal illnesses, it never suggests active euthanasia as a way of ending their pain and misery. In addition, by what standard can it be shown that bearing the burden of the infirm and dying is not good for society? This experience can benefit individuals and society, especially by helping people to develop the virtues of patience and perseverance.

Moreover, opponents of mercy killing denounce the contention that the needs of society require active euthanasia. Such a utilitarian position (seeking the greatest "good" for the maximum number of people) would also license infanticide, suicide, abortion, senicide (murder of the senile), in fact, any killing thought to benefit society. What norms can be used to judge whether an individual is in a "hopeless" state and only burdens society? To whom should such a decision be entrusted?

Those who reject active euthanasia question whether a person in intense pain who requests death really knows what he wants. Many who ask to die are in excrutiating agony, or delirious states, or are so affected mentally by their illness that their judgment is distorted. Moreover, the person who wants to be killed may not really understand the medical facts of his case. And even if a person in a comatose state has previously devised a "living will," can we be sure that he would want his life terminated under his present circumstances?

Finally, opponents of mercy killing believe that not all those deemed incurably ill actually are. They point to wrong diagnoses, spontaneous remission, and the possibility of new treatments. Doctors are not infallible. Even medical experts make mistakes. Christians also believe that divine healing is possible for the terminally ill. The Bible records numerous examples of miraculous healing and even several resurrections from the dead. Leaders of anti-euthanasia forces grant that only a small number of individuals are spared through such means, but they insist that because restoration is possible no sufferer of an apparently fatal illness should be deprived of his life.

Christians also inject one other consideration into discussion of euthanasia. While much of the contemporary debate over euthanasia assumes a naturalistic perspective, which implies that death is the end of life, the annihilation of the individual, Christians assert that death is the beginning of a new life. By definition, life on earth is temporary and transitory; the Christian's ultimate goal and destiny is the life to come. Such a perspective enables Christians to defend the sanctity of human life while also offering hope of heaven to the dying.

Conclusion

In summary, advocates of active euthanasia maintain that mercy killing differs from murder because it has the interest of the recipient and society at heart. Thus it should be permitted for severely retarded individuals (who have never attained personhood), for individuals in comatose states (who have ceased to be persons), and for completely rational individuals who ask to die, because they find life physically or psychologically unbearable. Supporters of euthanasia contend that individual liberty and dignity, reduction of suffering, and social expediency all justify this approach. Believing that no ultimate norms prohibit active euthanasia, many naturalists consider only situational factors (the condition of the terminally ill) and the motivational factors (the desires of relatives and the terminally ill themselves). Christians who support this approach do so because they believe that the Bible does not explicitly prohibit active euthanasia and therefore in some cases situational factors (intense suffering and costs to society) and motivational considerations (love for the individual involved) make this course of action the most morally responsible.

Opponents argue that mercy killing should not be allowed under any circumstances. The commandments of God regarding the sanctity and dignity of human life (normative factors), and the potential for abuse, the needs of society, and the possibilities of misdiagnosis, of misinterpreting the desires of the terminally ill, and of finding new cures and miraculous healing (situational and existential factors) require Christians to oppose the practice. While recognizing that it is sometimes difficult to distinguish active from passive euthanasia, most Christians sharply renounce the former because they believe it contradicts divine norms.

Homosexuality

Introduction
Our analysis of homosexuality focuses on two major questions. One is How does a person become a homosexual (or committed to living a homosexual lifestyle)? Are individuals born homosexuals, do psychological traits predispose people to become homosexuals, or do they choose that sexual orientation by reacting to particular cues in their environment? A second, related issue revolves around what civil rights homosexuals should have in contemporary society. Should society legalize their sexual practices? Should homosexuals be allowed to marry? Should society discriminate against them in any way—in jobs, immigration, the armed services, or housing? We will evaluate both of these issues in light of biblical teaching about homosexuality and the two ethical triads.

Although homosexuality has been practiced since ancient times, no society has ever legalized homosexual marriage or fully condoned homosexual acts. Throughout human history most homosexuals have kept their sexual orientation and practices secret. While this continues to be true even in contemporary America, a vocal minority of homosexuals in our country has organized a crusade to press for civil rights. Born in New York City in 1969, the Gay Liberation movement has widely publicized the goals, lifestyles, and values of contemporary homosexuals. Although the outbreak of AIDS (Acquired Immune Deficiency Syndrome) in the 1980s among homosexuals has stymied their progress, this campaign has produced greater acceptance and civil rights for homosexuals. Experts estimate that about 2-3 percent of Americans are practicing homosexuals. Others who hold this sexual preference, however, do not actively practice it, and many of those who do have not publicly admitted that they are homosexuals.

Nevertheless, more and more homosexuals are coming "out of the closet" and living openly. As never before, during the last decade they have established communities, operated bars, and organized churches in large cities and small towns across America. Meanwhile they have founded a nationwide network of organizations that provide counseling and companionship for both professed and clandestine homosexuals.

Sources of Homosexuality

There is a close connection between people's beliefs about the origins of homosexuality and their moral evaluation of that practice. If a person is biologically programmed to prefer homosexual relationships or is so thoroughly conditioned by environmental influences that he cannot help becoming a homosexual, then presumably we cannot properly hold him morally responsible. If, however, a person is not born or made homosexual, but rather actively chooses that sexual orientation, then his choice may be properly subjected to moral evaluation, criticism, and legal structures.

Influenced by philosophical naturalism and recent empirical research, most contemporary psychologists and sociologists consider homosexuality to be caused, not willed. Abandoning the long-held view that homosexuality is a mental illness or a moral perversion, a learned behavior that therapy can remedy, these professionals believe that homosexuality is neither a sickness nor a chosen behavior. Following Alfred Kinsey, whose path-breaking studies of human sexuality were published in 1947 and 1952, they argue that no sexual acts are "unnatural" or morally wrong. They use a variety of biological, psychological, and sociological theories to explain the causes of homosexuality. The argument that this orientation is hereditary rests largely on twin studies. Several investigators have shown that identical (one-egg) twins are more likely to have the same sexual preference than fraternal (two-egg) twins. However, family and friends are much more likely to treat identical twins alike, and thus their similarities may be due to environment rather than heredity.[33]

Rejecting hereditary explanations, most contemporary therapists prefer sociopsychological ones. Many argue that certain parenting styles encourage children to become homosexuals. Research

33. See Richard A. Fowler and H. Wayne House, *The Christian Confronts His Culture* (Chicago: Moody Press, 1983).

indicates that male homosexuals frequently have domineering, possessive mothers and ineffectual or hostile fathers. The primary problem with this theory, however, is that many homosexuals do not come from families with these characteristics, while many heterosexuals do.

Other academicians explain homosexuality as resulting from self-definition. Society encourages homosexual encounters by making associations with the same sex less painful and embarrassing than relationships with the opposite sex. Widespread belief that homosexuality and heterosexuality are mutually exclusive categories leads many who engage in exploratory homosexual behavior to define themselves as homosexuals. This prompts them to develop relationships with other homosexuals, strengthening their gay self-concept.

Christians today are divided over whether homosexuals are born, are made, or actively choose their orientation. They also disagree over what the Bible teaches about homosexuality. Christians who maintain that the Bible explicitly condemns the practice conclude that those who engage in homosexual acts must choose to do so. Other Christians, however, argue either that the Bible does not disapprove of the way that homosexuality is usually practiced in contemporary society or else that today's radically different social conditions make the Bible's teachings on this subject no longer relevant. Many of them contend that homosexuality springs from either genetic influences or socialization rather than from personal choice.

Believing that the Bible considers homosexuality to be a moral perversion, Christians for centuries have opposed its practice, and most continue to do so today. Homosexuality is wrong, most fundamentally, because heterosexuality is God's intended pattern for human beings. God created individuals "male and female" (Gen. 1:27). God made a woman, Eve, not another man, to be a helpmeet and companion for Adam. The Bible repeatedly assumes and affirms heterosexuality as God's order of creation. Only heterosexual relationships can bear children and thus fulfill the cultural mandate to "be fruitful and multiply" (Gen. 1:28). Homosexual relations can never bring the completeness and unity that heterosexual intercourse involves. A result of man's fall into sin, like death, war, pride, greed, and divorce, homosexuality perverts God's original purpose for human beings. Consequently, the Bible denounces all homosexual acts as it does heterosexual promiscuity.

Several biblical passages display God's disapproval of homosexuality. Genesis 19 describes the destruction of Sodom, and Judges 19 the punishment of the residents of Gibeah for the homosexual acts they committed. Leviticus 18:22 and 20:13 declare homosexuality to be an "abomination" deserving death. I Corinthians 6:9-10 and I Timothy 1:8-11 depict homosexuality as a violation of God's moral law worthy of keeping offenders from inheriting God's kingdom. Paul wrote to Roman Christians that homosexuality is "unnatural" and "indecent" (1:27-28). Convictions that the Bible is God's inspired, authoritative revelation, that its moral teachings are valid for all times and places, and that the Scriptures do not distinguish among different types of homosexual activity have lead many Christians to conclude that all practice of homosexuality is morally wrong. Consequently, they argue that while psychological and sociological factors may influence people to engage in homosexual acts, people are not coerced but rather choose to commit such acts. Thus Christians urge society not to accept gay behavior as normal or simply different, as merely an alternative lifestyle or "sexual preference." Being gay is not imposed upon people by God, fate, or environmental conditioning.

Other Christians reject this assessment of homosexuality. While agreeing that the Bible opposes homosexuality, they argue that the Bible is so conditioned by the cultural setting in which it was written that some of its teachings must be rejected. Contemporary theological, psychological, and sociological analysis shows homosexuality not to be the perversion the Bible declares it to be, but rather a relationship that can be mutually fulfilling and enriching. Because modern research and rational reflection have demonstrated homosexuality to be caused, not willed, and because so many homosexual relationships are "faithful, tender, respectful and hopeful," its practice is considered moral and should not be proscribed.

Other theologians argue instead that the Bible does not oppose the contemporary practice of homosexuality. They believe (1) that the Scriptures condemn perversion (a person born heterosexual who engages in homosexual acts) but not inversion (a person born homosexual who practices that orientation) or (2) that only certain kinds of homosexual practices are forbidden (especially pederasty—older men having intercourse with younger boys) not all homosexual practices or (3) that the texts that supposedly reprove homosexual acts actually censure other practices.

In *The New Testament and the Homosexual* Robin Scroggs vehemently argues the second position. If the setting of the biblical writers is not reasonably similar to the contemporary context, he contends, then their commands are not relevant for today. "Paul's judgments," he writes, "may be eternally valid but can, nevertheless, be valid only against what he opposed." Scroggs concludes that Paul denounced only homosexual acts between older men and boys in the ancient Greco-Roman world. This, therefore, does not imply that Paul would condemn caring and mutual relationships between consenting adults, which Scroggs maintains, is the primary form of homosexuality today.[34] Evangelical feminists Letha Scanzoni and Virginia Mollenkott agree that the "idea of a life-long homosexual orientation or 'condition' is never mentioned in the Bible. . . ." Consequently, they believe that the Bible cannot be used to reprove a "permanent, committed relationship of love between homosexuals analogous to heterosexual marriage."[35]

Those who take the third option argue that biblical passages traditionally thought to censure homosexuality actually denounce other practices. God condemns Sodom and Gibeah not for their homosexuality but for their lack of hospitality. The holiness code in Leviticus reproves homosexual acts not as intrinsically wrong but for wasting male semen and producing ceremonial uncleanliness, neither of which is a contemporary concern. New Testament passages castigate homosexual promiscuity, and pederasty, the association of homosexuality with the worship of idols, and temple

34. Robin Scroggs, *The New Testament and the Homosexual* (Philadelphia: Fortress Press, 1983), p. 125.
35. Letha Scanzoni and Virginia Mollencott, *Is the Homosexual My Neighbor? Another Christian View* (New York: Harper and Row, 1978), pp. 71-72.

prostitution—not homosexuality itself. Summarizing the case, one scholar maintains that "every text dealing with homosexual activity also refers to aggravating circumstances such as idolatry, sacred prostitution, promiscuity, violent rape, seduction of children, and violation of guests' rights. As a result, one can never be sure to what extent the condemnation is of homosexual activities as such or only of homosexual activities under these circumstances."[36] Such Christians argue that contemporary homosexuality that involves idolatry, rape, or promiscuity is indeed contrary to biblical teaching, but that loving and faithful homosexual relationships can embody genuine Christian values.

In summary, we have discussed several major positions on homosexuality, which spring from different ethical presuppositions. Believing that no absolute standards or universal norms govern behavior, naturalists urge society to accept homosexuality as a normal practice. Because this orientation results from genetic or social influences and therefore is "natural" for some human beings, naturalists argue that homosexuality is morally laudable or at least morally neutral. While homosexual relations involving coercion (rape, incest) should be opposed, all homosexual acts between consenting adults should be approved. In short, because no transcendent values oppose homosexual practice, it is considered acceptable under the proper situation (mutual consent) and the correct motivation (concern for the well-being of one's partner).

Christians who believe that the Bible provides absolute norms that are valid for all times, places, and circumstances, and that the Bible does not differentiate among various kinds of homosexual activity, strongly oppose all forms of homosexuality, including long-term relationships between committed partners. Changing social circumstances and models of homosexuality do not override biblical injunctions against this practice. In other words, the biblical norms prohibit all homosexual acts no matter what situations or motivations are involved. No context or rationale could possibly make the practice of homosexuality morally correct.

The findings of the modern social sciences, the campaign of the

36. John McNeill, *The Church and the Homosexual* (Kansas City: Shedd, Andrews and McMeel, 1976), p. 60.

Gay Liberation movement, and their study of the Scriptures convince a second group of Christians that today's homosexuality is very different from that of biblical times. In their view, the scriptural norms disapprove of coercive and promiscuous homosexual acts but allow homosexual relationships that involve mutual love and commitment. Nevertheless, such efforts to assign alternative meanings to passages condemning homosexuality clash with the most obvious and soundest interpretations of the biblical texts.

Civil Rights

The question of homosexual civil rights is very complex. Throughout history homosexuals have often been persecuted. While most Western European countries today permit homosexual acts between consenting adults, most American states have outlawed homosexual behavior in both public and private settings. Each year several thousand persons discovered to be homosexuals or to have participated in homosexual acts are separated from the United States armed forces, usually with an "undesirable" discharge. Frequently homosexuals are evicted from privately owned housing and are discriminated against in hiring. Moreover, the federal government prohibits professed homosexuals from immigrating to America. For decades homosexuals suffered from police harassment, beatings and robberies, and social stigma. Pressure from the Gay Rights movement has helped homosexuals to gain more civil rights and social approval. More than half of U.S. states have repealed their sodomy statutes, and many corporations and government agencies have adopted antidiscriminatory policies toward homosexuals. The AIDS epidemic has intensified public concern about the practice of homosexuality and has caused many to suggest that some form of testing for this virus be made mandatory.

Gay leaders argue that homosexuals are just another disadvantaged group—like blacks, Chicanos, women, the poor—and therefore should not be discriminated against. Those who believe homosexuality to be a genetic fact, like being left-handed or redhaired, or a product of irresistible environmental conditioning logically conclude that gays should have full civil rights. Even those who consider homosexuality a choice but see no absolute norms for judging such a choice maintain that society has no valid ground for legislating against homosexual practices. Legal repression, they contend, will never eliminate homosexuality because the law cannot change an individual's sexual preference.

Those who maintain that the Scriptures condemn the practice of homosexuality disagree over whether civil penalties should be applied to homosexual acts and over whether professed homosexuals should have full civil rights. Singer Anita Bryant's crusade in 1977 in Dade County, Florida, and similar campaigns led to the repeal of gay rights ordinances in various communities. Supporters of these efforts argue that because homosexuality violates the traditional moral values of marriage, family, and heterosexual love and threatens social stability, its practice should be restricted by legislation and penalized. While gender, ethnicity, race, and often religion result from birth, a gay lifestyle, they assert, results from individual choice. Consequently, gay rights are not parallel to civil rights for women, blacks, and other minorities. Laws protecting gay rights would put an official stamp of approval on homosexual behavior, declaring this unnatural and immoral behavior to be acceptable and proper.

Other Christians, though also believing that the Bible opposes the practice of homosexuality, argue that this should not preclude homosexuals from having complete civil rights. They maintain that while the church should discriminate against individuals on the basis of their private moral acts, society should not. These Christians advocate a principled pluralism, which should allow groups with different world views to establish their own educational institutions, labor organizations, and political parties to promote their own beliefs. Such a system could free us from some of the more thorny problems involving homosexual rights, such as whether homosexuals should be allowed to teach in public elementary schools.

In conclusion, we believe that the Bible clearly opposes all types of homosexual practice. We urge Christians, however, not to succumb to misconceptions about homosexuals: that they are all effeminate; that they are all the same (they share no distinct and consistent personality type and are employed in almost every sector of the economy); that they are frequent child-molestors; that they are all promiscuous; or that they can always be cured of their homosexual orientation by a Christian conversion experience. While God can and does help Christian homosexuals to change, many of them do not. Such persons must be counseled to abstain from homosexual activity. Rejecting homophobia (fear of homosexuals), we must act in loving ways toward all homosexuals and provide teaching and counseling that strengthens and supports those who are willing to change.

For Further Reading

General

Anderson, J. N. D. *Issues of Life and Death. Abortion, Birth Control, Capital Punishment and Euthanasia*. Downers Grove, Ill.: Inter-Varsity Press, 1977.

Davis, John Jefferson. *Evangelical Ethics*. Phillipsburg, N.J.: Presbyterian and Reformed, 1985.

Abortion

Brown, Harold O. J. *Death Before Birth*. Nashville: Thomas Nelson, 1977.

Burtschaell, James T. *Rachel Weeping: the Case Against Abortion*. San Francisco: Harper and Row, 1984.

Davis, John Jefferson. *Abortion and the Christian: What Every Believer Should Know*. Phillipsburg, N.J.: Presbyterian and Reformed, 1984.

Davis, Ron Lee. *A Time for Compassion: A Call to Cherish and Protect Life*. Old Tappan, N.J.: Fleming H. Revell, 1986.

Nathanson, Bernard, and Richard Ostling. *Aborting America*. New York: Pinnacle, 1979.

Wennberg, Robert N. *Life in the Balance: Exploring the Abortion Controversy*. Grand Rapids: Eerdmans, 1985.

Young, Curt. *The Least of These*. Chicago: Moody Press, 1983.

Euthanasia

Eareckson, Joni. *A Step Further.* Grand Rapids: Zondervan, 1978.

Kluge, Eike-Henner. *The Ethics of Deliberate Death.* Port Washington, N.Y.: Kennikat Press, 1981.

Koop, C. Everett. *The Right to Live: the Right to Die.* Wheaton, Ill.: Tyndale, 1976.

Maguire, Daniel. *Death by Choice.* Garden City, N.J.: Image Books, 1984.

Homosexuality

Bahnsen, Greg. *Homosexuality: A Biblical View.* Grand Rapids: Baker, 1978.

Fowler, Richard A. and H. Wayne House. *The Christian Confronts His Culture.* Chicago: Moody Press, 1983.

Keysor, Charles, ed. *What You Should Know About Homosexuals.* Grand Rapids: Zondervan, 1979.

Kirk, Jerry. *The Homosexual Crisis in the Mainline Church: a Presbyterian Minister Speaks Out.* Nashville: Thomas Nelson, 1978.

McNeill, John. *The Church and the Homosexual.* Kansas City: Shedd, Andrews and McMeel, 1976.

Malloy, Edward. *Homosexuality and the Christian Way of Life.* New York: University Press of America, 1981.

Scroggs, Robin. *The New Testament and the Homosexual: Contextual Background for the Contemporary Debate.* Philadelphia: Fortress Press, 1983.

Epilogue

Gary Scott Smith

In the two volumes of *Building a Christian World View* we have attempted to develop a consistent, coherent, and biblical understanding of the universe and our life in it. We have sought to help Christians think in holistic and interrelated ways about the nature and basis of knowledge, the attributes and actions of God, the nature and role of human beings, the origin and structure of the cosmos, the purpose and pattern of society, and the source and principles of ethics. Our intention, however, is not simply to guide you in biblical ways of thinking but also to challenge you to apply your insights to your living. The Scriptures declare that out of the heart come the issues of life. That is, our actions always spring from what we believe and cherish. Throughout the Bible attitudes and actions, thought and conduct, are repeatedly joined. God declares that believing the right doctrines and professing the correct words are not sufficient. We must also act upon what we believe. Faithful response to God's norms involves obedient living in the world. With this in mind, let us consider some of the implications of our study for Christian action in society.

John Calvin proclaimed that the task of Christians is "to make the invisible kingdom of God visible." The Bible clearly teaches that God is building His kingdom in this world in this age. Jesus began His public ministry by commanding people to repent because the kingdom of God was at hand (Mark 1:14). His subsequent life and teaching both brought the kingdom to earth in great power and demonstrated that kingdom's presence. Jesus declared that His casting out of demons displayed the coming of God's kingdom

(Matt. 12:28-29). This, along with His overcoming Satan's temptations in the wilderness and the success of the mission of the seventy (see Luke 4 and 10), offered positive proof that Satan's power on earth was limited and inferior to God's. The New Testament also stresses that Christ's power to work miracles, His preaching of the gospel, and believers' possession of salvation testify to God's new kingdom order. By dying upon the cross, rising from the dead, and ascending to heaven Christ advanced the kingdom of God. His death paid the price for human sin and reconciled to God the Father all those who trust Him as Savior and Lord. Through the resurrection Christ triumphed over the devil, demonstrating that death and all the power of evil could not contain Him. In the ascension, Christ went to the right hand of His Father both to rule over the nations of the world and to be our mediator with God the Father.

God's kingdom, as many theologians have pointed out, has both present and future aspects. It is manifest in our world in the ways discussed above. It is partly but not totally fulfilled. Only when Christ comes again and establishes the new heavens and the new earth will God's kingdom be complete. Nevertheless, in this age our task is to advance God's kingdom. The parable of the mustard seed (Matt. 13:31-32) teaches that the kingdom begins small but is constantly growing and will someday dominate the earth. We must seek to understand the nature of the kingdom, discern its presence in our world, and further it by our acts.

In the Lord's Prayer we ask that God's will be done on earth as it is in heaven. Since God's will is completely done in heaven, we are praying that it be done fully on earth. By directing us to pray in this manner, Jesus implies that there are things going on in heaven that He wants to see happening on earth. Christians therefore are to embody, to put into practice, what is occurring in heaven. Jesus commands us to "seek first His [God's] kingdom and His righteousness" (Matt. 6:33), and the apostle Paul directs us to "seek the things that are above" (Col. 3:1, RSV). We are God's ambassadors in a world of phenomenal need. As His agents, we should fulfill His agenda by building His kingdom, which includes ministering to the physical and spiritual needs of human beings, and caring for the good earth. Before discussing some of the specific implications of our role as kingdom workers, three general points must be made.

First, only those who have been born anew, born from above (see John 3:3), can effectively serve as the agents of God's kingdom. God's new order requires new people. Only those who accept Christ as Savior and Lord, who commit themselves to Him, understand that God is building a kingdom and desire to become its ambassadors. To be a Christian means to renounce all rights to your own life and give Jesus preeminence. Without the radical transformation that the Holy Spirit brings through regeneration, human beings will not be motivated to advance God's new order.

Second, the power of the Holy Spirit is also essential to the task of building the kingdom. Christ has commissioned us to preach the gospel to all nations, to make disciples and to transform society. With every commissioning in the Bible there is an empowering. Christ tells us that as we go forth in His name, He will go with us. He promises that the Holy Spirit, the Comforter, will dwell within us, and inspire our efforts. Consistently in the book of Acts the phrase "filled with the Holy Spirit" is used in connection with power for service (see Acts 2:14; 4:7-8, 31; 6:3; 7:55; 13:9). Paul teaches us in Galatians that the Holy Spirit abides in us, directs our prayers and produces fruit in us. He challenges us to live and walk in the Spirit (see Gal. 4:6; 5:16, 18, 22, 25).

Third, all Christians are called to serve God through their vocations in the world. God expects all believers to be His agents in the world, not simply pastors, missionaries, and others in "full time Christian service." We can properly distinguish between ecclesiastical and nonecclesiastical vocations, but we cannot properly distinguish between Christian and non-Christian (or neutral) vocations. There are not two classes of Christians—those who serve God through their careers and those whose careers do not matter to God. In the Bible we meet farmers and fishermen, tent-makers and tax collectors, merchants and homemakers, prophets and kings, people who do many different kinds of work. The Scriptures urge us to work heartily in our callings as unto the Lord (Col. 3:23; see also Eccl. 9:10; Prov. 14:23; Rom. 12:11). Any job that provides a product or a service that people genuinely need, that in some way enriches human life on earth, can be a means of doing God's work on earth and advancing His kingdom.

God is a builder. He is building a kingdom. Since we are created in God's image and likeness we too are builders. He commands all of us to build to His honor and glory, to use our work to serve Him and other human beings. In the Garden of Eden God assigned our first parents the tasks of filling the earth, sustaining life, and having dominion over all creation. While the fall and the presence of sin in the world and our lives have made that task more difficult, sin's intrusion has not cancelled our mandate to subdue the earth and build God's kingdom. Work is in no way degrading. Both God the Father and God the Son work. They have been involved in acts of creating, sustaining, and interpreting the universe. Labor is natural for human beings made in God's image. It is our task and glory. Work is meant to be the main way by which we offer our lives as a service to God.

We challenge you who are college students to evaluate prayerfully the majors you have chosen and the career path you are pursuing. Why have you chosen this vocation? Does your envisioned vocation suit your talents? Does it offer you work you will enjoy? Can you serve God effectively through this vocation? Will your work improve life for the poor, oppressed, and disadvantaged? Has God directed you to prepare for work in this field?

Thus far we have argued that Christians are called to build God's kingdom on earth, to seek to transform their sphere of influence. We now turn our attention to specific areas where we can seek to bring cultural life into conformity with biblical norms. During the last century forces of secularization have influenced Western nations to base their corporate and institutional life more on secular than on Christian principles. At the same time, many Christians have limited the areas in which they attempt to follow biblical principles faithfully. Many believers have restricted the gospel's teachings to their church, family, and leisure activities. They have thought that biblical norms in such areas as politics and the state, economics and work, education and society are not relevant to contemporary life.

The Bible was written in a particular context (agrarian Israel of two to three thousand years ago), and parts of the Old Testament are addressed specifically to Israel as a theocratic nation (directly under God's rule). Because cultural conditions have changed dramatically and because, since the coming of Christ, God works in the world primarily through the church, not a particular nation, some of the Bible's provisions, especially certain regulations of the Old Testament, are no longer valid. Christ's provision of redemption fulfilled and therefore cancelled the ceremonial laws of the Old Testament. Despite differences, however, much continuity exists between the Old and New Covenants. The general principles and norms revealed in the Scriptures (both Old and New Testament) continue to serve as guidelines for organizing and conducting both public and private life in the twentieth century.

Through His act of creation God established basic structures to direct and shape life. Humanity rebelled against God's creational norms and developed distorted social institutions and relationships. Through His revealed Word, the Bible, God intends to reorder these institutions and relationships. The Bible therefore contains directives, models, and laws for structuring social institutions and guiding individual Christians in their participation in public life.

God instituted marriage and family in the Garden of Eden as He created Eve to be Adam's companion and helper and commanded them to be fruitful and multiply (Gen. 1:28). Through the partnership of marriage men and women can effectively serve the Lord, other human beings, and one another. While God does call some persons to be single, he intends the family to be the basic social and spiritual building block of both church and society. Parents are expected to nurture their children, providing for their physical, material, social, intellectual, and spiritual needs. God commands children to respect and honor their parents (Exod. 20:12; Eph. 6:1) and parents to discipline their children (Prov. 3:12; 29:15; I Tim. 3:4; Heb. 12:5-11).

We urge those who are dating and developing relationships with potential mates to study biblical teaching about marriage and the family. Understand the tremendous opportunity and obligations involved in marriage. Seek the Lord's will in choosing a marriage partner. As you contemplate marriage with a particular individual, consider your personality types, interests, commitments, and goals. Explore together how your union might enhance your service to God and the world. The Bible directs Christians to marry fellow believers. Marrying someone who does not share your commitment to Christ will undoubtedly produce conflicts over priorities. Before marrying, seek out counseling from a competent minister. If and when you do marry, strive to build your relationship upon your mutual devotion to the Lord. If the Lord brings children into your life, consider them to be a trust from Him. Take seriously your responsibility to oversee and direct their development. Establish a home that glorifies Jesus Christ and demonstrates His love to one another and to the world.

In addition to establishing the institutions of marriage and family, God also ordained the state. Its primary task is to preserve order, regulate social interactions, and promote and insure justice in society (see Pss. 58:1; 72:1-2, 12, 14; 82:1-4; Isa. 31:1-2; Jer. 23:5; Rom. 1-4; I Pet. 2:14). The Old Testament prophets repeatedly chastised Israel and other nations for failing to practice justice, act righteously, and deal equitably with all their citizens. The state should direct public policy so as to enable people to fulfill their many God-given offices and callings to society as parents, children, teachers, students, citizens, church members, workers, and so on.

Christians then should encourage the state to promote justice in society. We should actively participate in the political process and support policies that insure fair and impartial treatment of all citizens. Because laws always reflect underlying moral principles, we should labor to base America's laws upon the biblical norms appropriate to a pluralistic culture in the New Testament age. Forming distinctively Christian political organizations and supporting avowedly Christian politicians is appropriate if those organizations and politicians seek to develop a genuinely biblical approach to politics. Often such organizations have uncritically adopted the political program of the right or left, without subjecting it to extensive analysis based upon biblical teaching. Christian politicians have all too frequently not used biblical categories and norms to devise a distinctive political philosophy. We should support elected officials, whether or not they profess faith in Christ, who support policies that promote biblical norms of justice and righteousness.

What should today's Christian college students do to prepare to serve the Lord faithfully in political life? You can take courses in political science and sociology so that you better understand America's political process and the issues facing our society. You can study the Scripture individually and corporately to see how its teachings apply to contemporary politics. You can carefully analyze political issues and candidates for office and vote wisely. After graduation you will have increased opportunity to work for candidates in campaigns, lobby elected officials, and even run for office. You can support Christian and secular organizations that seek to influence our government to adopt responsible and humane policies in such areas as peace, freedom, security, world hunger, civil rights, abortion, and euthanasia.

In addition to calling the state to practice justice and deal fairly with all its citizens, Christians should work actively to develop educational institutions and programs that inculcate a biblical world view and prepare people to respond obediently to the Lord in all areas of life. Christians are commanded to raise their children "in the nurture and admonition of the Lord." The church and the school should aid parents in providing for the physical, emotional, intellectual, and spiritual development of their children.

Public schools from Puritan New England to the Civil War were largely based upon a biblical understanding of the world and life. Since the 1870s this biblical foundation of the public schools has largely been eroded and replaced by a nebulous secular humanism. Today America's public schools are no longer distinctively Christian. Concerned Christian parents have responded to this development in a number of ways. Some have decided to teach their children at home. Others have exposed the humanistic orientation of today's schools and encouraged them once again to promote Judeo-Christian values. Still others have founded their own schools, which base their entire curriculum and program upon biblical principles. These schools attempt to teach children to be faithful caretakers of God's good earth and ambassadors of His gospel of grace and love.

We challenge readers to serve the Lord in the realm of education. Investigate Christian schools. Prayerfully consider supporting them financially and by sending your children. Take your responsibility for your children's development seriously. Work with your school and church to help your children learn to love the Lord, appreciate and understand His world, and help others.

Before the Civil War most American colleges were controlled by Christian denominations. They sought to teach a biblical world view and to prepare students to serve Christ through their vocations. During the past one hundred years distinctively Christian colleges have become a decided minority among American educational institutions. Such colleges often publish doctrinal statements affirming their beliefs, hold chapel services, require religion classes, maintain high moral standards, and encourage students to live by biblical values. But the college that seeks to be genuinely Christian does much more. It attempts to recognize Christ as Lord over every aspect of the institution, from athletics to dormitory life to classroom instruction. In the Christian college a biblical understanding of all life should underlie the entire curriculum, from chemistry to computers to communication arts. Because facts are not neutral but have meaning only in contexts, and because presuppositions direct everyone's investigation and explanation of life, the Christian college should base its instruction upon biblical assumptions about God, humanity, knowledge, and the cosmos.

Christian students are called to serve God through all aspects of their educational experience. Your primary task is to give Jesus Christ preeminence in your life, in all that you do. As you study ask: How should I be changed through these learning opportunities? How can they better prepare me to proclaim the gospel, correct injustice, abolish hunger and illiteracy, eradicate poverty, and further world peace? Later as you serve God through your vocation, support Christian colleges by your prayers, finances, and recruitment efforts.

Unfortunately, at this time there are few consistently Christian universities in America. Since universities provide substantial intellectual stimulation, research, and leadership for our nation, the gospel can transform American culture only if we establish more

Christian universities. To reshape the thinking, values, and ethos of America, to engage more constructively in the battle of ideas going on in our nation, we need the resources and minds that best flourish in a community of Christian scholars.

A third institution that plays a vital role in God's growing kingdom is the church. Although the church should not be equated with the kingdom—God's kingdom being much broader and more extensive than the institutional church—nonetheless, through its ministry of preaching the Word and administering the sacraments the church contributes greatly to kingdom work. In many ways the church serves as the source and inspiration for Christian efforts in other areas of culture. Through worship, prayer, Bible study, preaching, and fellowship the church instructs and empowers Christians to serve God in the world. Christian congregations are called to minister to those in spiritual and material need. Both evangelism and social action are important parts of the church's task. In several large American cities major congregations and parachurch ministries have joined forces to combat poverty, urban blight, racism, substance abuse, and many other problems. Their efforts have won many to Christ and have significantly improved urban life in many ways. Smaller congregations often have great impacts as well. Many of them are involved deeply in evangelism, housing projects and food pantries for the poor, drug rehabilitation programs, and prison ministries. Some of these congregations accomplish a great deal because they only accept as members persons who commit themselves to working diligently in one area of their community outreach.

We challenge you to be part of a congregation that meets your spiritual needs and provides you with avenues of ministry in the world. The church should be a vital part of your life, teaching you the Word of God, providing you with Christian fellowship, and preparing you to serve the poor, homeless, sick, and oppressed.

During the last decade many sociologists and historians have argued that an evangelical renaissance is taking place in America. About one-third of adult Americans claim to be born again. Evangelical books, television networks and programs, radio stations, congregations, schools, and organizations have proliferated.

Significant numbers of politicians, including several presidents and presidential candidates, have professed faith in Jesus Christ. The signs of evangelical influence are everywhere. Unfortunately, in some ways the evangelical renaissance has been superficial. Many social problems continue to afflict America: abortion, child abuse, divorce, homosexuality, adultery, poverty, racism, hunger, homelessness, crime, substance abuse, and militarism. Relativistic, pragmatic, or hedonistic principles and goals still direct much of our nation's education, politics, morality, and social practices. If the present evangelical resurgence is to become another "great awakening" like the awakenings of the eighteenth and nineteenth centuries (see chap. 8), then Christians must increase their efforts to combat these problems and to reshape America's institutional life.

In other words, we must redouble our attempt to proclaim and embody the kingdom of God, to make visible and concrete what God is doing in heaven. Our goal is to create a society where justice and *shalom* prevail. God wants our nation and our world to experience peace in all its aspects (personal, social, national, and international) and health in all its forms (physical, psychological, spiritual, and material). Such a peaceable kingdom with its fruits of righteousness and joy would indeed fulfill God's design for humanity.

While Christians have never achieved such a society, wherever the gospel has been faithfully and zealously preached, great changes have occurred. During the first three centuries A.D. Christians significantly reshaped the mighty Roman Empire. The preaching of Martin Luther and John Calvin led to major revivals of biblical Christianity and vastly improved social conditions in the sixteenth century. In the eighteenth century the Holy Spirit used John and Charles Wesley to breathe fresh life into English Christianity and thus saved the British from their own version of the French Revolution. During the nineteenth century a great awakening swept the United States, rejuvenating many congregations and bringing countless conversions. The many voluntary societies it spawned tackled numerous social problems and produced great benefits. Around the turn of the twentieth century Abraham Kuyper, a theologian, pastor, professor, and statesman, helped to place churches, schools, government, and social practices in the Netherlands on a more firm biblical basis. Examples could be multiplied. The point is that God is building His kingdom on earth and we are His workers. Let us build with confidence, enthusiasm, and joy.

Scripture Index

General Index